Fortunate Son

★

Fortunate Son

★

THE AUTOBIOGRAPHY OF
LEWIS B. PULLER, JR.

GROVE WEIDENFELD
New York

Thanks to Lynn Barnett, for being with me from
the start.—Lewis B. Puller, Jr.

Published by Grove Weidenfeld
A division of Grove Press, Inc.
841 Broadway
New York, NY 10003-4793

Published in Canada by General Publishing Company, Ltd.

LIBRARY OF CONGRESS CATALOGING-IN-PUBLICATION DATA

Puller, Lewis B.
Fortunate son : the autobiography of Lewis B. Puller, Jr.—1st ed.
p.   cm.
ISBN 0-8021-1218-8 (alk. paper) : $21.95
1. Puller, Lewis B.   2. Vietnamese Conflict, 1961–1975—Veterans—
United States.   3. Vietnamese Conflict, 1961–1975—Personal
narratives, American.   4. Veterans, Disabled—United States—
Biography.   5. United States. Marine Corps Biography.   6. Marines—
United States—Biography.   I. Title.
DS559.73.U6P85   1991
959.704'3373—dc20   91-4463
                                              CIP

Manufactured in the United States of America

Printed on acid-free paper

Designed by Kathryn Parise

First Edition 1991

3 5 7 9 10 8 6 4

for Toddy

Some folks inherit star spangled eyes;
    ooh, they send you down to war.
And when you ask them "How much should we give?"
    they only answer more! more! more!

It ain't me, it ain't me;
    I ain't no military son.
It ain't me, it ain't me;
    I ain't no fortunate one.

"Fortunate Son" by John Fogerty
of Creedence Clearwater Revival

Part One

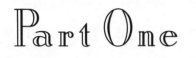

★

I FIRST NOTICED my father's tattoo the summer he returned from the Korean War. We had just moved from Virginia to the marine base at Camp Pendleton, California. Mother had asked me to awaken him from an afternoon nap, and as I entered their bedroom and stood beside his sleeping figure, my eyes were drawn to the blue globe and anchor on his right upper arm. When I extended my hand to trace its outline with my finger, he awakened, and acquiescing to the curiosity of a five-year-old, he playfully flexed his bicep and tousled my hair with his free left hand.

I had no idea that the object of my fascination was the emblem of the Marine Corps, the organization to which my father had already dedicated more than thirty of his fifty-three years. I did know that it must be important, because my mother had a piece of gold and silver jewelry in the same shape as Father's tattoo, and she wore it frequently when she got dressed up. Later I learned that Mother loved the gold and silver pin and despised the tattoo.

There were other things I noticed about my father in the summer and fall of 1951, a time during which he made a special effort to be accessible to his only son and to make up for his absence during the war. My father was born before the turn of the century, the third of four children and the elder son. His father was a traveling salesman whose battle with cancer had been lost by the time Father was ten. His grandfather had been killed by Union fire at Kelly's Ford in Virginia during the Civil War, and his boyhood heroes, long before he became a role model for a newer generation of Americans, had been Robert E. Lee and Stonewall Jackson. When Father came home from his fifth and last war, Lee and Jackson remained in his eyes the standard against which all military leaders were measured, and I remember kneeling with him and invoking their hallowed names in my bedtime prayers before he tucked me in.

My father had been promoted to the rank of brigadier general after leading the First Marine Regiment of the First Marine Division in the retreat from the Chosin Reservoir through Koto-ri just before Christmas 1950. The breakout came to be regarded as a classic in the annals of modern American military warfare. For his role in holding together the rear guard during some of the bloodiest fighting of the war, my father was recognized for heroic leadership, and his elevation to flag rank was assured.

After the engagement ended, Mother told me, Father had escaped from a trap set by the Red Chinese, but I could not envision his being caught in a device similar to the one I baited with lettuce in the apple orchard behind my grandmother's home in Virginia, where we waited out the war. He had sent me war mementos: two Korean swords, an enemy helmet and bugle, and several medals, which arrived in silk-lined blue boxes. Affectionately known among his beloved marines as "the old man" or "Chesty" for the way he carried himself when marching, he must have known that the combat taking place on the frozen wastes and ridges of Korea would be his last, and even then he was passing on to me the proud traditions of his profession.

For my sixth birthday, near the end of the summer, he gave me a .22-caliber single-shot rifle, which he had modified by sawing the stock in half to accommodate my narrow shoulders and short arms. On the butt he had stenciled my name, Lewis B. Puller, Jr., and the added touch filled me with a pride of ownership and a certainty that I had the best father in the world. He also gave me a cleaning kit, and I became familiar with the caustic smells of cleaning solvent and oil before I could hold the rifle steady enough to hit a target. After we had practiced on paper targets and tin cans, he took me into the brown hills around our home in search of California jackrabbits.

At first I struggled to match his long-legged gait, but after he realized that I could not keep up, he slowed his pace and began circumventing the steeper hills. Even then I tired easily, and my aching legs diverted my attention from our elusive quarry. Throughout the several months that we hunted together in the Camp Pendleton countryside, I never once came close to hitting a rabbit; but my father puffed silently on his pipe each time I missed, and on those occasions when he bagged game, I was allowed to carry our trophies the last hundred yards back home.

======= ☆ =======

In early February, as my twin sister, Martha, and I were beginning the second half of our first year of grade school and our older sister, Virginia, was a seemingly adult sixth grader, a parade was held to honor my father's heroism at the Chosin Reservoir. I was permitted to go along with Mother, and she held my hand as we stood at the end of a sun-drenched parade ground and waited for the ceremony to end. When the last drumbeat sounded and the standard-bearers had retired the colors, my father strode from the field on which he had just been honored and knelt briefly to let me view the object of the morning's pageantry. A gold star in lieu of his fifth Navy Cross, the most ever earned by any one marine and our country's second-highest award for valor, now joined the panoply of ribbons that covered most of his left chest.

The memory of that frozen instant more than three decades ago is as fresh and firmly fixed in my mind today as any of my most vivid boyhood recollections. I remember little else of the events surrounding that indelible moment, and at age six, I was certainly incapable of understanding its historical meaning, but on that now distant drill field beneath the glare of a Southern California sun, I had first begun to grasp the concept of battlefield glory and with it sensed a commitment to a calling over which I would be powerless.

======= ☆ =======

At Camp Pendleton Father commanded the Third Marine Brigade and was charged with training fresh troops for the denouement being played out along the thirty-eighth parallel in Korea. On several occasions he and his jeep driver, Sergeant Orville Jones, took me with them to observe war games and field exercises in Pendleton's scrub-dotted boondocks. I was naturally fascinated by the maneuvers of khaki-clad marines and the smoke and thunder of mock warfare.

Back at home after one exercise my father set up a pup tent for me in the backyard of our family quarters, and I used it as a base of operations for imaginary war games of my own. Martha was at first a willing participant in my martial flights of fancy, and from my headquarters behind the tent flaps, I issued orders and directed her on dangerous missions until she tired of the game and seriously depleted my troop supply. Accustomed as I had become to seeing my father's commands carried out instantaneously and without question by a host of military subordinates, I was chagrined that my one soldier would mutiny in the heat of battle and leave me defenseless and without a chain of command. By dinner, of course, I had forgiven her insurrection and made my battle plan for the next day's activities.

One day I accompanied my father to the pistol range, sitting in the backseat directly behind Sergeant Jones, my father next to me on the passenger side. While my father nodded off, I annoyed Jones with a multitude of childish questions, which he answered as best he could, every so often admonishing me to keep my voice down so that my father could catch up on his sleep.

When we got to the range, I was given cotton to muffle the sound of the pistol fire, but I held my hands over my ears anyway while my father and the other shooters fired round after round into the rectangular targets. As my father shot, the other marines gathered to watch him, and I noted that the .45-caliber pistol jumped in his hand each time he squeezed the trigger. After he had finished, he reloaded his weapon, placed me on the firing line, and instructed me to hold it tightly with both hands. Anticipating a kick similar to that of my rifle, I squeezed off a round and was dismayed that the weapon jumped from my hands and struck me in the eye.

Stung by the blow from the pistol and embarrassed by my own ineptitude, I wanted to cry, but before I could vent my tears, my father had placed the .45 back in my hands. He then steadied my hands with his own, and together we fired the remaining rounds from the ammunition clip. After we had finished, I was given the task of policing the area of spent cartridges, and for the rest of the afternoon I was kidded about the mouse on my right eye. Later I had time to reflect on my growing respect for handguns, but for most of the ride home I was preoccupied with the newly acquired awareness that a boy did not cry in the presence of grown men.

═══ ☆ ═══

In the summer of 1952 my father was transferred to the Marine Corps Recruit Depot in San Diego, and our family moved into one of the ample sets of general officers' quarters on the base. There was a small sign in the front yard that announced my father's name and rank, and an armed sentry patrolled the sidewalk that ran past our home.

For the first time I began to take note of the support level that accompanied general officer status, and it seemed to me that all at once we were inundated with people who ran the house and assisted my mother and father. In addition to a cook, a butler, and a gardener, who kept the house and grounds in immaculate condition, my father had a military aide as well as Sergeant Jones, who continued to serve as his driver and all-purpose errand runner. Father also had a barge at his disposal, and on a few occasions, when his job entailed its use and I was allowed to tag along, I was in awe of the two sailors who stood watch on its stern. Straight-backed and expressionless in their white starched uniforms, they maintained rigid stances with their legs slightly spread and their hands folded behind them, and I could not fathom what kept them from toppling into the sea as the boat skipped over the water toward our destination.

The Marine Corps Recruit Depot, like its East Coast counterpart, Parris Island, was a port of entry for brand-new marines on their way toward service in the Fleet Marine Force. Their training was intense and demanding, and as Martha and I explored the base after school and on weekends, we frequently stumbled upon these young men with their funny bald heads doing calisthenics or being browbeaten by screaming red-faced men in wide-brimmed hats. As often as not the recruits were chanting as they jogged from one scene of humiliation to the next, and their presence became such a part of my daily life that I never questioned their plight.

When finally my language began to take on some of the flavor of the drill instructors who led them, my father stepped in and restricted the free run that I had formerly had of the base. Despite his stern measures, some intermingling with the troops remained unavoidable, since we had to pass by the barracks and parade ground on our way to the base swimming pool and movie theater.

At the swimming pool, where Martha and I took our first lessons, the instructors were enlisted marines who taught the recruits and the dependents of the military personnel assigned to the base. Pool hours were staggered so that we did not share pool time with servicemen, but as we waited for the enlisted marines to clear the pool each day so that we could begin our lessons, I remember being impressed by the enormous muscles on some of them and by the grotesque tattoos that seemed to adorn many of them. Fire-breathing dragons and coiled serpents completely covered the chests of many of the swimmers, and it was not uncommon to see each of the knotted forearms and biceps of some men sporting several tattoos of various sizes and colors. Compared with many of them, my father's tattoo now seemed as insignificant as a smudge on a magic slate, and I wondered if it was painful to undergo such extensive needlework.

By the time Martha and I had completed several lessons, she had advanced to the point where she was doing laps alone while I was still flailing about in the shallow end. It was not the only time in our growing up together that the discrepancy between our levels of athletic prowess would mortify me, and I was grateful that the tattooed marines had gone on to other endeavors and were not able to compare us. At the conclusion of the lessons I had finally gotten to the point where the deep end had lost its terror for me, but by then, of course, my twin was doing swan dives and jackknifes off the diving board.

At about the time that Martha was discovering her propensity for water sports and I was learning the true meaning of shame, Father decided that she and I needed another means of locomotion. He bought us each shiny new bicycles, a red one for her and a blue one for me, but while I sat and daydreamed about the adventures about to be undertaken on my new toy, my sister mounted hers and within minutes was racing around the neighborhood. It took several days and extensive coaching and coaxing from Father before I mastered my own two-wheeler, but when I reached that magic moment when I was upright on my own and moving through the wind, I quickly forgot my earlier humiliation. When I chanced a look over my shoulder, my father's chest was still heaving from the effort of running alongside me, but his hands were clasped over his head in victory and a broad smile stretched across his face.

That fall Father made a trip back to the East Coast on Marine Corps business. He had, by then, become much in demand as a speaker at Marine Corps reunions, and the travel required by his job, coupled with his many appearances at quasi Marine Corps functions, seemed to keep him on the road constantly. It also kept Mother in a state of near hysteria because she never knew when one of his outspoken criticisms of the military, often made without any seeming regard for his own best interests, would appear in the newspapers. On this particular trip he ran into the man to whom we had given our cocker spaniel puppy two years earlier, when we had moved from Virginia to Camp Pendleton. The man had recently divorced, and unable to care properly for the dog, he asked my father to take her back. When Father returned to San Diego, he had Fidget in tow, and Martha, Virginia, and I were roused from our beds to come downstairs and get reacquainted with the dog we had never expected to see again. When she saw us, pandemonium broke loose in the kitchen as she darted about, licking our faces and barking out her joy. It was as though she had been gone for a week rather than two years. Father had always believed that every boy should have a dog, and despite having broken the rules by bringing Fidget back on a military transport, he knew that he had made the right decision. We also used the occasion to exact a promise from him that henceforth we would take Fidget with us when we moved.

That Christmas Father gave me an electric train and several sets of toy soldiers. I never acquired the mechanical skills necessary to synchronize the various transformers, switches, and locomotives, but the green plywood table that held the track served as an ideal battleground for my toy soldiers. Before long I had built my armies up to several hundred pieces, and Father found time to take me to dime stores and hobby shops to find new men. As the word spread of my collection, his friends and acquaintances began to give me additional pieces, and a British colonel who visited briefly with us sent me several Tower of London beefeaters and two mounted cavalry officers that I especially liked.

Father had a strong preference for the Civil War soldiers, and he often helped me arrange the blue and gray Billy Yanks and Johnny Rebs as I concocted my strategies and maneuvered my armies. He was proud of his grandfather's role in the war he referred to as the War Between the States, and looking back, I can see that he had an almost mystical respect for many of its generals and wished that he could have apprenticed with them. I, of course, had no understanding of the suffering or sacrifice he knew to be a major part of warfare, and after we had arranged the pieces to his satisfaction, he invariably withdrew from the fracas before I began firing my toy cannons and knocking over my mock combatants with the marbles I threw at them to simulate incoming artillery fire. The electric train had been a far more expensive gift, but it did not allow me the flights of fantasy I experienced with my tabletop warriors, and my father never commented when it became dusty with disuse and finally was moved back into its cardboard box to make room for my advancing hordes.

In August 1953, with the Korean War ended, Father was promoted to major general, and the sign in our front yard was repainted to reflect his new rank. We had to mute our celebration because the general who lived across the street was not selected for promotion, but all in all, times were good and our lives were happy. Father had sufficiently decompressed from his Korean War experience that he was no longer making the kinds of inflammatory statements about the conduct of the war that had gotten him into trouble in the past, including one that haunted him for years to the effect that whiskey and beer would make troops fight better than ice cream and soft training. The promotion to major general was proof that he was on the track toward at least a possible shot at becoming commandant of the Marine Corps and fulfilling a lifelong ambition.

On weekends he sometimes had time to play baseball with me in the side yard of our quarters, and for our games of catch he used an ancient first baseman's mitt that Mother said he had owned since long before they were married. He also took us to the San Diego Zoo, where we rode the train together, and on special occasions there were afternoon excursions to the movies. *Gunga Din*, an oldie by 1953, was his favorite, but I was also entranced by the derring-do and swordsmanship of *Prince Valiant* and *King of the Khyber Rifles*. For my eighth birthday, just after he made major general, he gave me a little rowboat with heavy gray painted oars, which I was not yet strong enough to handle on my own, and when we took it out together, he rowed while Fidget and I crowded together in the bow. He also decided, shortly after my eighth birthday, that I was old enough to learn the fundamentals of close-order drill, and for several weeks Sergeant Jones attempted to teach me how to march, a task that Father finally canceled when he realized that the effort was going nowhere.

In July 1954, just before Martha and I started fourth grade, we moved from San Diego to Camp Lejeune, North Carolina, where Father was to take command of the Second Marine Division. Mother did most of the driving in the week that it took us to complete the journey, but I was so preoccupied with the panorama outside my backseat window and so used to seeing Father driven that I attached no significance to my mother's helmsmanship. In the rear seat Martha, Virginia, and I rotated the window seats, and we shuffled Fidget about as best we could when the cramped space became too burdensome.

I was amazed at the vast expanse of desert dotted only with scrub brush and gnarled cactus plants that flew past my window, and the sight of real Indians in mud hovels along the roadside set my imagination racing and the dog yelping. In Flagstaff, Arizona, there was an annual tribal competition taking place when we passed through, and Father allowed us to stay up past our bedtime and, by the reflected light of huge bonfires, watch the ceremonial dances and athletic feats of the painted warriors. I felt as if I had been transported from the audience of a western movie into the heat of the action on the screen, and when the Indians chanted, I pressed closely against my father's side.

Shortly before our trip ended, we managed to get two flat tires at the same time, and I noticed that Mother seemed worried about Father as we waited for help at the side of the road. I had never before seen her express any concern about his health, and the solicitude for him only half hidden on my mother's face made me vaguely uneasy. He was fifty-six years old, and the thought crossed my mind that things went on between my parents in which my sisters and I were not included. Later I would learn that Father suffered from high blood pressure, but even if his condition had been explained to me, I probably would not have grasped its ominous overtones.

At Camp Lejeune we were moved into an enclave of four or five sets of general officers' quarters separated from the rest of the lower-ranking officers' residences by a little park filled with pine trees and playground equipment. The general officers' quarters were in a row parallel to the New River, and they abutted a golf course on the back side so that the overall effect was one of seclusion and privacy. Our house was the second from the end farthest from the park, and I had my own bedroom, which was on the second floor and looked out on the river.

Mother and Father had the one air-conditioned bedroom in the house, and because it was so sultry when we first occupied the house, they permitted me to set up a cot in their bedroom and take up temporary residence there until we had become acclimated to the North Carolina summer. After several weeks of my spending nights at the foot of my parents' bed, Father suggested to me that perhaps it was time to consider a different sleeping arrangement. When I told him I was perfectly happy where I was, he made his point more forcefully, and I was unceremoniously moved to my own bedroom. A few days earlier I had found a bag of strange-looking rubber sheathlike devices on my father's dresser, but not until a year or two later did I realize that their presence had a bearing on my ejection from my parents' bedroom.

As with the house in San Diego, our new surroundings were supported and maintained by a butler, a cook, several yard workers, and my father's military aide and his driver. There were plenty of other children for my sisters and me to play with, but when we finished our games in the park, the other children went home in one direction and my sisters and I took an opposite tack. When we had visitors over for the first time, they were invariably struck by the contrast between our home and their own quarters, and Martha and I had to struggle to overcome the awkwardness caused by our father's lofty status as the division commander. On several occasions I got into fistfights with other boys who exorcised their jealousy by taunting us, and my father's solution after seeing me come home several times with a bloody nose was to sign me up for the youth league boxing team. His action only served to make matters worse because it legitimized the bloody noses, and it increased my mortification by assuring that I was now getting my nose bloodied by boys who were my own size. When basketball season rolled around, I hid the boxing gloves he had given me so that he would not consider sending me back to the ring the following year.

A couple of months after Father assumed command of the Second Division, our family had a scare that helped explain Mother's concern for his health while we were driving across the country. A week after my ninth birthday Father had inspected a battalion of marines that was being sent overseas, and the searing heat from the midday sun caused several of the troops to drop in their tracks while awaiting inspection. That evening Father was out late, and the next morning he conducted a strenuous inspection of base warehouses whose concrete and steel construction retained most of the summer heat and left the building interiors like ovens. After the inspection was completed, he returned to his office, but he felt ill and was taken to the hospital, where his aide noticed that his coordination was poor and his color pale. After he was seen by the duty doctor, he lapsed into unconsciousness and began convulsing. He was sedated, placed in an oxygen tent, and carefully monitored, and by early morning he had stabilized and his condition seemed much improved.

Mother spent the night at the hospital, and the next morning, when he had regained consciousness, my sisters and I were allowed in for a visit. He seemed perfectly normal to me, although he was somewhat weak, and it was distracting to try to talk to him through the cellophanelike tent that encased his upper body. We were not allowed to stay long; but he held my hand when I reached under the tent, and he told me to take care of Mother and my sisters until he came home. I left his room feeling that my father had had a minor setback and that in a few days he would be as good as new. In fact, he had suffered a cerebral vascular thrombosis, a stroke, and he had experienced another more severe episode after reaching the hospital. There was no paralysis and no residuals, but Chesty Puller, the living legend who every marine thought was indestructible had shown his Achilles' heel, and from that point on his military career was on a downward spiral.

When Father came home, he took a few days of convalescent leave; but there were no physical manifestations of his illness, and I quickly forgot about it. Martha and I were busy getting adjusted to our new elementary school, and I spent my spare time trying to advance through the ranks of my Cub Scout den and accumulating points for merit badges. Within a short time of his discharge from the hospital, Father was operating at the same pace he had maintained before the stroke, and except for an occasional uncharacteristic tenseness on Mother's part, our lives seemed the same.

One morning in the fall, as Martha and I were preparing to go to school and Mother and Father were finishing their breakfast, I went from the dining room into the adjacent kitchen to warm myself by the stove. Crumpton, the butler, was at the sink doing the breakfast dishes, and as I backed up to the stove, my shirttail came to rest on one of the stove's burners. Within seconds the back of my shirt was in flames, and I began screaming and beating on Crumpton's back as the fire ate through my undershirt and began consuming my skin. When Crumpton turned around and, with eyes as large as the teacups he was washing, saw what had happened, he grabbed a dish towel and began beating on my back. A split second later the swinging door from the dining room to the kitchen came off its hinges, and my father, gal-vanized by my screaming, was beside me. He ripped the shards of burning shirt from my body with his hands and extinguished the fire; but by then my back was a patchwork of first-, second-, and third-degree burns, and I was on the verge of going into shock.

Mother drove us to the hospital because it was faster than waiting for an ambulance, and my father sat in the backseat with me and held a white bed sheet around my upper body. As waves of searing pain swept up my back, my father held me tightly and encouraged me to scream as loudly as I wanted. His hands were charred and blistered from ripping off my shirt, but his eyes had an intensity and his jaw a set that I had never seen before. Within minutes of arriving at the hospital, I was taken into surgery and given an anesthetic that mercifully put out the conflagration that my nerve ends had told me was raging on my back. When I awoke, I was swaddled in a white bandage from my neck to my waist, and I was embarrassed because I was naked from the waist down.

The doctors assured me and my parents that aside from the danger of infection, I was going to be okay, but for years I would have to wear a T-shirt with my bathing suit when I went out in the sun. Fortunately the infection never developed, and after several days I was allowed to go home with instructions to return for dressing changes. As my back healed, the itching nearly drove me crazy, but I quickly learned to ease my discomfort by rubbing one of my mother's knitting needles back and forth between the bandage and the healing skin between my shoulder blades. Father joked about my agility with the knitting needles and about my upstaging him by arranging a hospital admission for myself; but I had seen the fear in his eyes when Mother was driving us to the emergency room, and I knew how relieved he was to see me recovering.

When word spread that my father had suffered a stroke, he received hundreds of letters and get-well cards from all over the country. Many came from marines with whom he had served or been associated, both officers and enlisted men, but others came from total strangers. Several times I overheard my parents discussing some of the more poignant letters he received, and he was deeply moved by the way people who knew him or knew of him expressed their regard for his achievements.

In early November a panel of navy doctors, convened to evaluate his fitness for duty, found him free of any residuals of the stroke and able to perform the duties of his rank. He was elated at the good news, but several days later his joy was cut short when he was ordered by the commandant of the Marine Corps to report to the Bethesda, Maryland, Naval Hospital for further evaluation. After two weeks in the hospital he was found unfit for duty and scheduled to go before a retirement board in early August. He returned home angry and bitter, and perhaps because he couldn't discuss the perceived unfairness of his situation with fellow marines, he vented his frustration on Mother. He had felt from the time of his illness that a coterie of senior officers in the Marine Corps was jealous of his celebrity and would use the stroke as a pretext to end his career. He viewed his summons to Bethesda after a board had already passed on his fitness as part of a conspiracy to do him in and was even critical of the commandant of the Marine Corps.

I was never told what words passed between my father and the commandant while he was away from us in Bethesda, but given Father's outspokenness and his sense of the injustice being done him, I am certain they were less than cordial. General Lemuel C. Shepherd, the commandant, had also been my godfather, and prior to Father's stroke, he regularly sent me birthday presents. After Father came back from Bethesda, I never received another gift or communication from my godfather, and for years I did not understand if or why he had abandoned me.

Father tried to have the findings of the Bethesda doctors reversed, pursuing every available appeal up the chain of command. It all was fruitless, and although he did not expect Marine Corps Headquarters in Washington, D.C., to intercede, he was disillusioned that no accommodations were made for him in view of his service record. General Shepherd wrote him several letters extolling his courage on the battlefield and acknowledging his legendary status as a troop leader and professional soldier, but he also indicated that he did not have the authority to reverse the proceedings that had taken place at Bethesda. Instead, he relieved Father of command of the Second Division and made him deputy commander of the base at Camp Lejeune for the time that it would take until his appeals were exhausted and his retirement papers were completed. Although he held the post for six months, until October 1955, the job was largely ceremonial and involved no real responsibility. During that time several United States senators, including John F. Kennedy of Massachusetts, wrote headquarters in Washington to ascertain why Chesty Puller was being retired, but even their intercession was to no avail.

At the end of that October Father's retirement became a reality, and he reported to the base commanding officer to receive the third star of a lieutenant general, the rank at which he was to retire. In a symbolic gesture of his appreciation for the enlisted men, whom he considered the backbone of the Marine Corps, he asked the senior noncom present rather than the senior officer to pin the star on his shoulder. When that was completed, he thanked his military aide and Sergeant Jones, accepted the three-star flag of his retirement rank, and made a short statement for the press saying that the enlisted men and junior officers of the Marine Corps were responsible for his rise from private to lieutenant general.

Only fifty-seven years old, he had served more than thirty-seven years in the Marine Corps, including more than twenty-six on foreign soil and in five wars. He was the most decorated man in the history of the Marine Corps, a living legend about whom General Shepherd had written, "Marines should always be inspired by that tradition which honors the name Puller as a symbol of fighting courage." Now he was being put out to pasture by the organization to which he had devoted all of his adult life. His health may have left the Marine Corps no other choice, but rejection in any form from an organization to which he had given so much was almost too painful to bear.

When he got back to our quarters after the morning's ceremony, Mother had the car packed, and Martha, the dog, and I waited in the driveway while he changed into civilian clothes. (Virginia was away at school.) There was a brief, emotional good-bye to the cook and butler, who had been helping pack our household effects for the last several days, and we then headed north toward the town in Virginia where my father had met my mother and where we had lived while he was fighting in Korea. It was quiet in the backseat as we left Camp Lejeune, but my sister and I were excited at the prospect of being with our grandmother for a few weeks while the house our parents had bought nearby was made ready for us.

———— ☆ ————

The sleepy little Virginia town of Saluda, although straddling a major north-south thoroughfare, was no more than a crossroads with a dozen or so small businesses and fifty or sixty houses. Had it not been my mother's birthplace, it would have seemed a strange setting for a man as famous as my father to have picked to spend his retirement years. There was so little industry and so few business opportunities that most of the young men and women moved away as soon as they finished school, and the inhabitants who remained were either old or un-enthusiastic about moving on. Yet the town, with its abundance of shade trees, ancient brick courthouse, and matchbook-size bank and post office, had a rustic appeal that beguiled those who paused long enough to take in its magnolia and honeysuckle scents. The surrounding countryside of small farms and woodlands was punctuated by a few clusters of single-family dwellings and an occasional business to service the needs of an agrarian community. Middlesex County, of which Saluda was the county seat, was bordered on the north by the Rappahannock River, and the rolling fields, woods, and farmlands between our home and the river sloped gradually toward its wide expanse.

The home Mother and Father had purchased was a modest three-bedroom cottage with dormer windows facing the highway through town. Mother loved it because it had three fireplaces and was surrounded by a knee-high wall of ivy, but it was in serious disrepair and took several years to restore. The previous owners, an alcoholic doctor and his morphine-addicted wife, had died within a short time of each other. They had been cremated, and according to rumor, their ashes were buried in urns beneath the birdbath in the front yard.

For months Martha and I lived in mortal dread of the ghosts of Dr. and Mrs. James, who supposedly searched for their bodies on moonlit nights. Mother and Father did their best to allay our fears, but there were nights in the lunar cycle when Fidget, Martha, and I huddled beneath the covers in my upstairs bedroom while unexplained noises in the walls of the house kindled our imaginations. The noises proved to be field mice that had moved in while the house was vacant, but Martha and I were convinced that there was sufficient room between the walls of our bedrooms for both the mice and the ghosts of Dr. and Mrs. James.

Tiny Saluda was a big change for all of us, and although the tensions from having to make major adjustments to our living situations occasionally spilled over, we grew closer as a family. With Virginia at a girls' school in Richmond, Martha and I, close to begin with, grew even closer because there were so few children around our own age.

Without a support staff our lives became much less pampered, and for the first time Martha and I were faced with household chores. Prior to Father's retirement, I had never made my own bed or shined my own shoes, and now I was expected to help maintain a home. There were times, early on, as I struggled beneath a load of firewood or raked leaves into a pile for burning, when I thought what a downward turn our fortunes had taken. Gradually, however, I began to take pride in my responsibilities, and as the house and grounds began responding to our nurturing, I felt real accomplishment. We never talked about Father's stroke after we moved to Saluda; but there was an unstated premise that he was unable to do any strenuous work around the house, and as I tried to step into the void, I puffed with pride to think that I was in a sense becoming the man of the house.

As the bond between Martha and me was strengthened when we entered our new world, so, too, did the bonding between my father and me intensify. Father had been working since the age of ten, when his own father died and he began trapping muskrats before school to supplement his mother's income. Now, after almost fifty years of working, he suddenly found himself with time on his hands and the opportunity to focus on his children. Most mornings Mother fixed us breakfast together before Martha and I boarded the bus for school, and at the conclusion of the day he was always there to share talk of our victories and defeats and to help us with our homework. Although he had completed only a year of college, he was quick with figures, and a lifetime of reading had developed his vocabulary to the point that I soon realized what an invaluable resource he could be for help with writing assignments.

Shortly after we moved to Saluda, I acquired an afternoon paper route, my first paying job, and Father drove me on my rounds one day when my bicycle had a flat tire. A few days later it rained, and he again came to my assistance. Thereafter he drove me every day he was free, and I came to depend on him for transportation and to enjoy our time together despite the fact that he was such a poor driver. Several times we wound up in ditches along unpaved roads leading to some of the more remote stops on my route, and I was always amazed at his complete unflappability in the face of predicaments of his own making.

Soon after Father's retirement *Esquire* magazine sent a writer and a photographer to Saluda to conduct an interview for an article about Chesty Puller's career and the circumstances surrounding his separation from the Marine Corps. I tried to insinuate myself into the living room, where the interview was being conducted, as often as I could, and I was as fascinated by the tape recorders and the zoom lenses of the men from *Esquire* as by the attention they lavished on my father. What emerged was a scathing indictment of a Marine Corps policy that had, in retiring my father, allowed the corps to squander one of its greatest resources. The article was entitled "Waste of an Old War Horse" and was accompanied by a full-page picture of my father's face. Also in the magazine was a layout of a bikini-clad model, and for several years after the article appeared, I devoted considerable time to both pieces. Mother, of course, saw my perusal of the magazine as an expression of fondness for my father and had no idea that my preoccupation with *Esquire* was in part glandular. At the age of eleven I had already decided that girls were far more interesting than boys, but I was woefully lacking in the skills necessary to pursue my interests. I think Father sensed my frustration almost as soon as I began to experience alien yearnings, but on those awkward occasions when he offered to sit down and explain the birds and bees to me, I was so embarrassed that I always rebuffed his offers. In the meantime, cheesecake such as I chanced upon in the pages of magazines like *Esquire* held the promise of wonderful possibilities for the future and was for years as close as I would come to the forbidden pleasures of the opposite sex.

An unanticipated result of our settling so close to a major highway was the easy access that it provided admirers who wished to visit my father. From the time we moved in until I went off to college eight years later, I remember a steady stream of callers who made their way to our front door to pay their respects to the Marine Corps's most famous warrior. He welcomed them all with a cordiality befitting his southern roots, but the marines among them received special attention and often were allowed to interrupt family meals and even to join us at the table. Mother occasionally became miffed at our lack of privacy and threatened to move us to a less accessible location; but she realized how much Father needed his loyal following, and she grudgingly put up with all but the most outrageous interruptions. Some of the marines who came to call had served with Father during World War I, in the banana wars of Haiti and Nicaragua, in the Pacific during World War II, or more recently in the frozen wastes of Korea, and I was spellbound as he and his colleagues exchanged war stories. It was always difficult for me to get Father to talk about exploits from his past when we were alone together; but the contact with old marine acquaintances served to loosen his tongue, and I hung on his reminiscences and on the stories of heroic feats ascribed to him by men with whom he had soldiered.

There were others whom he did not know who came to bask in the reflected glory of a legendary figure, or simply to shake the hand of a man they admired so much. Among them all, however, the well-meaning and the ne'er-do-wells, those who had served and those whose motives were self-serving, there was a common thread of adulation. I decided early on that I wanted men to feel toward me the way they felt toward my father, as throughout my youth I witnessed examples of hero worship toward him that would have befitted the denizens of Mount Olympus. By the time I reached my teens I had grown accustomed to having strangers approach our table in restaurants to tell my father how much they admired him, and on numerous occasions, when we traveled to Richmond on shopping trips, men we did not know would cross the street to shake his hand.

=== ☆ ===

Six months after Father retired, a tragedy befell the Marine Corps that for a few days later that summer required his return to active duty and to the national limelight. On April 8, 1956, Staff Sergeant Matthew C. McKeon, a Marine Corps drill instructor at Parris Island, South Carolina, led a platoon of recruits on a disciplinary night march through the swamps around the depot. As he led them across the channel known as Ribbon Creek, several of the men panicked in the unexpectedly high waters of the tidal inlet, and before it was over, six young men had drowned.

Within days the tragedy had escalated into a nationwide controversy, and with the Marine Corps and its training methods under attack, Father felt that Sergeant McKeon was about to be offered up as a sacrificial lamb. He deplored the loss of the six young men; but he believed that the recruit training structure was sound, and he wanted Sergeant McKeon to get a fair trial. He also felt that the honor of the Marine Corps was at stake, and when he was recalled to active duty several months later to appear as a witness at the trial, he was eager to go.

On the afternoon he was poised to leave for South Carolina, after he had donned his uniform and packed his bags, a neighbor called to report that several days earlier she had seen me smoking cigarettes with an older boy behind a barn near her house. The report was true, and before Father left to catch his plane, he walked up to the vacant lot where I was playing touch football with the older boy who had given me the cigarettes and some other friends. The game came to an abrupt halt when the players spotted my father with his gleaming stars and rows of military ribbons, and before anyone moved, my father had administered such a tongue-lashing to me and my teenaged friend that the friend's knees actually knocked together. I was mortified as I watched him turn on his heel and leave, but the other boys were too stunned to make light of my humiliation. My friend never offered me another cigarette, and my father never again mentioned the incident. I had never seen him so angry, and although I continued to experiment with cigarettes, I was very careful with my smoking from that day forward.

My father went to Parris Island, and in an hour of testimony that was chronicled in the *New York Times*, he defended the training methods of the Marine Corps and, by implication, the drill instructor who had employed them with such tragic consequences. Sergeant McKeon was ultimately found guilty of negligent homicide, but he was acquitted of the more serious charge of manslaughter in part because of my father's testimony. More important to my father, however, was the justification he felt he had provided for the harsh training methods he considered necessary to prepare troops for combat.

We met him at the airport in Richmond when he returned home, and I knew by the way he confidently strode through the crowd of cameras, photographers, and newsmen on his way to the car that he was pleased with his performance at Parris Island. Apparently most Americans agreed, for in the weeks and months that followed, he received hundreds of phone calls, telegrams, and letters praising him for coming to the defense of the Marine Corps.

I realized then that bitter as he was for the way he perceived himself to have been treated by the higher-ups in Marine Corps Headquarters, he was incapable of sitting idly by while his beloved corps was under attack. His testimony also reinforced the perception that he was a marines' marine who cared far more about the enlisted men than he did about the high-ranking officers. After his return from Parris Island, there was a noticeable increase in the number of well-wishers appearing at our front door, but by then Mother seemed to have resigned herself to the inevitability of their constant interruptions.

I listened in on my father's conversations with his colleagues and acquaintances while I was growing up, and I unconsciously adopted his politics and philosophy as my own. Most of the admirers who came to share his wisdom were already predisposed to accept his words as gospel; Father's personality was so strong and his delivery so forceful that I saw very few people who ever seemed to express disagreement with his stands on issues. I came to believe, as a youngster, that his opinions were sacrosanct, and it was easy for me to clothe myself with his values. My sisters and I, despite being Episcopalians, attended Catholic schools while Father was on active duty. In those schools we were inculcated with a strong anti-Communist bias by the nuns and priests who taught our daily lessons. Father shared that bias, and by the time I was nine or ten, I firmly believed that Joseph Stalin was the incarnation of evil and that the United States was locked in a death struggle with the Soviet Union that would decide the fate of the free world.

A year after my father retired from the Marine Corps, the Hungarian Revolution took place, and as Russian tanks rolled through the streets of Budapest, my father espoused the cause of the Hungarian "freedom fighters" and decried the gutlessness of a neutral American foreign policy that would not come to the aid of the Hungarians. It seemed to me, with my sophisticated fifth-grade perspective, that Father was entirely right, and I began to see clearly that as a patriotic American I would have the duty later in life to help stem the Red tide. Obviously a country such as the Soviet Union, which would send heavily armed tanks to do combat with men wielding bottles of gasoline, did not fight fairly, and the Hungarian Revolution, as I experienced it through my father's eyes and the pictures in *Life* magazine, reinforced my recently acquired view of communism. It also showed me that there were real reasons for the air-raid drills Martha and I had participated in at school.

=== ☆ ===

For the first three years after we moved to Saluda, Martha and I went to the same local public schools, and we gradually accustomed ourselves to life in the country. Martha took up horseback riding and water skiing, and in no time at all she was as proficient at those activities as she was at swimming and diving. I played Little League baseball, but even with the shiny new glove Father bought me in Richmond, I could do no better than play substitute second base. While Martha was collecting blue ribbons for her equestrianship and effortlessly jumping wakes behind powerboats in the Urbana Creek north of Saluda, I struggled to maintain a .200 batting average. Father never gave any indication that her athletic accomplishments were superior to mine. In fact, the day I accidentally hit a triple along the first-base foul line, he seemed to glow with pride while I stood in stunned disbelief atop third base and watched him in the bleachers.

We also hunted together as we had five years earlier in the hills of Camp Pendleton. By now, having moved up from a twenty-two to a twelve-gauge shotgun, I could easily keep up with my father as we stalked through the woodlands and open fields around Saluda, looking for rabbits and squirrels. In California I had been amazed that my father could walk so fast and so far while I seemed always to be out of breath or trying to ignore the woodenness in my legs. Now, however, as he neared sixty years of age and I was moving into adolescence, the roles were reversed, and he was the one who needed frequent stops to renew his strength. He still had a good enough eye and quick enough reflexes to be able to bring down a flushed quail or a moving rabbit, but I was beginning to understand that when he paused to listen for game or check his bearings, he was really buying time against the encroachments of old age.

On special occasions he took me goose hunting on the plantation of a dear friend with whom he had gone to the Virginia Military Institute forty years earlier, and I became schooled in southern courtesy as I watched these two old men defer to each other on what seemed to me to be the most insignificant points of hunting etiquette. My father always offered Mr. Lafferty the geese we bagged, which he in turn always refused; I wondered the first time it happened why our geese were being proffered to a man whose estate was home to tens of thousands of geese. One cold December morning when my father and I hunted alone in one of Mr. Lafferty's blinds, I shot a goose that had landed amid the decoys and the corn stubble in my line of fire. My father was horrified that I had shot a stationary bird, and he admonished me not to tell anyone that my quarry had not been brought down on the wing. I was stung by his criticism, and my enthusiasm over my trophy quickly evaporated, even though I had learned a painful lesson about sportsmanship and also gained an insight into my father's code of honor.

We also hunted deer together at the naval weapons station in nearby Yorktown, Virginia, where every Saturday morning during hunting season a highly organized deer drive was conducted. The hunting party was divided into hunters and drivers, who alternately took turns driving the deer out of the woods or waiting for them in stands. Aside from the deer, Father was the center of attention during these hunts, and he and I were always given choice stands, where the deer were most likely to exit from the woods.

On my first hunt, the winter after I turned eleven, I was daydreaming on my stand when a spike buck suddenly crashed through the underbrush between my father's stand and my own. As the deer veered across an open space thirty yards in front of my position, I raised my shotgun and squeezed off one round, several pellets of which caught him in the neck and head and brought him down. I had killed my first deer, a rite of passage that Father considered essential to the development of a young boy growing up in the country, and for the rest of the day he proudly told each of the hunters who stopped to congratulate us how I had killed my first deer at an earlier age than he. I was as proud as if I had just shot a grizzly bear with a bow and arrow, and for weeks after we got home, Father told and retold the story of my first deer kill to anyone who would listen, including all the customers on my paper route.

As I approached adolescence, I began to notice how my parents were attempting to monitor my progress and imbue me with their values. Sundays we all rode to the Episcopal church three miles from Saluda, where my sisters, my father, my grandmother, and I always sat in the fifth pew from the front on the right-hand side. Mother was a soprano in the choir and at age fifty still sang like a nightingale. The rest of the choir was average, but on a good Sunday, when Mother was in top form, I listened raptly and waited for the chill bumps to subside along my back and arms as she held the high notes of her solos. Father, on the other hand, had a singing voice like a frog's, which all his children inherited, but we followed his lead and sang lustily over our shared hymnals. Religion was a mainstay of Mother's life, and although Father was not as zealous as she in his stewardship of our spiritual direction, we were expected to go to church regularly, say prayers at our meals, and participate in church projects.

My father rarely discussed religion with my sisters or me, but I knew by his example that he valued highly the spiritual side of life. Years later, when I was about to depart for college, he took me aside and suggested that in the absence of a well-defined moral code of my own, I would do well to follow the example of the Ten Commandments. It was a brief lecture that I am certain he felt uncomfortable with yet obligated to make, but it was so uncharacteristic of him that I have a vivid recollection of the conversation.

Aside from our religious orientation, good manners were an element in our upbringing that Mother and Father considered important. I was taught early to stand when adults entered a room and to help ladies with their chairs or with car doors. We never interrupted grown-ups in conversations, and when addressing them, we always ended our responses with "sir" or "ma'am." Father taught me to squeeze a man's hand firmly when I shook hands and to look people straight in the eye when we were talking. He valued personal appearances and good grooming, and until I left for college, I never went more than a few weeks without a haircut. When I was in seventh grade, he taught me how to tie a necktie, and from then on I was expected to be properly dressed in coat and tie for special occasions.

I was equally aware of how I looked to others. In seventh grade I was fitted for braces by an orthodontist in Richmond, and on the way home in the car my teeth hurt and I was depressed. I had gotten eyeglasses only a few months earlier to correct my nearsightedness, and the braces coming so quickly after the glasses were more than my fragile psyche could handle. Father noticed my despondency and suggested that we stop on the outskirts of Richmond for cheeseburgers and ice cream. With my sore teeth I could manage neither, so while Mother and Father were finishing their meal in the drugstore where we stopped, I wandered over to the magazine stand and began browsing.

Before I had gotten two pages into the magazine I had selected, a burly white-collared druggist appeared at my side, snatched the magazine from my hand, and began browbeating me for reading the magazine without paying for it. I was totally bewildered by his attitude, but before I could retreat or apologize, I saw out of the corner of my eye that my father had risen from his booth and was advancing toward the druggist. His teeth were tightly clenched, as were his fists, and there was fire in his eyes as he came to rest with his face not six inches from the druggist's. Before he spoke, I looked at my mother, who with her eyes closed in the vinyl booth appeared to be praying, and then I looked at the druggist, who was at least fifty pounds heavier and thirty years younger than my father.

"Leave the boy alone," my father growled, in a voice gone hard, "or you and I can go outside and settle this."

For a moment the druggist said nothing as his face blanched until it was the color of his collar.

"Excuse me, sir," he finally stammered, and he retreated to the safety of the cash register.

My father never mentioned the episode again, but I played the scene over and over as we completed our journey back to Saluda. I found it strange that my teeth had stopped hurting, but I found it stranger still that while the incident in the drugstore was unfolding, Mother had reacted as if she had seen my father behave similarly on other occasions.

At the beginning of eighth grade I became a day student at Christchurch School for Boys, an Episcopal boarding school that was located adjacent to our church, and for the first time since starting grade school, I was in a private school while Martha remained in the local public school. Every day after school, when I got home, Martha sat me down and demanded to know what wondrous things I had encountered in my dealings with the other boys, and until the novelty of my stories wore off, I was able to exact favors from her for my reports. I embellished freely in order to keep her feeding the dog and doing my household chores, but I was for the most part as fascinated as she by the sophisticated older boys from Washington or Richmond with whom I now mingled on a daily basis.

I was, at age thirteen, a ninety-pound stick of a boy with braces and glasses, but the glandular changes just beginning in my body held out the hope, however remote, that one day I would have body hair and the musculature of some of the juniors and seniors I so admired. For years Father had been keeping track of Martha's and my heights by periodically marking and dating them in pencil on the living room wall, and he often expressed the wish that I would exceed his height and reach six feet. Sometime during my eighth-grade year I finally grew taller than Martha, but it was several more years before I could look my father level in the eye.

At Christchurch I threw myself into my studies, partly to compensate for not being a capable athlete. I did well academically and quickly gained a reputation as one of the bright boys. In the afternoons I played on the lower-school football, basketball, and baseball teams, and I was able to start at several sports because there were only forty boys in the eighth and ninth grades. Father came to most of the home games, and I was embarrassed that he took such an interest in my small victories; but the other boys regarded him as the national celebrity that he was and readily accepted his presence.

Before one of the basketball games in the winter of my first year at Christchurch, I realized, as I was getting my uniform out of my locker, that I had taken my athletic supporter home to be washed and left it there. It was not a matter of any consequence, and I simply donned my uniform over my Jockey shorts and forgot all about it. When my father arrived for the game, the forgotten jockstrap was hanging halfway out of his hip pocket, and although he seemed oblivious of the telltale symbol of my approaching manhood, I could not have been any more mortified if he had shown up nude and passed out contraceptives to all my teammates. He was proud that he had a son to carry on the Puller name and saw no need for discretion in his effort to protect the family jewels.

For the first two years at Christchurch I was too young to drive, and I rode to school in the mornings with one of the custodians at the school who lived in Saluda. Father always awakened us in time to join him for breakfast at the kitchen table, and in the evening after sports he picked me up beside the school gym. He was interested in my development, and though he did not pry, he was eager to hear the adolescent ramblings of his son.

One day in late January of my first year at Christchurch, he did not return my greeting when he picked me up, and I could tell by the way he clutched the steering wheel as I was getting in that something had gone wrong at home. When I was seated, he put his hand on my shoulder and told me that he had buried Fidget earlier that afternoon. I sat quietly and listened as he recounted how the dog had walked with him to the post office and then been run over by a speeding motorist as they crossed the street on the way home. According to Father, she had

26

died without suffering, and he had buried her beneath a walnut tree at the back edge of our property.

Neither of us talked on the way home; but tears stung my face, which I averted so that Father would not see them, and my throat felt like raw meat. When we got home, he walked with me to the grave and stood silently beside me. Fidget and I had been inseparable, and I did not realize until she was gone how much I had loved her. After a few minutes my father put his hand gently on my elbow and led me away from the darkness of the grave and toward the lighted kitchen, where Mother was preparing dinner.

=== ☆ ===

As I grew older and began the sometimes painful process by which a son distances himself from his father in preparation for striking out on his own, I began to realize that my father the man and my father the legend were not always one and the same. The legend was all-powerful, fearless in the face of any challenge or adversity, and incapable of mistakes in judgment or unfairness in dealings with lesser mortals. The man, like most men approaching their twilight years, was not as strong as he had once been, occasionally showed signs of self-doubt, and made his share of errors when interacting with other people. From the time I was a little boy, he had delighted in balling up his fists and playfully going several rounds with me. He continued the game after I started high school; but by the time I was fifteen or sixteen my reflexes had become sharper than his, and I became uncomfortable exchanging mock punches with him.

One day after a few minutes of horseplay, during which he had exerted himself too strenuously, I accidentally bloodied his lip. The game ended immediately, but as he stood in the middle of our living room with his chest heaving and his handkerchief pressed against his mouth, I felt as if I had committed blasphemy. We continued to box following that episode; but neither of us had our heart in the game, and after one or two feints and jabs there was always some pretext for quitting.

I also began to be bothered by the waste of my father's considerable talent and the inordinate amount of time he spent on trivial undertakings. Of all the adults with whom I had ever come in contact, my own father was the most famous, yet it seemed to me that he did almost no productive work after he retired. My friends all had working fathers who left their homes every morning, and though most of them did not have glamorous jobs, they at least had someplace to go and some interest outside the house. My own father, on the other hand, spent hours sitting at the dining room table playing solitaire or rereading books that he had owned for many years. Mother was busy running the house and raising Virginia, Martha, and me, while there were days during which my father did nothing more than make an occasional trip to the corner store or fetch the mail.

He was easy to have around the house and was almost totally undemanding of his children, but it seemed to me that this living legend should have more important things to do than serve as an errand boy for our mother. I did not realize that the Marine Corps had been his whole life and that in committing himself so totally to its mission, he had never had time for hobbies or other outside interests. I also did not see until I was much older that my father's stroke had taken a physical toll on him that he would never acknowledge.

═══ ☆ ═══

In the middle of my junior year in high school my father awakened one night in intense pain. My mother called for the family doctor and then came to my bedroom with the alarming news. I could tell by her expression that he was seriously ill, and I immediately got dressed and went down to their bedroom. When the doctor arrived, he did a cursory examination, diagnosed the source of the pain as an enlarged prostate, and summoned an ambulance. I rode in the ambulance with my father to the Portsmouth Naval Hospital, which was two hours away, and Mother followed us in the family car with the doctor and a member of the rescue squad who served as her driver.

My father held tightly to my hand for most of the trip, and I could tell that he was in agony, although his only complaint was that he was not allowed to smoke in the ambulance. After he was admitted, the decision was made to do an emergency prostate removal, and for several weeks during his recovery he was given painkillers and nightly sedations.

When he returned home, he was unable to sleep at night, and because I was often up late doing homework at the dining table, he played solitaire at the other end of the table while I burned the midnight oil. He was restless after the operation, a combination, I think, of withdrawal from sleeping pills and the indignity he had suffered to his manhood, and he spent as much time pacing the dining room to the living room and back as he did manipulating the cards.

I felt close to him at that crisis point in his life, partly because in his vulnerable state I did not feel that I was looking up at him and partly because we were two males sharing the same late hours alone together. At any rate, I finally realized that he wanted to talk, and for perhaps seven or eight days in that winter of 1962 I was able to communicate with my father as I never had before. He told me that he was fearful about aging and the inevitably declining state of his health, and about how he never wanted to be a burden to his family. I listened as best I could to an old man reveal feelings that he never had expressed before. He also told me that he was counting on me to carry on when he was gone and how proud he was to have a son to continue the Puller name. We did not talk about the military or my attempting to follow in his footsteps, but even then there were some unstated assumptions about the course my life would take.

Several years earlier, shortly after his retirement, we had gone to Williamsburg for an outing, and he had taken me to see a short film about the American Revolution called *The Story of a Patriot*, which was shown continuously to tourists visiting the information center. At the conclusion of the film the main character watches a group of young men who have just enlisted to go fight the British, and he swells with pride when he sees his son among the ranks of the newly enlisted.

My father's enchantment with that scene registered powerfully on my young psyche, and without his ever saying another word, I knew that someday I would be enlisting in some as yet undetermined cause. Now, five or six years later, as I shared the dining table of our home with the man I loved like no other in the world, I wanted desperately to be what he expected me to be. It took me years to realize that I could never hope to emulate the legend that was Chesty Puller, but I knew even then that I loved the man far more than the legend.

II

★

IN THE AUTUMN OF 1967 with the lengthening shadow of the Vietnam War spreading a chill across America, I moved on from the carefree pursuits of undergraduate life at the College of William and Mary and joined the Marine Corps. Like my father, who had enlisted fifty years earlier during the war to end all wars, I traveled from a rural Virginia town to the Marine Corps recruiting station in nearby Richmond in search of something larger than myself. I had drifted through the previous four years, drinking beer and chasing girls with a singleness of purpose that belied my lack of meaningful direction, and now, on the threshold of manhood and with war as a backdrop, I realized that the time had come to put frivolity aside.

William and Mary in the months prior to my departure was still the sleepy southern campus whose quaintness had attracted me four years earlier. When my companions and I were not cramming for exams, parties on fraternity row and pickup bridge games in the student lounge filled our idle time, while our minds were more absorbed with the fledgling fantasies of the uninitiated than with global politics or foreign affairs. The carnage taking place in Southeast Asia had remained a distant and nonintrusive reality for all but the most perceptive of us, insulated as we were by youth and an inexperience born of our middle-class backgrounds, and the campus unrest that was beginning to roil its way east from Berkeley had yet to register in Williamsburg.

There were, however, signs of a more ominous nature. The networks had begun reporting the rising casualty tolls on the nightly news, and a previously unrecognized stridency seemed to color the political dialogue coming out of Washington. Fellow students who had planned on careers in accounting or business administration occasionally spoke of teaching for a few years after graduation, and at social gatherings over the summer I had met several young men who were on their way north to Canada and a sanctuary of sorts. A few others, from military families for the most part, shared my opinion that the war in Vietnam was but another manifestation of the domino theory and were boyishly anxious to do their part to stem the tide of Communist aggression. Against this background, I viewed the graduation that ended my student draft deferment and qualified me for the Marine Corps officer candidate program as an opportunity rather than a burden.

As I entered the recruiter's office, I was acutely aware of the impact that my name would have on the sergeant whose duty it would be to convince me of the golden opportunities that a hitch in the Marine Corps could provide. "The Marine Corps Builds Men," the decal on his office divider proclaimed, and I, in my youthful exuberance, never paused to consider that the corps might do the opposite. When he realized who I was, the sergeant dispensed with his usual sales pitch and concentrated on the mechanics of becoming the recruiter who signed up Chesty Puller's son.

I had already been reclassified 1-A by the Selective Service System and so had entered the pool of young men whose legacy was to be the most potentially shattering experience yet encountered by the male members of the post–World War II baby boom. I had also completed a cursory physical and mental qualification test in the process of being reclassified, and the Marine Corps now subjected me to a more rigorous examination to establish my fitness to enter its officer candidate program. The recruiter also telephoned Marine Corps Headquarters in Washington, D.C., to obtain a waiver for my poor eyesight, and the authority on the other end of the line at first demurred but then acquiesced when he realized that if he stood firm, the corps could fail to sign up the son of its most famous marine because of a technicality.

Several days later, after the paperwork had been completed and the oath of allegiance administered, I returned to Saluda to await orders to Quantico for basic training. My older sister's husband, Captain Bill

Dabney, was already serving a tour as a marine infantry company commander in Vietnam, and she, too, was back at home sitting out our generation's initial venture into war. Our mother, despite the luxury of having two of her three children living at home for a short time, was all too familiar with my sister's situation as she, too, had returned to the same town to be with our grandmother under similar circumstances during World War II and the Korean War. For my part, I did not share our neighbors' sympathy for my sister's plight. Her husband was pursuing a career that he had freely chosen, and I had been taught that war was both an opportunity and an obligation for any man who embraced the military calling. I would be following in my brother-in-law's footsteps within a year, and my concept of mortality was at that time so rudimentary that I hardly considered the possibility that either of us might not return. Furthermore, after a childhood diet of Hemingway novels and John Wayne movies along with my father's example, I viewed my own prospects, if not with eagerness, at least with equanimity.

In the weeks prior to my departure for Officer Candidate School, I embarked on a crash course of physical conditioning. I had wrestled and played football in high school; but the four years of abuse to which I subjected my body in college had left me woefully out of shape, and I knew that my instructors at Quantico would be doubly alert to any signs of mental or physical weakness. At that time I was far more fearful of the Marine Corps than of the North Vietnamese or Vietcong, and the idea of failing made me push myself to the point of exhaustion. My two daily workouts emphasized running and upper-body conditioning, and although I started in relatively poor shape, I was surprised how quickly my muscles began to firm up after a four-year layoff. I also began to pay far more attention to the newspapers and nightly news broadcasts about Southeast Asia. My sister's letters from her husband also helped slake a growing thirst for firsthand knowledge of the war. In a sense I was beginning to prepare myself psychologically as well as physically for what was to come.

I occasionally interrupted my self-imposed regimen to return to the William and Mary campus in Williamsburg for weekend respites, but I had already begun to feel out of place among my former cohorts and fraternity brothers who had not yet graduated. The camaraderie of the fraternity now seemed almost trivial, and although I often drank myself to the point of oblivion, I could not escape the feeling that for me the carefree celebrations of youth could not be recaptured. Then, too,

I found it peculiar that so few of my peers were following the path I had chosen, but I attributed our different courses to my own military background and did not look for ulterior motives.

Of all my friends and acquaintances at William and Mary, only one had been touched by the war for which I was headed. Byron Speer, the president of a neighboring fraternity, whose dreams of manhood I had been privileged to share in frequent late-night bull sessions, had preceded me into the Marine Corps and had been killed within months of his arrival in Vietnam the previous June. His death saddened me and brought home the intimations of mortality with which most of my circle were blessedly unfamiliar.

Even as estrangement from my companions of the previous four years made me uneasy, a new relationship began to blossom that eased these uncomfortable feelings. One evening I returned from a workout to find that my twin sister had arrived for the weekend with her new roommate. They had gone to Mary Washington College together and now taught school in that area of northern Virginia where I would be undergoing basic training. I was attracted immediately to this raven-haired young woman, and although neither of us contemplated anything of a serious nature, the timing was such that we both were vulnerable. By the end of the weekend I knew that I would see more of her, and I marveled at the stroke of fortune that would place us in such close proximity while I attended OCS.

During this waiting time my father had remained characteristically closemouthed about my future in the Marine Corps. He had come to Richmond for my swearing in and had stood at my side among the popping flashbulbs as I took the oath of allegiance. He had wanted me to follow him to the Virginia Military Institute; but he had not pressed the issue when it came time for me to select a college, and he similarly did not overtly attempt to influence my decision to enter the Marine Corps. I, of course, knew that he was immensely proud of me for having chosen to follow his example, but a tacit understanding between us made words unnecessary. I felt an urgent and compelling need to prove myself worthy of his name, and he, in the twilight of a military career that had spanned almost forty years, wished that he could go in my stead. As I said my good-byes and prepared to leave for Quantico, he kissed me squarely on the lips and held me tightly in his arms.

I reported in to Officer Candidate School as late in the day as was acceptable. It was a blustery Sunday evening shortly before Thanksgiving. I was hung over from having overcelebrated my last weekend as a civilian, and I felt completely out of place in my tweed sport coat and brown wing tips. I had been forewarned never to say "sir" to an enlisted man and always to say "sir" to an officer, and after breaking the first part of the rule at each clerk's station as I was being processed, I managed to violate the last part with predictable results when, at the end of the line, I was turned over to an irate Captain Gretter, who was to be my principal tormentor for the next ten weeks. When told that I was a "miserable shit-eating college boy who would never be an officer in this Marine Corps," I wanted nothing so much as to disappear into my shaving kit, and I was overcome with gratitude when ordered to move outside and into a roughshod formation of woebegone college boys who obviously had suffered similar humiliation from Captain Gretter. As I stood there in the dark trying to be as inconspicuous as possible, I overheard two large sergeants conversing animatedly about who among this miserable collection of pukes could possibly be Chesty Puller's son, and I wondered if I had taken on more than I could handle.

When the last candidates in our platoon completed their paperwork, our platoon sergeant and sergeant instructor briefly introduced themselves. They then made it perfectly clear that they and Captain Gretter would be doing the thinking for us for the next two and one-half months and that we could forget we had even earned the diplomas that were for most of us our only tangible accomplishment in life. Staff Sergeant Brown was a burly black man who later earned a Navy Cross for heroism in Vietnam, and his military bearing made it obvious that he would brook no disrespect. Sergeant Sorg, his assistant, was a toothless Swede who looked menacing enough for his role, but his words left a serious doubt in my mind about whether he was capable of doing anyone's thinking, including his own. While Sorg marched us, if such a term could be used to describe our halting gait, to our barracks along the banks of the Potomac River, I was grateful for the cover of darkness, but fearful that I had delivered myself into the hands of megalomaniacs.

Before turning in, we were assigned bunks, footlockers, and wall lockers in a narrow squad bay whose well-worn deck glistened from the countless scrubbings it had endured from previous officer candidates. As I stored my few allowable belongings, I dared look around for the first time at the faces of my platoon mates. Most appeared to be recent college graduates, although a few were enlisted men who had shown promise in earlier assignments and been recommended for Officer

Candidate School without college degrees. There was even a Vietnam veteran whose two rows of ribbons, including two Purple Hearts, immediately accorded him a godlike status he probably neither deserved nor wanted. There were also a couple of relatively older lawyers whose enlistment terms ensured that they would be heading back to their law firms while the rest of us headed for Vietnam.

Before dawn the next morning Sergeant Sorg awakened us by rolling a corrugated metal trash can the length of the squad bay between the double-deck bunks that lined both bulkheads. We sprang from our bunks and assumed positions of attention at the foot of our bunks while Sorg paced up and down the aisle, explaining the day's agenda and reminding us that as officer candidates we were the lowest form of scum in the Marine Corps. We spent that first day largely being hurried from one line to another to draw the basic gear we would need for our initial training and filling out endless forms, which would no doubt be filed away and never read again. We double-timed to every supply station as a unit, with Sergeant Sorg harassing us all the way, and by the end of the day, when our civilian clothes had been replaced by Marine Corps green and our varied hairstyles reduced to a uniform baldness, there was very little to tell us apart. From the start the emphasis seemed to be on eliminating our individual idiosyncrasies and developing a group character. There was to be only one way, the Marine Corps way, as Sergeant Sorg reiterated, and if we could not accept its terms, unequivocally and without question, the Marine Corps would not accept us as officers. I also quickly realized that the constant rushing from one place to the next, while it did not improve efficiency since we invariably waited after we arrived, did increase tension and was designed to reduce our ranks of their weaker members. When viewed as a game, it became easier to endure.

Midway through the first day, as I was standing in yet another line waiting for boots, a scrawny sergeant instructor from another platoon backed me up against a bulkhead and demanded to know if I knew the significance of the blue and white ribbon over his left breast pocket. He had been awarded the Navy Cross for assaulting an enemy position with an entrenching tool on a tour in Vietnam and seemed to be directing the same frenzied intensity at me that had impelled him at the North Vietnamese, one pure moment of valor that, it seemed to me, would remain forever the focus of his life. When I acknowledged the award, he screamed at me that he intended to earn five more and thereby eclipse the record of Chesty Puller. I have often wondered if that strange young man, barely out of his teens, died in pursuit of an impossible dream. His act of courage was certainly greater than anything to which I aspired at that time, but I did recognize a kindred element in its motivation.

The next morning Captain Gretter began interviewing each candidate in the platoon in his office adjacent to our squad bay. His pattern was to leave the day-to-day details of our training to Staff Sergeant Brown and Sergeant Sorg, and for that reason he rarely came into our living area. His participation in any aspect of our training therefore meant that that particular item on the agenda had special significance and was a clue that we had best perform well. As I entered his office for my interview and assumed a position of attention front and center of his desk, I felt that a year had passed since my first disastrous meeting with him only a day and a half earlier. He took his time completing whatever paperwork he had been poring over when I entered and then, capping his pen, acknowledged my presence for the first time.

"Candidate Puller," he began, "you will receive no preferential treatment while here because of your relationship to your father. If anything," he continued, "I consider your presence in my platoon an irritant rather than an honor because it will require additional effort on my part and because every swinging dick in this green machine is going to be eyeballing you. I am personally going to take it upon myself to see that you meet the qualifications of an officer in spades. Do I make myself clear?" he finished.

Having learned my lesson earlier in the week, I this time managed a firm "Yes, sir," and did not allow my eyes to wander from the spot on the wall directly behind his head where they had been riveted since his harangue began. I do not know how he conducted himself when interviewing the rest of the platoon, but he certainly laid his cards on the table when dealing with me. Had our roles been reversed, I probably would have taken the same tack, but I was nevertheless seething inside that he would imply that I might attempt to take advantage of my father's name.

The interviews over, Captain Gretter assembled us for a run in our newly acquired crimson and gold PT garb and set such a pace that he left all but the couple of college track stars strewn in his wake like so much flotsam and jetsam. As I dry heaved between my legs three-quarters of the way through the run, I would have felt completely humiliated but for the fact that half the platoon shared my predicament. There was no question but that Captain Gretter was in command.

Once the routine of OCS became familiar and we learned what was expected, it became more tolerable. Each day started before sunup with five minutes of calisthenics, followed by a morning formation, chow in the mess hall, and an endless series of classes both indoors and outdoors. There was considerable time spent in physical conditioning and in drilling on the parade ground, but the real goal of Officer Candidate School was a testing of our physical, mental, and psychological limits rather than a grounding in military fundamentals. That was to come later, in Basic School, for those of us who earned lieutenants' bars, but for now the Marine Corps wanted only to see how far we could be pushed.

There were academic tests to ascertain our ability to absorb written instruction, positions of leadership, or billets, in which each of us served for brief periods to test our judgment and responsibility, and an assortment of grueling physical hurdles that, if not overcome, would doom us to enlisted status. Once a week there was a forced march of varying length, usually four to eight miles, in which each of the four platoons undergoing training took part. We were quickly made to realize that successful completion of this item of our training was the standard against which the rest of the week's performance would be measured, and the psychological pressure to do well was enormous.

For the first march we were assembled in a flat staging area by platoon. Each of us carried a full complement of combat gear, including a bulky pack, a hard hat, canteens, and a rifle. Although our instructors, both officers and enlisted, carried far less gear, they would cover more ground in the course of the march since they would be constantly scurrying back and forth along the lines, urging stragglers to close ranks and maintain platoon integrity. Captain Gretter was, of course, squarely in his element and looking forward with immense satisfaction to our misery. We had also been told that it was far easier to march in the first or second platoon since there was an inevitable accordion effect and the third and fourth platoons' members had to spend a lot of time running just to keep up with those who preceded.

As the march began, my platoon had drawn third place, an ominous sign, and it seemed we were running from the start. The route began with a series of three increasingly steep hills, whose severe angulations had to have been designed by a sadistic engineer rather than by God, and by the time we reached the crest of the middle hill, my calf and thigh muscles felt as if they had been transformed into Silly Putty. Sweat filled every crevice of my body, and amazingly, the top of my boxer shorts seemed to be riding just beneath my armpits. My pack straps dug deeply into my shoulders, and my spine seemed to have achieved a remarkable curvature I would have thought possible only in a contortionist. Although I and a dozen other unfortunates managed to struggle up the next hill, leaving some in worse shape scattered in our wake, a waiting cadre of officers immediately branded us as stragglers, and we were disqualified from completing the march with the rest of the company. As we were ignominiously set apart from our peers, I felt an almost visceral humiliation and resolved never to straggle on another march. Captain Gretter did not deign so much as to look at us, no doubt considering it a personal insult that we had disgraced his platoon, and I would have preferred by far the profane tirades that were his usual stock-in-trade.

Although our training schedule made no allowance for Thanksgiving that autumn, we were given liberty a couple of weeks later from Saturday at noon until Sunday night. My sister's roommate, Toddy, picked me up in the parking lot outside the barracks and laughed uproariously at the contrast between my tweed coat and my bald head. I hid my self-consciousness as best I could and entertained the brief thought that civilian clothing was for me beginning to lose its fit. Besides, Toddy was delivering me from the hands of Captain Gretter and his minions for twenty-four hours, and her willingness to pick me up was the most encouraging sign I had seen in weeks. My mother, sensing that I would be spending the time at my sister and Toddy's apartment, had sent money for a fancy meal, and the roast beef and red wine we enjoyed that night were far more sumptuous than anything I could have ordered in a five-star restaurant.

Later we went to see *Bonnie and Clyde*, shared popcorn, and held hands like a couple of high school kids, while Faye Dunaway and Warren Beatty shot the bejesus out of everything in sight. As I went to sleep on the couch in the apartment living room that night, I sensed that the softness of this incredible woman was going to give me the strength to make it through the rest of Officer Candidate School. I kissed her good-bye on Sunday evening in the same parking lot where she had received me only a day earlier and woefully realized that I was falling in love at a time when emotional independence might well be the more prudent course.

Halfway through the ten-week course our platoon underwent an evaluation in the course of which the unsatisfactory performers were culled from the program and the marginal ones were put on notice that they had best shape up. The tension prior to notification was tremendous, but once the results became known, those of us who had performed satisfactorily were on sounder footing and became more self-assured. I was, at that crucial halfway point, meeting all the physical demands, including a fairly decent performance on the obstacle course and a much-improved score on the physical fitness test. I even managed to knock down an opponent twenty pounds heavier than I was in the pugil stick competition, and I thought I noticed the trace of a smile on Captain Gretter's otherwise grim visage when my stunned adversary's knees buckled in our combat with these weighted and padded clubs.

Staff Sergeant Brown taught us to try to divorce our minds from the pain in our bodies while navigating the hill trail by the simple expedient of sucking Life Savers and imagining ourselves in a more pleasant situation, and from that moment on I fantasized that the finish line for each successful hike was the middle of Toddy's apartment. On one particularly grueling march, during which rain had so slicked the sides of the trail that it was almost impossible to achieve enough traction to maintain momentum, I was foundering and in danger of once more becoming a straggler when a hand on my butt provided the necessary impetus to best the increasing resistance of the offending hill. As I reached the top, I realized from Sergeant Sorg's toothless grin that he had provided the boost, and I wondered if it was my own determination or my name that had prompted him to make such an uncharacteristic gesture. From that point on, my apprehension of the hill trail vanished, and although the weariness of my legs was an inevitable accompaniment to each succeeding hike, I never again allowed Gretter, Brown, or Sorg to read the exhaustion on my face.

By the end of OCS I had developed a hardness and a confidence of which I had not thought myself capable. I had lost ten pounds despite consuming more food than ever before in my life, and the flabbiness developed over four years of dissolution had been replaced by hard edges and new muscle. I found that I had actually come to enjoy the unsolvable problems and pitfalls placed before me, and if I could not master them, I at least developed a capacity to appear to know what I was doing. The brown bars and commission of a second lieutenant and leader of marines were within my grasp. I had been bred for them, I had earned them, and nobody was going to deprive me of them. On the last march prior to commissioning, I practically ran from start to finish, and my defiant gaze at Captain Gretter at its completion was, of course, exactly the reaction he had been trying to elicit from me for ten weeks.

The night before we were commissioned, Staff Sergeant Brown and Sergeant Sorg had a keg party for the platoon in the barracks. We had spent the day turning in the gear we had used in the course of our training and in squaring away the squad bay, which had housed us for the previous two and one-half months. After our uniforms were readied for the next day's ceremonies, we gathered with the sergeants and invited enlisted staff who had participated in our training and began to drink beer. At first our efforts at socializing were tentative and stilted since we were used to dealing with the sergeants as our supervisors, but as the beer began to loosen our tongues and inhibitions, a feeling of camaraderie began to develop.

Sorg and Brown had known from the start that the day would come when, if they did their jobs well, we would outrank them, and their pride at having molded us from collegiate dandies into marine officers spilled over to the group, as so, of course, did a good deal of beer. Somewhere amid the horseplay and backslapping one of us had the cloth name tag that branded us as candidates ripped from the shirt pocket of his green utilities, and within minutes not a name tag was intact. When mine was removed, the entire enlisted assemblage seemed to have the same thought at once, and they all raced upstairs to my wall locker to gather all my name tags as souvenirs. I realized then, I think for the first time, and through the glow of too much beer, how much admiration for my father they all had suppressed while our training was in progress.

Since most of us would be going directly to Basic School after our commissioning the next day, the remainder of the evening did not degenerate into maudlin good-byes. We were simply moving on together, and our mood was ebullient at having survived an ordeal and earned our bars. Even the lawyers who were returning to civilian life as reservists were treated charitably. At that point none of us could have known how easily they were getting off when compared with the experience many of us would be facing shortly. Much later in the evening I summoned the courage to thank Sorg for having given me that push weeks earlier on the hill trail, and he covered his embarrassment by telling the other staff that he had really been trying to push me off the trail rather than up the hill.

As we slumbered off to our bunks for the last wake-up at OCS, I overheard one drunken staff sergeant from another platoon tell Brown that 75 percent of us who chose the infantry would be dead or wounded within six months of arriving in Vietnam, but even his somber words could not dull my elation.

═ ☆ ═

The next morning, as we readied our winter greens for the commissioning ceremony and took care of the last-minute details associated with any change of duty stations, Sorg entered the squad bay and requested rather than demanded that we assume positions of attention one last time at the foot of our bunks. He saluted each of us and collected the customary dollar that is the traditional right of the first enlisted man to salute a newly commissioned officer in the Marine Corps. Although we would not become officers technically for several more hours, no one objected to Sorg's manipulation of the schedule, and I smiled wryly that this barely literate sergeant was fleecing a platoon of college graduates out of twenty-eight dollars. As I passed him the crisp one-dollar bill I had readied for the occasion, I marveled that he, Brown, and Gretter were no longer the titans I had regarded with such awe earlier in the fall.

═ ☆ ═

My parents and older sister were already seated in the auditorium when I arrived just prior to the commissioning ceremony. Only Martha was missing—a distant wedding necessitated her being away for the weekend. Toddy had lent me her car but had decided to forgo the actual ceremony, feeling that it would be presumptuous to horn in on what should be essentially a family celebration. Neither her parents nor mine realized yet that we had been spending most of our spare time together since the beginning of OCS, and as I greeted my mother and father, I was already looking past the first hours of my lieutenancy to a very special evening with the woman whose encouragement had sustained me through my often self-doubting passage from civilian to military life.

Following a short speech by a Marine Corps general who opined that the hardest two ranks to make in the Marine Corps were brigadier general and second lieutenant, we were sworn in en masse, after which Virginia helped my father pin on my lieutenant's bars. He beamed proudly, and I spent a good part of the rest of the afternoon self-consciously either looking at my own shoulders or looking for enlisted men whose salutes I could return.

Jimmy Stewart's stepson Ron McLean, although in another platoon, was also commissioned that afternoon, and the famous actor had come down for the ceremony. The four of us had our picture taken together for the *New York Times*, and the attention directed toward Stewart and my father nearly eclipsed any special recognition we lowly lieutenants might have merited. Less than a year later the clear-eyed young McLean, who had earned the respect of all of us by the quiet way he handled his relationship to a legendary figure, was dead, a statistic among the group of young men who by now were forfeiting their lives in Vietnam at a rate that had become unacceptable to most Americans.

A short reception followed our passage into officer status, and I was grateful that Captain Gretter did not mention my difficulties on the hill trail to my father. I made certain that Sorg and Brown, who were milling on the periphery of the crowd surrounding my father, had an opportunity to meet him, and they each looked as if the hand of God had been extended when he reached out to greet them. He thanked them warmly for the instruction they had given me in that self-effacing way that had secured his devotion among enlisted men everywhere, and I marveled at the way he was able to shift the focus from himself to them.

I never saw Sorg or Brown again, but I hope my parting handshakes with them conveyed some of the feeling that my father was able to express so easily. Captain Gretter, ever the commander, took me aside before the reception ended and grudgingly acknowledged the unique burden I had shouldered during the previous ten weeks. Despite his overture, I could see that he was thinking that I would yet be tested in a manner that all the training in the world could never hope to approximate, but at least we parted with mutual respect. I walked my parents to their car for the trip back to Saluda, and I checked my watch to make certain I had time to sign in at Basic School and still pick up a bottle of Wild Turkey before the package store closed.

Basic School, located just across the base, was all but deserted when I arrived later that afternoon. Our class was not to begin officially until Monday, and most of us from OCS were so hell-bent on celebrating our new status that we simply signed in, stored our gear in our assigned living quarters, and headed for Georgetown or the nearest watering hole. Because my twin sister was out of town, Toddy and I would have the apartment to ourselves, and I was feeling on top of the world as I looked back over the day's activities and toward the remainder of the weekend. I had survived the ordeal of basic training, disappointing neither my father nor myself, and I had read in his face that morning as he pinned on my bars a familial pride that transcended time and place. I felt as if I were on the verge of fulfilling a destiny that had its origins many generations back in our family history. It was fitting that time and circumstance had so conspired as to make me an officer in the Marine Corps during a period of war, and if I was by temperament not suited to assuming the mantle of leadership, I certainly was by birth.

Toddy's embrace when she opened the door to her apartment was so ardent that I almost dropped the bottle of Wild Turkey. I was elated that she shared my sense of accomplishment, and I quickly filled her in on the morning's activities, including our having met Jimmy Stewart and my father's pride. We toasted each other with the outrageously expensive liquor, laughing at the incongruity of drinking it from jelly jars, and I facetiously promised her fine crystal if she would only love, honor, and obey me. After a candlelit dinner served on the apartment card table, we did the dishes and continued our conversation on the living room sofa. I had never felt closer to or more comfortable with a woman, and when there was nothing remaining to be said, I carried her into the bedroom for the first time. Tomorrow I could begin thinking about the obligations and responsibilities that would attend my passage into the officer ranks; but for tonight I was a young man in love, and with Toddy beside me there was not a cloud on the horizon.

=== ☆ ===

Although we were the most junior officers in the Marine Corps when we arrived at Basic School on Sunday night, we were nevertheless finally officers, and there was none of the overwhelming fear that played such a large role in our first night at Officer Candidate School. Besides my classmates from OCS, there was a smattering of lieutenants from other commissioning programs and others who for various reasons had delayed their entry into active duty. One lieutenant, whom I did not know, was killed in an automobile accident on his way to the school, and while I could not fully mourn the loss of a stranger, for me his death cast a pall on the first few days of our training and proved to be an omen for events to come. Early in the week there was a memorial service for him, which we all were required to attend, and the pervasive sadness of the occasion seemed odd to me since none of us knew him. On reflection I can see that the combination of his youth and the realization that we had lost one of our own set the tone for his memorial service. Even after only ten weeks in the corps we were developing an esprit that dictated that we properly honor our dead.

Initially, for me, one of the most striking contrasts between Basic School and Officer Candidate School was our living accommodations. While a bunk bed, a footlocker, and a wall locker had been the Marine

Corps's only concessions to our comfort as candidates, as officers we now had rooms with real doors, and although there were three of us assigned to each room, we could at least shut out the rest of the platoon at the end of the day. Because a dining hall, laundry service, and a bar were also located in the building that housed us, we were relatively self-contained, and after the regimen of OCS, it felt positively civilized to be able to repair to the Hawkins room, the in-house watering hole, for a few beers and war stories at the conclusion of a day of training.

The curriculum was divided equally between classroom instruction and field training, with more time being spent outdoors as the training progressed. The entire course in the winter of 1968 had been shortened from nine months to twenty-one weeks with about one Saturday free each month. The reason for the concentration of the course was obvious, if seldom talked about, as we toiled through fourteen-hour workdays attempting to master the skills that would be matters of life and death in our next assignments. Since casualties were so high among our graduates, our own hectic training schedule was largely dictated by the staggering attrition rate among the young lieutenants already in Vietnam whom we were being groomed to replace, and although we groused at the frantic pace, we recognized its necessity.

There was, of course, another striking difference between OCS and Basic School that preyed on all our minds. As candidates we focused only on the completion of the course, recognizing that the petty harassment would cease when we became officers and that privilege would accompany rank as we moved into our second level of training. In Basic, however, the tendency was to focus not on the present but on how to apply the presently learned skills to the gathering storm in Southeast Asia, and with the mind-set engendered by the certainty of our next assignments, there was a deadly seriousness with which we approached our calling. Over and over again our instructors reminded us that the road to hell was paved with the bones of young lieutenants who had made mistakes, and while their admonitions were perhaps unnecessary, they were keenly effective as attention getters.

Our Basic School platoons were each commanded by a captain who had already served a tour in Vietnam. My platoon's company commander was the antithesis of Captain Gretter: a college graduate rather than a mustang. His stoic exterior and lack of warmth never permitted us to know exactly where we stood with him. Perhaps the jobs of OCS platoon commander and Basic platoon commander required different approaches, the former being a leader and the latter an administrator, but I much preferred the profane outbursts of Captain Gretter to the bloodless admonitions of Captain Leroy. Then, too, Captain Leroy, although a Vietnam veteran, had not experienced the trial by fire like most of the other platoon commanders. I believe that his lack of combat experience made him reluctant to express emotions in the simulated combat situations that were such a large part of our training. In any event, our personalities did not mesh, and I felt suffocated by his fixation on minor details when what I really felt I needed to know was how to stay alive and keep my troops alive in the coming year. Our enlisted instructors, on the other hand, all were seasoned combat veterans who had hands-on experience with the curriculum they were teaching, and although their grammar and diction were no match for Captain Leroy's, I listened carefully as they explained how to read the markings on a Vietcong trail or treat a sucking chest wound.

As the routine of Basic School became established, I found myself spending virtually all of my minimal spare time with Toddy in nearby Woodbridge or the surrounding area. Martha's fiancé was by now a marine company commander in Vietnam, and she was too preoccupied with worry over his safety to be concerned about my constant presence. A number of married lieutenants in our class had apartments in the same complex, and I gradually drifted into a pattern of commuting back and forth to Basic School with them several times a week. On weekends Toddy and I took trips into the countryside or were together in Georgetown, and while neither of us was comfortable with our makeshift arrangement, it was far more tolerable for me than being without her. Her presence in my life also made the grueling regimen of Basic less onerous, although I worried that I was beginning to develop a dependency on her that was completely unlike anything I had ever experienced with any other woman. At that point the idea of marriage seemed out of the question to both of us, and we rarely talked about the future and the unspeakable possibilities inherent in my next assignment, preferring instead to seize what little time we had and live that to the fullest.

— ☆ —

In late January 1968, several weeks after my Basic School class had begun, the Vietnam War suddenly escalated as North Vietnamese regulars and Vietcong guerrillas began a coordinated assault on hamlets and cities throughout the provinces of South Vietnam. Up to that time the war had been characterized by more or less sporadic bursts of activity with a steady but slowly mounting escalation throughout all South Vietnam. This was different. The North Vietnamese offensive shook the foundations of Middle America, and outside the theater of war the reverberations were probably felt nowhere more strongly than at Basic School. The Tet offensive had begun, and as the ancient citadel of the city of Hue fell into Communist hands with an attendant massacre of thousands of innocent citizens, the magnitude of what we had signed on for registered ominously with my classmates.

The task of retaking Hue was given primarily to the Marine Corps, and in twenty-six days of bloody block-by-block, street-by-street, house-by-house nonstop combat, the once-peaceful and beautiful imperial capital was transformed into a slaughterhouse. When it was over and the city had been liberated and in part reduced to rubble, five thousand enemy soldiers had been killed, three thousand marines and ARVNs (Army of the Republic of Vietnam) had become casualties, and almost all the marines who participated in the battle had been killed or wounded, including Martha's future husband, who sustained a leg wound. For his role as a company commander during the bloody siege, Michael P. Downs was awarded a Silver Star. Dozens of similar awards were made following the battle for Hue in which the conspicuous gallantry of young marine officers and enlisted men simply continued and confirmed the proud but costly tradition of the Marine Corps.

After the Tet offensive, the media stepped up its reporting of the rising toll of weekly casualties, and the networks provided graphic footage of the firefights they were able to film; but the war, at least in my mind, was still a television war, the horror of which I was as yet unable to comprehend fully. Despite the fact that by now twenty thousand Americans had given their lives in pursuit of a foreign policy for which much of America was rapidly losing its stomach and for which there was no apparent end in sight, I still knew only one person who had been killed in the war. In addition, the OCS and Basic School classes were so self-contained that contact between marines in different classes was infrequent. As a consequence, we were spared the psychic trauma of personally knowing the dead lieutenants who had in many cases occupied our own physical space only weeks or months earlier.

Nevertheless, Tet gave the Vietnam War an immediacy that had theretofore been lacking, and my fellow marines responded to it in different ways. Some saw the stepped-up pace of the war as a challenge and in their youthful exuberance welcomed the chance to prove themselves worthy of the uniform. Others surveyed the situation with an eye toward the number of junior officers being killed or wounded each week and began scrambling about for military occupational specialties that offered insulation from combat. I began to notice, for the first time, the graffiti that had been carved into classroom desktops by anonymous students from earlier classes.

"Why die? Go Supply," one admonished, while another advised, "Motor T and out in three." A third put it simply: "What the fuck, drive a truck." The opposite viewpoint also was made by some gung ho student, who wrote for the more bloodthirsty of us, "War is our business and business is good."

Somewhat ironically, as our concern over the military occupational specialties into which we would be channeled grew with the rising casualty toll, our options became more and more limited until, for some classes at the height of the war, they were nonexistent. The Marine Corps had a duty to field combat officers, and if that duty required that every officer in a Basic School class become an O-3 infantry officer, that is precisely what would happen.

I had joined the Marine Corps with the intention of becoming a combat platoon leader, and nothing that happened during Tet in any way altered my determination. I could not have faced my father, or lived with myself, if I had chosen an easier way. For me, therefore, there was no moral dilemma or soul-searching agony when it came time to list my preferences. My choice of specialization was infantry, my choice of duty was Vietnam, and the Marine Corps was more than happy to oblige me. Shortly before our selections were made, Basic School hosted a career-night cocktail party, during which officers from the various career branches were available to discuss our options over meatballs and shrimp cocktails. The infantry officer adviser told us with a perfectly straight face that since we had to spend a tour in Vietnam anyway, we might as well find out what the war was really about by selecting his specialty and seeing a little action. The logic of his position seemed irrefutable to me, and I happily reported to Toddy that I had found a man who had been through it and still shared my views. She listened politely but made no comment.

As Basic School progressed and our technical proficiency grew, I found that there were aspects of the training that I actually enjoyed. Each of us fired every weapon in the Marine Corps arsenal from the smallest handgun to the largest artillery piece, and we assembled and disassembled most of them until their cycles of functioning became second nature. After our assignments had been made, virtually all the leadership billets for the various field problems were meted out to those of us who had been selected as infantry and artillery officers, and while the rest of the class had an easier go of it, there was considerable satisfaction in leading a patrol to a successful conclusion or coordinating a company-size helicopter assault.

Looking back, I can see now that the Marine Corps instilled in us a pride and professionalism more closely akin to a calling than an occupation and that many of us actually looked forward to our inevitable baptism by fire. There were, of course, times when we questioned our ability to master the sheer volume of information we were expected to absorb or when bone-numbing weariness would drive us to despondency, but it seemed that at each critical juncture, when the class was on the verge of mutiny, the Marine Corps would back off or offer some reward designed to boost our spirits. When all else failed and I was overcome by the feeling that the Marine Corps dictated all my choices in life, there were always Toddy's waiting arms to provide the solace that nothing else could come close to approximating.

One weekend in late winter a group of us planned an outing at a country farmhouse on a river near my family home. Toddy and I, my Basic School roommate and his date, and several other young lieutenants and their ladies planned to meet at the semiabandoned estate deep in the heart of the Tidewater and simply bask in the luxury of an entire weekend away from Basic School. Each couple took responsibility for a number of the chores associated with the undertaking, and we all chipped in for groceries and a supply of liquor. By the time Toddy and I arrived on Friday night, a roaring fire had been built in the kitchen fireplace, and our anticipation was such that we quickly joined in the convivial mood of the group. From time to time throughout the weekend couples disappeared into the far reaches of the rambling old house, only to return to the communal table and warmth of the kitchen. There was no talk of war or preparation for it on Friday and Saturday, and the idyllic setting along the shores of the Rappahannock contributed to our sense of well-being.

Late Saturday afternoon, in the long shadows of what had been a brilliant winter sky, Toddy and I strolled hand in hand to the edge of the river, and there, beside the gnarled trunk of an old oak, I for the first time in my life told a woman that I loved her and did not think I could live without her. We held each other closely, and from that point on the carefree part of our relationship was over. For the first time we acknowledged that there was no turning back without irreparable damage to each of us.

On the trip back on Sunday Toddy was uncharacteristically subdued, and I concentrated on the driving, leaving her to her thoughts. We felt as close as ever, and we continued to respond to each other's bodies as we had ever since I held her the night of my commissioning; but I could tell that her mind was at a crossroads, and I resolved to remain silent, having perhaps already confessed too much the previous day. I knew that I had placed her in an awkward position by expressing the depth of my feeling and that it was difficult enough asking a twenty-two-year-old woman to sustain such a serious relationship, much less one with a man who was so soon going to be off to war. It had been a wonderful two days, but as we pulled into her apartment parking lot, there was an extra weightiness to the usual end of weekend letdown. I kissed her hard on the lips and made a lame excuse to get back to Basic School to prepare for the next day's activities.

There was a field problem that next week for which I had been assigned a leadership billet, and virtually all my time was taken up with preparing for and then helping head the exercises. Because I was so busy, I did not see Toddy for several days, and when I next showed up at her apartment, it was obvious to me that our separation had helped her sort things out. She was again her usual cheerful self, and I was careful not to upset the chemistry between us by making any professions of love. We graded homework papers together for her fourth grade and went into Washington to see *The Graduate* with Dustin Hoffman. We held hands and ate popcorn as we had on our first movie date, and by the end of the evening I had begun to feel that my admissions of the previous week had not damaged our relationship. In fact, I felt terrific that she was apparently willing to keep seeing me despite my being hopelessly in love with her and possessive to the point of annoyance. We slept together again that night, and I decided that part of the tension between us could be softened by spending less time at her apartment. As I drifted off, it occurred to me that a weekend at William and Mary might provide just the change of scenery to get our minds off Basic School and the Marine Corps. As usual, I met my ride before sunup the next morning as it pulled up to the curb, so that neither Toddy nor my sister would be awakened.

Several weeks later, when the Marine Corps gave us our next free Saturday, Toddy and I made the two-and-a-half-hour journey to Williamsburg. She had been receptive to the idea of meeting some of my old fraternity brothers when I first broached the idea of an excursion, perhaps as much to get away from the relentlessly military surroundings as anything else, but I also suspected that she wanted to get a fix on what I had been like in my pre–Marine Corps days. I had not been back to William and Mary since becoming an officer, and I was anxious to parade my new status as well as have an opportunity to show her off. We also arranged to drive up to my parents' house to spend the night after the Saturday evening fraternity party, and although my mother and father had already met Toddy several times, their impressions of her had been made before our relationship began to get serious.

Our spirits were high when we arrived on campus. Time was now so precious and the future so uncertain we had anticipated especially keenly this brief return to an untroubled past. The evening started well enough as I proudly introduced Toddy to my old cronies, and I marveled at her ability to draw them into conversation and put them at ease. Her occasional sideways glances at me sometimes indicated that she disapproved of this or that particular fraternity brother, but all her criticisms were offered and taken with good humor. As the evening wore on, however, and the beer flowed more freely, I began to sense the widening gulf between the boy I had left behind only a few short months ago and the man I was becoming. For my former classmates the coming maelstrom was no more than a topic of idle conversation, far less interesting than next week's football game or keg party, and although I realized that my interests and priorities had been similar before I was graduated, the experience left me isolated from my former schoolmates and alone in my awkwardness. It was also additional evidence of how desperately I needed this remarkable woman.

On the trip to my parents' house after the party she must have sensed the discomfort I was feeling about the friends who had once seemed so close to me. While she gently chided me about my selection of companions, she listened closely as I tried to explain how alien the familiar had become. When we reached my family home, I was grateful that my parents had not waited up for us. I fixed us each a strong nightcap, and we embraced before retiring to separate bedrooms, as required by the gentility of my mother's southern upbringing.

The next morning my father was in fine spirits as he presided over a huge country breakfast of fried apples, sausage, and scrambled eggs. Mother spent the meal scurrying from kitchen to dining table and concentrating on the logistics of keeping everything hot and in plentiful supply, but I could tell that she was keeping a watchful eye on Toddy. They both thought that Toddy had been an ideal roommate for my sister and a fine young lady, but my entry into the equation was obviously causing them to rethink their opinion of her. I winked at Toddy and played footsie with her under the table while my father reminisced about his Basic School days forty years before.

It was my first chance since I had become a lieutenant to talk at length with the family. While Toddy found the discussion of my father's early life fascinating, I knew that she was also grateful that the conversation had not focused on her. My father could not understand why the Vietnam War seemed to be going so badly and was full of ideas for giving the marines a free hand and bombing Hanoi. He had tried to get recalled to active duty a couple of years earlier, when Vietnam first began to heat up, and I listened patiently, since most of his questions required no answers of me. I knew that he was enjoying himself despite his frustrations over the war, and I was in turn delighted that he and Toddy warmed to each other so quickly. My mother withheld any sign of approval of Toddy's and my relationship, but I was thrilled that Father proffered his so readily. Later, as we prepared to leave, he walked us out to the car and made a point of telling Toddy that she was always welcome in his home with or without any of his children, and I knew that he had gained another fan for life.

The middle weeks of Basic School settled into a predictable routine after the Tet offensive. Other classes had started behind ours so that we were no longer the most junior officers in the Marine Corps, although the distinction was meaningless since we would continue to view ourselves as raw lieutenants until we had faced combat. Nevertheless, most of us had gained enough confidence that we no longer blindly accepted the textbook approach to solving a field problem.

One night patrol when I was the patrol leader, I quickly sized up the most likely location for our ersatz enemy, who had been given our patrol routes in advance, to set up their ambush. I therefore altered the route without informing the umpires on the exercise, and we managed to return to our headquarters early and without taking any casualties. The other side, of course, cried foul and was furious, but I was ultimately given points for showing initiative and scored well on the problem. In addition, the other officers who made up the patrol were delighted since we were able to return from the field several hours ahead of the rest of the class.

We worked hard and partied hard throughout Basic School, but as the realization that all our pretend warfare would be for real in a few short months began to register, some of our leisure-time activities became bizarre. The bachelors in the class generally performed the more outlandish stunts since they did not have the restraining influence of spouses, although neither group set a precedent for decorous behavior. One young lieutenant, Ken Shelleman, who was later killed in Vietnam, bought a red Lincoln Continental convertible whose sticker price exceeded his yearly salary, and he drove it to Ocean City or points north every weekend. He routinely gassed his chariot up at the end of the week's training, bought a case of Lancer's wine, and drove as far as he could get from Quantico while still allowing himself just enough time to return for Monday morning formation. While we never learned what he did on his weekend forays, we understood the reason for his weekly ritual and cheered each time he returned safely. Since I was not married but pretty much living as if I were, Toddy and I initially socialized in both circles. Gradually, however, we began to sever our ties with the more boisterous students, preferring to put on a stack of Glenn Yarborough records and simply spend time together.

Soon after our trip to Williamsburg Toddy showed up unexpectedly one day in the middle of the week at the Basic School bachelor officers' quarters (BOQ), and although I was delighted to see her, her unannounced visit was completely out of character. I was summoned from my quarters and could tell immediately by her worried look as I met her in the lounge that something was wrong. She held my hands tightly and told me that she had just come from the doctor's office, where she had tested positively for pregnancy. Our country outing on the shores of the Rappahannock River had had an unintended result, and although I was taken completely by surprise, the news did not upset me. I knew that I loved her and believed that she loved me. Her pregnancy simply meant that we would marry now rather than when and if I returned from Vietnam. After my initial shock I asked her to marry me. The smile that replaced her worried look was all the answer I needed. We retired to the Hawkins room, where I bought several rounds of drinks, and began to ponder my rapidly changing circumstances. We were going to be a family, and even if the timing was a little off, I still considered myself a very fortunate young man.

That weekend we traveled to nearby Fort Belvoir, Virginia, where her father, an army colonel, and her mother were stationed. I barely knew them but had the unenviable task of informing them that I not only had gotten their daughter pregnant but was going to marry her and then go off to war, leaving them to care for her while I was gone. Toddy's mother promptly excused herself to regain her composure, and her father's apoplectic look convinced me that we should take a walk while they got used to the news. When we returned, they had calmed themselves enough to wish us happiness, but I was a long way from calling them Mom and Dad. My own mother's reaction was, if anything, even less sanguine than that of Toddy's parents and for years remained an impediment to any rapport between the two most influential women in my life. From the onset my father accepted our situation with love and understanding, and his concern for both of us at that early crisis in our lives was a bulwark of strength that sustained us both in the midst of criticism from other family members.

The succeeding Friday night we were married by the Quantico base chaplain in a simple ceremony in his quarters. I had hurriedly purchased a plain gold band, which I almost dropped at several points during our exchange of vows, and my bride, though nervous almost to the point of fainting, looked lovely in a white linen suit that her mother had bought for the occasion. A friend of Toddy's, whose husband was a marine lieutenant already in Vietnam, arranged a small reception, to which we invited Toddy's parents, my twin sister, and a few friends who were in the area, including some of our Basic School colleagues. One of the women who had been invited was awaiting the return from Vietnam of her marine husband, who had just had both of his feet blown off by an enemy land mine, and I remember thinking how bravely she appeared to be handling their terrible misfortune. Another guest, a Turkish exchange lieutenant who knew very little of American customs but believed in the direct approach, propositioned the hostess, but aside from that, the reception went smoothly with champagne toasts from all our friends. The next morning before sunup I was in the field for an all-day land navigation problem, while Toddy went to find us an apartment of our own. Although we both were relieved to be done with the madness of getting married, it had been an incredibly brief honeymoon.

Our newlyweds' apartment had one bedroom and a living room/dining room area with rented furniture so flimsy as to appear not to be weight-bearing; but it was our first home, and we felt as if we were living in the lap of luxury. I quickly discovered that my wife was an excellent cook, and we soon invited her parents to dinner. After several rounds of drinks Colonel Todd and I discovered that we could tolerate each other, and by the end of a bottle of wine bought specially for dinner and after-dinner liqueurs, he actually asked me to call him by his first name. Toddy and her mother raised their eyebrows while Bob and I raised our glasses to seal our new familiarity.

With the coming of spring and a home of sorts to return to every night, the pace of Basic School seemed to quicken. Toddy continued to teach until the end of the school year, and I was busy with the final assortment of amphibious landings, mock wars, and helicopter assaults. By June my fellow lieutenants and I had absorbed most of the technical expertise necessary to be combat platoon leaders, and we looked forward to Vietnam with mixed feelings of dread and fascination. I could call in fire missions or medical evacuations with equal facility, plot and lead patrols, and otherwise perform the duties of a junior infantry officer. I, of course, had no idea how I would react in a couple of months when I began to play for keeps; but neither did most of my colleagues, and we all affected an air of bravado as we led the textbook exercises that could only remotely approximate the reality of combat. Nevertheless, the Marine Corps had prepared us as well as possible short of actually shooting at us.

There was no formal graduation from Basic School. Whereas we had worked to become officers at Officer Candidate School and to be recognized in an appropriate commissioning ceremony, we simply finished the prescribed regimen of Basic, cleaned out the rooms we had been assigned, and picked up our next set of orders. Some of our class went on to Pensacola, Florida, for training as pilots, some to Fort Sill, Oklahoma, for training as artillery officers, and some to Monterey, California, for language school, but the vast majority of those who had been selected into the infantry were given twenty days' leave to be followed by a report date to the West Coast for processing to Vietnam. Two of our class members were placed on legal hold to testify in a murder trial and never got to Vietnam, and several others who had demonstrated exceptional ability were sent to Ranger School. I was one of the privileged majority who would be leading troops in combat in just a month, and I felt a keen sense of irony when the lance corporal/clerk who processed my orders turned out to be one of the officer candidates who had flunked out of my OCS class. His reward for failure would be a safe stateside tour of duty behind a typewriter, and although I would not have traded places with him for anything, he was living proof of the Marine Corps axiom that the shitbirds get the easy assignments.

Toddy and I broke the short-term lease on our apartment as soon as Basic School ended, and we had the movers store our few items of furniture and other household goods in her parents' attic. I was grateful that she would be living with them while I was overseas and that she would have help in caring for our child. After some initial morning sickness her pregnancy was proceeding normally, and now she would occasionally wake me in the middle of the night to feel the baby kick. We were completely in awe of the gathering life we had created and spent countless hours trying to decide on a girl's name that we both liked; we were in agreement that the child would be named for my father if it happened to be a boy. On the flyleaf of the copy of his autobiography, *Marine: The Life of Lewis B. "Chesty" Puller*, that he had given me when it was published years earlier, my father had written that he was the last of his line and that he wanted at least two grandsons from me. He was like a child himself at the prospect of achieving the first half of his wish, and although my mother was mortified that Toddy's pregnancy was so obvious, we reveled in his enjoyment and ignored her.

We had planned to spend some of my leave time with each set of parents with a trip to Williamsburg and Virginia Beach for the marriage of a fraternity brother sandwiched in between. After I got our household effects relocated to Toddy's parents, my sole responsibility for the remainder of my leave was to board a plane for the West Coast in accordance with my orders. I had already packed a duffel bag and valet pack, which would be the only items I carried to Southeast Asia, and I had made out an allotment so that most of my pay would go to Toddy while I was gone. I had also written a standard will while at Basic School, as had virtually all my classmates, and although writing it was an unpleasant reminder of our uncertain future, I was glad the Marine Corps had insisted that we plan for the worst. Toddy's knuckles had whitened appreciably when I gave her the document, and she put it away for safekeeping without even scanning its contents. It seemed to me almost surreal that we would be obviating the problems of intestacy by writing a will with the ink barely dry on our marriage license and a birth certificate in the offing.

As we drove to Virginia Beach after spending a couple of days with my wife's parents, we both were looking forward to a few days of relative idleness. My pre-Vietnam leave was our first real vacation together, and we intended to enjoy every minute of it. Unfortunately my next assignment was never out of our minds and cast a damper on the entire holiday. At Basic School and in the military community generally, everyone had been absorbed with the war effort, and it was difficult to become despondent about having to go since everyone else either had just returned from Vietnam or was just preparing to go. In the civilian world, however, it was as if the war barely existed, and I quickly began to feel resentful toward the young men my age on the beach and in the bars whose lives would be unaffected by the war. Curiously I felt even more resentful toward the few military types (a coast guard post was nearby) I did meet while on leave who, through circumstance or design, were going to sit out the war in the carnival atmosphere of Virginia Beach.

One night while at the beach, we attended a party at the apartment of a young coast guard officer who was an acquaintance of my about-to-be-married fraternity brother. Our host was an affable enough young man who went out of his way to make Toddy and me comfortable in strange surroundings, and I probably abused his hospitality by making too many trips to the beer keg he had bought for the party; but I still could not get over the contrast between our situations. We both were uniformed servicemen of roughly the same age, yet one of us would shortly be looking into the jaws of death on an almost daily basis, while the other would be polishing his surfboard in air-conditioned comfort. I thought wryly of the differing degrees of sacrifices demanded of a pig and a chicken when forced to contribute to a breakfast of ham and eggs. I never saw him again, but I have since then seen many whose military tours were of a similar nature, and many of them have bitterly resented the interruption of their civilian status.

Toddy and I were relieved to head for nearby Fort Monroe in Hampton for my friend's wedding after only a few days. The distress we were experiencing had become achingly palpable, and I almost began to wish I had been ordered straight to Vietnam from Basic School. Since the bride was an army daughter, Ernie and Marian's wedding at least put us back in a military community. In the officers' club during the rehearsal dinner, I saw a young captain whose leg had been so badly deformed by a war wound that I found it remarkable that the limb was still capable of bearing weight. I said nothing to Toddy about the anatomical miracle I had witnessed when I returned to my seat, but unnerved by the sight, I also wasted no time in tossing down several glasses of wine.

After the wedding Toddy and I spent a night in Ernie and Marian's apartment in Williamsburg, which was vacant while they honey-mooned. I felt a tinge of resentment toward my old fraternity brother and roommate, who had just completed the traditional wedding ceremony that Toddy and I didn't have and who was being spared military service because of a teaching deferment, but I was grateful that we were able to use his apartment. Williamsburg in late summer with college not yet back in session was deserted, and I felt an unfamiliar hollowness not inconsistent with the empty classroom buildings, dormitories, and fraternity lodges that I pointed out to Toddy as landmarks on my journey toward manhood. That night I drank too much beer, listened over and over to Richard Harris's plaintive rendition of "MacArthur Park," and was unable even in my lady's arms to dispel the feeling of desolation that was welling up in my heart.

The next day we drove to Saluda to spend a final few days with my family before my departure. Martha had driven down from northern Virginia, and because the family home was crowded, Toddy and I were lodged in a nearby motel. From the moment we arrived, a steady stream of visitors trekked in and out of my parents' home, bringing gifts of food in the southern manner, wished me a safe tour in Vietnam, and discreetly eyed Toddy's not-so-delicate condition. The men all told me how they had served in the Big War or the Korean conflict, and while the wives bustled about in the kitchen, each veteran seemed to feel a need to take me aside and conspiratorially whisper that I should keep my head down while overseas. I did my best to stay drunk for most of the visit, and Toddy and I seized on any pretense to hole up in our motel room when the visitors like the summer weather became too stifling.

As always when the family was reunited in Saluda, we spent a lot of time at the dining table, a gorgeous mahogany antique that could seat a dozen people comfortably and that had once belonged to Robert E. Lee's aide-de-camp. Father presided at the head of the table with Mother at the opposite end nearest the kitchen. Out of habit I sat on one side of the table with my sisters across from me, and Toddy, the newest member of the family, was, after much discussion, placed between my father and me. The cuisine, as befitted a Tidewater Virginia town only minutes from several rivers, consisted largely of the delicious local seafood and shellfish that I had been raised on but that put Toddy's already queasy stomach in an uproar. Aside from the usual seating arrangements and the standard bill of fare, however, the atmosphere at meals was different in the summer of 1968. Mother spent an inordinate amount of time in the kitchen, refusing to come to grips with my imminent departure or Toddy's pregnancy, and Father seemed to be lost in his own thoughts. My sisters' husband and fiancé were still in Vietnam, although they had survived the most dangerous parts of their tours at a time when I would be beginning mine. That would leave Father, the only real warrior in the family, at home with the women, and although at his age that was exactly where he belonged, it nevertheless must have been a source of humiliation for a man whose every instinct demanded that he be in the fracas. Virginia, though rarely demonstrative, did her best to keep the mood of our gathering from degenerating into total despair, but Martha, to whom I was particularly close, was a basket case from the time she arrived.

On the morning Toddy and I were to leave Saluda for her parents' home in northern Virginia, I took my sisters aside for an almost unbearable discussion. My father's sister had established before her death a trust fund the interest on which accrued to him during his lifetime, with the principal to be divided among his living children at the time of his death. As is frequently the case with such arrangements, it was drawn too precisely and with such an eye toward tax consequences that any deviation from normal life expectancies of the beneficiaries would cause unintended results. In my case, it meant that if I died in Vietnam and my wife gave birth to a male child, my father's namesake would be cut off from a rightful legacy. When I made my sisters promise to disregard the fine print in the instrument and see that Toddy and our child got my share, they both burst into tears and at that point would probably have agreed to almost anything else I asked. It was the first, last, and only discussion I had with either of them about the possibility of my own early death and seemed to tap a wellspring of emotion whose power overwhelmed all three of us.

After I had finished packing the car, got Toddy comfortably settled in the passenger's seat, and mumbled some awkward assurances to my mother and sisters about how quickly we would be together again, I turned toward my father for our farewell. As we stood facing each other beneath the spreading boughs of a weeping willow tree in the backyard of my boyhood home, the alarming thought crossed my mind that I might never again see this suddenly fragile old man, not because I might die in Vietnam but because he might not survive my tour. He tried to tell me again and for the thousandth time the parable of the Spartan mother who, on sending her own son off to war, advised him to come back with his shield or on it, but he was unable to complete the quote. His final words trailed off, and his shoulders shook as he took me in his arms, and we both tried to take from each other the solace and the strength that had suddenly abandoned us. Finally and after what seemed an eternity, we broke our embrace, and my mother led him back into the house with tears streaming down both their cheeks. I mechanically got into the car, wiped the tears from my own face, and tried to ease the pain in my aching throat as we silently headed north toward Washington. It was the first time I had ever seen my father cry.

On the trip up Route 17 I began to have the distinct feeling that my psyche was unraveling. I had not seen my wife smile in days, could not stand even to be near those few people in my life to whom I had the most intense attachments, and my father's tears had completely unnerved me. Now, as we passed the open fields that took their sustenance from the river that paralleled our route, traveled past the clapboard houses that dotted the surrounding countryside, and negotiated curve after curve on the two-lane blacktop I had driven hundreds of times, I felt as if the moving panorama were being offered to my view for the last time. I resolved never again to take the view for granted should I be so fortunate as ever to pass this way again, a prospect that, given my present mood and circumstances, appeared unlikely.

By the time we cleared Fredericksburg, traveled the more unfamiliar length of Route 1, and pulled into the Todds' driveway at Fort Belvoir, I was ready for something to revive my flagging spirits. Toddy and I had barely spoken for the entire trip, but at the start she had placed her hand firmly over mine on the gearshift as I tried to work my way through the emotions of departure. Now I grimly realized that there would be one more painful good-bye before I could get on with the war. Tonight would be our last together before she put me on the plane to San Francisco and Vietnam. Her parents had bought steaks for all of us and a bottle of my favorite scotch to help take the sting out of the evening. They had also invited their next-door neighbors over for drinks before dinner, and while I was flattered that my in-laws wanted to introduce me to their friends, I wasn't much in the mood for polite chitchat. As the scotch began to warm my stomach, however, I saw the wisdom of having company over to keep the conversation away from the more gloomy thoughts that, though unstated, were on all our minds. I found it curious that neither my father-in-law nor his neighbor, both professional soldiers near the end of their careers, had yet served in Vietnam, although Colonel Todd had volunteered to do so. After all, I reasoned through the scotch, a soldier's purpose was to

serve his country in time of war, and when my host and his guest agreed
between themselves that neither of them would want to assume the role
for which I had volunteered, the thought entered my mind that either
some Marine Corps officers took their calling more seriously than some
army officers or that there was information about the war available to
these two men to which I was not privy.

Later that night, after the neighbors had gone home and the steaks
had been grilled and eaten, the four of us settled down in the den for a
nightcap. Toddy and I were exhausted from the frantic pace of our
vacation and the emotional roller coaster we had been riding for the last
several days, but her parents wanted to assure us that she and the baby
would be properly cared for while I was in Vietnam. They also wanted
me to know that their daughter and grandchild could continue to live
with them if I should die in Vietnam, and although their last offer was
made while Toddy was out of the room, the stiffness in our voices when
she returned gave away the subject. More than once in the last month
Toddy had complained to me that she felt she was constantly coming in
on the tail end of conversations in which she had every right to be
included, and this was obviously yet another example. It occurred to
me that this vulnerable-looking female had hidden sources of strength
that became fairly obvious when she got her dander up, and I felt
suddenly grateful to her parents for the independence they had helped
her achieve. I had developed a genuine affection for the Todds in the
short time I had known them, and as we put away our brandy snifters
and prepared for bed, there was a warmth in our embrace that was
more than casual.

Our last night together was, up until that point in my life, one of the
worst I had ever endured. After we retired to our bedroom and were
finally alone for the last time, all the false bravado I had been using as a
shield for much of the summer deserted me. There seemed to be
nothing either of us could say to comfort the other, and although I had
intended to make love to my wife in some sort of soldier-goes-to-war
scenario, I could not bear even to touch her. When Shakespeare wrote
that parting is such sweet sorrow, he had obviously never left a pregnant wife with whom he was deeply in love to go off and fight a war.
After all efforts at communication had been exhausted, we finally
assumed postures of feigned sleep with our backs to each other and so
passed the remainder of the night in restless misery. The next morning
at daybreak we both were up, bleary-eyed and exhausted but grateful to
be able to escape a bed which that night had served neither of the two
main purposes for which a bed was intended.

Toddy's mother fixed us a fine breakfast, which for some reason I approached as though I had not eaten for days, but my wife barely touched her plate. All the previous night's tossing and turning must have kindled my appetite, and I concentrated on the mounds of sausage and eggs placed before me while doing my best to avoid Toddy's downcast eyes. It felt good to be back in uniform for the flight to San Francisco, and until it was time to leave for Dulles International Airport, I busied myself doing small errands and attending to last-minute details. My duffel bag and officer's valet pack were already packed, but we both managed to keep busy and stay out of each other's way. I decided to take my watch, which was a fairly expensive Hamilton I had won in a college poker game, but I did take off the family crest signet ring my father had given me for college graduation and left it with Toddy. I wanted to make sure our child would eventually get something personal of mine if I failed to return. Again there was no need to explain to Toddy the motivation that prompted my passing the ring to her, and she nodded silently and put it away for safekeeping.

As had my mother and father, the Todds walked us out to the car, wished me luck, and again assured me that my wife and child would be well cared for. Toddy drove to the airport while I hid behind my sunglasses, and although I would have preferred that she drop me off at the main entrance, she insisted on parking the car and seeing me to my departure gate. The terminal contained a smattering of soldiers, sailors, airmen, and marines, who, like me, were either leaving for or returning from Southeast Asia, but for the most part the other passengers appeared to be civilians on business trips or summer vacationers.

I self-consciously eyed the rows of ribbons worn by the returning veterans and loathed the insouciance of the remaining travelers, but I was relieved that my flight was on time and that the agony of this last departure would soon be over. Toddy, only five feet tall to begin with and halfway through her pregnancy, had never looked smaller or more forlorn to me, and the brave front she tried to project served only to make her appear that much more vulnerable. I squeezed her as tightly as I dared and wondered how this spunky little woman, whom I had barely known a year, had completely taken over my life. As I turned to take my place on the boarding vehicle, I did my best to hide my tears from the enlisted men already on board and felt exactly as I imagined a drowning man who has just lost his grip on a lifeline must feel.

As soon as my plane became airborne, I ordered two scotches on the rocks, which I finished in rapid succession. I actually felt relieved to be separated from Toddy and my family after so many gut-wrenching farewells. I knew that if I were going to function efficiently for, or indeed survive, the next year, I would have to clear my head of the emotional baggage I was now carrying and concentrate on being a marine. Toddy's absence would make that easier. The combination of the midday scotch and the previous night's lack of sleep soon had me nodding, and by the time the flight movie began I was well on my way to a much needed nap. As I drifted off, I noted that the title of the movie was *In Enemy Country.*

The airport in San Francisco, unlike the one I had left a few hours earlier, was awash with servicemen on their way into or out of Vietnam, and as I surveyed the bustling throng of green and khaki all around me, I could feel myself being drawn inexorably closer to the war. If Scott McKenzie's gentle people with flowers in their hair were truly typical of San Francisco, according to the words of the popular song, I remember thinking, they all must have been holed up in the Haight-Ashbury, because they certainly were not providing much business to the airlines. On the other hand, the government was providing plenty of business, and my pulse quickened as I contemplated the next few days.

There was a military shuttle bus service from the airport to the transit facility in the navy bachelor officers' quarters at nearby Treasure Island. With time on my hands I ordered a sandwich and several drinks at the club bar and listened to a few war stories from some of the old salts who appeared to be permanent fixtures there. I also called Toddy to let her know I had arrived safely and to speak with her one last time before going out of the country. As I hung up the phone, I was sorry I had called since she already sounded depressed and remote. Separated less than a day, we both had begun to detach ourselves emotionally from each other, and I was angry at myself for having made an unnecessary and painful call. I bought two beers to go at the bar and drank them alone in my room before turning in for the evening. I would not need a wake-up since the unfamiliar setting and the absence of my wife assured me of another fitful night's sleep.

The next morning, as I prepared to check out of the BOQ and take the return shuttle to the airport, I noted bemusedly that the ensign in the room adjacent to mine had left a note on his door asking to be awakened at ten o'clock for his waterskiing lesson. Undoubtedly, the lesson would contribute in some very real measure to his development as a naval officer; but I was reminded of my coast guard acquaintance and his surfboard of a few days earlier, and I marveled anew at the differing levels of sacrifice demanded of those who pursue the military calling.

Back at the airport, I was delighted to find a Basic School classmate whose orders were similar enough to mine that we would be traveling on the same plane up to Seattle and then on to Camp Hanson, Okinawa. After that he would be going to the Third Marine Division and I to the First, my father's old outfit. For now I welcomed Joe as a long-lost friend. Ever the workhorse, he spent most of the flight reviewing notes he had taken in Basic School while I read a copy of *Rosemary's Baby* that I had picked up in the airport newsstand and studied my fellow passengers. All of us were marines, in uniform and on our way to war. We all were young and scared, but as green as we were, many affected a swagger to cover self-doubt. I also noted that the officers and enlisted men sat in different sections of the plane. I didn't notice any particular condescension on the part of the officers or deference on the part of the enlisted men, but it just seemed that our training dictated that we remain apart.

Seattle was the last home stop. For many on our manifest it would be their first trip away from American soil, and for some lesser number their last, and Joe and I decided to memorialize the occasion with a few beers while the plane was being readied. Besides, there would be no liquor served on the plane. For all of my self-doubt and insecurity, I was beginning to feel like John Wayne in a World War II movie, as I, a marine lieutenant in uniform and on his way to war, bellied up to the bar in the Seattle airport cocktail lounge. When I nonchalantly took my wallet from my pants pocket and ordered the local favorite, the waitress completely destroyed the mood by loudly demanding proof of my age before she would serve me. I drank my beer in silence and humiliation as everyone within hearing range guffawed. I also left no tip as we headed back to our plane, and wondered what John Wayne would have done.

In Okinawa, after an interminable flight, Joe and I checked into another transient facility at Camp Hanson. There were many signs of the war's proximity. Most of the marines who were leaving the war zone, either temporarily or to return to the States, wore jungle utilities that were lightweight loose-fitting uniforms with deep pockets attached to the pants rather than inside them. They also wore marine green skivvies and T-shirts and floppy bush hats, and many had mustaches as well, which in 1968 were not permitted stateside. A fair number also wore purple ribbons over their left breast pockets. Most of the Purple Heart recipients bore no visible wounds, confirming my naive, stereotypical view of the Hollywood war wound that enters and exits human flesh with minimal damage. I quickly learned that the more seriously wounded had already been sent back to the States, while those I was meeting bore minor wounds and were rotating back into Vietnam after short periods of recuperation.

Many of the young single officers, immediately after arriving at Camp Hanson, headed straight for the bathhouses and massage parlors just outside the gate, which since our first days of Basic School we all had heard compared favorably with heaven. Inexpensive whores, I realized from reading Hemingway and Jones, were an inevitable accompaniment of war, but if Joe's account of his night on the town was to be believed, Okinawa had elevated prostitution to an art form. I decided to avoid the temptation downtown and spent most of my spare time for the two days we were in Okinawa in the officers' club, where for twenty-five cents a female barber gave me a haircut and a neck and shoulder massage that in itself bordered on the erotic. There were also drinks for a dime each during happy hour, first-run movies twenty-four hours a day for free on a screen beside the bar, and, for those who wanted to spend money, an assortment of one-armed bandits, into which I pumped my last twenty dollars.

The next stop was Vietnam, and I knew I would have no use for money where I was headed. Finally the Marine Corps, as if to justify the existence of such a place, arranged a couple of mandatory briefings, designed to acquaint us with the big picture and overall strategy of the war. The young captain, who so efficiently and with such certainty pointed out the exact locations of various North Vietnamese units in South Vietnam and the locations of the South Vietnamese and American units that were countering them, left me with the uneasy realization that I would soon be one of the pawns who provided the intelligence for their bloodless equations. It was difficult to look at pins on a map and at the same time envision them as a group of men who would shortly be trying to end my life.

Joe and I parted company in Okinawa, and I made the last leg of my flight into Vietnam alone. It looked lush and tropical from the air with the foliage along the coastline forming a curve against the blue waters of the South China Sea. As our plane came to a halt on the runway in Da Nang and we descended onto the tarmac, I fully expected to be met by a hail of bullets. Instead I was slapped in the face by a steamy heat of such intensity that I felt as if I had stepped into a sauna. My uniform was instantly drenched with perspiration, and the fetid air was visible in all directions as it shimmered up from the ground and gave an eerie wavering appearance to everything it warmed.

III

★

"WELCOME TO VIETNAM," the stewardesses called after us as we left the plane and boarded trucks for the short trip to the main terminal. They were the last attractive round-eyed women I saw until my odyssey was completed and I was headed in the other direction. As we filed through the gate into the terminal, a group of marines and soldiers standing woodenly at the edge of the tarmac caught my eye. They were rail-thin combat veterans on their way home, some just a few days away from battle. Most wore several rows of ribbons on their chests. There appeared to be no interaction among the group of about two dozen, and the majority had expressionless faces with fixed, unfocused eyes set in hollow sockets. A chill danced its way up my sweat-soaked spine, and I felt fear for the first time since entering Vietnam.

Once I was in Da Nang the seemingly haphazard process by which I was transferred down to my unit went fairly smoothly. At the terminal we were instructed to exchange what dollars we had remaining for military scrip, given a brief orientation, and sent to division for further briefings. I was assigned to the Second Battalion of the First Marine Regiment of the First Marine Division, and after I received my orders, I and a dozen other new lieutenants were given a cursory welcome to Vietnam by the division commanding general in his office. As we stood at ease in front of his desk and dutifully nodded our agreement with a pep talk he had probably delivered to hundreds of green lieutenants, I was struck by the contrast between the air-conditioning in his office and the heat outside, to which I did not think I would ever grow accustomed. At the end of his speech he mentioned that he had served under my father early in his own career, making the color rise in my cheeks. The other lieutenants appeared not to notice the personal reference, and I knew in the back of my mind that in a day or two when I got my own command, the troops would be judging me on my own merits rather than on my lineage. At least in the war zone, I was going to get a chance to be my own man rather than Chesty Puller's son, and while the general's remark was complimentary, I was glad the other lieutenants did not pick up on it.

We were given another "big picture" briefing while at division, complete with wall-size maps and overlays, again pointing out the last-known positions of various enemy units. This time, however, the bad guys were practically at our back door, and I listened much more attentively. Finally we were given a copy of the rules of engagement and made to sign a statement saying we had read them and agreed to abide by them. The document was fairly voluminous and outlined various Geneva conventions for the conduct of war. I read it out of curiosity but realized that the clerk who handed us our copies was simply following regulations and did not expect us to take it seriously. It seemed odd to me that warring countries would expect their troops to kill each other in a gentlemanly and humane manner, and odder still that the Marine Corps would require its junior officers to undertake such an exercise in hypocrisy.

That night I found yet another transient facility, a Quonset hut with several bare cots, and I stored my valet pack and duffel bag beneath the nearest empty one. The building's only redeeming features were its proximity to a makeshift officers' club, actually another Quonset hut with a bar, and to a shower with hot, running water. The next morning I would be flying in a C-130 north to regional headquarters at Phu Bai, but for now I was going to take advantage of the local amenities, sparse though they might be. I headed for the club, reminding myself at the door that if I wore my cover through the portal, in accord with military tradition, I would be required to buy a round of drinks for everyone inside. With cover firmly in hand I ordered a salty dog (vodka in a glass with a salted rim) at the bar and settled in to watch the activity at a nearby table where several rear-echelon overweight middle-aged officers were trying to entice a couple of world-weary bar girls to come back to their quarters for a party. On the stool next to me an older captain, up from the ranks, who worked in motor transport and had so far that night had far too much to drink, repeatedly asked me why any young man in his right mind with a college education would want to be an infantry officer in the Marine Corps. After several more salty dogs, I finally shut him up by telling him that I was Chesty Puller's son and took my leave to prepare for the big day ahead.

The next morning I flew to Phu Bai. The C-130 had none of the comforts of commercial jetliners; but a plane ride, however lacking in amenities, meant that I would reach my unit more quickly than if I proceeded by jeep, and I was getting anxious to get to my platoon. I found a canvas seat along the bulkhead and, in looking around, was amazed to see that most of the passengers were civilians. Included among them were Vietnamese locals, who seemed to be traveling with a cortege of barnyard animals, and an Australian rock band that I assumed was going to be doing a USO show. The plane struck me as hopelessly overloaded and seemed to struggle to become airborne. The crew members all sported pearl-handled revolvers that they wore slung low on the hips in fast-draw holsters, aviator sunglasses, and mustaches and affected an air of boredom with what for them was just another milk run, but they did keep order among the cackle of chickens and crying babies. I held tightly to my valet pack and duffel bag for most of the hop and prayed that I would not be bitten by a rabid dog or accidentally shot by one of the gunslinging sergeants.

Regimental headquarters at Phu Bai was a collection of makeshift plywood buildings, where I checked in with the headquarters clerical staff. I was told that I would be reporting the next day to my battalion, which was located a few kilometers away at the mouth of the Cua Viet River. I was also given a place to store my gear and overnight accommodations and told to come back later that afternoon to meet the regimental commanding officer. In the meantime, it was suggested that I might want to start scrounging for gear since equipment was in short supply. After futilely trying to requisition field gear through Marine Corps channels, I finally found most of what I needed at a nearby army unit. The only boots the Marine Corps had available were size six and size eleven, and I smiled wryly as I slipped on the nine and a half I scrounged from the army. We had been taught at Basic School that if we obtained gear outside normal channels, the integrity of the supply process would be compromised, but when it came down to a choice between the system and my immediate needs, I had no hesitations. Decked out in jungle utilities and with proper boots and a sidearm, I finally began to feel as if I were no longer the greenest marine in Vietnam. I also ran into Ken Shelleman, the lieutenant from my Basic School class with the red convertible. Ken had gotten to the regiment a day ahead of me and had already scoped out the best available watering holes. As it turned out, we were going to be assigned to different companies in the same battalion, and we immediately agreed to get together for a drink that evening after we had been briefed by the regimental CO.

The briefing was the same basic pep talk I had received at division, including an allusion to my father's illustrious name. The colonel pointed out that my father had commanded the First Marine Division seventeen years earlier during the retreat from the Chosin Reservoir and that it was fitting that I now serve in the same division. I, of course, had already grasped the historical implication of my assignment although my father and I served in vastly different capacities. When he assumed command of the regiment, he had thirty-two years of service and four Navy Crosses. He had earned his fifth for the retreat from the frozen Chosin, a bittersweet culmination to a career that had included more than twenty-six years of foreign service. On the other hand, I was a brand-new second lieutenant with a year of service, who had never commanded anything larger than a Boy Scout troop, and while I appreciated the personal reference, I did not feel up to any sort of comparison with my father. I wished desperately that I could simply assume command of my platoon without any more references to him, and I was grateful that the only other lieutenant within earshot of this conversation was Ken Shelleman, who knew my feelings.

The colonel went on to tell us that a week in the bush would serve as a far better snapping-in than anything he could say by way of an introductory briefing. He told us that he had arranged for a chopper to drop us off at battalion the next day, wished us luck, and suggested that we might want to have a few drinks that evening since it would be our last free night for as far ahead as we cared to project. Neither Ken nor I needed any convincing, and as we left the colonel's sandbagged command post, it occurred to me that as we proceeded down the chain of command, the living accommodations were becoming less and less hospitable. No one had shot at me yet, but I did not expect to see air-conditioning again for quite some time.

The next morning Ken and I, red-eyed from overindulging, reported to the colonel's helicopter pad. To my surprise, Bill Dabney, who had commanded a company at Khe Sanh, was waiting to see me off. He was at the tail end of his tour and had lost twenty pounds, but he appeared healthy and carried my gear to the waiting helicopter, whose whirling rotor blades all but ruled out conversation. We exchanged good-byes as best we could in the chopper's prop wash, and within minutes I was airborne and headed downriver to my battalion. It seemed to me a good sign that Bill did not have that expressionless stare I had seen on the faces of my first combat veterans, and I was pleased that he would be able to report to Toddy that he had left me in good health. The helicopter pilot put us down in the wrong location several kilometers past our unit, and we were fortunate to find a navy launch to carry us back upriver to the battalion site.

The Second Battalion of the First Marine Regiment of the First Marine Division, when I joined it, was deployed in a large semicircle with the open part of the area backing up to the Cua Viet River. After Ken and I disembarked, we reported directly to battalion headquarters, temporarily located in a bombed-out Vietnamese temple. The battalion had just moved south from Khe Sanh, and to judge by the feeble repairs to the temple headquarters, nobody expected to stay long. Large flaps of canvas covered the holes in the walls and ceiling and were held in place by sandbags and rope, while empty mortar crates had been pieced together in a jigsaw fashion to cover the mud floor. We were met by the battalion executive officer, Major Wright, who gave us yet another briefing and told me that I would be joining Golf Company the next day and be given command of its third platoon. Major Wright was a no-nonsense professional whom I liked immediately, although I wondered why he appeared to be running the show. As it turned out, the new battalion CO had just come on board and, like me, would need some time to learn the ropes and get snapped in before imparting his particular brand of leadership to his new command.

═══ ☆ ═══

That afternoon I walked the perimeter of the battalion base camp and tried to get a feel for the lay of the land, which was relatively flat and open with wide grassy expanses punctuated with tree lines. The nearest city, Dong Ha, was only a short distance away, but the area around our base of operations was sparsely populated and used primarily for farming. Water and electricity were supplied by a water point and portable generators, and with such primitive utilities the river was a godsend for our laundry and bathing needs. Meals, when we were not in the field, would be cooked on gas stoves and served from an open mess tent. Sleeping accommodations were in makeshift hooches along the perimeter lines, which we would be manning when not out on patrol. All in all, I thought, as I completed the trace of our area, the amenities of my new surroundings would appear quite refined if viewed from the perspective of a caveman.

Ken Shelleman had been assigned to another company after our briefing by Major Wright, but our paths crossed again later that afternoon at battalion supply, where we were given field gear, compasses, maps, K-bar knives, and poncho liners and inflatable mattresses. The mattresses, affectionately known as rubber ladies, kept one a couple of inches off the ground and provided some insulation from the cold and wet but were far too bulky to carry out into the field. The poncho liners, on the other hand, weighed only a few ounces, could easily be rolled up and tied down to the top of a pack, and, more important, would dry out in a couple of hours in the sun.

I resolved to find a whetstone for sharpening the newly issued K-bar, whose edge barely left a scratch as I ran it over my thumbnail. I had brought with me from the States a knife that my father had used as a young officer; but it had no sheath, and I decided that the K-bar would suffice until I could have one made. Ken and I were given floppy bush hats and took turns posing for each other before we parted again. I was beginning to feel quite salty with my new gear, and I adjusted and readjusted the bush hat to affect a more menacing appearance. Now all I needed was a mustache, a ten-pound weight loss, and a couple of firefights, and I would be the meanest mother in the green machine.

Later that evening I sat in the battalion command post and listened as various units in the field called in situation reports. I was anxious to take command of my own platoon but also apprehensive lest I display any sign of weakness that would compromise my ability to command. I also had some nagging doubts about my mastery of the technical aspects of small-unit leadership, and I prayed that I would have some time to learn my job before we made contact with the enemy. As I watched the intelligence units map the progress called in by the commanders in the field, I was grateful that the evening was uneventful.

My own unit, Golf Company, had been out for several days, so I did not really know what to expect, but I did pick up two pieces of disturbing information about the third platoon from the top sergeant. It was presently being led by a staff sergeant, who had assumed command several months earlier, when the lieutenant in command had accidentally shot his radio operator in the back while cleaning his pistol. The radio operator was wearing a flak jacket, and the wound was superficial; but the young lieutenant was relieved of duty on the spot, according to the top sergeant who was filling me in.

I feared that the inept performance of the platoon's previous lieutenant would probably incline its members to prejudge me, another green lieutenant, whom they could manage quite well without. The situation also meant that I would be taking command from a combat veteran, albeit enlisted, who had a successful record with the platoon over the last several months and that for him my arrival meant a demotion. He would continue to be my platoon sergeant, and I knew that his experience would be invaluable to me; but I also knew that I would have to handle our relationship delicately and make it clear from the start that I did not intend to engage in a power struggle over leadership of the platoon.

The second piece of information was far more alarming. Three days earlier, in the course of a night patrol, the man walking point for the third platoon had been killed. As he led the platoon toward a checkpoint, a burst of automatic-weapons fire stitched a pattern on his torso, extending from his crotch to his forehead. The impact of the bullets, coming at point-blank range, propelled him backward across the space between him and the next man in line, and he was dead before he hit the ground. There were no other shots fired, no further contact, and the incident was over in a few minutes.

Staff Sergeant Phil Leslie had immediately pulled the platoon into a defensive configuration and called in artillery. For the rest of the night a steel curtain of harassing and interdicting fire surrounded his platoon and insulated it from an unknown and unseen enemy. At daylight a medevac chopper was called in to carry the body to graves registration, and a few spent shell casings from an AK-47 assault rifle were found; but there was no other evidence of the enemy's presence. The rest of the platoon was, of course, demoralized, badly shaken, and extremely pissed off. Leslie had reacted in a professional manner, but his men had been bested without any opportunity for retribution.

The next day Golf Company was resupplied in the field, and I caught a ride out to my unit in the vehicle that was hauling the water wagon. Fortunately we also brought out the mail since a surefire way to get the troops' attention was to hold a mail call. The company skipper, Captain Clyde Woods, came over and identified himself. He wore no insignia or other markings. When I saluted smartly, I was told in no uncertain terms that I could stow the formality and the salutes as he did not care to be pointed out to any VC snipers who might be looking for officer trophies. Woods was a big man, heavily muscled with broad shoulders and an easy smile, and I liked him from the start, although my cheeks were still burning about the salute.

He walked me over to the third platoon's area while the troops were filling their canteens and getting their mail and introduced me to Staff Sergeant Leslie, the acting platoon commander, who was cordial enough, considering that I was about to take over his platoon. We shook hands, and I decided to let him continue running the platoon until we got back to battalion the next day. Leslie was a former two-hundred-pounder who had lost fifty of that during his eight months in the bush, and his deliberately slow manner of speaking belied a shrewdness developed over seven years in the Marine Corps. I knew from the looks that he and Captain Woods exchanged when I told him to continue to march that my initial decision was correct, and I felt that professional jealousy was not going to be a factor in our relationship.

The third platoon was a surly bunch of teenage misfits who were mildly curious but completely unimpressed by my arrival. They were on a midday break from the heat of the August sun when I arrived with the water wagon and were lolling about in a loosely formed semicircle with every fourth or fifth man facing outward to avoid being caught by snipers. Many had taken off their flak jackets and their shirts to get some relief from the heat, and all had their packs, rifles, and other gear neatly stacked and within easy reach.

At first glance they appeared nonchalant, but after making a rapid scan of some of the troops making up the perimeter, I could see that months of living in the bush had sharpened their reactions to a fine edge. There was very little wasted motion in their movements, and while all their faces appeared boyish, most had a cast that made them seem years older. I turned down Sergeant Leslie's offer to assemble the three squads making up the platoon for a formal introduction. I planned to hold a rifle inspection as soon as possible after we returned from the bush, and I knew that there was no rush to get to know my men.

In addition to three squads of eight or more men, each with a leader, there were a three-man machine-gun team and a mortar section of like number assigned to the third platoon. We were, in Sergeant Leslie's words, "loaded for bear." We also had two corpsmen and a platoon guide, who could stand in for Leslie if he became disabled. Finally, a radio operator filled out my complement of marines, so that at present strength there were about forty of us. The squads were under strength because of casualties whose replacements had not yet arrived, but the presence of the machine-gun team and the mortar section alerted me that this was a unit that, though used to traveling light, could turn out a heavy volume of firepower very quickly.

Leslie summoned our command group: Corporal Turner, the platoon guide; Corporal Watson, the radio operator; and Doc Ellis, the senior corpsman, to meet me while the rest of the platoon were reading their mail. Corporal Turner was a huge black man who rarely stopped talking and joking but was easily recognizable as a born leader. He sported one gold earring, which was balanced by a marble-size piece of shrapnel lodged just beneath the skin on the opposite side of his neck. He had chosen the earring for its power to make people focus on his face when he was speaking, he informed me, and although the shrapnel had chosen him in a firefight some months earlier, he had decided not to have it removed when he realized that it had the same effect as the gold earring. Watson was a laconic redhead from Bristol, Virginia, whose powerful shoulders made it apparent why he had been chosen as radioman. He was new at his job, having replaced the radio operator who was inadvertently shot by the lieutenant whose place I was taking, but Leslie thought he was going to make a good radioman. The corpsman, Doc Ellis, was a dedicated professional whose diminutive size made his black-rimmed glasses and mustache appear enormous, but he had already proved himself countless times in tending to the wounded under fire.

While Watson and Ellis pulled self-consciously on their cigarettes, Corporal Turner was not in the least intimidated by my rank and immediately caught me off guard by asking directly what it was like to be the son of the corps's most famous marine. When I responded that he should be more concerned over what it was going to be like to be commanded by one of the corps's greenest lieutenants, the others joined in the laughter, and the ice was broken. Most of them never mentioned my father again.

My decision to allow Sergeant Leslie to continue to lead the platoon was of little consequence that day since I was invited to travel with Captain Woods for the rest of the patrol. Woods obviously wanted to make a preliminary judgment of my abilities as a small-unit leader before entrusting me with one of his platoons. As short as he was on lieutenants, it probably would have taken a display of monumental incompetence on my part to have been denied a command. When the order came to saddle up, I was amazed at how quickly the entire company was on its feet and moving. One man in my platoon had found a human skull somewhere and was tossing it up and down like a baseball when Captain Woods first took me over to meet Leslie. The rest of the platoon seemed not to give any import to his little game or even to notice it, but I was riveted as the skull was tossed into the air and caught. As we began the order of march, I looked over my shoulder in time to see the young man shatter the skull against the base of a concrete post. Hate was written clearly across his face, I supposed from the unavenged loss of a comrade earlier in the week, but the first words that crossed my mind were "Alas! poor Yorick."

We moved out with the first platoon in the lead, followed by Captain Woods's command group, which now included me, and the remaining two platoons back and spread to either side so that the entire formation from the front resembled a reversed fork with the two tines facing the rear. The terrain was flat and open, and the sky was cloudless so that communication and unit integrity were not difficult to maintain. The chance of enemy contact had been forecast as remote, and Captain Woods spent a lot of time that afternoon checking my fundamental skills. He put me through the paces handling the radio and plotting resections from known landmarks to see that we were on course. As I gained familiarity with the map and saw to it that the company's checkpoints were called in to battalion headquarters, I could feel myself gaining confidence.

We stopped briefly just before dark and moved the entire company several hundred meters into a nighttime defensive perimeter atop a raised berm between two rice paddies. Captain Woods had an artillery spotter who plotted pre-positioned artillery targets around our location as insurance against enemy penetration, and after we had checked the company perimeter to make certain that we could not be infiltrated and that our claymore mines were properly placed, we settled in for the night. I had brought no rations to the field and in any event had been too busy to notice hunger until we stopped, but now with nothing to do until dawn I was ravenous. Most of the company had eaten just before our final move while it was still light, heating the contents of their C ration cans with heat tabs or small pieces of plastic explosive called C-4. Sergeant Leslie came over from the third platoon with a can of beans and franks for me that I readily accepted. I ate them cold greedily, shoveling the beans and pieces of meat into my mouth with a plastic spoon, as Leslie pointed out how much better they would taste if heated. Captain Woods joined in his good-natured chiding as I got my first lesson in field comfort. Food can be eaten hot only during daylight hours since the light from heat tabs and plastique can be spotted by the enemy. I would remember next time, but hungry as I was and as newly acquainted to C rations, even cold, the grub tasted delicious.

We took turns standing two-hour radio watches for the rest of the night, and I marveled at how quickly and how easily those in our command post who were not on alert could get to sleep. I was not used to the uncomfortable ground or the soggy surroundings and was also not yet tired enough to drift off at any opportunity. It seemed strange to me on my first full day that I had not seen a North Vietnamese Army (NVA) soldier or a Vietcong guerrilla or indeed any sign of war. To be sure, with darkness the mosquitoes had come in swarms, but those were not the hostiles I had been trained to fight. When dawn came, I was red-eyed, covered with bites, and eagerly anticipating a return to battalion, where I could get a hot meal and a shave.

When we returned from the field, Captain Woods officially gave me command of the third platoon, and Leslie and I, after getting cleaned up, walked over to the battalion mess area to get some chow and discuss how I was going to manage the platoon. Although it was not yet mealtime, the kitchen staff readily supplied us with the last meal's leftovers and all the milk we could drink. After we had eaten, I bummed a cigarette from a nearby marine and after the first few drags decided to requisition a carton of Pall Malls from the packets that were supplied free to troops in the field. I had stopped smoking a year earlier, when I was getting in shape for Officer Candidate School, but somehow it seemed silly now to worry about its long-range health implications with thirteen months in Nam ahead. I told Leslie that he was to stay close at my side for the immediate future and that as the platoon's operation became more familiar to me, I would be assuming more control, to which he readily nodded agreement. I also instructed him to have each squad assemble for a rifle inspection, and I had him stagger the times so that the process would not take on too much formality. I wanted to have a few words individually with each of the men, and I needed to see how much discipline they were imposing on themselves. A rifle inspection seemed the ideal way to form a quick judgment.

The next time we went on patrol, it would be as my lone platoon rather than in a company. But for the next twenty-four hours our responsibility was to stand lines in an assigned section of the battalion perimeter. Our section was bounded on the left by the river and on the right by another platoon and stretched about four hundred meters. The area before us was flat and unobstructed so that daytime surveillance was not difficult, but even a greenhorn like me could see that our lines could be easily breached at night, considering a gap of thirty or forty meters between men, even if half the platoon were standing watch. The men had dug fighting holes along the perimeter and pitched their tents just to the rear so that access back and forth was easy. The real problem was keeping tired marines who had just come back from patrol alert when it was quiet. I was quite uneasy about our vulnerability as the setup did not conform in any way to the field manuals' examples of defensive perimeters with their interlocking fields of fire. My apprehension was heightened by the lack of wire and sandbags fortifying our position. Sergeant Leslie did not seem too concerned, however, especially since there were no sizable enemy units reported in our area, and I took some comfort from his assessment.

Since my platoon was spread out along the perimeter by squads, it was an easy matter to conduct my rifle inspection and troop the line at the same time. I started with the first squad, which was positioned closest to the river, and worked my way back up to the makeshift hooch that Leslie, Watson, and I were occupying at the opposite end of the line. I was pleased that their weapons were clean and that each marine had been assigned a different field of fire. Sergeant Leslie had obviously been doing a good job of running the platoon.

All the men were young, about half with high school diplomas, in good health, and seemingly respectful of me or at least of the position I occupied. They probably also realized that if they got out of line, Leslie would take them to task. With a couple of exceptions they appeared pretty much as I had expected. The machine-gun team had a forty-year-old man who was completely bald and it seemed to me somewhat mentally deficient. His nickname was Pappy, and as Leslie explained to me later, he had entered the Marine Corps through an ill-conceived program called Project 100,000, which was designed to give hard-core unemployed civilians a skill that they could use after their military service. The other members of his team took care of Pappy, and he could keep up with his much younger comrades; but I had a hard time figuring out how his skills with a machine gun were going to help him earn a living after the Marine Corps. The platoon was predominantly white with a handful of Hispanics and blacks, and if there was a common thread that united them, it was their lower-middle-class backgrounds. Many were from the South and from rural areas of the country, but there were a couple of city boys who good-naturedly teased the farmers about their lack of sophistication.

When I got back to my hooch after conducting the inspection, I complimented Sergeant Leslie on the condition of the platoon and made a couple of suggestions about moving the machine gun to a more commanding position, which he agreed to. I also directed him to have the men spend some time filling sandbags for their foxholes and asked him to talk to the battalion supply officer about getting us more concertina wire for the front of our positions. The hooch that he had put together for us was a pathetic structure comprised of two-by-fours, sandbags, tent flaps, and sheets of plastic that had once served as wrappings for artillery rounds. It worked well enough in dry weather, but as I discovered that night, it offered only minimal protection from rain. We spent a good part of the night rearranging the plastic sheets as the rain collected in pools on our makeshift ceiling and burst through. In the morning we both were soaked to the skin, and I felt as if we had been the only two unarmed men in an all-night water-balloon fight. I felt a little better as the sun began to dry my clothes, but in my first letter home to Toddy, which I wrote that morning, I gave her the address of my unit and asked her to put a rain suit at the top of her list of items to send me in a care package.

That afternoon and for the next several days the third platoon conducted short-range patrols, and I assumed a more commanding role as the week wore on. Captain Woods assigned routes that were fairly short and within several thousand meters, or klicks, of the battalion to give me a chance to get broken in, probably so that he could send help if necessary, but the week went by without any enemy contact. The weather, in contrast with our first night of standing watch, was beautiful, though hot, without a cloud in the sky, and I developed a burn on my neck and arms that eventually sloughed off like pieces of peanut brittle, leaving large pink patches. The biggest problem in leading patrols, other than making certain that we stayed on course and hit our checkpoints, was keeping the men properly spaced. They tended to bunch up when the terrain was rough or visibility was poor and to get too far apart when we were moving quickly or they were tired. If they were too close to each other, one booby trap or mortar round would cause multiple casualties, and if they were too spread out, they tended to lose contact and were difficult to maneuver. It was a constant challenge to get them properly synchronized, and I could hardly imagine what sort of havoc enemy artillery or small-arms fire would have on my efforts to maintain any semblance of control. Sergeant Leslie was, of course, a big help, and by the end of the week we had each begun to develop a feel for what the other was doing without any overt communication between us.

In that short time I had increased my cigarette consumption to several packs a day, betraying a tenseness that I hoped did not communicate itself to my men in other ways. I began, too, to think that the patrols could not function properly unless I was in contact with whoever was walking point. That meant that I was never more than two or three men back from the front of the patrol and far more apt to be caught in the killing zone should we be ambushed or trigger a land mine. Leslie warned me repeatedly that I should rotate my position in the patrol route, but as long as we were not making contact, I thought that I could run things far more smoothly from the front, where I could see what was happening and could correct any deviations from our proper azimuths. In any event, Leslie became resigned to taking a position toward the back of the patrols as time wore on, and I felt more secure knowing that he was covering my rear. He had already been leading patrols for months before I arrived in country and there was no Marine Corps regulation that required that he press his luck.

One of our primary missions, as we patrolled in northern I Corps, was to prevent the enemy from firing rockets and launching mortars into the vulnerable city of Dong Ha. The attempt to interdict those missiles at their launch sites required us to spend most of our time in the field. We patrolled as a platoon during the day, moved into a nighttime perimeter as darkness was descending, and then sent out squad-size patrols at night. It was demanding, uncomfortable work with the psychological pressures of imminent enemy contact ever on our minds. We ate and drank only what we carried, slept fitfully in quickly dug fighting holes, and tried not to remain stationary long enough for the enemy to find us. Our routine was broken periodically by a return to the womb of the battalion compound for resupply, but even then we had lines to stand so that there was never any real relief. I was pleased that no missiles had been fired into Dong Ha from my patrol area, but I also began to feel after a couple of weeks that the war had passed us by and the enemy was purposely ignoring us. The troops probably knew better, and the memory of their slain comrade smoldered in their minds. It also kept everyone on edge. That was desirable but tiring.

Late one afternoon toward the end of my second week, near where that last casualty had been incurred, we came across the badly decomposed corpse of an NVA soldier. He had no pack, weapon, or other gear but was readily identified by the rotting uniform that hung from his body. He was also lying in an open, exposed area as if he had simply dropped in his tracks or crawled as far as he could after being wounded. Leslie was elated at our grotesque find and wanted to claim the hapless soldier as a casualty of the fire mission he had called in the night the third platoon sustained its loss, but there was no way to validate his assumption. At any rate I could tell that my men felt somewhat vindicated by our grisly trophy, and some of them would have mutilated his body further but for the fact that there was so little of it left. As it was, I had to restrain one young marine from urinating on the corpse. I was shocked by the vehemence of their hatred toward a now-inanimate object and their lack of respect for the dead. Sergeant Leslie told me after we had buried the corpse in a shallow grave that I would soon understand, but shaken by the experience, I did not want to lose that much of myself. I could not help thinking that somewhere that dead NVA soldier had a family who would never know what had happened to him, but I naturally kept my feelings to myself.

Several days later Captain Woods assigned me a mechanized patrol using a tank and two amtracs. Checkpoints would be farther apart since we could cover more ground, but other than that and the fact that we would be riding rather than walking, the basic mission was the same. I think the skipper sensed that my men were becoming weary from so many foot patrols. I had never led a mechanized patrol before, even in Basic School, and I was apprehensive about having the responsibility for the cumbersome vehicles, but as I briefed the squad leaders on riding assignments, it was apparent that they considered our mission a sort of holiday excursion. Riding was better than walking, and any small enemy unit would be foolhardy to take us on with so much added firepower. Also, the patrol would probably be completed fairly quickly, giving the platoon some much-needed time off.

Everybody was still in a festive mood as we boarded our newfound locomotion, and headed out of the battalion compound. Almost immediately the first signs of trouble developed. The drivers, as it turned out, had gotten used to sitting in their vehicles inside the battalion perimeter and had absolutely no knowledge of the terrain beyond the wire. I realized it was going to be a bad day when the vehicles had trouble getting through wire that was no obstacle to a foot patrol. I rode with one squad and the machine-gun team in the lead amtrac, followed by the tank and other amtrac, which contained Sergeant Leslie and the rest of the platoon. I was disoriented when we finally succeeded in breaking out of the compound, since the patrol finally began where it was easiest to negotiate the wire, not where I thought we would exit. Then, to add to my distress, my compass needle began to swing wildly because of the surrounding metal, making it almost impossible to find our first checkpoint. Luckily Sergeant Leslie could navigate the area from memory, but even with his guidance, we wound up hitting our checkpoints in the reverse of their assigned order.

Finally, just as I thought my mortification was complete, I succeeded in getting one of the amtracs firmly mired in a swamp, and we spent the next hour towing it free. As we limped back to the battalion compound, I was completely absorbed in how badly the patrol had gone when suddenly the entire platoon began firing from the moving convoy. Convinced that we had finally made enemy contact, I shouldered my rifle and turned toward the firing only to discover that a large pig was running alongside the amtrac. It was bleeding from a dozen bullet holes and collapsed beside us just as Leslie and I succeeded in restoring fire discipline. The animal had been scared from its resting place by the noise of the tank and, in its haste to flee, offered a perfect target as it ran alongside. Leslie was furious at this spontaneous shooting, and I realized for the first time how difficult it could be to impose order on a bunch of edgy teenage marines. We finished off the pig with a pistol round behind the ear and called in the incident to Captain Woods, who had heard the commotion from inside the wire. He downplayed the incident as well as the debacle that I had made of the patrol, but for weeks I chafed at the thought that my platoon's first live contact was with an unarmed pig. We left the animal where we had slaughtered it, and curiously no irate farmer ever showed up to demand reparations.

A few days after the episode with the pig, the composition of the platoon changed with the return of two men who had been wounded earlier and sent to the rear to recuperate. Cowboy was a rancher from Idaho and had been the platoon radio operator before he was wounded. Since we were breaking in Watson to be the new radioman and Cowboy had already humped the heavy radio for several months, Leslie and I decided to make him a squad leader. His new job was equally as important but involved less risk of injury, and he readily agreed to take the second squad, whose leader was rotating home. Ski was a lanky city boy whose catlike grace and quick reflexes made him a natural for walking point, and although we tried to rotate positions as much as possible, his point experience was invaluable. Both men had incurred only minor wounds, and their return improved the unit's efficiency and did wonders for morale. Unfortunately the third platoon got an additional replacement when Cowboy and Ski returned.

Corporal Hitch was a forty-three-year-old former staff sergeant who had mouthed off to an officer and been busted. When he refused to back down and apologize, he was taken out of his soft billet as a supply sergeant and assigned to the field. He came to me with seventeen years in the Marine Corps, but as could be expected, he was completely out of shape and, unlike Pappy, unable to keep up on difficult patrols. I complained to Captain Woods that Hitch had no business being in the bush and could well endanger the rest of us but was told to hold my horses until a deal could be cut at battalion to cover the problem. I sent him down to the second squad, where Cowboy could keep an eye on him. Theoretically that should have been no problem since he was twice as old as anyone else in the squad and stood out like a sore thumb. With his time in the corps, some of the troops assumed that he knew what he was doing; that could not have been farther from the truth.

After the third platoon acquired Hitch, Cowboy, and Ski, one of our first assignments involved a two-day patrol by amtrac across the Cua Viet River to a friendly hamlet, actually, more of a goodwill mission than a patrol. We were to be dropped off in the ville by the amtracs, meet with the village chief to get an assessment of enemy activity in his province, and provide some rudimentary medical help to his people. We would spend the night there and be picked up by the amtracs the next morning for the return trip back across the river. I was given a Vietnamese interpreter, and the corpsmen loaded up with extra medical supplies to hand out to the local populace. I had not seen the far side of the river, and since the locals were supposed to be friendly, the platoon actually looked forward to our excursion. Fortunately the amtrac drivers had been there and this time knew where we were going. One marine fell or got knocked off the vehicle as we crossed the river and with his flak jacket and full complement of gear probably would have drowned had we not succeeded in reeling him in, but otherwise the trip went smoothly.

The village chief and a small contingent of Popular Forces met us as we disembarked at the entrance to the hamlet. Headquarters was a small whitewashed structure that also served as a town hall and armory. Although the chief had fortified it with some sandbags and a few rolls of concertina wire spread around the perimeter, I feared it could not withstand much of an attack. His dozen or so troops were poorly armed with pistols and carbines and made a great show of appearing busy when we arrived, but my advice to them would have been to surrender immediately if attacked by any force larger than a squad. I surmised that the chief had all the muscle he needed, to live well off the sweat of his villagers, but his days were numbered if the VC or NVA decided that it did not want him around. He was pleased to have us hold sick call, which would improve his political standing, and he was hospitable throughout our stay.

After the usual amenities and a gift of a carton of American ciga-rettes, I told him through my interpreter that we were going to proceed through his village and hold the sick call at the other end, returning in time to meet with him before dark. He insisted that he be allowed to arrange a banquet that evening for Sergeant Leslie and me and three or four others of my choosing, and though I fretted about leaving my platoon alone for even a short time, Leslie took me aside and told me that our host would lose face if we did not accept. When I did so, he smiled broadly and shuffled off to begin preparations for the meal, while Leslie and I licked our chops as we fantasized an Oriental banquet.

The village itself consisted of several hundred thatched-roof houses spread along either side of a narrow dirt lane in more or less a straight line. The villagers supported themselves by farming and river com-merce, and they were open and friendly toward our goodwill mission. One young boy adopted me as soon as we began our journey to the other end of the village and signified his claim to the other urchins who followed in our wake by holding on tightly to my hand. Chickens strutted about freely, and the village appeared to me to be quite pros-perous with no sign of civil unrest. By the time the platoon had made its way to the outskirts of town, we had attracted a sizable crowd, mostly women, children, and old men, and I gave no particular thought to the absence of young men. The side of the river that we had come from had been so sparsely settled that it was almost eerie, and it was pleasant for a change to mix with the population whom we were supposed to be saving from communism.

As we exited the village, I had the platoon set up in a loose perimeter in an open field beyond the last hut, and the two corpsmen began treating the sick. At first the curious villagers were shy, but as one or two of the bolder children, coaxed by cigarettes and candy, came forward, they quickly lost their fear. Most of their ailments were of a minor nature, skin infections and stomach disorders caused by parasites. As the corpsmen began to work their magic, they were quickly swamped, and we had to force the crowd out of the perimeter and into a semblance of a waiting line. I became concerned that once inside the perimeter, some of the women and children would begin stealing our gear, and indeed, my marines soon found children attempting to carry off anything they could get their hands on. I finally announced that if we found one more child attempting to fleece us, I would have the corpsmen pack their medical kits. The threat seemed to work. Some of the more enterprising children now began to barter cookies and other homemade sweets for C rations and cigarettes, and by the end of the sick call some marines were paying exorbitant sums of money to these children for the same items they could have gotten earlier for next to nothing. The young lad who had adopted me took it upon himself to protect me from these young vendors, but he obviously also had his eye on my pack and rations. As we saddled up and prepared to hike back to the village compound, I gave him several tins of meat and fruit, but I stopped short of giving him my cigarettes. I was still new enough in country to find the sight of eight-year-old boys smoking cigarettes unsettling.

When we got back to our starting point, the platoon set up for the night around the compound. As a rule, we moved just as darkness fell to avoid giving away our location; but there had been no sign of enemy activity, and I thought we should take advantage of what little protection the compound offered. After I had checked the perimeter, Leslie, the interpreter, and I went to meet with the village chief and his entourage. The room was sparsely furnished with a table, a couple of chairs, and several racks of rifles. The chief motioned me to sit in one chair while he took the other and our subordinates stood. The conversation was stilted and of little intelligence value, but a necessary formality. He insisted that there were no VC or VC sympathizers in the village, had never been any, and none would be permitted in the future, and with each assertion he excitedly clasped the butt of his sidearm. We smoked some of the cigarettes I had given him earlier and drank glasses of tepid tea, while he tried to elicit a promise from me to requisition some more concertina wire for the compound's defenses. He also seemed to think that he had done me a favor by allowing my corpsmen to treat his people. That perplexed me until I realized that his collaboration might be risky if the VC infrastructure in the area was strong. If that were the case, however, he had probably gotten permission from the enemy to allow our sick call and most of the medical supplies we left with Doc Ellis's patients would wind up in the hands of the VC.

After it became obvious that I was going to learn nothing more and that he was going to get no more concessions, we ended the meeting, and he sent a guide with me to gather up our group for the banquet. I decided to take Sergeant Leslie, Doc Ellis, the senior corpsman, since he had done most of the work that day, Watson, whom I would need to keep radio contact with the platoon, and the interpreter. Corporal Turner was unhappy about being left behind but understood that a responsible party had to be left in charge of the platoon, and he admonished us to eat carefully as our party of five left, following our guide to a nearby thatched hut.

The meal was served on a low table around which we tried to make ourselves comfortable sitting on the floor. Smiling women filled and refilled our plates with unidentifiable meats, vegetables, and rice and a pungent sauce that masked the taste of everything. I later found out that the principal component of the sauce was chicken blood, which explained its horrible taste, but there was no refusing our smiling hostesses, who, oblivious of our protestations, continued to glop food onto our plates. There were also tea and strong spirits, which we were successful in refusing because of our mission. After an hour and a half we begged off, explaining that my company commander would never condone a more prolonged absence from my bivouacked marines. As we rose to go, we were surprised to be presented with a bill, which was, in addition, completely out of proportion to the fare we had been served. We pooled our scrip and paid begrudgingly, but everyone in the room knew we had been taken.

Corporal Turner was relieved to see us and had a good laugh at our expense when Sergeant Leslie told him how we had been burned over the cost of our meal. I was still fuming at the way the villagers had tried to take advantage of us at every opportunity and could just imagine the village chief smoking my cigarettes with his cronies and joking about how he had put one over on the Americans. To make matters worse, a light rain fell all night, and while my men and I were huddled beneath our poncho liners, I knew that our hosts were dry and warm. I stood a radio watch and then tried to get some sleep; but the dampness and cold made rest almost impossible, and I dozed fitfully. At least the amtracs would be there first thing in the morning to carry us back across the river, I thought, where we could concentrate on search and destroy rather than placate and pacify.

Sometime after midnight Sergeant Leslie shook me awake, and I could sense urgency in his voice. Corporal Hitch had detected movement in front of his squad's position and believed that the enemy was probing our lines. I knew that the village had been curfewed for tonight, so anything out there had to be unfriendly, and I had Leslie pass the word for full alert. My heart raced at the prospect of catching a couple of guerrillas coming through the wire, but I prayed that they were not an advance party for a larger unit. Hitch was by now beside himself and convinced that a frontal assault was about to be launched directly at his position when I scurried over to join him. He animatedly pointed out what appeared to be three crouched figures just beyond the wire and told me that he had been watching them move closer for the last hour. I could not fathom why the three perfectly plain silhouettes were so still and so in open view. After observing them with Hitch for a few minutes, I decided to fire a few rounds at them to force their hand. I squeezed off several rounds at each target, but when my fusillade evoked no response, it finally dawned on me that Hitch's quarry existed only in our heads. We called in an illumination round from the artillery battery that was supporting us to be certain that Hitch was not mistaken, and as the round descended and briefly lit up the terrain the three figures turned out to be small shrubs. Within minutes most of the marines who were not on watch were again sound asleep, and any shreds of credibility Hitch might still have had were squandered.

When daybreak came, we dried our poncho liners in the sun, policed our area, and waited for the amtracs. The trip back was uneventful, and I was beginning to wonder after our latest caper if there were indeed any enemy soldiers in South Vietnam. I had been in command of the third platoon for about three weeks, and our only confirmed kills were a pig and three bushes. Although I dreaded the prospect of my first firefight, I knew that it was inevitable, and I wanted to get it over with. Back at battalion Sergeant Leslie and I briefed Captain Woods on our goodwill mission, and I expressed my frustration at the windmill tilting we had been doing up until now. He assured us that something much bigger on the drawing board would soon give us all the action we would want or could handle. Sergeant Leslie and I exchanged glances but did not press the matter, since we were already embarrassed for having called in a fire mission to illuminate some shrubbery. We also decided not to tell the platoon, which was already rife with rumors over our anticipated move south. Leslie and I agreed that Woods's hint of action would only fuel the rumor mill, which already had us living in air-conditioned Quonset huts when we rotated into the Da Nang area.

A day or two later Captain Woods summoned the company's lieutenants and platoon sergeants, and it was obvious from the way he set his jaw that his earlier words had been in earnest. The battalion was indeed about to move south, he said, but before we moved, we were going to be helilifted up into the demilitarized zone (DMZ) in a surprise airborne assault. As he described the mission, the pencils and pads came out, and we began mentally formulating the regulation five-paragraph orders we would give our platoons. In theory the mission appeared simple. The platoon would board a helicopter at a specified landing zone at daybreak the next morning, disembark at preplanned grid coordinates in the DMZ, follow a route of march through several objectives to another landing zone, and be picked up by helicopter for the return trip.

I was the newest and the greenest lieutenant in the company, but none of us had ever been up into the no-man's-land of the DMZ, so in a sense we all were starting even. The commander of the second platoon, Lieutenant John Zier, had been in country six or seven months, and he and I had already struck up a rapport since both our wives were waiting for us in the Washington area. Even he with his experience was somber at the prospect of our undertaking. He was a large man, six feet three and 230 pounds before the heat of Vietnam had whittled 30 pounds from his muscular frame, and I had taken delight on previous occasions from his bull-in-the-china-shop approach to life. If John Zier was worried, I knew that I should be also, but a part of me was looking forward to the next day.

Late that afternoon, after I had briefed the platoon and given them the order of march for our maneuver, B-52 bombers began to prep the area of our operation. For the next several hours an air strike was in operation, and plane after plane jettisoned its payload of two-thousand-pound bombs into the DMZ wilderness. From our position on the ground outside Dong Ha we could not see or hear the planes, but each time one of the bombs detonated, the ground around us reverberated as if an iron fist had been pounded into a steel carpet. The sound resembled thunder, and I could not fathom how any creature could live through such a devastating barrage. "Get some," my marines would yell as the pilots went about their deadly business, and there was not a man in the battalion who did not pray that the air strikes would crush the life from every living organism in the area into which we would be flown at dawn.

The next morning at daybreak the three platoons boarded helicopters and headed north. We traveled fairly low to the ground in tight configurations of three choppers to a company. My men were packed like sardines along the sides of the lead chopper, and from my position near the door gunner I could watch the vegetation below. As we neared our destination, we passed over several camouflaged North Vietnamese antiaircraft emplacements. I could see the guns swivel and hear the steady pop of .50-caliber rounds, and I suddenly realized that we were under fire. Several rounds passed through the fuselage of our chopper. One went through the canteen on the web belt of the marine sitting next to me without giving him anything more than a wet lap and a bad scare. He passed his ruined canteen up to the crew chief and crossed himself as we moved out of range of the enemy gunner, but we both realized that the round could have cut him in half if it had been six inches farther to the right.

Ten minutes later our chopper banked steeply to the left, and the ground, which had been below us, seemed to have turned sideways. The vegetation of the landing zone, flattened by the rotating blades, met us, and with a thump we were on the ground and being pushed out of the back and down the tail ramp by an agitated crew chief. I had been taught at Basic School to ask the crew chief for the direction in which the nose of the chopper was pointing for orientation, but amid the noise and confusion of disembarking marines, he could not hear me.

Within seconds the chopper was again airborne and headed back to Dong Ha, while my platoon and I were left alone in the soggy vegetation. The noise of the helicopter blades was replaced by the steady cackle of Watson's radio as adjacent units tried to come up on the same frequency and make contact, and my men fanned out in a broad circle to secure our area and await word from the skipper to move out. After we had regained some semblance of organization and I had determined our bearings, it had just occurred to me that the landing had been quiet when suddenly the first squad began firing its weapons. I could not see its target, but as the volume of fire peaked and then died out, I realized that we had made contact. A breathless marine then made his way over to me to report that his squad had killed two NVA soldiers as they fled our perimeter.

Both the dead soldiers were unarmed except for Chinese hand grenades in their packs, and as I surveyed their bullet-riddled bodies, it seemed strange to me that they had survived the two-thousand-pound bombs the day before only to be done in by rifle rounds. One of the soldiers was wearing gold-rimmed John Lennon-style glasses, and I wondered if he had known that his glasses were a part of the uniform of the peace movement back home and if he had ever listened to the music of the Beatles. The other dead soldier had a picture of a woman among his possessions. The third platoon now had its first legitimate kills since my arrival, and, in accordance with battalion policy, the marines who actually got the credit would receive in-country R & R.

When the word came over the radio from Captain Woods to move out, we covered the faces of the dead soldiers with their uniform shirts and, having neither the time nor the inclination to bury them, left them where they had fallen. Our first objective was the crest of a steep, heavily wooded hill directly to our south. The skipper wanted to get a better vantage point from which to view the surrounding countryside, and the hilltop facing us seemed ideal until we started to climb. I moved my platoon out in the standard one-squad-up, two-back formation, but the foliage was so dense and the incline so steep that we were hardly able to progress.

As we hacked our way up the hill, visual contact between squads also worsened until we were forced to resort to single file. Almost immediately Corporal Hitch collapsed from the heat, which had become unbearable after the morning cloud cover had lifted. A combat photographer who had been assigned to us at the last minute also became a heat casualty, even though he had only a camera to carry. Both Hitch and the photographer had to be carried back to our original landing zone to await a medevac chopper, and we waited in place for an hour while the bird made its way to them. I never saw Hitch again, but he (and the photographer) had compromised our mission by the delay. His collapse proved I had been correct in asking Captain Woods to have him removed from my command and from the bush.

We finally reached our first objective with the rest of the company strung out behind us like an unraveled spool of communications wire, every man out of breath and drenched with sweat. The squad leaders were kept busy trying to keep their charges from going to their canteens at every opportunity. Doc Ellis estimated the heat to be 110 degrees. Men simply sank to their knees whenever the platoon paused. I had never been so consumed with thirst in my life. Watson reported to the skipper that we had crested the hill, and several minutes later a huffing and puffing Captain Woods emerged with his radioman from the underbrush behind us to eye the terrain.

Half a dozen bomb craters pockmarked the slope of the hill and the valley between our position and the next hill, and the smell of fresh dirt and cordite from the giant holes filled and irritated our nostrils. The crater nearest us was about twenty feet in diameter and nearly as deep, and as Captain Woods and I peered into its sharply sloping sides, we could see a single NVA boot sitting at the bottom with a severed leg protruding from it. Nausea seized me briefly, but there was not enough liquid remaining in my body to bring anything up.

The skipper called in a situation report over the battalion net and summoned the other two platoon leaders for a quick conference. Even Zier, with his athletic build and incredible stamina, moved as though he were walking through molasses. The other lieutenant made no effort to hide his fatigue. Neither of their platoons had made enemy contact, but we all were too exhausted to waste energy discussing my kills as we tried to concentrate on Captain Woods's plan of action.

I was instructed to flank the valley below us with my platoon and cut across the ridgeline of the next hill. When my objective was secured, Captain Woods and the remaining two platoons would come on line, cross the valley frontally, and join us as they had at our first objective. My assignment, of course, meant that the third platoon would have twice as far to walk as the other two platoons and that if the next hill was occupied, we could easily be decimated, but I knew Woods was banking on no enemy unit's having remained intact after the B-52s.

"His bank, my ass," I thought as I acknowledged my orders and prepared to get the platoon up and moving. As always, the men grumbled but obeyed. Our flanking maneuver took well over an hour, but the first part of it was downhill, and since the second hill was not nearly as steep or as thick with underbrush, we did not have to work nearly as hard to cover the ground. There was no sign of life, and the surroundings took on an otherworldly aura without so much as a bird chirp coming from the abundant wilderness.

From the ridgeline of the second hill, I could see down into another valley and up a third hill to the south, and I could also see the rest of the company on the hill we had just vacated. The terrain seemed to consist of nothing but hills and valleys, and I knew that an entire North Vietnamese army could be lying in wait beyond any one of them; but I was at least relieved to be able to call Captain Woods and tell him that we had secured our objective without incident.

Our platoon used the half hour it took the rest of the company to cross the valley to take a breather and eat some chow. I wolfed down a can of cling peaches that tasted better than anything I had eaten in my entire life. As I tilted my head back to drain the last drop of liquid into my mouth, Ellis warned me to slow down, but undaunted, I then licked the inside of the can. We had not eaten since coming into this godawful inferno, and the troops were dehydrated and near exhaustion. I had less than a canteen of water left, and many of the men were even lower than I despite their wearing from three to five canteens each. We were going to start taking casualties in droves if we did not get some relief, and for once I prayed for rain in Vietnam.

As Captain Woods arrived, I could tell that he was ready to throw in the towel as he vainly searched for clouds to block out the midafternoon sun, which had become our worst enemy. When he announced to the command group that we were going to clear a landing zone in the valley below and call in the helicopters, our relief was palpable. As I passed the word to my platoon, they seemed rejuvenated by knowing the end of the mission was at hand. A scouting party of volunteers was hastily assembled and sent directly across our prepared landing zone to climb the last hill they would ever have to hump in the DMZ. When they signaled that it was secure, the rest of us descended into the valley, staked out a landing zone, and began clearing it of trees and shrubbery.

There were only a couple of hours of daylight left, and the men worked like dervishes, despite their exhaustion, when they realized that if we could not get the choppers in soon, we would have to spend the night. A dozen men hacked away with machetes, felling the small trees and bushes that others stepped in to carry off to the side. There was only enough flatland for one chopper to land at a time, and no one wanted to be the last to board; but Captain Woods placed my platoon first since we had been on point all day.

As the sun weakened and a usable landing zone began to take shape, several of my men discovered a tunnel hidden by underbrush in the side of the hill. I was surprised at the number of men who volunteered to serve as tunnel rats since there was no way of knowing what was inside, but the element of the unknown seemed to spark the enthusiasm of some of the men. After a volunteer was selected, we tossed a couple of grenades into the shaft. The volunteer's quick foray produced nothing but some sacks of rice and medical supplies from an American pharmaceutical company. Apparently the shaft was used only for storage, which was a relief to me but a disappointment to the tunnel rat, who was looking for the in-country R&R that a kill would bring him. I was also disillusioned that NVA soldiers would have access to American medical supplies, but Captain Woods credited our find to the machinations of the black market or to wholesale purchases through a neutral country.

We sealed off the tunnel entrance with a plastic explosive charge and settled in to wait for the choppers. I gave the squads the order in which they were to board for the ride home, and anxious marines spent the next hour looking and listening for signs of our deliverance. We had no idea how the other companies of the battalion were faring and at that point cared even less, since the paramount thought on everyone's mind was to get the hell out of the DMZ before the enemy figured out where we were and came sweeping in from the surrounding hills or, worse yet, targeted our position and began lobbing in mortar rounds. The longer we remained in place, the more vulnerable we became, and I also knew that the last chopper out was the one in most danger since the first pickups would give away our position.

Finally, after what seemed like an eternity, the faint clacking of helicopter blades became audible in the distance and intensified into a roar as the choppers appeared on the horizon and came sweeping toward us. Within seconds of the lead chopper's swoop into the landing zone, my men and I had scrambled aboard and were airborne, and I watched with admiration as a second chopper that had been hovering above us repeated the process for the second platoon. When the third bird had picked up the last of the company, the three of them came on line and swung south toward Dong Ha and more hospitable surroundings.

It was almost dark, and we all were too exhausted to try to make our voices heard above the whirling blades and rushing air; but Sergeant Leslie gave me the thumbs-up, and more than one tired marine gave thanks to God that he had almost made it through another day in Vietnam. I leaned wearily against the bulkhead behind me and watched the young marine opposite me absentmindedly clean his fingernails with his bush knife. Suddenly I realized that it was August 18, my twenty-third birthday.

When we disembarked near Dong Ha, there seemed to have been no provisions made for our return, and the company fell out on the side of the landing zone and awaited further orders. A water wagon was driven up and the platoons lined up to refill their canteens and slosh water on one another. Somebody spotted a pallet of C rations, which was quickly cannibalized, and within minutes the glow of heat tabs dotted our formation as hungry marines, their thirst slaked by the water resupply, now filled their bellies with the stolen food. A rear-echelon supply sergeant considered raising a squawk when he realized that we had pirated his rations but then thought better of interfering with marines who had just returned from a combat mission. Many of the men fell asleep as soon as they had eaten, but I continued to gulp cup after cup of water, feeling as if my parched throat could never get enough.

Later that evening we were loaded onto a navy barge and transported back down the Cua Viet River to Mai Xa Thi, our original location. It was cool in the open boat beneath a cloudless sky, and though we were packed in tight, my marines found ways to be comfortable. Many used their helmets or packs as pillows and sprawled lazily on the crowded deck, making small talk or gazing at the stars. The coolness and tranquility of the evening were a pleasant contrast to the heat and confusion of our mission, as the boat plowed quietly through the black water. Like all infantrymen we were content to be traveling by any mode of transportation other than shank's mare.

I smoked quietly and thought with mixed feelings about the enemy soldiers my platoon had killed. I was proud that we had gotten two kills since that reflected favorably on the platoon and was good for morale, but I was ashamed that we had basically shot unarmed men as they fled from us. We had been trained to kill anything that moved in the unfriendly environs of the DMZ, and it was far better to be safe than sorry; but I still wished that the two soldiers had been armed to the teeth and charging our position when we wasted them.

I felt vaguely unclean in an unidentifiable way, and I was also bothered by the fact that our first two kills had absolutely no say in the manner and timing of their deaths. Had we landed one klick farther over or proceeded in a different direction, they would probably be sleeping now or marking time, I thought, until they were rotated back to Hanoi. I wondered if it was a soldier's lot always to fall victim to circumstances beyond his control.

When we unloaded at Mai Xa Thi, we were given the rest of the evening and the following day off. Our lines were located near the rear-echelon cooks and motor pool maggots, and it was simple justice that they spell us for a few hours. The men unloaded their packs and weapons, and after being warned by Sergeant Leslie not to get too far out of line, they shuffled off in groups of twos and threes to look for mischief.

Leslie and I went over to battalion headquarters to see how the rest of the companies had made out, but intelligence was still very poor. At least one platoon had missed its dustoff and was going to be camping out in the DMZ, and the other companies were still en route from Dong Ha. Apparently there had been sporadic contact like ours, but no one had gotten into trouble with a large enemy unit. The gunny gave Leslie and me cold beers that we shared with Captain Woods when he came in. He congratulated us on the kills and on being on point all day, but from his tone it was obvious he was disappointed not to have made more contact. Our time at Mai Xa Thi was almost over, and Captain Woods had wanted to leave "Victor Charles" and "Luke the Gook" something to remember us by; but as I savored the coldness of my beer, I felt that my day had been full enough.

The next day, with the battalion all present and accounted for, the rumor mill resumed full operation. The straight scoop, as relayed to us by Captain Woods, was that we were to proceed south by truck within the next few days to relieve a battalion outside Da Nang. The troops were unwilling to believe the truth, however, and one story even had us parachuting into Hanoi.

═══ ☆ ═══

I went for a swim and washed my clothes in the Cua Viet. That was accomplished most efficiently by wading into the river, fully clad, with a bar of soap, scrubbing down, and then stripping. Water had never felt so good, and Sergeant Leslie and I allowed ourselves some extra time to soak off the black dirt of the DMZ before emerging and wringing out our utilities.

We spent the remainder of the day luxuriating beneath the same sun that had almost killed us a day earlier, cleaning our weapons and drinking beer, and by midafternoon my morale had vastly improved. I wrote my wife and my father, telling them of our anticipated move south but omitting any references to danger or discomfort. That evening the company feasted on a sumptuous meal of minute steaks, fried eggs, and Kool-Aid. This was our last night at Mai Xa Thi, and after dinner Lieutenant Zier, our platoon sergeants, and I smoked cigarettes in the darkness outside the mess area, conjecturing about living conditions at Camp 413 in the Da Nang tactical area of responsibility (TAOR). An advance party had already been sent south to start the transition, and I was looking forward to the trip and to seeing something of the countryside between Dong Ha and Da Nang.

Breaking camp is an easy matter for an infantry platoon. When the word came that we were moving out, we quickly refilled our packs and duffel bags and loaded onto a convoy of six-bys for the truck ride south. I felt oddly naked as I looked back at our empty area of operations and unmanned lines, but of course, my reaction was irrational since there was now nothing to protect.

The route to Da Nang was along narrow, unpaved roads heavily traveled by Vietnamese civilians, who grudgingly gave way to the advancing trucks. Ancient black sedans, filled to capacity and going north, passed us occasionally, as did all manner of open trucks and buses loaded down with chickens, pigs, and wicker baskets. There were also men and women on bicycles and the ubiquitous travelers who bobbed along, balancing baskets on each end of poles slung across their shoulders. Rice paddies and open fields filled the landscape between the little hamlets. Passing through these, we were forced to slow down, and I watched farmers and young children work the water buffaloes that, though docile with the peasants, would not allow marines near them. The rest of the platoon sat sandwiched together on the benches that lined the rear of the truck, and at each stopping point they were besieged by youngsters with their hands outstretched, begging for food and cigarettes.

We also passed through the outskirts of Hue, the ancient and hauntingly beautiful town that had been the focus of the Tet offensive only months earlier, and the havoc there was a graphic reminder of the obscenity of war. Everywhere we looked, the rubble of bombed-out crumbling buildings contrasted starkly with the still-beautiful tree-lined boulevards and picturesque gardens. It was not difficult to imagine the bloody carnage that had taken place so recently, but it was still possible to be moved by the timeless tranquility the ancient citadel somehow inspired.

By contrast, Da Nang, at least the area to which we were trucked, was an armed camp of hastily constructed plywood and canvas buildings laid out to meet the needs of a rapidly expanding military presence with no regard for aesthetics. We were deposited in a transient area of tin-roofed shacks with an outdoor shower facility and an adjacent mess hall, and as the platoon disembarked and the men began stretching their cramped legs, I could see them eye the showers approvingly through the dust and grime left on their faces by the day's ride. Captain Woods scheduled a morning formation and then gave the men liberty for the rest of the day and evening. It was evident from the murmur that went up that most of the troops had not had liberty in a rear area in months.

Leslie gave the platoon his standard warning about staying out of trouble, and then he, Lieutenant Zier, and I stashed our gear in the officers' shack and began the all-important search for food and drink. We first showered with the troops and then gorged ourselves on cheeseburgers with real lettuce and tomato. Leslie and I stopped eating after two burgers each and watched in amazement as the huge Zier consumed two more. It was comforting to know that this carnivore would be with us for the balance of the evening if anyone should challenge our right to be drunk and in Da Nang.

The NCO club where we eventually settled in was small and dingy, but it had an ample supply of cold beer and enough old salts that the odds favored the same sea stories with variations being oft repeated over drinks. The walls were covered with nude pinup girls, and my loins quickly reminded me of how long my sex life had been on hold. As in the case of most military clubs, the regulars were typically rear-echelon types who were nearing the end of their careers and whom in this instance the fickle finger had dealt one last tour in Vietnam. Some of them had cut their teeth in Korea, and when they realized that I was Chesty Puller's son, the bullshit factor took a dramatic upturn. I was embarrassed at first that Leslie, Zier, and I were given free beer in honor of my father, but as we got into our cups, I rationalized that given the type of work we were doing and the infrequency of our visits to any club, we deserved free beer.

Toward midnight I autographed cocktail napkins for every marine in the bar who was plastered enough to think my signature was of any value, and Leslie, Zier, and I, oblivious of all rank differences, staggered off arm in arm to our quarters. We were met at the entrance by a huge black enlisted marine who, though very drunk and disoriented, still managed to convey the impression that he was not going to allow us into our own quarters. His hulk filled the entire doorframe. While Sergeant Leslie and I argued over whether we should shoot him or have him court-martialed, Lieutenant Zier, in a voice suddenly gone hard, told the intruder that he owed it to himself to disappear. Zier's clenched fists and bulging biceps were persuasive, and as the man stepped down from his perch and vanished, I suddenly sobered up. It was also obvious that Zier had not spent a good portion of his life lifting weights just to look good at the beach.

At daybreak a badly hung-over third platoon fell out to complete the last leg of our trip. We boarded the trucks and headed down the main service road to Camp 413. There we were chopped to the Third Battalion, Twenty-seventh Marine Regiment, to succeed it in the Da Nang TAOR. Camp 413 was a triangular enclosure bounded by man-made berms and containing the standard assortment of plywood buildings and tin Quonset huts.

Our mission was to conduct offensive operations within the Da Nang TAOR, to "locate and destroy enemy bases and logistic installations and to deploy our forces to provide defense of the Da Nang Vital Area and military complex with emphasis on routes of approach to probable rocket/mortar launch positions." To put it simply, my platoon was to conduct patrols and set ambushes so that the enemy would have a more difficult time using Da Nang for target practice. The enemy, on the other hand, had as its primary mission setting booby traps and ambushes for my patrols, so that they could more easily lob ordnance into Da Nang and its incredibly busy airfield.

When we arrived at Camp 413, the lieutenants were assigned a hardback where we could store our gear and rest when in from patrol, and each of the platoons was also assigned a hardback. Third Battalion, Twenty-seventh Marines stayed in place for the first four days after our arrival to teach us its method of operation. It was crowded in the rear, but during those four days my platoon participated in joint night patrols with a platoon from the Twenty-seventh Marines, getting a feel for the lay of the land before striking out on our own.

The patrolling here was considerably different from that at Dong Ha, as our unit found out the first time we went on a joint night patrol with the platoon from the Twenty-seventh. My counterpart was a staff sergeant rather than a lieutenant, a bad sign right off since it indicated officer attrition, and we all sensed that the Da Nang TAOR was a bad-news sector.

Even more ominous, the point man, the platoon leader, and many of the other men carried probe sticks, long, slender poles, with which they tentatively poked the ground ahead of them. This indicated not only the threat of numerous booby traps and land mines but also the fact that we were operating in an area that belonged to the enemy most of the time. Although our first patrol went smoothly, when we returned to our base camp in the morning, the other platoon's point man took Sergeant Leslie and me aside and told us that if we learned nothing else from our time out with him, we would be well served always to remember the probe sticks. He had been assigned to his platoon for nine months, most of it in the Da Nang area, and in that time he had seen all but a handful of his comrades killed or wounded by small arms and booby traps. Farther north, at Dong Ha, the possibility of encountering a large-scale NVA force that could decimate an entire platoon in one action had created enormous psychological pressure, but it was beginning to appear that farther south around Da Nang the same pressure was going to be maintained by an unseen enemy that would try to pick us off one or two men at a time with booby traps, snipers, and small-scale hit-and-run ambushes. Both approaches were equally lethal, but the frustration in the Da Nang area would be greater because of the near impossibility of retaliation.

After the Twenty-seventh Marines had departed, Golf Company quickly settled into a routine. The company had a central command post group that floated, sometimes in the field but more often in the Camp 413 compound, and the three platoons of the company rotated around it. Every two days my platoon was supposed to be shifted to one of the positions of the other platoons; that involved hiking back to Camp 413 from the field, getting resupplied, and hiking back out to where the next platoon was located.

The most desirable rotation site was a small compound where the main service road from Camp 413 met the Tu Cau River. A solid wooden bridge carried heavy civilian and military commerce across the river, and the platoon that occupied the compound was responsible for ensuring that the bridge remained intact. A large wooden tower that afforded a panoramic view of the surrounding countryside, as well as a means of monitoring enemy movement within our TAOR, had been built within the compound. The bridge had sandbagged emplacements at either end manned by a squad of marines, and floodlights, to spot enemy demolition teams, had been installed along its sides and understructure. The troops considered bridge duty an easy assignment because there were no long-range patrols and they could bathe in the river.

The men pitched lean-tos around the barbed-wire perimeter, and aside from having to be alert to the possibility of attack, they had ample time to spend sandbagging their positions. Sergeant Leslie and I did not view bridge duty in quite the same way that the troops saw it, although we were grateful to be able to remain stationary for a couple of days at a time. We knew that the bridge was considered a choice target by the Vietcong, and while duty was pleasant enough as long as the enemy chose to suffer our presence, the VC knew exactly where we were and could pick its own time to mass for an attack. Furthermore, the troops tended to get lax as their comfort level rose, and it was difficult to keep them at a fighting edge when they were not getting daily reminders that there was a war going on.

Of the other two locations within our TAOR, one was viewed with dread by all but the insane among us. Both areas involved constant patrolling among a populace that seemed overwhelmingly sympathetic to the Communists, but the area known as the Riviera was the worst and gave the third platoon its rudest introduction to the Da Nang area. The Riviera was a narrow strip of sand and hedgerows along the coast of the South China Sea just east of Camp 413.

Access to the area was obtained through either a couple of enemy-held villages or a huge rice paddy in which the water was often waist-high after rains. The paddy was lower than the surrounding area and gave enemy snipers vantage points from which to shoot at G Company platoons as they entered or exited the Riviera. There was also the very real possibility that a seriously wounded marine would drown where he fell if his comrades were pinned down by a heavy volume of fire, and in any event, casualties had to be carried through the paddy before a helicopter could be called in for a medevac. Access through the villes was not much better since an intricate network of thick tree lines and dense foliage punctuated by small clearings gave the enemy excellent ambush sites. We were always vulnerable getting in or out of the Riviera because the Vietcong knew exactly where we were. We either telegraphed our routes as we made our way through the rice paddy or alerted hostile villagers as we passed their thatched huts and garden plots.

I had learned secondhand of the dangers of the Riviera from our predecessors. No doubt our host patrol unit had not wanted to press its luck at the end of its tour by giving us a firsthand introduction. We were therefore on our own the first time we left the battalion compound and crossed the big paddy just before sunup. The men were skittish, and I could read the apprehension on their faces as they waded through the rain-clogged rice paddy, their rifles held aloft. I followed in the sudsy wake of the man walking point. When we had cleared the paddy, I breathed more easily and had the men check themselves for leeches. Doc Ellis used the tip of his cigarette to unfasten several of the repulsive creatures from various legs and arms.

After we had regained the high ground, the arid expanse of the landscape before us did not seem nearly so formidable as it had only an hour earlier in the predawn shadows. On the far side of the paddy some of the men joked about the nervous Nellies in the platoon from the Twenty-seventh Marines, but most reserved judgment. Captain Woods had purposely given us a lot of ground to cover on our first venture into the area so that we could quickly familiarize ourselves with a wide territory; but he had included only a few checkpoints, and I had a freer hand than usual in picking the routes to our objectives.

I had decided to follow the high ground toward the northern perimeter of our area of operations, cross over the sandy open area toward the South China Sea, and come back down the shoreline, using a wooded area along the beach for maximum protection. The first leg of the mission went smoothly, and we made our way up the sandy high ground without encountering any resistance. We could see small villes below us to our west with farmers working their crops, but the villagers, except for an occasional small child who stared curiously, seemed to ignore us. As the sun grew higher, the clear blue surface of the South China Sea shimmered brilliantly to our east, and my men and I perspired freely as we worked to negotiate the sandy hills.

At our first checkpoint, around midday, I called in our position to battalion, and the men spread out in a wide circle to get some relief from the sun and eat C rations. With the panoramic view afforded by our high position, I thought it unlikely that we could be ambushed, and I had Leslie pass the word that we would stay until the heat of the day subsided. The squads assigned sentries to monitor possible avenues of approach, and many of the men who were not on watch rigged sunscreens with their poncho liners and quickly fell asleep. Sergeant Leslie and I studied maps and the terrain for any clues to what we might encounter on the next leg of the patrol.

After a couple of hours I gave the word to saddle up, and the squad that had been walking point changed places with another squad as we prepared to come down from the high ground and move east toward the coast. The second leg was shorter than the first, but off the high ground we were much more vulnerable. In descent we moved more quickly, trying to stay in the open as short a time as possible.

Within an hour we had reached a tiny fishing village of about two dozen huts. I called in our second checkpoint while the platoon reconnoitered the ville for any signs of enemy activity and posted sentries. There was one rickety old boat in which I would not have felt safe in a swimming pool, much less the open waters of the South China Sea, but displayed at the entrance, it was obviously the pride of the ville. Several old men were busy with machetes, chopping up firewood to be bundled for the market, and they continued at their chores seemingly oblivious of my men's searching.

After the troops had found nothing suspicious, both groups seemed to become more relaxed, and as usual the children made the first friendly overtures. My men gave the villagers candy and cigarettes, and the corpsmen treated minor ailments for some of the townspeople who were not too timid to come forward. We had arrived as the village was preparing its evening meal, and when some of the men passed out cans of C rations, several families invited us to share their meals. It was the first time I had seen birds' heads and rice served together, but I hid my revulsion and was grateful that we were being accorded such a friendly reception. We had completed the better part of a day in a supposedly hostile area, had encountered no enemy resistance, and the first civilians with whom we had come in contact had shown every sign of being cooperative. As dark began to settle, I thanked our guests as best I could and got the men on their feet and in patrol formation to move out of the village and into a nighttime defensive perimeter. As we filed out of the village, I had rotated the order of march, with the third squad of the day now assuming the lead, and since we were going to be traveling only a few hundred meters, Leslie and I were trying a new man, Lance Corporal George Barton, on point. We had used Barton on point only a few times before and knew that he had quick reflexes and good instincts, but because he lacked experience and was nervous, I had shortened the interval between his place in the patrol and mine, and I concentrated on his movements and the area ahead of us. Sergeant Leslie was traveling with the rearmost squad. When we had cleared the village by about a hundred meters, the rear of the patrol suddenly came under small-arms fire from the village we had just left. Leslie and the lag squad quickly returned fire in the direction of the muzzle flashes, which were clearly visible in the descending dark, and whoever had been firing at us broke contact.

We incurred no casualties; but the bullets were hitting just behind the men in the rear, and they quickened their pace to get out of range. The men in the front had stopped advancing to try to determine what was happening, and another fifteen minutes had passed by the time we got unbunched. I disappointed some angry marines by not allowing them to return to the village for retaliation, but I knew that I should not break mission discipline. It was hard to believe that the same villagers who had just shared their meal with us would now allow us to be used

101

for target practice, but under the circumstances there was no way we could return and still keep our patrol schedule.

I had learned a valuable lesson about concentrating on the rear as well as the front, but the problem of harassing fire as we exited supposedly friendly villes continued to vex us whenever we patrolled the Riviera. It also reinforced the attitude among the troops that all Vietnamese were enemies, even though we realized that there was probably no way unarmed civilians could prevent the Vietcong from sweeping in behind us and taking potshots.

When we got under way again, it was dark, and the terrain abruptly changed from the sandy open area we had been negotiating all day to a series of checkerboard rice paddies with one- or two-foot-high berms enclosing each square. As we advanced along our route, I was absorbed in thinking about our brief skirmish. We had gotten our first introduction to the methods of the local Vietcong cadre. As I mechanically slogged along in Barton's footsteps, I wondered when we would be hit again.

About ten meters from the intersection of a paddy dike our path was paralleling with another that ran perpendicular to it, I saw Barton's back stiffen, and the air was suddenly filled with the sound of automatic-weapons fire. Barton had heard the click of an AK-47 safety being turned off only meters away, and as he and the enemy soldier facing him opened fire at each other simultaneously and at point-blank range, I realized that we had walked head-on into a Vietcong ambush.

As I dropped to my knees, a string of bright red tracer rounds, like a length of neon tubing, passed waist-high down the berm beside me. It was obvious that if I had been on the berm instead of in the paddy beside it, I would have been eviscerated. Within seconds the rest of the ambush team somewhere off to our left directed its fire across the path of the tracer rounds and into our flank, but Barton and I were shielded from the lethal barrage by the paddy dike we had dropped behind. The fire from our left subsided, but a ball of flame suddenly burst in the paddy between me and the marine behind me, and I thought momentarily that we were under attack from the right flank as well. When I realized that the explosion had been a grenade lobbed into our position by the enemy soldiers to our left who could not hit us with direct fire, I pulled a grenade from my belt, yanked out the pin, and heaved it from my knees with a hook-shot motion in the direction of the enemy. After what seemed like an interminable amount of time, during which I thought I had thrown a dud, the grenade finally detonated and was followed by silence.

For the first time I heard moaning from the marine behind me and realized that he had been hit. My cries of "Corpsman up, corpsman up!" were answered almost immediately by Doc Ellis, who ran in a crouching position, medical kit in hand, to administer first aid to the wounded marine. The man had been hit in the head by grenade shrapnel, and as Ellis bandaged his head, he told me that the fragments had struck a glancing blow and that the wounds appeared superficial.

Probably not five minutes had elapsed between the time of the first shots' being fired and the enemy's breaking contact in response to my grenade toss, but it had seemed like an eternity. Sergeant Leslie had by now worked his way up to my position, and as I regained my wits, I had him pull all three squads into a tight perimeter facing outward and using the natural protection of the paddy dikes as insulation from whoever might still be lurking in the dark. After the wounded man and Doc Ellis assured me that a medevac was unnecessary, I called in a situation report to Captain Woods, who gave us permission to sit tight until first light. The squads placed claymore mines in front of their positions, and we passed a sleepless and soggy night; but the Vietcong had apparently had enough and did not attack our perimeter.

We had been in the Riviera one day, the platoon had been hit fore and aft, and I was not at all certain that I was going to be able to take this kind of action on a regular basis. At some point during the night I became aware of how close I had come to being killed, and I made my way over to a badly shaken Barton, who was also wide-awake, and thanked him for having saved my life.

In the morning we found the shell casings from the tracer rounds and some beaten-down foliage but no other signs of an enemy presence. It seemed remarkable to me that Barton and the enemy soldier had opened up on each other with automatic-weapons fire at almost point-blank range yet neither had been hit. The Vietcong ambush team had prepared its lethal trap with the idea that we would be walking along the top of the paddy dike, and the first burst of fire had been presighted along that path. As a result, Barton and the unseen soldier probably missed firing into each other's chests by about a foot, and the paddy dike on which we were to have died had been instead a life-saving buffer. I had hoped that Barton's quick reaction or my grenade would have inflicted some damage on the enemy; but we found no blood trails, and we were extremely fortunate to have gotten through the encounter with only one minor casualty, considering that the VC had initiated the contact and caught us off guard.

Four or five of the men volunteered to walk our casualty back to the battalion aid station, and I let them do so. We still had another half day's work to do, and it would have been foolish to take any chances with a head wound. I wondered why the men, aside from being concerned about their comrade, would volunteer to break loose from the safety of the platoon, but I smiled to myself as I realized that they would be getting out of the bush three or four hours ahead of the rest of the platoon by taking a direct route back. I was beginning to realize that while my marines were capable of incredible acts of bravery, they would incur almost any risk to gain a few hours of slack time in the rear. That was why the battalion policy of in-country R&R for enemy kills worked so well, and that was why they had to be rewarded when they performed well and admonished when they failed to do what was expected of them. I was worried that five men were now going to risk being overrun by a larger unit, but since they were doing the unexpected in splitting off from the platoon, any encounter would probably be by chance rather than by design. I sent a radioman with them so that they could report back when they reached the battalion area and so that we could come to their assistance if they got into trouble.

As we proceeded south along the coast, just before turning inland for the trek back to Camp 413, we passed a leper colony that we had heard described as a haven of Vietcong sympathizers. We had been instructed not to enter it under any circumstances; that was fine with the platoon since most of us held the usual misconceptions about the contagion of the disease. The colony housed several hundred men and women who went about their business in total disregard of my men when we stopped at the edge of their camp to fill our canteens. I was morbidly curious about the inmates but from the periphery most of them appeared perfectly normal. Nevertheless, it was rumored that since marines were banned from entering the colony, the Vietcong used it as a staging area and supply point, and we had been told that we could expect trouble.

Fortunately there were no more surprises for the third platoon that afternoon, and I breathed more easily when our volunteer party radioed to report that it had made it safely back to camp and that our casualty was not seriously wounded. Thus we completed our first Riviera patrol, returning via the village of Viem Dong, instead of recrossing the big rice paddy. I waited at the compound entrance to make certain that all the patrol made it safely inside and that its weapons were unloaded, and then Sergeant Leslie and I went in search of a cold beer. We both expressed the wish that the next two days at the Tu Cau bridge would be less exciting than the last two had been.

IV

THE TU CAU BRIDGE was a good hour's march from Camp 413, but the company gunny had managed to scrounge trucks from the motor pool to transport us to the river the following morning. The platoon was feeling good as we disembarked, both because we were going to be in one place for the rest of the day and because we had one-upped the green machine by arriving at our new destination by truck rather than on foot. I had my squads assume the positions of the men we were relieving, and after their commander gave us a brief orientation, his platoon boarded the six-bys we had arrived in and headed back to Camp 413. I had been told that we could cut some slack at the bridge and rest up for the final rotation in the area northwest of Camp 413, which, though dangerous, did not have the reputation of the Riviera.

After I had walked the perimeter of the compound and checked the guard posts at either end of the bridge, Sergeant Leslie and I stored our gear in the command bunker, which we shared with a young engineer corporal who seemed to be permanently assigned to the Tu Cau bridge. His only responsibility seemed to be to turn the floodlights on at night and off in the morning and keep the generators operational, and since he knew he had found an easy job, he at least tried to do it well so that he would not be sent off to an infantry unit. We all envied him his soft duty, but I was grateful to have someone with us who already knew the eccentricities of the bridge. I therefore let him remain in the bunker, but I moved him off to one corner so that Leslie and I could flop in the best location and so that he would realize that his time at the bridge did not accord him any favored status. Sergeant Leslie chided me good-naturedly for throwing my weight around at the expense of an enlisted man, but he too realized that after what we had just gone through, our engineer's comfort was not a priority.

Because the bridge was on a major artery, we had more contact with civilians than we had had at any time since my arrival. Within hours of our settling in, local vendors were swarming among us, and the troops, much to my disapproval, were willing buyers. I tried to limit commerce to the open area along the road outside the compound, and I was adamant in not allowing anyone to loiter once he or she was on the bridge, but the merchants were ingenious and persistent. Invariably the food salesmen would begin their pitch by offering me free samples, and they had a staggering array of American black-market products, including all kinds of canned goods, sodas, and snack foods, for which they demanded exorbitant prices. I rejected all offers of goods as bribes, and tried to be as uncooperative as possible, but Sergeant Leslie patiently explained to me that the Vietnamese way of doing business was meant to honor me and not to demonstrate that I could be bought. I finally weakened and accepted a free haircut from an itinerant barber, whom I also allowed into the compound to perform a much-needed service on my shaggy charges, some of whom had not had haircuts in weeks. He beamed broadly as he shaved our heads and pocketed our military scrip, but when he offered to return that evening with a full complement of party girls, he quickly found himself outside the compound.

There was a Korean whose gimmick was English Bibles at sixty dollars a crack, which he would then mail to loved ones in the States. He had a letter signed by a general that authorized him to move more freely among the troops. I figured that his chances of success were minimal since sixty dollars was the equivalent of several weeks' pay for most of the troops, but in the hour before Leslie and I decided to disregard the letter and consign him to the fate of the barber, he actually completed five sales. Leslie and I agreed that Christianity had been good for our Korean friend, and we wondered what sort of arrangement he had made farther up the line to have gotten the cooperation of the brass.

Our two days at the bridge were a welcome respite, and I used some of my free time to catch up on correspondence. I had been writing to Toddy every chance I got since getting into Vietnam, often between patrols and in pencil so that the wetness would not smear my penmanship, but I now had some time to write my father and a couple of old fraternity brothers, whom I shamelessly begged to send scotch in well-sealed plastic bottles.

I had probably not written my father half a dozen letters in my previous four years of college, but now that I had embarked on a rite of passage that was not only fraught with peril but also similar to the one he had undertaken as a fledgling lieutenant fifty years earlier in the jungles of Haiti and Nicaragua, I felt an urgent need to share some of my experiences with him. Oddly enough, after having been under fire and forced to react in several life-or-death situations, I now felt much closer to my father, though geographically I had never been farther from him. It was almost as if a door had been opened to a world that I had often heard discussed but had never experienced, and the experience of combat now freed me to pour my soul out to the one man I most wanted to emulate.

While at the bridge I received my first mail from Toddy, a packet of nine letters that, though sent under separate cover over the last month, all managed to arrive at the same time. She also sent the rain suit I had requested in an earlier letter and a jar of pistachio nuts. The rain suit did not keep out the rain, but it was useful in keeping the water that was already next to my skin warm. Sergeant Leslie and I shared the pistachios as well as the news of my wife's burgeoning pregnancy, and we both had a good laugh over one of her complaints that television viewing had been mediocre since my departure. Leslie volunteered that he would be satisfied just watching commercials, which I reported to Toddy.

The rain suit came in particularly handy the second day of our Tu Cau assignment when a typhoon almost destroyed the bridge. The first day had been clear and hot, and I allowed the platoon to go down to the river in shifts for needed baths and to launder their clothes. Much to the amusement of the local populace, many of the men used the occasion to try to bronze their birthday suits. It began raining that night, however, and by morning heavy winds and a torrential downpour had all but obliterated our view of the river. The rain also made lookout duty on the bridge meaningless since it was not possible to see the approach of any potential saboteurs, and we finally resorted to tossing grenades into the water every half hour to discourage anyone who might have wished to take advantage of the situation. The bridge had naturally been built at a narrow point, and at the height of the storm the water was rising nearly a foot an hour. For a while we thought we were going to lose the bridge to nature rather than the enemy; but when the river crested later that afternoon, to within a couple of feet of the road, the structure held, and by evening our fears and the angry waters were subsiding.

We left the Tu Cau bridge the next morning convinced that its defense was far preferable to the Riviera. We returned to Camp 413 just long enough to resupply before returning to the field in the area northwest of the compound. We were once again in a geographically unfamiliar area, and with conflicting reports on enemy activity, we again felt our way cautiously. The topography of the area was similar to the Riviera's, with large, open areas of sandy, brush-covered hills broken up by hedgerows, tree lines, and occasional hamlets surrounded by rice paddies and other cultivated plots. The rain from the storm had slackened but still beat uncomfortably against our faces when the wind gusted. Visibility was poor, causing the men to bunch together to maintain contact.

For the first part of the afternoon we patrolled without any signs of the enemy, but as we were moving into our nighttime position at dark, the by now familiar crack of AK-47s and their accompanying muzzle flashes provided a rude welcome. We were under fire by several snipers from a tree line in the distance, and their rounds were widely scattered and off target in the rain and approaching dark; but I hurried the platoon into our perimeter as several dozen nearly spent rounds pockmarked the sand behind us. Our position for the night was a V-shaped draw, which provided good protection against assaults from the flanks once the platoon had dug in along the high sides of the two hills that formed the V. During the night I sent out short patrols, primarily to discourage the Vietcong from probing our position. Sergeant Leslie and I commiserated in the dark that it was beginning to look as if we were going to take hostile fire every time we left the battalion compound to patrol.

The following dawn, as we prepared to break camp, one of the men discovered a booby trap at the vertex of the draw, where the two hills came together. The device consisted of a C ration can holding a grenade with its pin removed so that the grenade's spoon was held in place by the side of the can. The can was rigged about knee high and located just to the side of the trail with a trip wire crossing the trail to an anchor on the other side. It was the first booby trap I had seen since coming in country, and though rigged crudely, it was fully as lethal as a more sophisticated device. If we had proceeded through the draw in the previous day's twilight rather than stopped to make camp, my point man and perhaps several others would probably have been maimed or killed. I reminded myself that the platoon had to become more disciplined at using probe sticks and staying off trails. I had our demolition man rig a time charge to blow the booby trap in place as we exited the draw.

As the last squad cleared our bivouac area and the platoon spread out across the terrain in patrol formation, the booby trap detonated harmlessly. Almost simultaneously we began taking fire again from a tree line adjacent to the area we had just left. Once more most of the rounds were short, but the volume was heavier than it had been the night before and included automatic-weapons fire. Obviously whoever had been shooting at us yesterday had gone for reinforcements during the night and had lain in wait for us, having figured out our probable route of march for the next day.

I picked up the pace as the rounds nipped at our heels, and the lag squad returned fire; but the enemy firing did not stop until one of the men in the squad fired a rocket into the tree line, which burst in an orange ball of flame and ended the contact from that quarter. By now those of us at the front of the patrol were almost running to get out of range of the marksmen in the tree line. As we approached another hedgerow that paralleled the main road back to Camp 413, I was panting and out of breath but relieved that our adversaries had miscalculated the range. Just as we slowed the pace to allow the rest of the unit to catch up, another explosion just in front of me rent the air, and my point man and the marine behind him collapsed into the sand.

In our haste to get away, we had tripped another booby trap, and I watched helplessly and in horror for a moment as the two wounded marines writhed in agony on the ground before me. The man who had triggered the booby trap was the worse wounded, and he bled from half a dozen shrapnel wounds, including a mean-looking gash in his neck. The second man was stunned by the explosion and had several minor nicks and cuts, but for the most part he had been shielded from the grenade fragments by the body of the man in front of him.

Within minutes the corpsmen were busy stanching the flow of blood, administering morphine shots, and applying battle dressings. As they worked over the wounded men, Doc Ellis advised me that although the wounds were not mortal, the men could not be moved and that we would need a dustoff. I had the platoon clear a landing zone and called for a medevac chopper as the squads took up positions on the zone's perimeter, which we had marked with red cloth panels we had made from an old mail sack and carried for such a situation.

Since the condition of the casualties was relatively stable, the call for the medevac was priority rather than emergency, and it seemed to take forever for the choppers to arrive. We tried to joke with the wounded men about their free lift out of the bush and the clean sheets they would be sleeping on later, and they struggled to appear brave and manly. Someone produced two cigars, and our wounded charges tried to smoke them between teeth clenched far more tightly than was necessary to hold the stogies, as I studied the sky for signs of the dustoff. Finally, after a couple of hours and several calls to Captain Woods, the faint clack of rotor blades became audible, and the choppers appeared as tiny specks on the horizon. When they drew closer, the noise became a roar, and the now rising sun glistened brightly on their green underbellies. I came up on the medevac frequency and, after establishing radio contact with the pilot, talked him into the landing zone while the escort gunship circled above, with the door gunner at the ready. I popped a green smoke grenade to mark the center of the zone, and thirty seconds later three of my men and I were racing through the swirling smoke to shovel our two casualties into the door of the ever so briefly grounded bird.

As the pilot lifted off, the crew chief and I exchanged thumbs-ups, and the two choppers angled off toward Da Nang, with only the beaten-down foliage from the prop wash and a few wisps of green smoke as evidence of their mission of mercy. It was eerily quiet as the choppers disappeared into the distance, and I wished for a moment that I had been on board one of them. Sergeant Leslie prodded me to get the platoon up and moving since every enemy unit in the area must now know exactly where we were. I had called in the medevac exactly as I had learned to do at Basic School, and technically the procedure had been accomplished flawlessly. The only problem was that real men, my men, had spilled real blood, and I was impotent to do anything other than curse the Vietcong and the Marine Corps for bringing me to this godawful wasteland.

When we returned to Camp 413 later that afternoon, the men were tired and angry. I could sense their mounting frustration as I performed the usual routine check of their weapons, but I didn't have a clue to how I could resolve the situation. We had been prepared for the Riviera, but not for the loss of two men in an area considered somewhat pacified.

To make matters worse, the word came down after our return that a marine from another platoon in the company had just been killed while crossing the big rice paddy into the Riviera. A big, likable blond in his late teens, whom I had chided on occasion about the easy life of an artilleryman, he had been the platoon's forward observer. Now he was dead before having reached twenty. He had taken a sniper round through the head while waiting for the lead element of his platoon to clear the paddy, and the scuttlebutt was that his lieutenant had gotten rattled and been unable to identify the enemy position for the artillery. At any rate, the marine had either died of his wounds or drowned in the same rice paddy through which we were going to have to make our way the next day, and some of the men saw it as an omen. Sergeant Leslie and I decided that as a precaution we would cross into the area under the cover of darkness, as we had on our last foray, but no one was looking forward to it.

Before dawn the next morning we were once more wading through the waist-deep muddy waters of the paddy, our rifles held high and our senses receptive to the slightest movement on the far bank. I had worked out a route of march with Captain Woods that more or less reversed the course we had taken on our first Riviera patrol, but for now I concentrated on getting across the paddy, praying that my platoon would not be fired at by snipers.

After we had cleared the paddy without incident and checked ourselves for the ever-present leeches, I began to feel pretty good about having crossed over twice without taking sniper fire. For a moment I thought that the predawn crossings were going to be the key, but Sergeant Leslie quickly deflated me by suggesting that it was just a question of time until the enemy countered our pattern with an equally deadly ploy. I knew he was right and, in an attempt to cover my baseless optimism, informed him we would be returning to Camp 413 the next day through one of the villes to the south of the paddy. Leslie nodded his agreement, but having just pointed out to me the folly of repeating the same march pattern, he did not need to voice the thought that we were going to be coming out of the Riviera the same way we had previously.

In the Riviera our route called for skirting Viem Dong, the little village at the south end of our TAOR, traveling directly east toward the

South China Sea, and then coming up the coast so that the leper colony would be to our west. A klick past the leper colony we would turn inland and cross the open area to the high ground that we had come down in the opposite direction on our earlier patrol. We would then make camp for the night and the next day proceed along the eastern spine of the hills back to Viem Dong for the crossing to Camp 413. It looked like a good route to me, and as Sergeant Leslie and I studied our maps while the day's first light dissipated the shadows before us, we each felt more confident now that we were somewhat familiar with the territory.

As we proceeded toward the coast, the reassuring sights and sounds of a rural area rousing itself from sleep belied the treachery of our journey, and I watched several farmers in the distance making their way into open fields while a solitary rooster crowed his regards to the rising sun. By the time we completed the first leg the temperature had risen a good twenty or thirty degrees, and although it was only midmorning, the men were already drinking freely from their canteens. There was a slight coastal breeze that kept the flies from lighting on our sweat-soaked bodies but did little to relieve the heat, and most of the men had removed their utility shirts and bundled them into their packs.

I had decided to use the wooded area adjacent to the beach for the next leg of our patrol for both shade and cover, although the going was more tedious. We stopped at noon to refill our canteens and sit out the midday heat, and many of the men used the break to catch up on the sleep we had lost by starting so early. Later in the afternoon, as we emerged from the woods, my point man spotted two pajama-clad men with rifles busy working at something atop a distant hill.

They had to be Vietcong cadre, no doubt arming a booby trap several hundred meters from us. Since we could not get any closer to them without alerting them, I summoned the platoon's best marksman, who could hardly contain himself at the prospect of a potential kill. Considering the wind and the distance, it was unlikely that he would hit one of the men, much less score a kill, but we encouraged him to concentrate on getting off just one shot. We all held our breath as he lined up his sights on the black pajama top of the man who afforded the fullest view. His shot was off the mark, and the two figures disappeared over the crest of the hill as the errant volley echoed back at us, but the rest of the platoon was elated that we had at least taken the offensive for a change. My marksman was chagrined that he had blown his opportunity, and while we all teased him with the usual clichés about not being able to hit the broad side of barns or bull's asses with bass fiddles, we knew that his chances had been slim. Unfortunately we had also given away our position to anyone within earshot, and we now had to cross an expanse of open area to get to the hills farther inland.

The leper colony had been quiet when we passed it in the woods, and it was possible that no one inside had seen us; but I now realized, as we turned our backs to the coast and to the colony, that word of our presence would spread quickly. I therefore hurried the platoon through the sand and shrubbery that stretched before us, hoping that we could reach the high ground before our adversaries had time to react. When we arrived an hour later, soaked with perspiration but intact, the platoon formed a perimeter around the crest of the highest vantage point, shed its gear, and began preparing the evening meal. There were only a couple of hours of daylight left and as soon as it began to darken, we were going to take up positions on the next hill over for the night. I called in a situation report on the battalion frequency while Sergeant Leslie opened beans and franks and heated them for the two of us.

We both felt pretty good as we spooned the bubbly mess from its green containers, but rather than be relaxed, I was vaguely uneasy that we had been in the Riviera for most of a day without having been sniped at or stumbling onto a booby trap. After we finished our meal, I buried the cans and cardboard containers in which the rations had been packaged, and Leslie checked the squads to make certain that the men had done likewise. We knew that the Vietcong could make booby traps out of our refuse, and there was no point in making their job easier for them. When Leslie returned, we smoked together and waited for the sun to move farther down on the horizon before breaking camp. Finally the blistering heat of the day had begun to subside, and when I breathed in the evening air and surveyed the landscape, the area seemed almost tranquil.

As I ground out my last cigarette of the day and gave the order to saddle up, the men began getting to their feet and donning their packs and flak jackets. Almost simultaneously the sickening whoosh of mortar rounds interrupted my mechanical direction, and suddenly our hilltop was the center of a fire storm. The first four or five rounds were long and impacted harmlessly on the reverse slope of the hill behind us, but as we dropped to our hands and knees, I sensed that the enemy mortarmen would quickly adjust their fire to compensate for their miscalculation. The firing seemed to be coming from a tree line near the leper colony and directly across the valley from us, and as I pondered our predicament, machine-gun fire began to sweep the down-slope in front of our position.

We were pinned down on the flat area atop a hill, but the angle was such that the automatic-weapons fire could not reach the men unless they rose from the prone position that by now most of the platoon had assumed. One young marine, who had joined the platoon just prior to our operation in the DMZ, suddenly stood up and began firing his rifle John Wayne fashion from the hip. Before I could pull him down beside me, a well-aimed round from the tree line leveled him and made further effort on my part unnecessary. Within seconds Doc Ellis was beside the wounded marine, medical kit in hand, and he quickly affixed a battle dressing to what turned out to be a minor head wound.

As I refocused my attention on the activity in the tree line, I realized that while the enemy machine gun was ineffective in reaching us, it would keep us from counterattacking. I also knew that the mortar fire was going to decimate us if we stayed put and allowed enemy soldiers time to adjust it. As if in response to my thought the next barrage began, and I could feel the whistling rounds working their way up the hill behind us. By now many of the marines on the forward edge of our line were returning fire from their prone positions, and because we were above the enemy soldiers, we could fire directly into the trees. Not long after the second barrage had begun, however, the tree line from which it was being directed suddenly exploded into balls of fire, and I belatedly realized that my own mortar team was laying down its own barrage of suppressing fire. Looking over my shoulder, I saw one of the team members on his knees holding the mortar tube against its baseplate while his two comrades were furiously shoveling rounds into its open end. Within seconds of our return fire, the enemy unit broke contact, and as we lay there in the stillness, I could hardly believe how desperate the situation had been just moments earlier. My mortar section's quick action had probably saved us from wholesale casualties, and I was horrified to realize that in the course of the firefight it had never occurred to *me* to order them to commence fire.

After it was over and we had regrouped, the squad leaders reported their situations. We had suffered only the one casualty, and Doc Ellis told me that the wounded marine would be able to complete the patrol with us and get further medical attention the next day, so we were spared the necessity of a nighttime medevac. By now the stars were sparkling overhead, but there was very little sparkle left in the third platoon as we abandoned our hilltop and gingerly advanced toward our nighttime position.

We dug in extra deep that night, and as Sergeant Leslie and I huddled in our fighting hole, we rehashed the experience we had just survived. Whoever had attacked us was well equipped and capable of laying down a volume of fire equal to our own. Because they had a machine gun and a mortar tube, they were probably North Vietnamese rather than Vietcong, and they definitely knew what they were doing. I shuddered to think what would have happened if their initial barrage had not overshot, if my own mortar section had not responded so well, or if the enemy had simply waited five more minutes and caught us spread out between the two hills. The permutations for disaster were endless, and Leslie advised me not to think about it; but I could not get over how I had completely forgotten my own mortar. I had not felt fear, and indeed, at the height of the activity I had a strange sensation of being outside my own body, detachedly observing the activity around me, but I knew that my butt had been saved by some fast-thinking kids for whom my respect had just taken a quantum leap.

The next day, as we headed back toward Camp 413, we passed Lieutenant Zier and his patrol, who had taken sniper fire as they crossed the big rice paddy on their way out to replace us. We gave our respective platoons a ten-minute break as we paused to exchange intelligence and smoke cigarettes together. At one point in our conversation we simply looked at each other and said, as if on cue, "This shit has got to stop."

The words uttered simultaneously by two exhausted and harried lieutenants seemed ludicrous for a moment, and we both burst into laughter; but the thought behind them was deadly serious. I had already had several men who were making up excuses to get out of the bush, and Lieutenant Zier told me that he was experiencing the same problem. Morale was at an all-time low, and if what we were doing was the textbook response to small-unit skirmishes, I still wasn't sure I wanted to be a part of it or, indeed, if I could even handle it.

When we got back to base camp later that afternoon, word was waiting for us that Lieutenant Zier's platoon had just stumbled into a minefield. Two men had been wounded initially, and when their comrades went to their assistance, they had detonated another mine, and three more, including Zier, had gone down. All five had been medevacked, and although preliminary reports indicated that John Zier, the bull whom I had come to regard as invincible, was in no danger of losing his life, it was uncertain if he would ever return to his unit. His twin brother, another marine lieutenant, had been wounded a few weeks earlier and sent back to the States, and I thought that John could easily have picked a better way to visit his brother. The more I thought about John Zier, the way in which he had been wounded, and the way in which we always seemed to be responding to an unseen enemy rather than initiating action on our own, the more depressed and frustrated I became. I finally wrote my wife a letter and went in search of Sergeant Leslie and a six-pack of warm beer.

Later in the day Captain Woods came over to the platoon commanders' hooch where Leslie and I were drinking beer and took a seat on Lieutenant Zier's cot. My spirits had been, if not lifted, at least dulled by the alcohol, and Leslie and I had to concentrate to make certain we were hearing the skipper correctly. At the end of the week my platoon was going to be temporarily attached to an ARVN company operating out of a compound just to the east of Marble Mountain, a klick or two farther inland.

Woods told us that we would be there for at least two weeks, and although he did not have any more information on the assignment, Sergeant Leslie and I barely managed to contain ourselves at the prospect of a change of duty. Captain Woods went on to tell us that the normal platoon rotation had been suspended until we returned from the ARVN company. My platoon would be patrolling for the next two days in the area to the northwest of the compound, and we would then serve as a blocking force along the main service road to the Tu Cau bridge for an ARVN sweep of the area adjacent to the road. We did not relish the idea of going back into the same area where I had lost two men less than a week before, but the realization that we were going to be able to avoid a return to the Riviera for at least a fortnight had us both dancing around the room as soon as Captain Woods headed back to the company hooch.

I had Leslie inform the platoon of our change of fortune, and when I went to the mess hall for chow that evening, I could tell by the broad grins on the faces of Corporal Turner, Cowboy, Barton, and some of the others that the news had not displeased them. We all realized that the next few days were not going to be fun, but the change in morale was remarkable now that we could get some respite from the Riviera patrols.

By the time we left Camp 413 the next morning, the sun was already well up, and it was obviously going to be another scorcher. We did not need the cover of darkness to reach the northwest area, so I had given the men time to get a hot breakfast. Mindful of our two casualties thereabouts, Leslie and I decided to vary our pattern, stay out of the open, where snipers and booby traps were more likely, and instead make our daytime stopovers in the hamlets, where we thought the enemy might be less likely to engage us for fear of hitting civilians.

In keeping with this experiment, I directed the marine walking point in front of me to turn west off the service road after we had gotten several hundred meters out of camp. We headed overland toward a ville that we had skirted on our earlier patrol and maintained a westward azimuth for several klicks. The vegetation was somewhat denser than in the Riviera, but we tried to stay off the trails and footpaths along our route for fear of mines and booby traps. As a result, our progress was slow, and by the time we reached the outskirts of the village we were soaking wet from fighting our way through the foliage. I had removed my utility shirt to get some relief from the heat at midmorning, but as a result my bare arms were covered with nicks and cuts from the vines and branches we had had to hack our way through. Because of our previous losses in the area, the platoon was in no mood to waste time winning hearts and minds, and when the villagers realized that we were going to be in their midst for several hours, they became inhospitable.

A cursory search failed to turn up any signs of Vietcong ordnance, but by now we had come to regard searches that yielded no results as evidence of good concealment rather than pro-American bias. As usual, there were no young males in the village, and the women and old men tried to ignore us, although their studied indifference bordered on overt hostility. When one of my men began unbuttoning his fly to relieve himself into a watering hole at the edge of the village, the shrieks of a couple of the locals almost precipitated an incident with considerable shoving on both sides until we realized that the stagnant-appearing little hole was the village water supply. I could not tell whether our hosts were more fearful of us or of Vietcong reprisals, but for the time that we were with them, none of the usual thawing out common when Doc Ellis and Coswell treated the sick and when my men passed out C rations and cigarettes took place. We all were suspicious and on edge, and the watering hole incident, which might ordinarily have ended in laughter, now only heightened the tension.

Everyone sensed that something was different about this particular ville. Sergeant Leslie and I discussed the strange vibes we were getting and decided to exit the village at midafternoon in the usual way, but then to double back under cover of darkness and set up a night ambush site at one of the hamlet entrances. I fully expected the platoon to be fired on as the last squad filed out of the ville, and in anticipation of contact I had instructed the lag squad to fire a rocket directly into the village if so much as one shot was fired in our direction.

We were allowed to depart in peace, perhaps because the villagers could sense our resolve and were reluctant to press their luck. I realized as we continued our patrol that I, at least, was becoming calloused and indifferent toward the very people we were supposedly trying to liberate, but it seemed to be the only way to assure our own survival. At any rate, I was relieved that we did not have to employ the rocket launchers, and I even managed a frozen smile in Sergeant Leslie's direction at the realization that fear and loathing from the people we were charged with protecting were more manageable emotions than indifference or scorn.

In taking our leave, we tried to make it appear that we had no intention of returning to the village, and Leslie and I made a pretense of poring over our maps, even studying them as we proceeded along our route. We traveled inland until we were well out of sight of the village, marched another five hundred meters as a precaution, and then tried to make ourselves as inconspicuous as possible while we holed up to wait for darkness. By now the platoon moved with a minimum of wasted motion and made its daytime base camp more or less automatically with little direction from Leslie or me.

The sky had darkened ominously in the hour or so it took us to move from the village to our stopping point, and by the time we were in place a heavy rain and howling wind had blocked out the searing sun. The rain was a nuisance; but at least it alleviated the heat, and I knew that it would provide additional cover as we moved back into the area of the village. We ate a soggy meal of cold C rations, and I wondered why I was even bothering with the unappetizing mess as beads of water dripped from my nose and glasses into the green can of processed meat in my left hand. Despite my discomfort, however, the mood of the platoon was upbeat, and I knew that the additional charge was due to our anticipation over assuming the role of the hunter rather than that of the quarry.

Before we moved out, the men blackened their faces, and each squad leader checked his unit to make certain that the telltale noises of metal against metal had been eliminated and that all weapons were in order. We retraced our route quickly, as soon as darkness fell, and were able to make good time since the trail was familiar and the rain and wind obviated the need to avoid making noise. In addition, we were not worried about being ambushed or booby-trapped since we had given the impression that we would be patrolling in the opposite direction.

I knew from our previous visit that a patchwork of garden plots enclosed by hedgerows lay adjacent to the village along the path by which we had exited, and I had decided to have the platoon set up in the one closest to the path so that we would have good surveillance of anyone leaving or entering the hamlet. We slipped into place inside the hedge without being seen or heard, and the men took up positions facing outward with the natural contour of the hedgerow as the perimeter of our camp. The foliage provided good camouflage, and after checking the squad positions and emplacement of claymore mines, I was satisfied that I had selected well. We could hear through the rain the muted sounds of the villagers settling in for the evening in nearby thatched huts. The acrid smell of smoldering cooking fires let us know that the evening meal had been completed.

Although the normal activity indicated that our return had been undetected, I also knew that any contact, however incidental, would blow our cover and quickly reverse the role of hunter and quarry. Throughout the next several hours the rain continued to fall, soaking both the men on watch and those trying to doze, but there was no sign of activity along the path. I had anticipated that the rain might cause the enemy to stay put, but I was also banking on the Vietcong's being curious about our afternoon visit and using the nighttime to gather intelligence in the village.

When nothing seemed to be happening, I decided around midnight to send a squad into the village for a look around. I had no trouble getting two volunteers from each squad, and I had Ski and Corporal Turner lead the patrol. Ski, with his natural agility, was a solid choice for this kind of cat-and-mouse activity, and I knew that Corporal Turner would keep things from getting out of hand if there was a confrontation with civilians.

As my ad hoc squad noiselessly filed out of our perimeter, the remaining members of the platoon, sensing that we were on the offensive again, stirred momentarily from their lethargy before settling back in to await the return. I huddled next to Watson, my radio operator, to get the first situation reports; but we both knew that the radio could be a dead giveaway, and I had instructed Corporal Turner to call in only if he got into a situation he couldn't handle. I was always most uncomfortable when the platoon was split up at nighttime, and I dreaded the prospect of having to go after a squad in trouble in the dead of night. At least the dread kept me wide-awake despite exhaustion. An hour after they had left, Turner came up on the radio net to whisper that Ski had observed some activity around one of the village hooches and was closing in, and I could tell by the spacing of his words that the game had taken a deadly turn. I was suddenly aware of the beads on my forehead—either rain or perspiration. After fifteen minutes, an eternity, Turner radioed again to report that the squad had taken a captive and was heading back to our perimeter. Within minutes an excited group of marines, flushed with success, came hurtling down the path out of the village, pushing a young man whom they had gagged and blindfolded. They paused in the path only long enough to make certain that we did not mistake them for enemies and then plunged headlong through the hedgerow, where their captive fell in a heap at my feet.

Ski was out of breath and trembling with excitement, and the young pajama-clad man he had in tow quaked through his blindfold as if he'd known the ax was descending. Ski gasped for air as he recounted the events of the last hour. The squad had posted two men at the entrance to the village when they began their probe, and two others had quickly made their way to the opposite end so that both avenues of escape were covered. The remaining four men fanned out, looking for signs of enemy activity. Ski, Turner, and their charges had spotted their captive running into one of the huts. They had pursued him inside, found him feigning sleep on a straw mat, and taken him as a prisoner on the assumption that since he was running around the village in the middle of the night and had tried to avoid them, he must have been a Vietcong.

The young man appeared to be in his early twenties, and he had not been in the village that afternoon; but other than his suspicious behavior there was no concrete evidence to link him to the Vietcong. A search of his living quarters had not turned up any enemy ordnance, and he had a valid identification card, although that could easily have been forged or purchased on the black market. But I had the gut feeling that our captive was at least a Vietcong sympathizer, if not a cadre member, especially since his village had been so hostile to us and he was apparently doing a little intelligence gathering of his own at a strange hour of the night. Sergeant Leslie agreed with my assessment, and we therefore decided to keep him bound and under watch for the remainder of the night and then have a squad escort him back to Camp 413 in the morning for interrogation by an intelligence unit.

Ski made certain that our captive was trussed tightly, perhaps more so than was necessary under the circumstances, and we removed the blindfold but left him gagged so that he could not give away our position. Because I was worried about retaliation from his comrades, we staked him out in the open so that he would probably be the first man hit if he were part of an enemy unit that decided to fire mortars or small arms. Several times during the remainder of the night Corporal Turner adjusted the young man's bonds to minimize his discomfort, although many of the men would have seized on the slightest provocation to end his mission permanently.

At daybreak I had Ski and the other men from the night squad except for Corporal Turner carry our prisoner back to battalion, with instructions to turn him over to the proper authorities and then wait for our return that night. I knew that he was probably going to be released and that my raiding party was going to be angry, and I at least wanted to give them a half day out of the bush as a reward for their initiative. Turner, of course, wanted to go too, but we both knew that the platoon could not afford to give him up at a time when the enemy was almost certain to make known its displeasure over the events of the night. My squad radioed back to us later in the morning that it had made it back safely. I never saw our prisoner again; but as I had predicted, he was released after interrogation, and if he had not been a Vietcong sympathizer before meeting us, he almost certainly became one afterward. If the incident were viewed one way, we had captured a probable member of an opposing force under suspicious circumstances and had dealt with him appropriately through the existing channels. From the opposite perspective, we had kidnapped a South Vietnamese civilian as he lay in his own bed and held him incommunicado for several hours.

Needless to say, our morning reception by the already hostile villagers was cool when we moved back into the hamlet. I had fully expected to be challenged to release a no doubt favorite son, but oddly the subject was never raised. Leslie and some of the men conjectured that the man had probably been a courier who was unknown to the village since there was no pleading wife or crying children to present his case, while another element of the platoon thought that the Vietcong grapevine had issued orders to ignore the situation and deal with it later.

At any rate, we all were uneasy, and I was especially nervous over the

121

prospect of spending the rest of the day in hostile territory with a platoon that was now less than full strength. Our strategy of staying close to the village and mingling with the local populace seemed to be working since we had not made enemy contact in the previous twenty-four hours, and I resolved, despite the strain, to stick to the same plan for the rest of the day.

There was another smaller ville of a half dozen thatched huts several hundred meters north of us, and Leslie and I thought it best to strike out in its direction, since we had pretty well worn out our welcome in our present location. Heading north, we were fired on by snipers before we had even cleared the ville, and although no one was hit, it was an unmistakable sign of worse to come.

Turner was so angry that he grabbed an old man and his young granddaughter and placed them in the column on the theory that the enemy would not risk firing at us with civilians in our midst. I made no move to stop him, and since the snipers stopped firing, I decided to keep our unwilling additions until we reached the next ville. The old man had lost an arm years before and waved his stump furiously at me, as if he thought that the missing limb would give me a change of heart, but the little girl seemed to realize that we were resolute and, taking her grandfather by his remaining hand, led us at double time into the smaller village. When we reached the outskirts, Corporal Turner removed his gold earring and gave it to the little girl, who pocketed it without a noticeable change of expression, turned abruptly on her heels, and headed back in the opposite direction. The thought crossed my mind that I was losing whatever decency I had brought with me to Vietnam, but I was too tired and too frustrated to entertain it for long. Besides, just ahead of us there was another village that had to be disrupted and bent to my will if we were going to survive another day.

Watson, Leslie, Turner, and I set up our headquarters group in a partially bombed-out temple around which the other four or five structures in the ville were arranged. My now-undermanned squads fanned out around the perimeter of the ville and after the customary search staked out positions and assigned watches. The hamlet was small and afforded good vision in all directions. By the time we set up, it was close to noon, and after Watson had radioed in our position, Leslie and I put our heads together to plan the remainder of the patrol that we had been improvising as we went along.

The village was almost empty save for some children and two pregnant women, and I assumed that everyone else was out tending the rice paddies, which were by now swollen with rain. The storm had passed, taking with it the cloud cover but leaving in its place a fiery sun and an excruciating humidity. The temple afforded some relief from the sun, and our presence there was less intrusive than it would have been if we had taken over someone's living quarters for a command center, but considering all the enmity we had aroused in the past day, the nuance probably went unappreciated. Leslie and Turner joked with the pregnant women about their big bellies, communicating with gestures what they could not with language, and the women were far more amiable than our earlier hosts. I thought ironically that they probably felt protected from a gang rape by my men because of their advanced pregnancies but shelved my flash of intuition as a symptom of growing paranoia.

The contour lines on my map indicated a large hill to the southeast of us and near the main service road that led back to camp. I had decided to stay put until dark and then make the hill our objective for a brief nighttime base camp. Leslie and I thought that we could reach it in about two hours and that it would give us a vantage point from which we could survey the road for another couple of hours before we headed into camp. In the meantime, there was nothing left to do but be alert for snipers, entertain the villagers, and try to catch some shut-eye to make up for what we had missed the night before. After a meal of beans and franks, I located a wooden pallet parallel to one of the walls of the temple and just inside the entrance and settled down for a nap. It was cooler in the shade, and just as I was dozing off, I could see Watson fidgeting with the radio on the dirt floor beside me.

Sometime later I was jolted from my sleep by the crack of rifle fire. The first round hit the wall beside me and showered my face and neck with plaster chips. I dived onto the floor, and Watson scurried for cover as several other rounds buzzed like hornets around us. Just as quickly as it had begun it was over, and whoever had gotten so close to the temple was now long gone. Watson had taken a round across the seat of his pants so close that it had made a slit in his trousers and raised a welt on the cheek of his buttocks. After he recovered from the shock of such a close call, he wanted me to put him in for a Purple Heart, but when Doc Ellis told him the near miss didn't require medical attention and Leslie pointed out that he would become the butt of numerous jokes if the word got around the company, he recanted. I had been asleep for an hour when the shots came, but resuming my nap was now out of the question. I rapidly smoked several cigarettes to calm my nerves while

Leslie went off to chew out the marines in the sector of our perimeter who had allowed the sniper to get close enough to kill their lieutenant and radio operator.

It was by now obvious that we had created a grudge situation by snatching our captive the day before, and any earlier doubts I might have had about his status were now dispelled. Unfortunately his interrogators back at battalion would make an independent determination based solely on his actions, and it would, I knew, be immaterial to them that his buddies were trying to settle the score. For the next several hours the village reverted to its normal level of activity, and I began to feel as if the sniping incident had taken place only in some sort of surreal daydream as I napped. By late afternoon the townspeople had begun returning from their errands and the women were preparing cooking fires for the evening meal. We would be moving out shortly, and as dark set in I decided to smoke one last cigarette before giving the order to saddle up.

As I struck the match and brought the flame to the Lucky Strike hanging between my lips, sniper fire erupted from a nearby tree line as if my action had been a cue. Leslie's dressing-down had had its intended effect, and this time my men were returning fire before I hit the ground. While rounds dug up the dirt around me, Turner suddenly appeared at my side and began firing a grenade launcher into the muzzle flashes coming from the tree line. I was at first grateful that he had come to my assistance until I realized that the snipers had shifted their fire to focus on the muzzle flashes from the grenade launcher beside me. Before I could signal Turner to shift his position away from the headquarters group, our adversaries had realized that they were going to get the worst of the fracas and abruptly broke contact.

In the ensuing confusion the villagers had disappeared into the cover of their huts, and Leslie and I, sensing that our enemies were now regrouping, decided to get the platoon moving before their target practice resumed. My men were only too glad to get going, and within minutes we had formed two columns and were humping our way toward the hill southeast of us. A couple of the men wanted to fire a rocket back into the village as a thank-you for its hospitality, but since we had seen nothing to indicate that the villagers were at fault and we were not being fired on as we departed, I restrained them. We were not interfered with as we made our way toward the main service road.

While the straps of my pack dug into my shoulders, I breathed more easily, knowing that at least we were headed in the general direction of Camp 413. It had been a rough two days, and with only one more stop to go, I was looking forward to a hot meal, a cold shower, and a couple of beers. I had always thought that getting shot at while lighting a cigarette was something that happened only in the movies, and I could not believe that it had actually happened to me. For a few moments I considered giving up smoking, but since there were so few pleasures in the bush, I dismissed the idea out of hand.

Attempting to ride herd on a platoon during a night movement was always more difficult than it was during the day, and the rapidly descending darkness had its usual effect as we worked our way toward our objective. Fortunately the darkness also meant that the chance of encountering snipers was minimal, and my point man was able to concentrate on maintaining a true azimuth while Leslie and I policed the formation. It was also easier to control the platoon with a half dozen fewer men, and as I checked my watch an hour into our journey, I realized that our time estimate for reaching the hill was just about right.

Fifteen minutes later the hill loomed into view, illuminated by a gibbous moon that had risen as the evening wore on. It sat alone and incongruous amid a flat expanse of greenery, and I raised a hand to halt our progress as we approached. It was unlikely that the hill would be occupied, but before I committed the platoon, I had two men do a quick circumnavigation to make certain that we did not get caught in the open by a force that would have the advantage of the high ground. When my scouts returned, we moved directly into the high ground and set up in a rough perimeter around the crest of the hill.

As we had anticipated, the view was unobstructed in all directions, and I was pleased with my selection as our command group set in on the summit. Turning toward Sergeant Leslie to comment on our choice, I could see the marine nearest to me on the periphery slipping off his pack. Just then an explosion broke the silence and a red flash filled the darkness in front of me. The force of the explosion spun me around and to the ground, and as I scrambled back to my knees, I could smell smoke and hear the young man moaning. When I attempted to refocus my vision on the wounded marine, my eyes were blurry, and as I touched my hand to my face, I realized that my glasses had been blown off by the blast. My face was also wet where I had placed my hand, and when I again brought my hand back toward my face, blood trickled between my fingers. At first I thought I had been hit in the head, but when my hand began to throb, I realized that my luck had been much better and that I had only taken a piece of shrapnel in the hand.

The marine who had set off the booby trap had been much less fortunate, and his body had absorbed most of the impact. One of his legs had been broken by the blast, and a piece of bone protruded obscenely from his pants at mid-thigh. His arm on the opposite side was riddled with shrapnel, as was much of his side, and by the time I had recovered enough to work my way over to his position, Ellis already was working frantically over him. Within minutes he had applied battle dressings to stem the bleeding, immobilized the broken leg, and injected the man with a dose of morphine. I ignored his offer to bind my hand, which by comparison looked like a razor nick, and turned toward Watson, my radio operator, who was already on the medevac net. When Ellis got our casualty stabilized, he informed me that there was a real danger of losing him if we did not get a prompt medevac, and I summoned the chopper as forcefully as I could. One of my men had a battery-operated strobe light, and as soon as we got the word that the medevac chopper was on the way, we set up a makeshift landing zone at the base of the hill in the center of which we dug a shallow hole for the strobe light. I had never called in a night medevac and was glad that we had the strobe light available to mark the spot for the chopper to make its pickup.

When the chopper came sweeping in ten minutes later, we activated the signal and informed the pilot how we were marking his landing zone. Four marines rolled our casualty into a poncho liner and carried him down the hill as the chopper made a direct landing on our marker. Within thirty seconds he had been placed on board and the helicopter lifted off. I watched for a few moments as the pilot arced his craft back toward Da Nang and was again seized by a desire to be on board and safely out of the dirty little war for which I was rapidly losing my enthusiasm. Leslie tapped me on the shoulder to bring me out of my reverie, and we had the platoon assume its original position at the top of the hill, where one more marine had almost lost his life for reasons I no longer seemed capable of articulating even to myself. It seemed fitting that I had lost my glasses and was losing my perspective on the war at about the same time, and although several men congratulated me on having earned my first Purple Heart, I was in no mood to respond to their remarks.

After another hour on our perch with no sign of enemy activity, I decided to call it quits and head the platoon for home. The loss of my glasses was far more disabling than the injury to my hand, and for once I took a position well back in the column as we paralleled the main service road into camp. As we entered the camp and headed to our company area, we passed a group of rear-echelon cooks and bakers who had just finished watching a movie on the outdoor screen they had rigged to help them with their boredom. The movie screen had been a sore subject with my men since it had first been erected because we had to troop directly by it on our way to and from the bush.

On this occasion one of the hapless cooks started to make a comment about grunts returning from war games, and several of my men pummeled him to the ground before he had finished his sentence. Leslie and Turner quickly ended the fracas, but even the most dim-witted among us shared the frustration that had triggered the outburst. We had just lost another casualty in defense of the domino theory, and there was nobody among us who was going to let a slight by a rear-echelon motherfucker go unanswered.

I went back to the officers' hooch, unloaded my gear, picked up my spare glasses, and then walked to the battalion aid station to have my hand bandaged. When I returned, the skipper and Sergeant Leslie were waiting for me with cold beer, and Captain Woods made small talk about my million-dollar wound while Leslie and I chugged several brews. Woods gave us the news that our casualty was going to live, but his time in the bush and probably in the Marine Corps as well was over. I felt like crying and wondered how my father had handled these kinds of situations. I sensed that I was going to have to get over feeling personally responsible every time one of my marines was wounded or I would go mad, but for now all I wanted was the oblivion that another gallon of beer would bring. Leslie proposed a toast to the green machine and its proud traditions, and after several more beers, I understood with remarkable clarity the meaning of the expression "Eat the apple and fuck the corps."

The next day my platoon was to take up a blocking position, along the road and adjacent to the Tu Cau bridge, for a sweeping movement by an ARVN unit. We did not have to be in place until early afternoon and our destination was only an hour's march, so we had the luxury of a relatively free morning. Leslie and I started the day by nursing our swollen heads over breakfast in the mess hall, and I spent most of the meal trying to replace the fluids in my system that the elixir of forget-fulness had exacted as its toll. Despite our aching heads, we were in a good mood since the day's activity would be a variation from our usual routine and since we would be going to our assignment with the ARVN company the following day. I had also gotten several more letters from my wife, reporting that our unborn child was waking her regularly in the middle of the night with some sort of prenatal exercise.

After Leslie and I had force-fed ourselves breakfast, I went back to the officers' hooch and wrote Toddy a short letter to let her know about my first Purple Heart. There was an unwritten policy in the battalion, honored more in the breach than in the observance, that the second Purple Heart was supposed to be a free ticket out of the bush, but the policy, of course, did not apply to officers. At any rate, I knew that I would not be able to live with myself if I used the excuse of a couple of cheap wounds to try to avoid my duty, and I would certainly never be able to face my father again under such a cloud. Nevertheless, it seemed harmless enough to contemplate that under different circumstances I would already be halfway toward a job in the rear.

I wrote Toddy about my injury, mainly so that she would know how insignificant the wound was and before the rumor mill had time to magnify it out of all proportion. I had tried in my letters to shelter her from the more alarming experiences I was undergoing, but since she was the only emotional outlet I had available, my moods occasionally darkened the letters home. In this particular missive I told her that I had lost only a few drops of blood but that I wanted her to hear the news from me before she heard from some other well-meaning source that both of my legs had been blown off. I closed with an admonition that she take good care of herself and our child and went off to round up the platoon for the march to the Tu Cau bridge.

Leslie was already waiting for me outside the enlisted hooches, and the men were milling about, making last-minute preparations for our venture, when I arrived. They were in the same upbeat mood that had prevailed at breakfast, and the marines who had started the fight the night before were basking in the new respect that their peers had accorded them. I said a few words about this being our last mission before the Marine Corps cut us some slack, and we shouldered our packs and weapons and headed out of the compound.

The September heat, like the last time we had left camp, was scorching, but since we were coming back that evening, we were not burdened by full packs and an overload of ordnance and so made good time along the roadbed. The platoon marched in two columns, one on each side of the road so that traffic could pass between us, and Leslie and

Turner flitted back and forth along the column, making certain that there were at least ten-meter intervals between the men. It was unlikely that we would detonate a land mine since the minesweepers from battalion had performed their daily sweep just before our departure, but we cautiously kept the interval anyway to avoid the loss of more than one man to the same mine.

══ ☆ ══

When we reached the bridge, I had the three squads set up along the road facing toward the Marble Mountain area. There was a tree line across an open area at our backs, and I dispatched several men to give it a quick search to make certain that we would not be ambushed from the rear. The bridge was occupied by another platoon and was not our responsibility; but I set up my command post directly adjacent to it so that it was to my right, and my own platoon was fanned out down the main service road to my left. I also kept the machine-gun team with me and had it sight its weapon down the center of the bridge span. Because we were in the open and unprotected from the sun or the enemy, I was somewhat apprehensive, but most of the men attempted to solve the heat problem by draping poncho liners across tent poles or small shrubs and taking shelter beneath them. If enemy soldiers were flushed out by the sweeping ARVNs later in the afternoon, they were also going to be in the open.

For several hours the only traffic on the road consisted of civilians whose business necessitated travel across the bridge, and my men amused themselves by flirting with the women and bartering with the merchants who passed their positions. As was often the case with South Vietnamese military units, the ARVNs never showed up, and late in the afternoon the word came down from battalion that their sweep had been scratched. There was a good deal of grumbling up and down the line about wasted effort and unreliable allies when the word was passed, but no one was disappointed at having avoided another enemy confrontation. We had hoped to be transported back to Camp 413 in six-bys; but when they, too, did not materialize, the grumbling intensified, and the platoon members repacked their temporary shelters and prepared to begin the journey home.

Just as we were saddling up, automatic-weapons fire erupted at the far end of the bridge in the Vietnamese section along the riverbank. The fire, which began sporadically from two or three isolated positions, quickly spread and intensified. Within minutes the platoon at the

129

bridge was returning fire, and as we dived for cover from the stray rounds hitting around us, I realized that a full-scale firefight was developing. When the shooting started, the civilians on the road and bridge dropped their packages and other belongings and headed for cover.

As I tried to figure out what to do next, I reached into a sack that had been dropped in front of the command post and pulled out a bottle of Vietnamese beer. By now my machine gunner and I could see North Vietnamese soldiers in green uniforms darting across the road at the far end of the bridge, and while he tried to draw a bead on the fleeting targets, I broke the end off the beer bottle and sampled the product. Strictly speaking, it was not our firefight, but we were marines who after months of being harassed by an unseen enemy were anxious for some revenge. My gunner, rather than firing wildly, was squeezing off two or three rounds at a time, and after he got the timing down of the enemy movement across the road, he winged one of the soldiers, and they stopped trying to cross the road.

I passed him the beer bottle as a compliment to his marksmanship, but before we could celebrate further, a fighter jet appeared on station and began making strafing runs at the cluster of buildings across the river where the firing had started. My platoon watched in awe, and several men actually stood up and cheered as the pilot skillfully maneuvered to fire his rockets into the embankment and the structures above it. His payload threw great clumps of black earth into the air, and for several seconds falling debris from his handiwork rained threateningly down on our position from all the way across the river. Several of the buildings collapsed like falling cards. Then smoke and dust filled the area as one of his targets burst into orange flames.

So intent were we on watching this display of aerial wizardry that I did not even notice that firing had begun behind us in the tree line that we had secured earlier, until several rounds screamed overhead and redirected my attention. The squad closest to my position reacted immediately and, after turning to face the threat behind us, laid down a volume of fire that saturated the tree line and badly damaged a house between it and our position. The enemy stopped firing as soon as our return fire began, and after both sides had stopped shooting, a woman emerged from the house, carrying a small child.

The little girl's arm had been blown off by one of my men who had fired into the house when he detected movement. We watched in horror as the woman made her way to the road with her little girl moaning in her arms. Both mother and daughter were covered with blood, and Watson began radioing frantically for a medevac as a corpsman went to their aid. The marine who had shot the little girl looked on in stunned disbelief and for the rest of the day was not able to respond to the simplest of commands. The little girl was not evacuated until half an hour later, when the enemy unit had retreated back through the cover of the partially destroyed village and when the platoon at the bridge had begun evacuating its half a dozen casualties and it was a simple matter to send the little girl and her mother with the wounded marines. My platoon had taken no casualties other than the young man who had shot the little girl. It was apparent that his psychic wounds would probably never heal.

After it was over, I was invited to view the bodies of the ten North Vietnamese soldiers who had lost their lives in what came to be known as the battle for the Tu Cau bridge. They were laid out in a row along the road for the rear-echelon intelligence types to view at their leisure, but the invitation had no appeal for me after having just viewed the mess we had made of an eight-year-old girl. We still had a long march back to Camp 413, and my sole casualty lagged badly behind the rest of the squad; but I made only a token effort to hurry him along. When we got home, he asked to see the chaplain, and he never returned to the platoon. There were some who muttered that he had simply found a convenient way to get out of the bush, but he had been a competent marine before the incident at the bridge took the sap out of him, and I knew that there was no place in my platoon for marines who were unable to put their sensitivities on hold.

Somebody higher in the chain of command was pleased with G Company's performance at the Tu Cau bridge, and transportation was made available to my platoon for our move the next day as a reward for the ten kills. We boarded amtracs at midmorning and were driven north on the main service road toward Marble Mountain. Nestled at the foot of the mountain was the village of Nui Kim Son, which we passed through before turning inland toward the ARVN company, with which we would make our home for the next couple of weeks.

The amtracs followed a narrow dirt road bordered by open fields and rice paddies for the last leg of our journey, and by noon we had reached our destination, a makeshift compound in the middle of no-where. The structure itself was circular with a ten-foot-high wall con-structed of dirt, mud, and enough supporting substructure to keep it upright. It had one entrance that faced the dirt road we traversed in approaching it. The perimeter was surrounded by a network of barbed wire that, although laid out symmetrically, did not appear sufficient to withstand the assaults of a determined enemy.

As I disembarked from the lead vehicle with half the platoon, and Leslie did likewise from the other, we were greeted by the ARVN company commander, a man four or five years older than I, whose command of the English language was remarkable. His uniform was freshly laundered, in contrast with my own. While my men gathered up their gear and slapped the dust from their uniforms, he invited his American friends inside his humble surroundings to share in the hospitality of his countrymen.

The inside of the compound was as squalid as I had expected, consisting of a small sandbagged command post. The very center was surrounded by a barren sort of courtyard of hard-packed dirt. The ARVN men had rigged crude shanties along the inside perimeter of the wall to serve as their own living quarters, and a few chickens and a dog roamed freely about the camp.

I was invited to share my ARVN host's cubicle in the command post, and I deposited my gear on a small bunk directly across from his. It was a five-foot-by-five-foot room with about enough clearance for an adult dwarf to stand comfortably. On the roof overhead his radio operator and senior enlisted men had fashioned their own living quarters, which were covered by a shelter half and some oddly rigged canvas. The two sets of quarters had the appearance of a box that had been placed on top of a box and then fortified with sandbags as an afterthought. Our area on the ground level was dark and damp with only a couple of openings in the sandbags for daytime light, but it appeared that at least I would be dry when it rained. There was also a small covered porch adjacent to the structure where we would take our meals and where a couple of enterprising ARVN soldiers had rigged hammocks that could be used at night and quickly taken down when we were eating or making plans. Watson installed his own hammock on the other side of the command post, and Leslie assigned my platoon positions by squad around the perimeter with the ARVN soldiers.

When everyone was settled in, the ARVN captain suggested that he, Sergeant Leslie, and I take tea together on his porch while he briefed us on the operation of his company. The tea was served lukewarm in C ration cans and was so diluted that it was barely amber-colored. Nevertheless, our Vietnamese host savored every drop, and Leslie and I exchanged winks and complimented him on its excellence.

Captain Thanh began by explaining to us that he had started his professional life as a schoolteacher but that the draft forced him to abandon his calling. Unlike our own draft, with its short span of obligation, Thanh was committed for the duration of the war and had no idea when he could get back to teaching. He told us he had learned his fluent English at Hue University and was honored to be able to communicate with us in our native tongue. I told him that we were honored to be the beneficiaries of his skill at our language and apologized for my lack of knowledge of Vietnamese. I could not help noting to myself that his English was better than that of three-quarters of the men in my platoon.

With the introductory amenities completed, Captain Thanh went on to tell us that he and his company had been in their present location for several months and were due for replacement within a week. The compound was their home base camp, and in the time they had been assigned to it, they had been frequently absent from it on two- to three-day operations with larger Vietnamese units. No doubt the new company would have the same sort of routine. In the meantime, he sent out one squad-size patrol at a staggered time each night, mainly to prevent an enemy unit from massing for an attack rather than to seek contact.

My sole assignments would be to send a squad from my platoon with his night patrols and to help out with the watches along the wall. He would give me the patrol route each afternoon when he received it from higher up. He closed by suggesting that the two of us could work through any problems that developed between his troops and mine but that he could tell by my obvious skills as a troop leader that such incidents would not be forthcoming. When the meeting ended, Leslie and I agreed that our Vietnamese host had the diplomatic skills of an ambassador and that his presence as the commander of a line unit was a bit incongruous.

After our session I briefed the squad leaders and weapons team leaders. The schedule was sinfully indolent compared with what we had become accustomed to. Each squad would patrol only every third night, and our days would be free. There was a Seabee battalion situated near Marble Mountain and Nui Kim Son, about an hour's walk to the east of us, and I planned to divide the platoon into two groups and allow one at a time to make the trek there for a hot meal and a shower. Otherwise we would be brought food, water, and mail by amtrac from Camp 413 along with requested logistic support.

I planned to use some of our free time to get the men who had been specially trained to teach their specialties to the other platoon members. For example, if Doc Ellis could teach the mortar section some basic medical procedures, I reasoned that one man could take another's place if he became a casualty and no one would be indispensable. I also planned to acquaint Corporal Turner and a selected few of the other men with rudiments of my own job so that one of them could take over if both Sergeant Leslie and I were wounded.

The platoon got along well with Captain Thanh and his ARVN company for the week that we were together primarily because of his leadership. Although he was worlds apart from his troops in terms of social class and education, he cared deeply about them and about his country, and that concern translated into a loyalty from his men that bordered on reverence. I also learned more about Vietnamese soldiers in that week than I had in all my prior time in Vietnam and gained a new respect for their integrity.

While our own needs were met by a daily trek to the Seabee compound, where we could eat like kings and buy personal supplies in the small PX, the ARVNs seemed to live off the land. Several times a day Captain Thanh dispatched men on mysterious missions, and they invariably returned with bags of rice, fresh seafood and produce, and other local delicacies. He dispensed these supplies to his unit leaders, who had them prepared in large cooking pots over open fires. I was always asked to share his table, and in return I gave him C rations and some of the booty that arrived in care packages from home. He was especially fond of Lipton tea and the Italian sausage that one of the men had been sent by his brother, a deli operator in the States. I in turn learned to eat snake, which was not bad once the bones were discarded, and I think on one occasion the hapless dog that had mysteriously disappeared after our third or fourth day there.

The Seabee compound where we received our daily hot meal and had access to showers was an oasis in the desert. Once again we were made aware of how luxurious life in the rear could be, but we dared not complain to the Seabees as long as they were willing to share their bounty. In the officers' mess steak and lobster were common fare, and on one occasion I even got frozen strawberries with my vanilla ice cream. Beer was also plentiful—and inexpensive—and I toted several cases back to our compound. The Seabees had free access to nightly entertainment and live acts that were part of the USO program, and they lived in air-conditioned comfort, which, though tantalizing after we had slogged in through the rice paddies and filth outside their fiefdom, was probably best left alone. In the course of one visit to the Seabees, a medical doctor in standard utilities stopped me to complain that several of my men had the beginning symptoms of immersion foot and that I should see to it that they kept their feet dry. He was a well-meaning sort who I am certain took his Hippocratic oath seriously, but he seemingly had no sense of life outside the wire. I knew that it would be pointless to explain to him that some of us involved in the war lived in the mud, bled in the mud, and would escape our fates only by surviving it or dying in the mud. I left him scratching his head as I excused myself without responding to his concerns and headed back to the bush, toting a case of warm beer.

The evening before Captain Thanh departed he gave me a particularly sumptuous dinner. There was a dish of tender white chunks of backfin crab and a meat course consisting of thin strips of steak in a brown sauce with rice. I did not recognize the animal from which the meat came, but at least I thought I could tell that it was not dog. I contributed a pint of scotch, lovingly sent by Toddy. After the meal and several carefully rationed drinks, we sat on sandbags outside his bunker and enjoyed the coolness of the evening.

He seemed, as usual, remarkably serene for a man whose country had been racked by war for such a long time, and as we smoked in the dark, I told him that part of my motivation in coming to Vietnam was to help his people have a choice of governments. I could see a smile play across his lips by the glow from his cigarette, but he did not respond for several minutes. Finally he told me that the Vietnamese people would outlast whatever government happened to be imposed on them and that he and I were powerless to affect the Vietnamese destiny. He thanked me for caring and told me to think occasionally of him and of his people when the war was no longer a concern of mine. I felt for a moment as if I were in the presence of a very old man instead of someone in his late twenties; but the feeling passed, and we finished the remaining scotch before turning in. I never saw or heard of Captain Thanh after he departed with his company the next morning, but he was a jewel, especially when compared with his replacement.

The new company arrived later that day, and this time I greeted the incoming commander at the compound entrance as Captain Thanh had greeted me. In the interval between one company's departure and the other's arrival, my men had, of course, taken over the most desirable living quarters vacated by the first group, and my platoon made it clear that they were now the old boys. I had also moved my gear to

Captain Thanh's bunk since the area above it was less susceptible to leaks during rainstorms, and Watson moved his radio and hammock to the porch area at the opposite side of the command post. Lieutenant Doan, Thanh's replacement, and his men had no inkling of the adjustments we had made, and we did not bother to apprise them; but I later got a laugh each time I watched Doan try to adjust his sleeping area to avoid the drips above his bunk.

Lieutenant Doan was a mustang, a former enlisted man in the Vietnamese army who had worked his way up to officer status, and as might be expected, he had none of the education or vision of Captain Thanh. He also spoke no English and made it clear from the start that he saw no need for anything beyond minimal communications between the two of us. He was a brutal man who beat his troops with a bamboo truncheon for the most insignificant infractions, and before he had been with us two days, I despised him as much as his own troops must have. From the moment he arrived, he seemed obsessed with improving the compound's defenses. He assigned extra watches to the perimeter at night and doubled the surrounding concertina wire, and I agreed with both improvements, although I wondered if Lieutenant Doan was motivated by fear in making them.

Since Lieutenant Doan did not seem to care for me except as an adversary in the domino games he played inveterately, I left him to his own men and began to take my meals with Sergeant Leslie or Corporal Turner. Despite the fact of the war and the necessity to send out the one nightly patrol and man the wall, after two weeks we had made no enemy contact and our routines had begun to take on the characteristics of garrison duty. The men had too much free time and were bored but were relatively easy to keep in check since we knew how fortunate we were not to be in the bush. The compound was located in a remote area surrounded by rice paddies, so the men had none of the diversions they had enjoyed at the Tu Cau bridge. I chose to ignore the daytime card games in which some of the poorer players lost the equivalent of a month's pay at a single session.

For my part, I became more reflective and passed the time reading, listening to the radio, and writing home. Among the books I read were *The Chosen*, by Chaim Potok, and *One Flew over the Cuckoo's Nest*, by Ken Kesey. I wrote my wife daily, along with a number of friends from my boyhood days, and I looked forward to letters from home as my lifeline to the world. I also wrote my father a fifteen-page letter full of information about the military aspects of my tour and the life-and-death situations we had faced. Given this strong new bond, I could probably have gone on for another fifteen pages, but I stopped writing when I realized that my fifteen pages exceeded the combined length of all the letters I had written to him in four years of college.

As I wrote, I looked inward at the way I had responded to the biggest challenge of my life, and my soul-searching convinced me that I did not want a military career. As a young man in college I had poorly defined but high expectations of myself, but now in the midst of chaos and uncertainty I developed enough insight to realize that I could be happy teaching school or plying a trade if only God would permit me to survive the war. I knew that I definitely did not enjoy the mantle of leadership that had been thrust upon me, and I agonized over the life-and-death decisions regarding my men that I was forced to make. In the process I began to develop mixed feelings toward the Marine Corps and my country, alternately loving and despising both, and I was confused by the ambivalence of my feelings toward both corps and country. A part of me had already begun to regard the enemy as some sort of inhuman cannon fodder. I realized that my reaction was a defense mechanism that allowed me to accept and dispense death and mutilation more readily, but I also knew that I was going to lose a part of my soul if that thinking progressed much further.

When I could no longer bear the reality of my own situation and the incivility of war, I took refuge in daydreams, and I spent hours fantasizing sexual liaisons with my bride and trying to recall every detail of the time we had had together. I wrote her of the all-consuming horniness of lonely warriors, and I looked forward to our reunion in Hawaii for R&R as if it were going to take place in the Garden of Eden. I also drank beer, usually in solitude and late at night, and although the alcohol did not raise my spirits as it had when I was a teenager, it freed me temporarily from the albatross of command. Corporal Turner noticed the amount of beer I was consuming and alluded to it briefly and good-naturedly, but I was running an efficient operation and paid no heed to his comments.

Sometime toward the middle of our stay with the ARVNs, my platoon was unexpectedly given a free afternoon at China Beach, news that the platoon received with cheers. Now made famous by television, China Beach was a resortlike military area along the coast of the South China Sea where marines who had distinguished themselves were given in-country R&R. The beach was magnificent with a wide swath of dazzling white sand that gently sloped toward the emerald waters of the sea. The coastline formed an arc, sweeping toward the north and with a backdrop of gorgeous mountains often shrouded in mist that was as breathtaking as a scene from *South Pacific*. The man-made structures along the beach, mostly corrugated tin Quonset huts, were far less appealing but catered efficiently to the demands of men temporarily at rest from the war.

My platoon hiked into the Seabee compound late in the morning of the day we were scheduled for our respite, leaving the ARVNs to fend for themselves, and we were then trucked to the beach area, where we checked our weapons into an armory before settling in for an afternoon of revelry. The surrender of our weapons made a few of the men uneasy, but it was a wise precaution, motivated by the same concerns that had required cowboys to check their guns with barkeepers in the Old West. Indeed, shortly after we arrived, we were told of a young marine who, unnerved by the pressure of the war, had sneaked his rifle into the beach area a few weeks earlier and opened fire on a group of sunbathers.

I had made two stipulations concerning my platoon's behavior: No marine was to act so outrageously as to be arrested by the military police, and at the end of the day each man was to be able to get back to the compound under his own power. Anything else was permissible, and the platoon, after its months of unremitting vigilance, quickly made it clear that it was going to approach, but not exceed, the limits of acceptable conduct. The recreation area contained both an officers' area and an enlisted area, and I had planned to drink with the men for an hour or two and then explore the officers' country. I had spent so much time living with the men, however, and was now having such a good time relaxing the normal barriers to fellowship necessitated by command that I quickly abandoned my original plan to go drink with some strange officers who meant nothing to me.

As Leslie, Turner, and I sat at a table in the canteen and quaffed beer after beer, my inhibitions lessened, and the other platoon members who had been drinking at tables around us gradually began approaching us and sharing our conviviality. Before long, several tables had been pulled together, and we luxuriated in the simple joys of cold beer, greasy cheeseburgers, french fries, and jukebox music. Emboldened by the beer, several of the men became pot-valiant enough to ask me what it was like being the son of Chesty Puller, and rather than being put off by their inquiries, I tried to let them know that as well as being a legend in the Marine Corps, he had been a wonderful father. When someone proposed a toast to Chesty Puller, the marines' marine, every man in our group stood and downed his beer. I was so moved by the tribute that I had to move away to get control of my emotions.

When I returned, the by now drunken marines were busy lying to each other about the remarkable feats they had heard attributed to my dad. Sergeant Leslie, with more time in the corps than any of the others, naturally won the contest hands down, and I contributed to his victory by confirming the authenticity of every story, no matter how outrageous.

After several hours of drinking cold beer, eating cafeteria-style food, and swapping stories, the platoon was as disabled as if we had taken heavy casualties in a firefight. Several fistfights broke out between my men and some of the rear-echelon types, but the altercations were resolved without the MPs and so did not violate my admonitions on acceptable behavior. One of my more drunken marines decided late in the afternoon to swim back to the States and had to be forcibly re-trieved from the South China Sea, but even he was forgiven.

When the time came for our departure, it took a herculean effort to round up the platoon and assemble it at the armory for the retrieval of our weapons. Even then I had to dispatch Corporal Turner to gather up several strays who had decided to spend the rest of their duty tour in the enlisted canteen at China Beach. Sergeant Leslie took upon himself the task of calling out the serial numbers of the rifles so that each weapon would wind up in the hands of its rightful owner, but the job, in his impaired state, proved impossible. I finally signed for the entire batch, and the men sorted out their weapons later, when they were able to remember their own serial numbers.

On the way back to the Seabee compound Leslie, Turner, and I debated how much our presence had improved the class of people at China Beach, while several inebriated marines sitting beside us on the truck bench shook their heads and wondered if the leadership of our platoon had lost its collective mind. By the time we hiked back to the ARVN, night was descending and the heat and exertion from the march had soaked the alcohol from our systems.

I called Lieutenant Doan over and tried to make him understand that we would post watches on the wall as usual that night but that my platoon had gotten a bad case of food poisoning at China Beach and that I would not be sending a squad on the nightly patrol. It was the first and only time during our stay that I did not provide a squad for the nightly patrol, but I saw no compelling reason to saddle up my men after such a pleasant day, and the squad whose turn it was to go was grateful. I left Doan protesting vehemently and waving a finger in my direction as I turned in for the evening, and the thought occurred to me that all Vietnamese, friend and foe, looked pretty much alike.

The next morning the amtracs resupplied us and also brought two new troops, who were casualty replacements. I was shocked at how fresh and green they appeared, but when I mentioned it to Sergeant Leslie as I turned them over for squad assignment, he smiled and pointed out that I had been in Vietnam for only two months myself. I considered myself a seasoned veteran and felt as if I had aged at least ten years. At that moment I understood for the first time the legend appearing in Magic Marker on some helmets I had seen early in my tour: "A day in the Nam is an eternity." I wondered how many eternities I could survive before the pressures of command finally broke me. We were going back to the real war before long, back to the Riviera and the maimings, and although the dread was unarticulated, to a man we all feared it. The new men were, of course, primed with gross exaggerations about the viciousness of the enemy and the equally exaggerated bravery of our unit. Nevertheless, I sensed a kernel of truth in the description of our enemy and noticed that despite the humor accompanying these tales, the training our new troops received was rendered with deadly seriousness.

Lieutenant Doan tried unsuccessfully to postpone our departure since he realized that my men were far more disciplined than his own. A few days before we were scheduled to rotate back to our regular command, the ARVNs left us for a daylong operation with a Vietnamese battalion. When the company returned well after dark, there were several men missing from its ranks and several others who wore fresh bandages. Doan's men were sullen and uncommunicative, and it was some time before I was able to understand that they had gotten the worst of a scrap with an NVA unit whose strength ARVN intelligence had grossly underestimated. Two men had been killed, and several others were wounded badly enough to require hospitalization.

Lieutenant Doan was preoccupied with his own losses, and when I asked for the patrol routes for that evening, he lashed out at me. He had been given no patrol orders for the evening, he explained heatedly. His troops had just been defeated in battle through no fault of his own, and in any event, if orders were forthcoming, he would disobey them because it was the eve of a Vietnamese religious holiday. I could understand his feelings but thought it foolish to allow the enemy an opportunity to approach our position without being challenged, and I volunteered to make up my own patrol routes and send out a squad unaccompanied by any of his men.

When I pointed out to him that we owed him a patrol because of the China Beach fiasco, he was able to swallow his pride and agree to my proposition. I found it paradoxical that a man who always needed an excuse to save face with his own men was willing to humiliate them by administering public beatings, but I kept my thoughts to myself since I had gotten my way. My men were delighted to be able to patrol without Doan's men, whom they considered useless at best and a danger to their own safety at worst. The ARVNs often smoked cigarettes and talked while on patrol. On one occasion my men had refused to accompany them until a Vietnamese soldier agreed to leave his transistor radio behind.

Turner theorized that the South Vietnamese soldiers had an agreement with their North Vietnamese counterparts whereby the ARVNs would make enough noise while on patrol that the enemy could locate and then purposely avoid them. He was never able to prove his preposterous theory, but it seemed a plausible explanation for the undisciplined behavior of Doan's company and for the fact that we had not had a single instance of enemy contact in all our nightly patrols.

Nevertheless, I was apprehensive about the nightly patrol both because it was going to be undermanned and because we had noticed an unusual and to me alarming amount of civilian activity in the rice paddies around the compound while the ARVNs had been out on their assignment. I decided to break the normal rotation and send Cowboy and his men since he was my most experienced squad leader, and although he complained about having to patrol two nights out of three, he understood my decision and was grateful for the absence of the ARVNs.

As he and his men checked their weapons before filing out of the compound, I put my hand on his shoulder and told him I had purposely shortened the patrol routes so that he would not have far to go if he ran into trouble. Cowboy responded with his usual bravado, but I could see the concern in his face as I gave him last-minute instructions to call in at the first sign of anything out of the ordinary. Leslie and I spelled each other on Watson's radio as Cowboy called in his checkpoints. After a couple of hours the patrol seemed to be proceeding smoothly, and I became less anxious. I decided to sleep for a while and instructed Sergeant Leslie to wake me when Cowboy radioed that he was coming back in through the wire.

About two in the morning Leslie shook me awake and, with a relieved expression on his face, informed me that Cowboy was a hundred meters outside the compound and had just requested permission to enter. Just as Leslie told me that he had given the go-ahead and had alerted the sentries on the wall, we were frozen in mid-conversation by the chattering of automatic-weapons fire. There were several long bursts, followed by some sporadic single shots, and as Leslie and I grabbed our rifles and moved toward the compound entrance, an excited and out-of-breath Cowboy ran through the opening and nearly bowled me over.

He was trembling and spoke wildly about sappers in the barbed wire. When I shook him quiet to ask if all his men were accounted for, he seemed not to understand me, but Leslie did a quick head count of the rest of the unit, all of whom by now had gotten in and were as shocked as Cowboy. I got on Watson's radio and called for an artillery mission of illumination rounds while Cowboy regained control and explained what had happened. In the meantime, Leslie had gotten the platoon on full alert, and all the men were scrambling to get to their positions in the wall. I cursed the artillery for taking so long as a terrified Lieutenant Doan, whom I had forgotten about completely, followed suit and began organizing his company.

Cowboy explained that the patrol had been a piece of cake up until the point where he had gotten permission from Sergeant Leslie to reenter the compound. As they approached the wire, they saw several almost naked bodies lying motionless in the concertina and assumed that the sentries had spotted and killed a squad of sappers (who would have removed their clothes to avoid being caught in the wire) trying to probe our lines. When Cowboy reached down to pick up the AK-47 rifle of the sapper closest to the entrance, the man jumped to his feet, and the marine behind Cowboy reflexively shot the rising figure in the chest and stomach. Cowboy lifted the red-hot barrel of the enemy soldier's rifle over his head as the dying man squeezed off a full clip of ammunition. As if for corroboration, Cowboy now showed me his burned hand.

At that point, he continued, all hell had broken loose as the other sappers got up and began trying to escape. Cowboy's squad exchanged fire with the fleeing men; but in the dark it was difficult to tell what was real and what was shadow, and he quickly broke contact and tried to get inside. The same survival instinct had motivated the rest of his squad, and within a minute or two they all were charging pell-mell through the concertina to the safety of the compound.

As he completed his story, an illumination round burst overhead, and I grabbed two men and headed through the wire to see for myself what was happening. I expected to find the enemy soldier lying dead or badly wounded in the wire where he had been felled, and not knowing what to expect beyond one dead or dying man, I had switched my rifle to fully automatic and kept my finger on the trigger. While I searched the wire for the sapper, more illumination rounds burst overhead, and the suddenly bright landscape took on an eerie surreal glow of shifting shadows and dark spots. The ground was littered with signs of an enemy presence. I almost tripped over a satchel charge and an unexploded bangalore torpedo that was going to be used to blow a path through the wire, but there was no enemy soldier. Four or five blood trails led from the wire toward the outer edge of the area illuminated by the artillery rounds, and I followed the spotty red markings of one while the light from the descending rounds flickered and faded. At the end of the trail a soldier, naked except for faded shorts, lay on his side with an AK-47 rifle nearby. He appeared to move as I worked my way toward him, but the movement could have been an illusion caused by the shadows. I emptied a magazine from my rifle into his prostrate body from about ten feet away and watched his body jerk as the rounds impacted. I reloaded and watched for several minutes; but there was no further movement, and as the light from the fire mission ended, the two marines with me gathered at my side and reported that there were no more bodies where the other blood trails disappeared into the bush.

We cautiously approached the dead sapper, who had bullet holes in his chest, stomach, and one forearm, and I passed his rifle to the man behind me and prodded him with my foot to make certain he was dead. The other marine and I then grabbed him by his legs to pull him back toward the compound. As we did our ghoulish work, his foot separated from his leg where another bullet had entered his body and came off in my hand. I got a grip farther up on his leg, and after several more minutes we succeeded in getting him through the wire, something he had been unable to do for himself while alive, and to the entrance of the compound.

We left our grisly trophy at the entrance and reentered the compound, where a furious Sergeant Leslie berated me for recklessly having gone outside the wire. Captain Woods was on Watson's radio, and I tried to explain to him what had happened while listening to Leslie's tirade with my other ear. Lieutenant Doan in the meantime strutted about the compound as if he and his men had by themselves repulsed a full-scale enemy attack, and I finally cut him off without any pretense of civility. I lit a cigarette and for the first time noticed blood on my hands and uniform from the dead sapper. As I inhaled deeply, it occurred to me that I would never know if I had just killed another human being. There was no pride in the thought since he was lying helpless when I had found him, but I felt no remorse either. I acknowledged to Leslie that I had acted rashly in leaving the compound and further that I had violated a canon of small-unit leadership by not staying with the main body of my command, which was potentially under attack, but there was no point in lingering over the issue. Sleep, of course, was out of the question, and we talked until dawn about the activities of the night.

Lieutenant Doan was certain that the sappers' attack had been meant as a distraction and that once they had penetrated our position, a far larger unit was to have swept over the wall on the opposite side of the compound and chewed us to pieces. His explanation was both frightening and unprovable, and I acknowledged it tersely. I did know for certain that if I had not scheduled my own patrol that evening, the sapper, once inside our position, would have tossed his satchel charge into the command post where Doan and I lay sleeping and it would have required a strainer to separate our mangled body parts. I made a conscious effort to steady my hands as I realized how close I had again come to being killed, and I understood exactly how Cowboy felt after his brush with death.

When the sun came up, Cowboy and I ventured outside to survey the skirmish site. The dead soldier was quite large and heavily muscled by Vietnamese standards, and we surmised that he must have been part of an elite unit with special physical requirements. As we admired his physique, Cowboy told me that he would not mind dying almost naked but that he would prefer to be engaged in a different sort of activity, and I was glad to see that he had regained enough composure to attempt levity. The landscape around the perimeter of the compound was littered with paraphernalia that the sappers had left behind as they fled, including several articles of clothing, a manual of some sort written in Vietnamese, and a North Vietnamese belt and buckle, which I picked up as a souvenir. We gathered up the items, including the torpedo and the satchel charge, and carried them back inside, and I gave the clothing and the belt to Cowboy's squad. To judge from the blood trails, his men had seriously wounded several of the escaping sappers, and I felt they deserved the trophies. I knew that we would be required to turn over the AK-47, the most desirable trophy, to intelligence and that it would wind up in the den of some rear-echelon officer who had never experienced the smell of death; but that was just the way the system worked, and there was no point in trying to buck it.

Sometime later that day, as the dead soldier began to stiffen and bloat, someone placed a cigarette in his mouth and an empty beer can in his hand. We left him in that state until the next day, when Lieutenant Doan came to me to complain that some of his soldiers were upset at our lack of respect for a dead Vietnamese, be he friend or foe. I had Leslie dispatch a burial party. Several days later I learned that my gravediggers had decapitated the body before burying it and had placed the head on a stake at the junction of two heavily traveled Vietnamese roads. I was angry that my instructions had not been followed, but I had none of the outrage over the desecration of the corpse I had experienced on first arriving in Vietnam, when one of my new charges had tried to urinate on a dead soldier. I justified the difference in my reactions on the grounds that this particular soldier had actually tried to kill me, but I knew inwardly that ice was forming in my heart. By week's end we had a firm date from Captain Woods for our return to our regular TAOR, and I knew that at least in the Riviera I would be too busy to take time to brood about my moral state.

The day that we traveled back to Camp 413, the amtracs arrived at midmorning with our replacement platoon, and its lieutenant and I exchanged intelligence about the commands we were each vacating. I advised him not to become complacent in light of what had happened to us and to rely on Lieutenant Doan as little as possible. He in turn told me that the VC had stepped up its level of activity in the Riviera, if such was possible, and that booby traps and snipings had become an almost daily encounter whenever a platoon ventured into the area. His platoon had suffered several casualties in the last few days alone. He strongly recommended that we use our probe sticks even in terrain that appeared safe. He also told me that the VC had succeeded in partially blowing up the Tu Cau bridge, which was now impassable for vehicular traffic.

As we traveled the dusty roads through Nui Kim Son and on toward Camp 413, I tried to sort out the information I had just received. The two weeks prior to our posting to the ARVNs had been a living hell, and it now appeared that we were headed back to more of the same. I knew that it was going to require extraordinary leadership to keep my men from becoming completely demoralized.

In anticipation of our return, my junior corpsman had already gone to regimental medical and told the doctors there that he could not take the pressure anymore and wanted to be removed from the bush. I was furious when his request was honored, but I was unable to reverse the decision since he was technically not in my command. Furthermore, we had no use for a man who had acknowledged cowardice, and I consoled myself with the thought that if the corpsman had remained, he probably would have cost us lives in the long run. His example, however, I knew well, could become contagious within my command.

During the last week we were with the ARVNs, one marine had come to me and complained of a mysterious foot ailment that he claimed made patrolling impossible, and there had been other isolated instances of malingering by a few of the men. I had Doc Ellis check out the complaining marine's feet, and when he informed me that our man was faking it, I offered the marine a choice. He could forgo the daily trip into the Seabee compound for hot chow and I would set up a night listening post outside our perimeter that he could man alone while his feet healed, or he could continue to patrol with his squad and I would forget the matter. After he had considered his options, he chose the latter course. The harshness of my response seemed to discourage further malingering.

Captain Woods confirmed the reports of increased enemy intensity when he briefed Sergeant Leslie and me that evening. He welcomed us back to the war, but the picture he painted was so bleak that Leslie and I could only shake our heads in dismay. There were rumors of a big shake-up in the battalion, including a possible change of command by the battalion commanding officer. In the meantime, we were to continue as before. Woods gave me my assignment for the next day, and I could only nod grimly at the prospect of leading my platoon once more through the big paddy of the Riviera. Almost by way of apology, he told me that one of the options being considered involved permanently moving a company into the area of the leper colony so that the passage problem could be minimized, but that, too, was for later.

As the skipper left to return to his own hooch, and I dispatched Leslie to pass the word to the men, he paused at the door to tell us that Lieutenant Zier had mended sufficiently that he would be returning to the company in a couple of weeks. I was delighted that my old stablemate was on the mend, but his recovery was the only bright spot in an otherwise dismal briefing.

For our first venture back into the Riviera, Captain Woods had decided on a company-size operation of one day's duration. My platoon and I were thrilled since the presence of two additional platoons, besides decreasing our chances of being overrun, would discourage snipers and small-scale ambushes. We felt right at home, if a bit apprehensive, as we waded across the big rice paddy before dawn, and as usual at that dark hour we crossed without incident. The skipper's plan was to move quickly to the coast, travel north until we reached the little fishing village, and then come back inland and complete the mission by retracing the route we had used earlier along the hilly area farthest from the sea. The operation was, in effect, a show of force during which we would cover a lot of ground and reorient ourselves to the area.

We stopped for a couple of hours in the woods adjacent to the leper colony, had a meal, and waited out the hottest part of the day, but the skipper, even during the break, seemed anxious to continue the march. Toward late afternoon, after we had crossed over to the hills and almost completed the last leg of the operation, I began to think that the earlier briefings I had gotten were in error since we had not seen one sign of enemy activity during the entire day. It was almost as if the VC were watching us but allowing us to move freely, and most of my men and I could not help feeling that when we returned as a smaller force, there would be hell to pay.

As we crossed through the last hedgerow before beginning our ascent into the big paddy, I heard a loud pop and thought that Vietcong snipers were finally making their presence known. The first pop was quickly followed by two more and the familiar cry of "Corpsman, up!" As I retraced my steps to see what had happened, I could see a fallen marine on the opposite side of the hedgerow. Approaching him, I realized with a sickening feeling that it was Sergeant Leslie, but though he was down, he did not appear to be seriously wounded. By now the entire company had backed up behind us, and the skipper made his way forward to Leslie's position just as I reached him from the opposite side.

Leslie explained to us that he had detonated a small booby trap in crossing through the hedgerow, and he turned sheepishly on his side to show us the hole in his pants where a shrapnel fragment had entered his buttock. Two other marines had also detonated booby traps, but the loads were weak and poorly placed, and they had escaped injury. Ellis by now had begun applying a battle dressing to Sergeant Leslie's damaged butt, and as the skipper and I prepared to call in a medevac, Leslie insisted that he could make it on his own back through the paddy and into camp. We acquiesced after Ellis assured us that a short walk would cause no further damage, and within minutes the company was up and moving again. Sergeant Leslie limped badly all the way in, and as soon as I had seen to it that my men were safely inside the wire, I had Doc Ellis take him to the battalion aid station.

An hour later the two of them appeared at my hooch with the worst of all possible news. My platoon sergeant was to pick up his gear and report back to the battalion aid station for medical evacuation. By now his leg had completely stiffened and Ellis had to support him as he attempted to walk. Despite the seriousness of the wound and the diagnosis he had been given of a four- to six-week recovery, he felt even worse that he was abandoning me and the platoon. I assured him that there was no other option, clapped him on the back with all the firmness I could muster, and jokingly reminded him to remember his buddies while he was drinking cold beer in the rear. As he hobbled off to pack his things, I felt that I had lost a brother. I was suddenly all alone, and though I knew he would return, the weight of command, already heavy, became crushing. I smashed my fist into the side of Zier's footlocker and swore at the emptiness around me until the pain subsided.

With Leslie incapacitated, I moved Corporal Turner to acting platoon sergeant, a position he was reluctant to assume, although he was clearly the only choice. Turner had almost as much time in the bush as Sergeant Leslie but lacked the training and the rank to take over the higher billet. He did, however, have obvious leadership potential and an abundance of courage, which I had come to realize were far more valuable than any lessons he could have learned in NCO school. When I summoned him to my hooch to advise him of his new status, I could tell that he was questioning his own ability to handle the job, and I ended his protestations by asking him if there was any other man in the platoon from whom he was prepared to take orders. With that out of the way I offered him a beer; but he was not yet ready to enter the familial sort of relationship that Sergeant Leslie and I had enjoyed, and he declined my offer. It was one thing, I knew, to acquiesce to a proposition that he could not refuse. It was something else for a black corporal to sit down and drink beer with a white lieutenant whose perspective up until now had been light-years away from his own.

Turner and I were to become much closer after we had been shot at a few more times; but for now he was keeping his distance, and I respected him for it. When he left my hooch to tell his buddies that he could no longer be one of them, I sympathized with his plight, but I knew that I had made the right decision for all of us. Fortunately we had come back into the platoon rotation at a point where Corporal Turner and I got a shakedown patrol in an area other than the Riviera, and I watched him closely for the two days we were out as he attempted to get used to his new role. I heard rumors that one of the black marines had accused Turner of selling out to whitey, but I didn't bother to investigate further since I knew that my new platoon sergeant would have his own way of putting an end to that kind of talk. It also seemed to have little effect on the way Turner took over his new responsibilities. As we reentered the compound after being out for two days, I jokingly told him that if he kept up the good work he was destined to wind up being a lifer in the white man's corps.

══ ☆ ══

In early October, as I was beginning my third month as commander of the third platoon, we returned to the Riviera for a two-day, one-night patrol. Barton, the young lance corporal who had saved my life earlier, had been acting strangely for several weeks. His bizarre behavior continued as we made our way into the area through the hamlet of Viem Dong at the southernmost edge of our TAOR. I knew that Barton had been trying to get reassigned out of the bush, and his comrades thought that the incident during which he had saved my life had so unnerved him that he had lost his usefulness as a marine. The explanation was plausible; but I owed him, and I had been trying especially hard to restore his self-confidence and his self-respect. Nevertheless, as we began our dreaded return to the Riviera, he complained of headaches and cold chills. Turner and the others thought that he was continuing his sandbagging act. Ellis could find nothing wrong with him, and after we had cleared Viem Dong, I pulled him over to the side of the trail and dressed him down for being a discredit to the unit. He stopped complaining for the remainder of the day, and by the time the sun was going down I was in an upbeat mood both because my talk with Barton had apparently worked out and because we had not met any enemy resistance.

That night we set our base camp up on a high bluff overlooking Viem Dong, and by the time darkness had fallen we were dug in and ready to send out squad patrols. Viem Dong was bad news, but we held

149

the high ground above it and I was half hoping that the Vietcong who controlled the ville would try to provoke an altercation. My two-month "eternity" and sense of the enemy left me feeling that an altercation was inevitable, and I preferred its onset where the terrain was favorable.

Around midnight, when I was readying a night patrol for a quick loop around the outskirts of the village below us, Barton began to moan softly from his fighting hole. At first the sound was barely audible, but as the night wore on, it became loud enough to give away our position. Once again Ellis could find no reason for his behavior, but by now Barton was not responding to us and seemed to be having convulsions. I canceled the squad patrol and put the platoon on full alert since it seemed that every Vietcong in the area would by now be homing in on Barton's outbursts. I also radioed Captain Woods, who instructed us to try to keep Barton quiet until daybreak. The men were ready to kill him for endangering their lives. Finally Corporal Turner and I laid him out in the bottom of his fighting hole and covered his mouth with a towel each time he began his routine. Barton was semi-lucid between convulsions, but the attacks were coming closer together and were increasing in strength.

By dawn we all were exhausted. I had the platoon prepare a landing zone in the nearest flatland and called in a routine medevac. I half carried and half dragged Barton to the zone and dropped him in the shade of a small tree as the sun worked its way up in the sky. Spittle dripped from his chin, and we both were covered with dirt from wrestling in the fighting hole all night; but at least he was in place to be boarded when the chopper arrived. After several hours and several more convulsions we changed the medevac to a tactical emergency, and the bird finally arrived. Medevac procedure necessitated sending another marine with our casualty since he was in no condition to explain his peculiar symptoms, and I selected a man from Barton's squad who was familiar with his situation. I had been holding Barton in my arms for much of the morning, and as the chopper set down, he seemed to stiffen in my arms and then relax. He had smiled up at me when I told him that his time in the bush was over. I wiped the saliva from his face in a last-minute gesture as we piled his body onto the chopper. As it lifted off, I was overcome with relief and the platoon was elated to be done with a man who had almost doomed us. I did not know until we got back to Camp 413 later that night that George Barton had died in my arms. Until the very end I thought that he was faking a medical condition to get out of the bush, and I shall carry to my own grave the guilt from the way I misread him in his last hours. With Barton gone and our patrol a full four or five hours behind schedule, I got permission from Captain Woods to alter the route in a way that would permit us to hit only one or two of our checkpoints and still make it back before dark. It was by now almost noon, and I decided to advance the platoon northward along a dirt road that ran between the woods abutting the beach area and the leper colony. On earlier patrols we had always used the cover of the woods, but we could make better time along the road. Since the enemy already knew where we were, I was gambling on speed and the fact that we had never used the road to neutralize the enemy's strategic advantage. The heat of the midday sun and the increased pace made for a demanding march, but the men were motivated by a desire to reach camp before dark and did not complain.

By the time we had completed the northern leg of the patrol, we all were out of breath and our uniforms were soaked with sweat, but we had met no resistance and had made up valuable time. Watson called in our first checkpoint, and I gave the men a fifteen-minute break, after which we moved inland across the open area toward the spine of hills we needed to traverse in the opposite direction. I had always felt naked in crossing this open area, and as we approached the first hill, I began to breathe more easily. The point man had gotten thirty meters in front of me by the time we reached the foot of the hill, and I knew that once we had reached the crest, we would be back in control.

As I called to him to slow his pace and allow the rest of us, who were strung out behind him, to close the gap, an automatic weapon opened fire from the top of the hill. The point man dropped immediately, as we all did, but I could see, as the enemy fire raked the sandy area between him and me, that he had taken a round in the leg. He lay there exposed and vulnerable as the fusillade tattooed the earth around us, and in the confusion I realized clearly that he was going to die if I could not alter the pattern of fire. I pulled myself to my feet and headed toward him; but the enemy gunner shifted his fire to meet my charge, and I dived behind a rotting log only ten or fifteen meters from where I had begun and then abandoned my only John Wayne–style feat of the war.

My movement had distracted the Vietcong soldier on the top of the hill from the wounded point man, and he poured round after round into the base of the log shielding my body. As I attempted to burrow into the sand behind the log, I looked down and saw a colony of red ants going about their business as if nothing were happening. I was fascinated by the little creatures only inches from my nose and knew that I must be losing my equilibrium to be thinking about ants while the terrain around me was being pockmarked with lead. I forced myself to refocus on the threat on the hill, and by now the marines behind me were returning fire.

Within minutes it was over, and the enemy gunner used the reverse slope of the hill to make his getaway while one of my fire teams scrambled up the near side. When we had secured the hill, I hurried over to the point and watched helplessly as Doc Ellis administered an injection of morphine and Watson called up the second helicopter medevac of the day. Our casualty had actually taken a round in the heel that had entered through the back of his boot. Ellis assured me that the wound was not life-threatening and that he would not lose the leg, but he could not walk and was in excruciating pain. I shared a cigarette with the wounded marine and made small talk while the narcotic worked its way into his system. Ellis filled out a medevac tag and tied it over his knee so that the attending doctor would be aware of the morphine injection. This time the chopper arrived within minutes of the time we had summoned it, and I helped load our casualty aboard in what was by now becoming a gruesomely routine maneuver.

After they had lifted off, Turner and I got the men back into formation, and we double-timed down the hilly route to the big paddy. The platoon was sullen as the darkening shadows lengthened around us, and in a funk of my own I made no effort to revive their flagging spirits. By the time we reached the paddy it was dark, and I signaled the patrol to follow me across without any pause. The darkness at least meant that the snipers had retired for the evening, and we waded abjectly across in silence. As always, I waited at the entrance to Camp 413 to check the men's weapons, but while there was relief in our return to a safe haven, there was no joy.

Back at my hooch I sank wearily onto my bunk without removing my boots or water-soaked utilities, and within seconds I was asleep. After what seemed like hours but was probably only twenty minutes, I was shaken awake by Captain Woods, who had dropped in to tell me of Barton's death. No one knew yet what had killed him, but Woods was careful to tell me that I was not responsible. At first I could not believe that he had actually died, but as my disbelief gave way to acceptance, I knew that Captain Woods's kind words would in the long run be irrelevant to the way I came to terms with the death of a man who had saved my life. I knew only that I had not been there when Barton needed me most, and I loathed myself almost as much as I loathed the war and the Marine Corps that were forcing me to serve in an increasingly repugnant role. We never did find out the cause of Barton's death.

Woods snapped me from my reverie by telling me that we all had had enough of this nickel-and-dime war of attrition in the Riviera and that he was planning an operation within the next several days. That would give me no solace tonight but would at least allow the score to be evened the next time we were the guests of Victor Charles. He patted me on the back and left me to my misery. I decided to get some chow and a six-pack of beer before writing Toddy a long letter. I badly needed to purge my soul, and for a moment I thought how comforting it would be to wallow in self-pity for a few pages. Instead I wrote a brief note telling Toddy I was fine, and I settled for part of the six-pack and an unappetizing meat sandwich that I scrounged from the mess hall. As I finished the letter and two of the cans of beer and settled down for a few hours of sleep, it occurred to me that I could not remember the color of my wife's eyes. I hoped that she would not see in mine what I had seen in the eyes of other battle-scarred veterans when next we met.

True to his word, Captain Woods devised an ambitious operation as a way to settle the score in the Riviera. He knew that it would be unacceptable from a political standpoint simply to level Viem Dong, the hamlet at the edge of the Riviera, a known Vietcong stronghold, from which we had been taking increasing amounts of hostile fire, but he also knew that our South Korean allies were free to operate without the political constraints that figured so heavily in all our planning. He therefore seized on the idea of a joint operation in which our company would be lifted at first light into the Riviera. We would then form a cordon around Viem Dong, and a South Korean company would sweep through the village and drive the unsuspecting enemy into our field of fire. Whatever else the Koreans did in the village was their own business, but with their reputation for brutality, we all knew that the village would be loath to support the Vietcong so openly in the future.

As Woods outlined the plan, in effect a cordon and search operation, for his platoon leaders and platoon sergeants a few days after our earlier conversation, I could see several of the men nod their heads and murmur approvingly. We could not be certain of engaging any of our enemies, of course, but our own risk was minimal. If our timing was right, the operation could turn out to be a turkey shoot. Beyond that we would be on the offensive for a change, and the morale boost to the troops would be of inestimable value. As I congratulated the skipper on his concept after our briefing and assured him that my men would do their part in its execution, I realized that my commander was savvy enough to use whatever resources were at hand.

The idea of a cordon and search was a fairly simple textbook maneuver with which any company commander would be familiar, but the expedient of using the Koreans to do our dirty work was the selling point of the operation that I knew convinced higher command to give Woods the green light. If we got our kills, we could take full credit, and if the ROKs became overzealous, we could plead our lack of control over an allied force. At any rate, the effect on Viem Dong was going to be devastating, and I felt ready for revenge as I hurried back to brief my squad leaders on the forthcoming activities.

The night before the operation was to take place the rain came down in great gusting sheets, and my men looked forward to remaining in their hooches and preparing for the next day. Instead we were given orders to commence a patrol so that our adversaries would not become suspicious because of our lack of activity. The men were not happy at the idea of trudging out to a meaningless ambush site, sitting in the rain for half an hour, and then returning to our starting point solely to satisfy the whim of some safe and dry intelligence expert, but as usual we grudgingly did as we were told. When we returned an hour and a half later, we were as wet as if we had sat all night in the squall outside, and instead of having a chance to get dried out, we were now going to march for another hour to the nearby army camp from which the operation would begin the next morning.

As we filed out of camp for the second time in the same evening, the men were grumbling loudly, and only the thought of the next day's payoff kept their complaints in bounds. We were cold and exhausted as we made our way through the wire into the base camp, and I could tell by the number of trip flares that the platoon set off (safely, since the other unit knew we were arriving) in clearing the wire that they were past the point of caring. Once inside, we were escorted to the helicopter pad from which we were to lift off in several hours. We settled down around its perimeter and huddled inside our ponchos as the rain pelted our helmets and hunched shoulders. The everyday tribulations of an infantryman were at best an ordeal, I recalled from some Basic School graffiti, and Turner and I shook our heads knowingly and tried to keep our cigarettes going in the rain. After I had made certain that my platoon was ready for the morning and that the squads understood the order of embarkation and their assignments once we deplaned, I

154

slipped off for a last-minute briefing in the command center where the skipper had set up temporary shop.

It was dry inside the sandbagged bunker, and though not a coffee drinker, I gladly accepted a steaming mug and used its warmth to dry my chapped hands. We had gone over our operational plan in detail previously, and there were no last-minute changes; but the lieutenants listened attentively as Captain Woods retraced his five-paragraph order. Though it was not discussed, we were keenly aware that our men were outside in the rain while we had the luxury of hot coffee and a dry bunker, and our attentiveness was in part a reaction to the guilt we felt over our differing circumstances. Beyond that, however, the air was charged with the electricity common to the ritual of preparation for a kill, and the adrenaline pumping in our veins masked our weariness.

Somewhere in the background a radio cackled and sputtered. A World Series game was in progress. Mickey Lolich was on the mound for the Detroit Tigers, who were in the process of taking a seven-game series from the St. Louis Cardinals, in the culmination of a season that would assure baseball immortality for a young right-hander named Denny McLain, with his thirty-one games. Our minds, however, were on a different sort of contest.

When Woods finished his briefing and answered what few questions there were, we reluctantly made our way back to the helicopter pad to wait for the first signs of dawn. The rain had stopped by then, and most of the men were dozing fitfully and using their packs or helmets for pillows. An hour before liftoff I had Turner wake my sleeping marines, and we ate our C rations. By the time we had finished the mindless routine of heating, eating, and policing, the word came down that the choppers were on their way, and I smoked one last cigarette before assembling the men by squads in their staging area.

As soon as our chopper alighted, the men raced to its yawning tailgate and piled aboard. I made certain we all were accounted for before taking a seat beside the door gunner and giving the crew chief the thumbs-up. As we lifted off, I felt the familiar pull in the pit of my stomach caused by our rapid ascent, and when we leveled off, I relaxed my hold on the side of the craft and watched the blur of foliage passing just beneath us. The sky was streaked with the red of the rising sun, and I realized, as I watched its reflection on the glassy surface of the South China Sea, that at least for today the rain was finished. The pilot nosed down in a clearing between the beach and Viem Dong after only a few minutes aloft, and we scrambled down the gangway and fanned out to take up our positions as he reversed his direction and banked up into the sky.

I concentrated as best I could on making certain that the two squads to my left were on line and in position to hook up with the platoon adjacent to them, but in the confusion and noise from the other helicopter around us, control was almost impossible. The skipper's position was to be atop the high bluff to our right, overlooking Viem Dong, where we had camped the night before Barton died. After I had gotten my men on line, my next assignment was to connect with his location. Watson followed closely in my tracks with the radio, but the two nearest men to us were at least twenty meters away on either side and for all intents and purposes out of hearing range. As we maneuvered, I scanned the area to my immediate front, which I had been neglecting in my effort to maintain platoon integrity.

Suddenly I saw a squad of green-uniformed North Vietnamese soldiers begin running out of the village and in my direction. They had apparently panicked when the helicopters began landing and were now probing for a way out of the noose we were drawing around them. As they advanced toward me, I was unable to get the attention of the marines near me, and it dawned on me, to my horror, that I was the only obstacle between them and freedom. I raised my rifle to my shoulder and attempted to draw a bead on the lead soldier; but my first bullet was off the mark, and when I pulled the trigger the second time, my rifle jammed. By now the North Vietnamese soldiers had spotted me, and several of them fired wildly in my direction until they abruptly altered their advance and veered off to my left. Standing alone with a malfunctioning weapon and seven enemy soldiers bearing down on me, I was at once seized by a fear that was palpable and all-encompassing. My throat became as dry as parchment, and beads of perspiration popped out on my forehead before coursing down my face. I turned abruptly, with Watson in tow, and ran as fast as I could toward the safety of the bluffs above Viem Dong, where the company headquarters party was to be located.

A narrow trail led up the hill to the headquarters group, and as I approached, it never occurred to me that the thirty meters between my course and the commanders' position had not been secured. I knew only that the firepower advantage of the NVA squad I had just encountered would be neutralized if I could reach the men milling at the crest of the hill. With only a few meters left to cover in my flight, a thunderous boom suddenly rent the air, and I was propelled upward with the acrid smell of cordite in my nostrils.

156

When I landed a few feet up the trail from the booby-trapped howitzer round that I had detonated, I felt as if I had been airborne forever. Colors and sound became muted, and although there was now a beehive of activity around me, all movement seemed to me to be in slow motion. I thought initially that the loss of my glasses in the explosion accounted for my blurred vision, and I had no idea that the pink mist that engulfed me had been caused by the vaporization of most of my right and left legs. As shock began to numb my body, I could see through a haze of pain that my right thumb and little finger were missing, as was most of my left hand, and I could smell the charred flesh, which extended from my right wrist upward to the elbow. I knew that I had finished serving my time in the hell of Vietnam.

As I drifted in and out of consciousness, I felt elated at the prospect of relinquishing my command and going home to my wife and unborn child. I did not understand why Watson, who was the first man to reach me, kept screaming, "Pray, Lieutenant, for God's sake, pray." I could not see the jagged shards of flesh and bone that had only moments before been my legs, and I did not realize until much later that I had been forever set apart from the rest of humanity.

For the next hour a frantic group of marines awaited the medevac chopper that was my only hope of deliverance and worked at keeping me alive. Doc Ellis knelt beside my broken body and with his thumbs kept my life from pouring out into the sand, until a tourniquet fashioned from a web belt was tied around my left stump and a towel was pressed tightly into the hole where my right thigh had joined my torso. My watch and rifle were destroyed by the blast, and my flak jacket was in tatters; but I did manage to turn my undamaged maps and command of the platoon over to Corporal Turner during one of my lucid intervals. I also gave explicit orders to all the marines and corpsmen hovering around me that my wife was not to be told of my injuries until after the baby was born. There was, of course, no possibility of compliance with my command, but the marines ministering to me assured me that my wishes would be honored.

Because we were on a company-size operation, there were six corpsmen in the immediate area around Viem Dong, and each of them carried a supply of blood expanders, which were designed to stabilize blood pressure until whole blood could be administered. As word spread of my injuries, each of the company's corpsmen passed his expanders to Doc Ellis, who used up the last of them while my men slapped at my face, tried to get me to drink water, and held cigarettes to my lips in an attempt to keep me awake. When the chopper finally arrived, I was placed on a stretcher and gently carried to its entrance, where a helmeted crew chief and medevac surgeon helped me aboard. Someone had located my left boot which still contained its bloody foot and that, too, was placed on the stretcher with me.

As the chopper began its race toward the triage of the naval support hospital in Da Nang, I was only moments from death, but I remember thinking clearly before losing consciousness that I was going to make it. I never again saw the third platoon of Golf Company, a remarkable group of young men with whom I had had the most intense male relationships of my life, and I felt guilty for years that I had abandoned them before our work was finished. I was to feel even worse that I was glad to be leaving them and that, in my mind, I had spent my last healthy moments in Vietnam running from the enemy. I came to feel that I had failed to prove myself worthy of my father's name, and broken in spirit as well as body, I was going to have to run a different gauntlet.

In the naval support hospital triage in Da Nang, located just down the road from the Seabee compound where I had feasted on frozen strawberries and ice cream only a few days earlier, the remainder of my clothes were cut away, massive transfusions were started directly into my jugular vein, and my severed foot was discarded. On arrival, my blood pressure had failed to register, but once it was restored and I was stabilized, I was wheeled into the operating room, where my left stump was debrided and left open, and the femoral artery, which was all that remained of my right leg, was clamped shut. The procedure was fairly simple because there was so little left to work with. I remember thinking, before I succumbed to the anesthesia, how clean and shiny the tiles in the operating room appeared, how cold the room was, and how worried the eyes all seemed above the green masks of the doctors and nurses who labored over me.

When I regained consciousness, I was in a clean bed with white sheets. An assortment of tubes carried liquids to and from my body, and when I reached up to remove the annoying one affixed to my nose, I found that I could not do so because both my hands were wrapped in bandages the size of boxing gloves. I understood the reason for my bandaged hands because I had seen my right hand with its missing thumb and little finger earlier, and I also knew that my left hand now retained only a thumb and half a forefinger. The word *prehensile* no longer applied to me. I did not yet know or knew only vaguely that I had lost my right leg at the torso and that only a six-inch stump remained of my left thigh. In addition to the damage to my extremities, I had lost massive portions of both buttocks, my scrotum had been split, I had sustained a dislocated shoulder and a ruptured eardrum, and smaller wounds from shell fragments peppered the remainder of my body. Only my face had been spared. It remarkably contained only one small blue line across my nose from a powder burn.

Back in the United States, where the attention of most Americans was occupied with the outcome of the World Series, the assistant commandant of the Marine Corps, General Lewis Walt, who had been one of my father's company commanders in World War II, called Saluda, Virginia, with the news of my wounding and followed up his conversation by coming down from Washington. A young marine officer was dispatched to Fort Belvoir to break the news to my wife. There was no one home at the Todd quarters when he arrived, but he alarmed neighbors, who alerted my father-in-law as soon as he returned home. He called and through official army channels was able to ascertain roughly what had happened.

Communications from both the army and Marine Corps were badly garbled in the first days after my wounding. My wife was at first told that I had lost only one leg and later that I had lost one leg below the knee and one above the knee. When she got the first message, she went straight to her father's pantry, poured a double shot of bourbon, and tossed it off in one motion. Already furious that she had been the last to receive the news, she spent a sleepless night after Walter Cronkite reported my injury on the "CBS Evening News." The next morning she traveled to Saluda to be with my parents. By the time she arrived, they had received a more accurate assessment of my injuries, and my wife was soon to discover that if I survived, as was doubtful, I would do so with "a bilateral above the knee/hip disarticulation." Numb with fear and exhaustion and seven months' pregnant, she took solace from the only male Puller who was still capable of standing on his own two feet.

Sometime later that week, before I was medevacked to Yokosuka, Japan, in the first stage of a painful journey home, a marine general and old family friend, Tommy Tompkins, made a special visit to my bedside to pin a Silver Star and Purple Heart on the pillow cradling my head. For the photo opportunity that accompanied the presentation and reading of my citation, the tube was removed from my nose and the photographer was careful to frame his shots of me from the waist up. Even in my delirious state I did not feel that I had earned a Silver Star, and I expressed my reservations repeatedly to Colonel Tom

McKenney, another old family friend who spent most of those first few critical days in Da Nang at my bedside. There was no such reservation about my eligibility for the Purple Heart, and while my first one may have been cheap, the second award could hardly have been paid for more dearly.

While I was still in Da Nang, a parade of young officers who had been my peers in Basic School made the obligatory trek to the hospital to see me, and the concern on each of their faces so alarmed me that I finally requested and was given a bottle of whiskey to help them through the experience. For my part, I was becoming dependent on massive injections of morphine to quell the phantom pain in my missing limbs and postpone the inevitable acceptance of my loss, so my visitors were forced to drink alone. Mike Downs, my future brother-in-law, who was on his way back to the States, rerouted his homeward path to spend a few minutes with me, and he told me years later that he had resigned himself to never seeing me alive again after he had completed his visit.

For the most part the medical personnel who attended me while I was in Da Nang, as well as those who treated me in Yokosuka, were dedicated professionals who worked tirelessly every day in a world of blood and gore that would have broken men and women of lesser stature. There were also Red Cross volunteers who spent hours at my side as I began, through a narcotic netherworld, to assimilate the magnitude of my physical loss. Several of these "doughnut dollies," as they were affectionately labeled, helped me with letters to my wife that I do not remember dictating but that she saved, along with all the other letters I had written as a virile young platoon leader, the youthful optimism of a newlywed just separated from his bride contrasting with the stark terror of a shattered war casualty who had as yet no frame of reference for a life without legs.

There was one exception to the caring individuals who nurtured me in those first days as I clung precariously to life, whom I was told about by Tom McKenney a year after I had returned to the States. A young doctor who objected generally to American involvement in the war, and specifically to the fact that he had been drafted, entered the triage shortly after I was carried in and began taking pictures of me. It was assumed that he was documenting the effects of trauma on newly wounded combatants, so no effort was made to stop him until later in the week, when he announced to some of his colleagues that he had gotten some great pictures of the Puller kid that he was going to use in antiwar lectures after rotating. His pictures were confiscated immediately. I have often wondered if he was ever able to separate his views on the war from his Hippocratic obligation toward the warriors who were fighting it.

My journey home was begun against the best medical advice, but because my father, who was himself in poor health, had begun talking about flying to Japan to meet me, a decision was made to send me home early. In Yokosuka I developed a stress ulcer as a result of the shock of being wounded, and two-thirds of my stomach had to be removed. The pain was excruciating, and I was not expected to survive the operation, which exposed a second ulcer once the surgeons got inside. In my debilitated state the second ulcer was considered inoperable, but remarkably it stopped bleeding on its own, and I was again stabilized. When we got under way again, I was assigned a nurse whose sole duty was to be available in case the exposed femoral artery in my right side ruptured.

A day later my plane set down at Andrews Air Force Base outside Washington, D.C. I had, in keeping with the parable of the Spartan soldier, returned on my shield. My temperature was 105 degrees, and I had not had a dressing change since leaving Japan. I was transferred to the base hospital near the terminal, where my wife and family had gathered and had begun steeling themselves to meet me.

There were no brass bands to greet me, no rousing renditions of "Stars and Stripes Forever," and no politicians to offer their support for a job well done. I was home, though, back in the United States after a splendid overseas tour that had not quite reached its third month. And I had avoided, for whatever reason, the fate of those casualties who were returning home in aluminum boxes.

V

★

BY THE TIME I had been made as presentable as possible it was late in the evening, and a nervous hospital commander, justifiably concerned that I might die on his watch, reluctantly agreed to let me receive visitors. In my precarious state it was decided that I should see only one family member at a time, and my father was the first to enter the room. He stood quietly at the foot of my bed for a few moments, surveyed the wreckage of his only son, and then, unable to maintain his stoic demeanor, began weeping silently. He moved to my side and grasped my shoulder as if that simple act of communion would stay the convulsions that now racked his stooped frame, and I in my helpless state was unable to reach out or otherwise console him. It was only the second time in my life that I had seen my father cry, and as the nurse led him from my room, I felt an aching in my heart that all but eclipsed the physical pain from my wounds.

After I had regained my own composure, my wife was allowed to see me, but having spent my emotional load with my father, my meeting with Toddy was, at least for me, less wrenching. When she bent to kiss me, the warmth of her lips against mine eased my grief, and I was mercifully unable to read the anguish and uncertainty that she hid behind a mask of grim determination. With the ice broken by the kiss and my inhibitions diminished by morphine, I asked her to raise her

162

skirt so that I could assess the state of her pregnancy, and when she complied, we smiled at each other conspiratorially over our handiwork. Years later she told me that she had prepared herself as best she could for the sight of my mangled body, but that the nose tube that pumped secretions from my ulcerous stomach had almost unnerved her.

After I had spent a few minutes alone with my wife, my nurse and doctor decided to permit the rest of my visitors to enter as a group. I was exhausted from the long flight, the unremitting pain that was by now a constant companion, and the effort required to talk to my wife and father, so the group's visit was a quick one. I was also receiving injections of morphine every three or four hours, and my memory of the remainder of the visit as well as of the events of the next several weeks remains clouded. My mother could not bear to look at me and as a defense mechanism tried to steer the conversation to the Detroit Tigers' victory in the World Series but stopped when I made it clear that I was not interested in baseball. I did, however, manage to exact a promise from her that she would give me my grandmother's diamond engagement ring to add to the solitary band I had given Toddy when we married, and although Toddy's embarrassment was acute when I broached the subject, I must have known that for once in my life I had the upper hand in bargaining with my mother. After our reunion was concluded and my family and in-laws retired to try to assimilate the magnitude of my injuries, I was given another injection of morphine and slept fitfully until another onslaught of pain cut through the narcotic.

In the morning my twin sister, who had stayed at home the previous evening because she had been assured that only my wife was going to be permitted to see me, came to the hospital with Toddy and my brother-in-law. She was furious that she had missed the earlier visit but was so unnerved at the prospect of seeing her closest blood relative *in extremis* that she talked incessantly. In anticipation of her visit I had asked my nurse to fashion a bra from two surgical face masks, which I then gave her as a continuation of a running joke commentary on her less than ample endowment. She managed a flicker of a smile through her tear-stained face as she accepted my offering, but her agony could not be concealed as she contemplated my near destruction. Later she confessed to me that her initial impulse on seeing me was to pray for my death and that she was ridden with guilt over that reaction. With Martha's visit the circle of family reunions was completed, and while none of us realized it, successive visits eventually became less strained, although my little joke with the bra was the last bit of levity I felt up to for some time, as my despair over my situation began to take hold.

I had been scheduled for transport to the Philadelphia Naval Hospital by ambulance later that morning, a trip of several hours' duration, but my pain was so intense and my energy so depleted that I recoiled at the thought of the long ride and begged for a helicopter. My request was agreed to by the base commander, who wanted nothing so much as to send me on my way and relinquish the responsibility for a level of medical care that his hospital was ill equipped to provide, and by noon I was flying north toward Philadelphia with my wife and family following by car. On arrival at the Philadelphia Naval Hospital I was taken immediately to the operating room and given general anesthesia while my wounds were debrided and my dressings changed. When Toddy arrived, the procedure had been completed and I had been transferred to the hospital intensive care unit, which was my home for the next month. Because of my father's reputation, the hospital commander made a point of welcoming my family to his facility, but he pulled no punches in conveying his assessment of my condition. According to him, my chances of survival through the critical next ten days were about 50 percent unless I contracted pneumonia, in which case I would almost certainly die. The good news was that if I survived, his surgeons would do an excellent job of putting me back together again.

In the fall of 1968 and throughout my hospitalization in Philadelphia, the government had given no thought to temporary lodging for the families of wounded servicemen, and my family checked into a motel near the hospital for that week, in what was the first of many agonizing and expensive stays. They were so concerned initially about my condition that the expense of the accommodations was simply regarded as a nuisance; but as time wore on, the economics of the situation became intolerable, and they began to double up on rooms or plan day visits from Washington. Later in my hospitalization, when I had recovered sufficiently to take an apartment near the hospital grounds, my wife remembered her early problems with costly motels and invited the wives of severely wounded patients to sleep over with us. It was bad enough to be shot to pieces in the service of your country; but it was outrageous then to be expected to sustain heavy outside costs associated with recovery, and Toddy and I were doubly sympathetic to the plight of the enlisted wives, for whom the extra costs were often an unbearable hardship.

At the end of that first weekend Toddy and our families returned to Virginia while my older sister remained at the hospital and began a five-day vigil at my bedside. I was out of my head from pain and morphine most of the time, and the doctors assured my family that there was no purpose to be served by their staying. In addition, Toddy was nearing the end of her pregnancy, and there was a very real danger that her anxiety and the shock caused by my wounding would precipitate an early delivery. She promised to return as soon as possible and even then left reluctantly, but I was too absorbed with my own suffering to enjoy the company for long of even those I loved most dearly. Because I was completely helpless and my hold on life was so tenuous, some unusual arrangements were made to accommodate me. I was placed alone in a windowless room near the nurses' station of the intensive care unit, and I was assigned three corpsmen, each of whom worked an eight-hour rotating shift.

One of the corpsmen, Ernie, was a compulsive liar who stole medications from the nurses' station and from the patients. He was finally court-martialed and given a bad-conduct discharge when his drug use became flagrant, but while he tended to me, my judgment was so impaired and my dependency so total that I was completely taken in by his dissembling. The second corpsman, Jack, was a manic depressive who even to me appeared so close to the verge of a nervous breakdown that it came as no surprise when he tried to slash his wrists and became a patient himself. Finally, there was McMonagle, a bear of a man who had absolutely no respect for any form of authority and who was uniformly despised by all the doctors and nurses. I liked him immediately, and his dedication to my care was a lifeline in the early desperate days of intensive care.

By the end of my first two weeks in the intensive care unit, the odds favoring my survival had improved considerably, although to the unpracticed eye the reverse must have seemed the case. Several times a day my bandages had to be changed, and without morphine the ordeal was so painful that I was quickly reduced to the level of a snarling animal. For a period of time I became convinced that the staff as well as my family had entered into a conspiracy designed solely to increase my torment, and I lashed out at all who dared enter my room. Because I threw up so much of what the corpsmen tried to spoon into my mouth, I simply began to refuse food, and when my weight dropped to less than sixty pounds, orders were issued that I be fed through the tube in my nose. I was also completely immobile and had to be rotated from

my back to my stomach and vice versa every three hours in a special
bed that employed two thin mattresses on a circular track and resembled a sandwich board more than a resting place. Despite the constant
turning, I developed bed sores from the pressure and the perspiration
with which I was constantly soaked, and by the time I had completed
my stay in intensive care I had open sores the size of quarters along my
backbone and pelvis.

At some point toward the end of the second week I was carried back
to the operating room, where split thickness skin grafts were taken
from my upper torso and used to close the gaping hole where my right
leg had connected to my body and to patch the wounds to my buttocks.
The plastic surgeon assured me after several days that the grafts were
taking and that I was recovering nicely despite my best efforts to thwart
his efforts by refusing to eat. For my part, I knew only that the operation necessitated a whole new area of bandages across the donor sites
on my upper body, and I cursed him for joining the conspiracy
against me.

Toward the end of my stay in intensive care I was moved from the
windowless room near the nurses' station to a more remote but more
cheery end room that my corpsmen referred to as the solarium. I was
its sole occupant, so remained as isolated in my new setting as I had
been in the old room. The few visitors who came to see me in both
rooms were required to don white dressing gowns to maintain a sterile
environment, an unintended result of which was that for weeks I lived
in a world without color. My principal contact with the outside world
was through a transistor radio that played pop music from the nightstand beside my bed, and I still get goose bumps when I hear
"Abraham, Martin and John" and "Little Green Apples," songs that the
disc jockeys in Philadelphia played over and over in the fall of 1968.

Once I was in my new surroundings, a decision was made to wean me
from the morphine, on which I had become psychologically, if not
physically, dependent, and I begged and then screamed for my shots as
the time between injections was lengthened and the dosage was de-
creased. Without the morphine to dull my senses, I had to face both
physical pain and the reality of my loss, and for several days I was
nothing more than a bundle of jagged nerve endings as my wife and
McMonagle stood by to mop my brow, feed me lime Life Savers, and
hold cigarettes to my lips. It was a period of my life during which I lost
all self-respect for not having the strength to carry myself with dignity,
and I loathed my country and the Marine Corps for having brought me
to such depths.

During the first month of my hospitalization I was confined to the electrically powered bed that rotated me as if on a roasting spit, and the combination of my injuries and lack of mobility left me as weak as a newborn baby. I deteriorated to the point where I could not lift my head from the pillow, and I developed a dangerous-looking bald spot on the back of my head where a bed sore was beginning to form. By the time the boxing glove–size bandages on my hands were removed at the end of the month, the muscles in my arms had atrophied to the extent that my elbows appeared huge in comparison with my forearms and biceps.

There were signs of progress, however, and a major improvement was the new freedom made possible by getting back what was left of my hands. Without the bandages I was at least able to scratch a few itches and mop my own face, although I was appalled at how badly my hands had been mangled. At first my fingers were so stiff and swollen that I could not manage a cigarette on my own, and an exasperated McMonagle, tired of catering to my need for nicotine, finally bought me an ivory roach clip that allowed me to smoke on my own but made the doctors and nurses suspect that we were smoking marijuana on the sly. He, of course, delighted in their suspicions and even increased them by introducing incense into my room to string them along further. The tube was also removed from my nose sometime during the month. That greatly cheered up Toddy and, more important, ended the staff's capacity to pump gruel into my stomach when I refused to eat.

In early November I was taken off the critical list and moved to the twelfth floor of the hospital. SOQ 12, sick officers' quarters 12, was the area of the hospital set aside for officers undergoing long-term hospitalization. The majority of its patients had been seriously wounded in Vietnam and would eventually be boarded out of the service, but there were also a few terminally ill cancer patients and the usual assortment of malingerers and misfits looking for a place to hide. McMonagle wheeled me up to my new quarters in the electric bed on which I had lain for the previous month, and it was a close call as to whether the intensive care unit personnel were more relieved to be done with the two of us or we with them. In any event, our reputation for obstreperousness had preceded us, and the head nurse, a Commander Zatzerine, met us at the entrance to her domain and made it clear that she allowed no shenanigans on her ward. McMonagle, in keeping with his style, adopted his best supercilious pose during her tirade, but after she had finished, we decided to give her the benefit of the doubt for the present.

I was moved into the room across from the nurses' station, a by now familiar locale, but since the move was carried out on a weekend when my roommate was on liberty, I was not to meet him until Monday morning. One of the other patients had placed a sign on the door to my room that read DUMB GRUNT IS FEELING GROOVY in anticipation of my arrival, and while McMonagle howled at this comment on my attitude, I did not find it the least bit amusing.

That evening, after I had been installed in my new room, Nurse Zatzerine paid me another visit. When she realized that I was still too absorbed with my own misery to want to engage her in conversation, she respected my mood and did not attempt to draw me out. Instead she fetched a bottle of Lysol and scrubbed my bed, an action that she could have ordered one of the corpsmen to perform. I was so impressed and so shocked by that simple gesture of humility that when she next took my hands in hers, I made no effort to protest. She studied each hand in some detail, gently tracing the cracks in the parchmentlike skin with her forefinger, and she then announced that we both were going to have to get to work on getting my hands back in shape.

From that moment on I was as meek as a lamb when dealing with this angel of mercy, and I even came to look forward to those occasions when she would bathe my mutilated hands in mineral oil and work loose the dead skin that made them appear even worse. I now understood why the other patients all loved her and why she was so frequently asked to join those who could get liberty for happy hours at the nearby officers' club. It was typical of the navy, however, that after she had established such a marvelous rapport with SOQ 12's patients, she was transferred to a job that limited her contact with patients.

On the Monday following my transfer to SOQ 12, many of the patients who were far enough along in the recuperation process to get weekend passes returned from liberty, including my roommate, Lieutenant Paul Barents, a double above-the-knee amputee. Lieutenant Barents had been raked across the knees by automatic-weapons fire while setting up an ambush in Vietnam eighteen months earlier, and his wounds were so severe that both legs had been amputated surgically. He had made remarkable progress, however, at adjusting to the wooden prostheses with which the hospital's limb and brace shop had outfitted him, and when he walked into our room that first Monday morning with only a cane to steady his balance, I was amazed to discover that a man with so little remaining of his legs could ambulate. He was a tall, wiry man with a neatly trimmed mustache and a deep, booming voice, and when I ignored the cheerful salutation with which he greeted me, he quickly realized that I was not yet ready to talk and he did not press the issue. Instead he took a seat, slipped his stumps out of the sockets of his prostheses, and transferred himself into the wheelchair beside his bed. He then placed his legs in a corner of the room, donned a pair of hospital pajamas, and, without another look in my direction, wheeled out of the room in pursuit of more congenial company.

After Paul had gone, I turned my head toward the corner of the room where he had left his legs and stared curiously at them for several minutes. They retained shoes, socks, and trousers, and it suddenly dawned on me that the proper procedure in saddling up with artificial limbs was first to dress the legs and then put them on. The pants had slipped down a bit around the thigh area of each leg after Paul had stacked them in the corner, and I could see expanses of shiny pink plastic above the knees where the trousers had come to rest at the knee joint. I remained despondent and withdrawn for the remainder of the day over the totality of my pain and helplessness; but a new emotion, hope, reentered my life when Paul Barents walked through our hospital room door that Monday morning, and while I despised his good humor and envied his freedom to come and go as he pleased, I knew that there was much to be learned from him.

When Paul returned later in the morning, I was still unwilling to let myself be drawn into conversation, but I listened attentively as he conversed with the hospital staff and some of the other patients who dropped in. He baited me by warning each of our visitors that efforts to communicate with me were useless, and many of our visitors followed his cue and made a game of my silence. Despite my sullenness, I did learn that Paul had an apartment near the hospital that he shared with his wife and that he would soon be retiring from the Marine Corps and entering the civilian job market. Chronic infections in his stumps had caused him to remain in the hospital far longer than normal for a double amputee, and his most current hospitalization was for what was expected to be one last revision of a stump that had once been at mid-calf level but was now well above his knee.

Because I was unable to turn myself over in bed or otherwise move around, I was particularly impressed by Paul's mobility and skill with his wheelchair. He could transfer from bed to chair in the blink of an eye, and when in the chair, he could pop wheelies, do 360-degree turns on a dime, and maneuver as if the chair were a natural extension of his body. He had also developed an extra measure of upper-body strength by using his arms to do the work of his legs, and throughout the short time that we roomed together, he was constantly challenging all comers to arm-wrestling contests and more often than not beating them. That evening Kathy, Paul's wife, dropped in to visit him, and as they discussed the operation he was to have later that week and their future plans, I was shocked to discover that they appeared to have a fairly normal relationship. Kathy was a slim, vivacious woman with delicate features and a ready smile, and as they talked, I eavesdropped and became aware that she was as dependent on Paul as he was on her.

Unable to sleep that evening, I lay awake and mulled over the events of the day and the utter lack of control I had over my life. Prior to my being moved into the room with Paul, the certainties in my life were finite and unappealing. I was turned in my bed every three hours, and in the mornings a corpsman shaved, bathed, and fed me. My dressings were then changed, and for the rest of the day various doctors and nurses poked and prodded me as if I were a side of beef in a meat market. I no longer had any idea of my own capabilities, and whatever dignity I once possessed had abandoned me as surely as my missing limbs. For several weeks I had been brooding over the idea of asking Toddy for a divorce since I did not feel that it was fair to force her into a lifetime of caring for a helpless cripple. I had in fact even considered suicide, but I now laughed, despite my melancholy, when I realized that I was incapable of throwing myself out of the partially open window only a few feet from my bed.

As I watched Paul sleeping peacefully in the bed across the room from me, I wished desperately for one night's rest free of pain or discomfort. It then occurred to me that Paul must have been through the same hell I was now experiencing, and he had survived the ordeal. He had also redefined his relationship with his wife in a positive manner and in a few weeks would be putting the Marine Corps and the Vietnam War behind him and looking for a job. By the time blessed sleep finally came, I had begrudgingly come to realize that I must undergo a drastic change in attitude to avoid spending the rest of my days as a miserable, lonely freak.

As Paul's roommate I was privy to many of the conversations he had with the other patients on SOQ 12, many of whom stopped by that first week to wish him luck on his operation. They were a diverse assortment of young marine and naval officers who entered our room in wheelchairs, on crutches, or using the unfamiliar prostheses that for many were to become lifelong companions. Varied in their backgrounds and personalities, they bore the scars of a war that, whatever its devastation, produced a bonding among them far more powerful in some ways than the ties of family kinship. Some, like Lieutenant Joe Beltzer, who had been wounded three times, treated their disabilities as affirmations of manhood and wore their wooden legs and eye patches as badges of honor, while others were truly shattered by the wounds they had suffered. Lieutenant Clebe McClary, who had lost an arm and an eye to a Vietcong satchel charge, turned to Christ to restore wholeness to his life, and Lieutenant Cal Goodman, who was now missing his legs, his testicles, and his right thumb, cursed God and anyone who was foolish enough to cross his path.

Although I did not participate at first in the banter that took place between Paul and his companions, I was naturally curious and listened carefully as they exchanged war stories and elaborated on the horrors of the hospital. Time and time again their conversations turned to Dr. Nicholas Cabot, the orthopedic surgeon who would be doing Paul's stump revision and who would later help to piece me back together. According to the scuttlebutt, Cabot was an expatriate Russian who as a youth had learned French in Hong Kong and, in addition to being a brilliant surgeon, spoke half a dozen languages fluently. He was also reputed to be a man so totally dedicated to the practice of pure medicine that human feelings and emotions had no meaning for him. As a result, his empathy with his patients was nil, and his bedside manner bordered on brutality. When Beltzer described Cabot's habit of ripping bandages from the amputation sites of wounded patients during morning rounds and the way that some of the patients next in line would hide in the linen closet to avoid his examination, I shuddered to think that this man was going to care for me. The rest of the group listening to Beltzer's description of decorated combat veterans cringing in some dark closet laughed uproariously as Beltzer described Cabot, but I could find no humor in the anecdote.

I first met the notorious Dr. Cabot the day before Paul's operation, when he dropped by to explain the procedure to Paul and to obtain his signature on the surgery consent form. The explanation was a formality since Paul had undergone numerous stump revisions in the course of his hospitalization, but after he had signed the form and returned it and the clipboard that held it in place, Dr. Cabot came over to my side of the room.

He began examining my left stump, which lay open and exposed as if freshly hacked by a meat cleaver, and only after he had completed his task did he bother to introduce himself. Still trembling from the kneading that he had given my stump, I extended my mangled right hand to acknowledge his belated introduction, but he ignored the gesture and began explaining the course of treatment he had in mind. His principal concern was the closure of my stump, and toward that end he informed me that the staff would be around later that day to place what remained of the limb in traction in preparation for the surgery that he planned to undertake within the next several weeks. He also told me that he considered the three-corpsmen rotation assigned to me a needless coddling that was probably motivated by my father's status but that he would allow it to continue until he had closed my stump. I could feel myself color at the reference to my father; but I did not argue the point, and I ignored the nod of agreement that passed between McMonagle and Paul.

As Dr. Cabot left the room, clipboard in hand and without so much as a final gesture in my direction, Paul Barents said to no one in particular that if certain unnamed patients were more open to communication, they could have been better prepared for our Good Samaritan. I found out later that in a parting shot Dr. Cabot stopped at the nurses' station on his way off the ward long enough to discontinue my morphine and write an order for the corpsmen to begin getting me out of bed and into a wheelchair. Apparently neither measure was of sufficient importance that he felt obliged to discuss it with me.

Paul spent most of the afternoon getting his work-up for surgery and consulting with the anesthesiologist and other team members who would be participating in the operation. I was alone, therefore, when the technicians from Dr. Cabot's service arrived to place me in traction. Because my stump was so short and a section of the femur extended outward from the surrounding tissue, Dr. Cabot's plan was to stretch the skin downward as far as possible so that he could preserve maximum length. By the time his technicians had finished their work, cords had been affixed to the sides of my stump with a thick adhesive tape, twined together, and draped over the foot of my bed, where a suspended metal plate kept the apparatus in place and kept pressure on the cords to stretch the skin. I was more immobile than ever by the time my rigging was completed, and the skin over my thigh felt as if it had been the principal ingredient in a taffy pull. When I called for morphine, Cabot's indifference to the pain of his charges was brought home to me, but he had at least prescribed in its place the analgesic Darvon, which I immediately began to abuse.

When Paul returned from his preop interviews shortly before dinner, I was basking in the euphoria of a Darvon high that, although short-lived, served its purpose, numbing the pain in my stump while I became accustomed to the stretching of my skin. He whistled sympathetically as he surveyed the torture instrument that had been connected to me in his absence, but he again chose to humor my sullenness and busied himself in his own part of the room.

When the time came for me to be turned from my back to my stomach, the corpsman who rotated my bed failed to realize that the traction weight had to be moved to the opposite end of the bed, and I yelled in pain until he corrected his mistake. The normally placid Paul added his voice to the uproar, and I was as surprised by his outburst as was the hapless corpsman, who made every effort to avoid us for the rest of the evening.

For several days after Paul's surgery he was as incapacitated and in as much pain as I, although to my mind he withstood the ordeal much more manfully than I. Kathy tried to be at his side for most of his lucid moments, and she brought thermos bottles of soup and broth to hasten his recovery. I felt like a Peeping Tom as the two of them worked through their pain, but in view of our proximity and immobility there was nothing I could do other than try to be as quiet and inconspicuous as possible.

While Paul was recovering from his operation, the corpsmen first tried to get me into a wheelchair. The model they selected was an enormous wooden structure with a wicker back and seat, which looked like a leftover from the Civil War. It was obviously designed more for comfort than mobility, but despite many readjustments of rubber rings and pillows to ease my pain, I could at first bear sitting in it for only a few minutes at a time. In mid-November I still had open bed sores along my spine and barely healed skin grafts across my buttocks, and I was so weak from my wounds and inactivity that the first few times I was placed in the wheelchair my head flopped over onto my shoulder as if it were connected to my torso by a Slinky. At less than sixty pounds I was so emaciated that I did not recognize myself the first time I was wheeled by a mirror, and I automatically reached for my face to make certain that it was mine. It was also difficult to move me with the weight attached to my stump, and the corpsmen had to concentrate so hard on just keeping me in an upright position once I was seated that there was no question of wheeling me anywhere outside the room.

Gradually, however, and despite my protests, I gained enough strength to remain in the chair for twenty- or thirty-minute stretches, and McMonagle took it upon himself to build up my endurance. At first he coaxed me into short trips up and down the length of the corridor, but he soon increased the range to the point where the two of us were careening all over the hospital like a couple of joyriding teenagers. He also frequently managed to be a good fifteen minutes from my room when my sitting period was supposed to end, and he laughed demonically as I cursed his stratagems and demanded to be taken back to my bed. "In no time at all, Lieutenant," he reminded me, "you will be pushing your own chair, and there will be no need for these outbursts, which ill become an officer."

One night a couple of weeks before Thanksgiving, I was paid a surprise visit by an old fraternity brother who had been graduated the previous year and was in Philadelphia for a business seminar. I was tired and depressed when he arrived, mainly because I could see no end to the torment I was enduring but also because Toddy's advanced pregnancy precluded her spending more time with me. Jeff and I had been close in college; but our shared experiences had been carefree and joyous, and I was as ill prepared for the tears that streamed down his face when he first saw me as he was for my grotesque condition.

McMonagle tried to relieve our awkwardness with small talk, but even his usually disarming sarcasm could not ease the painful strangeness that now replaced Jeff's and my bygone familiarity, and the visit was a disaster. Like the good trooper he was, Jeff came back the following night with a box of chocolates, but our second visit was not much smoother than the first. After he had gone, Paul and McMonagle tried to explain to me that early visits from old friends were bound to be painful, but I chose not to share my tears and turned my head away from them and toward the open window on the opposite side of the room. Later I was able to understand that if the sight of my own body was shocking to me, it had to be even more so for those with whom I had been close, and I wondered anew why Toddy would want to remain with me.

On the Friday before Thanksgiving my father-in-law called from Fort Belvoir with the news that Toddy had given birth to our son, Lewis Burwell Puller III, whom she was already affectionately calling Lewpy. She had gone into labor the previous night, sending the Todd household into an uproar because the baby was not due until late December; but the delivery was a textbook performance, and Colonel Todd informed me proudly that mother and son were doing fine. By the time I had absorbed the news that I was a father and gotten back to my wife by phone later in the day, my flagging spirits had taken a sharp turn upward and I had completely abandoned the idea of leaving her. We were a real family, and despite the rocky start, I could tell, as I talked to my wife, that this child was God-sent and destined to solidify our marriage.

I also learned in the course of the conversation that Toddy had *lost* fifteen pounds during what had otherwise been a routine pregnancy, and I was chagrined at my own selfishness for failing to recognize the physical toll that my wounding had exacted from her. After we had finished talking and made plans for me to see my son, I had McMonagle take me to the hospital post exchange, where I purchased the largest box of cigars I could find. When I offered one to Paul later in the afternoon, it was the first time I had spoken civilly to him since we had been rooming together.

"Thanks, Lew," he replied as he accepted my offering and clapped me on the back. "I thought you were never going to talk."

Back home in Saluda, my own father cried yet again when informed that his namesake had arrived safely, but unlike the two earlier occasions when I had shared his sorrow, this time his tears were of joy.

Before I got the opportunity to see my son for the first time, Thanksgiving came and went. Paul had recovered enough for outpatient status, and alone and blue, I spent the holiday in the doldrums. McMonagle tried to cheer me up by making wisecracks about the unappetizing Thanksgiving dinner that he chopped into bite-size pieces on the tray beside my bed, but I was in no mood for either his quips or the processed turkey. I was finally eating solid food after weeks of being sustained through tubes; but my badly damaged stomach was in such a state that I was always uncomfortable after meals, and I frequently vomited if I ate the slightest bit too much. When McMonagle began a mock-serious lecture on gratitude and the starving multitudes in Africa, I was tempted to demonstrate the queasiness of my stomach for his benefit.

I was also quite disturbed by the boisterous activity that had been going on all day on the street twelve floors below my window. A constant flow of traffic had shuttled spectators to and from the John F. Kennedy Memorial Stadium for the Army-Navy game, and I could not reconcile the differing circumstances of the mob outside with the suffering of my platoon back in Vietnam. It seemed insane that men I knew should be groveling in the mud or being blown to bits while most of America was concentrating on point spreads. When Toddy called me that evening, after she and her family had celebrated her first day home from the hospital with the baby, I begged her to come visit me as soon as possible.

Ten days later, on the weekend before Dr. Cabot had scheduled my surgery, Toddy and her parents made the trip up from Fort Belvoir to let me meet our son, and the hospital's commanding officer made a room available to us adjacent to his office on the first floor. When word came that they had arrived, McMonagle wheeled me down in my rickety chair, and we were ushered into the room where the Todds were having coffee and Toddy sat holding the baby. As we entered, they rose to meet us, and after kissing me, my wife folded back the blanket to let me see our baby. I could not believe that he was so tiny and wrinkled, and it was a toss-up as to which of us was more helpless.

I was too frail to take him in my arms, but Toddy proudly pointed out the features that she considered especially good, and I instinctively knew that I had real competition for the first time since we had begun dating. While we chatted, she nursed him, and although I was not particularly impressed by his scrawny condition, I had never seen my wife look more radiant. As the baby suckled, I felt a possessiveness toward both of them that was unlike anything I had ever felt prior to Lewis's arrival. I also felt a stirring in my loins as I watched my wife and much to my amazement realized that I was aroused and as much in need of Toddy as the baby at her breast. When I began to show signs of tiring, the Todds wisely decided to cut short their visit. They left, and I spent the remainder of the afternoon in wonderment that I had become a father. McMonagle had a few choice comments about Toddy's remarkable endowment, but I was too dazed by the events of the day to rebuke him for being out of line.

Dr. Cabot closed my stump the following Wednesday in a lengthy operation that had life-threatening and unexpected consequences. The procedure seemed to go smoothly enough as he rounded off the femur, reshaped the exposed muscle and tissue, and closed the wound with a lattice of sutures that resembled the laces on a football. Unfortunately the stump ruptured later in the recovery room while I was still under the anesthesia, and I was rushed back to the operating room and stabilized with a dozen units of blood while Cabot and his team worked frantically to undo the damage. When I finally awoke two days later back in the intensive care unit, a nervous McMonagle was on duty at my side. He congratulated me on scaring the daylights out of the entire orthopedic surgery service, but even in my semilucid state I could read the concern through his sarcasm. For the first few dressing changes after I was taken back to SOQ 12, I was given Demerol intravenously to counter the excruciating pain in my stump, and Dr. Cabot actually performed the procedure himself. Despite my agony, I thought I detected an unfamiliar gentleness as he handled my stump, but it was so slight that I continued to pray for an acceleration of his scheduled retirement from the navy.

Once I had recovered from the effects of surgery and was released from traction, my world began to expand. The corpsmen assigned to me, including McMonagle, were transferred to other jobs, and I reluctantly began to assume new responsibilities for my own care. With McMonagle's departure I felt the loss of a friend who had helped me through the darkest hours, but I was also relieved to be done with my dependency upon a man whose insufferable arrogance seemed to have no bounds. He continued to visit me for many months after being reassigned; but we both came to realize that the basis of our relationship had changed, and we eventually lost touch.

Paul's final operation was also a success, and shortly before he left the hospital for the last time, I was transferred from my electric bed to a regular hospital bed. With considerable effort and Paul's encouragement I managed to turn myself over in bed for the first time since being wounded, and I grinned proudly at my achievement while Paul centered me on the mattress. From that day forward I was able to sleep more or less regularly, and my newly found ability to turn over in bed began the healing of my bed sores.

On the day that Paul was scheduled to check out of the hospital, I was wheeled back to my room from a postoperative evaluation and pushed over to my bunk, where I waited for the corpsmen to help me back into bed. To my surprise, Paul dismissed them and announced that he had a parting gift for me. He then wheeled to the foot of the bed, hoisted himself onto the mattress, and grabbed me by my pajama top.

"It is time, Lew," he said, "for you to learn to do this on your own." As I got his drift, I pushed downward on the armrests of the chair while he pulled me up by my armpits.

As we fell over into the middle of the bed in a jumble of stumps, Paul collected himself and climbed back into his own chair. When I realized that I had gotten into bed more or less on my own, I was elated, and Paul, flushed with success and laughing raucously, made me practice the exercise on my own several more times before he was satisfied. I lay in bed gasping with exhaustion and excitement at the end of my lesson, but I knew I had made another great stride toward independence and could hardly wait to call Toddy and tell her the good news. When Kathy arrived to take Paul home to their apartment in nearby New Jersey, we shook hands, and I thanked him for his help. Words were a totally insufficient means of communicating my appreciation for all that he had done for me, and Kathy looked away as her husband and I embraced. I knew that Toddy and I would be seeing a lot more of Paul and Kathy Barents, and I was grateful that he had been there to show me the way.

=== ☆ ===

After I learned to get in and out of bed on my own, it quickly became obvious that I needed to learn how to push myself in the wheelchair. When Cabot was told that I could transfer from bed to chair without help, he instructed the SOQ 12 staff to stop helping me around the ward, and I sulked in my room for several days rather than venture out on my own. I also complained to the nurses and corpsmen that there was no way I could navigate the bulky wooden chair I had originally been provided. Rather than argue the point, they replaced the ancient model with a standard folding chair and continued to ignore my calls for help. When I finally decided to strike out on my own, it took me fifteen minutes to propel myself the length of the hall and back.

The staff and some of the more mobile patients gathered around the nurses' station ignored me as I wheeled by them on my way down to the visitors' sitting room, but when I returned from my initial trip, exhausted and sweating freely, they clapped and whistled as if I had just run a four-minute mile. From then on I was able to move about more freely on the ward and visit with my neighbors, and the contact with the other patients lessened my self-preoccupation. I was amazed at how many young officers had been wounded and at the severity and extent of their injuries, but when I voiced my feelings, several of them bluntly told me that I needed to get down to the enlisted wards to see the real spoils of war. The Philadelphia Naval Hospital was the last duty station for most marines and sailors from the East Coast who had lost limbs in Vietnam, and in the late sixties business was booming.

As the Christmas holidays approached, Dr. Cabot wrote yet another order designed to increase my misery, and I soon found myself being carted off to physical therapy every morning and occupational therapy every afternoon. The PT staff was set up to help with the rehabilitation of lower-extremity amputees, and the OT staff performed the same function for young men who had upper-extremity losses. Some patients got to participate in both programs, and although we did not come close to being a majority, there were enough of us that our presence was not considered unusual by those familiar with the hospital.

It was a standard comment for patients to say to new arrivals that if you were feeling sorry for yourself, you could always look around and find someone whose wounds were more grotesque. In my case, that search was more demanding than it was for most, but just as many people came to question how I could have survived my injuries, so I was able to find a few hideously wounded men whose survival I could not believe. Double amputees were less common than single amputees, but it was not a unique event when a marine would arrive who had lost both his limbs or who had lost his eyesight in addition to an arm or leg.

I, like most who had experienced a devastating loss, was bitter and frustrated over what had happened to me, but from the start I was grateful that my genitalia had been spared. As a twenty-three-year-old male with a healthy and attractive young wife, I could not imagine a life without sex, and by the time I started on my rehabilitation, sex was very much on my mind. I did not know how I was going to accommodate my needs or those of my wife or, indeed, if she would still want me, but I knew that it was not going to be too much longer before I was going to find out.

On the morning I was first taken to physical therapy, I was apprehensive yet excited to be beginning a new phase of my hospitalization. PT and OT were located in a remote part of the hospital a considerable distance from SOQ 12, and I was pushed to the unit by one of the ward corpsmen, who returned for me later in the morning. Eventually I became strong enough to wheel the entire distance on my own, but for the first few weeks the corpsman gave me a push, or another more healthy mobile patient detailed to patient escort duty assisted me.

When we arrived, the daily routine was already in progress, and the unit was astir with activity. Some of the patients were working out or lifting weights on wooden tables along one wall, while others took turns walking between parallel bars on the wooden legs or with the braces that had been made for them in the nearby limb shop. The more accomplished patients practiced outside the parallel bars, and there was an oversize mirror in one corner of the unit in which they could observe themselves as they worked. There was also a set of stairs, an assortment of exercise machines, and a large mat on which the amputees learned how to stand after a fall. Several smaller rooms were connected to the main unit, and I could see that one contained a narrow exercise pool and another a whirlpool bath. With the exception of the attendants, virtually every man in the room had missing or badly damaged limbs.

When my corpsman and I entered the room, a redheaded woman in a blue smock rose from the desk where she was doing paperwork and came across the room to greet us.

"My name is Commander Shaughnessey," she said, extending her right hand to grip my forearm, "and you must be Lieutenant Puller. I am in charge of physical therapy," she continued, "and we might as well get started."

Her grip on my arm was viselike, and in the next hour my suspicions were confirmed that this Irish firebrand was going to whip me into shape. That first morning was spent in assessing my condition and capabilities; but by the end of the period she had thoroughly exhausted me, and I wondered what the therapy was going to be like when I began to exercise in earnest. The next day we started doing bench presses with a wooden cane to which she could attach sandbags of varying weights; the most I could manage was three pounds on each end. She also had a form of isometric exercise in which I used different muscles to push against her arms, and when I was unable to budge her, she taunted me about not being able to beat a woman. When I first attempted to do push-ups, lying flat on one of the exercise tables, I was barely able to raise my chest to the point where my arms were fully extended, and she forced me to continue the effort until I could not move my chest from the surface of the table at all.

As a final insult, on our first full day of rehab, she had me placed on the exercise mat and then began a game of catch with a towel she had rolled up and taped. At first she tossed the towel directly to me in a slow, easy manner, and I could catch most of her throws without losing my balance and toppling over onto the mat. Gradually, however, she picked up the pace and increased the range until I was reaching wildly for every throw and, more often than not, winding up in a heap on the mat. I was furious that I could not throw the towel back at her as hard as she threw it at me, and I tried desperately to smack her in the face. When she finally put a halt to my torment, I was soaked with sweat, humiliated, and ready to kill her.

"Balance and strength, Lieutenant. Balance and strength," she said. "We must increase your strength and improve your balance if we are ever going to get you up and walking."

Occupational therapy was far less demanding for me because compared with most of the upper-extremity amputees, the damage to my hands was minor. On my left hand I still had the thumb and half a forefinger, and on my right hand, though missing most of the thumb and little finger, I still had the middle digits. Combined, they amounted to almost a whole hand, and what I could not do with one hand, I could sometimes accomplish when I put them together. The OT unit was located in a smaller room adjacent to physical therapy and, like PT, was directed by a commissioned officer who was assisted by a staff largely comprised of enlisted personnel. In the winter of 1968 there were far fewer patients on the OT service than on PT because of the enemy's use of booby traps and land mines, triggered by men walking over them.

The nature of the therapy was different in OT since arms and hands perform much more delicate and complicated functions than legs and feet. In Shaughnessey's domain we did hard, demanding work that left us sore and exhausted, while in OT the tasks were often less physically demanding, but equally frustrating. It was grueling to try to lift the increasingly heavy weights that Shaughnessey added as my weight lifting progressed, but there were times in OT when I felt like screaming as I tried to learn how to button clothes or to thread a needle.

When I arrived for my first afternoon session, my attention was caught by a young man who had no hands playing Ping-Pong. In place of his hands were two hooks that he used to grasp the paddle, and I watched in awe as he moved the paddle from one hook to the other and practiced batting the ball with each device. There was also a wedding band on a chain around his neck, which bounced against his chest as he returned his opponent's serves, and I immediately felt encouraged to find another badly maimed serviceman who still had his marriage.

"Jim is one of our star pupils," said the therapist as she greeted me, "and you should see how quickly he can assemble a model airplane."

As I looked around, the room seemed more like a hobby shop than a rehabilitation unit, and my gaze settled on a table filled with models in various stages of completion. There was also an enormous loom, which I never saw in use the entire time I was on the service, and a pool table that was constantly in use. As in PT, all the patients had missing or disfigured limbs, although there were only two or three others in wheelchairs.

My first assignment was to write a sentence on a piece of paper. After trying out a number of new grips made necessary by my missing thumb, I squeezed the pen between my second and third fingers and wrote, "I love you, Toddy," in a scrawl I could barely recognize.

After a few days of double sessions of therapy, I began to feel as if I were on a never-ending carousel. If I was not doing push-ups for Shaughnessey or putting together jigsaw puzzles in OT, I was being shuffled back and forth between the two units or waiting for a pusher from patient escort. It was probably good that I was almost too busy to have time to think, but I resented being so completely under the control of a network of doctors and nurses to whom I often felt I was nothing but another case study. When Cabot put me on a beer ration to try to increase my weight, I drank several cans a night and topped them off with prescribed sleeping pills. My resulting incoherence so alarmed the staff that the sleeping pills were discontinued; but I continued to drink the beer, and by Christmas I had added 5 pounds to my 60-pound frame. I had weighed almost 160 pounds when I entered the Marine Corps, and although I never came close to weighing that again, I still needed to gain another 40 pounds.

One day shortly before Christmas I received a letter from one of the men in my platoon. Corporal Morgan had been a quiet, almost intro-spective marine who had kept his distance from me while we served together. I did not know him well, but he had worked out satisfactorily as a fire-team leader in his squad and had shown leadership potential, and at Leslie's suggestion I had promoted him to squad leader just before I was wounded. As I opened his letter, I was excited to be hearing from one of my men but surprised that Morgan would be the first man to make contact with me.

In the first few paragraphs he brought me up-to-date on how the platoon was faring, who had been wounded since I left, and who had rotated back to the States. He then wrote that the third platoon would probably be spending Christmas in the Riviera and that it was a hell of a place to be spending any time, much less Christmas. In his closing paragraphs he described a recent night ambush in which the platoon had shot several Vietcong soldiers who, though badly wounded, had managed to drag themselves into a rice paddy under the cover of darkness. In the morning, when it was light, Morgan had followed their blood trails into the paddy and located the enemy soldiers. He wrote that he had finished them off with his rifle, trying to make up for all of the dead and wounded men that the third platoon had suffered, but that nobody could ever kill enough Vietcong to make up for that. As I finished the letter, I shuddered at the thought of Morgan's grisly act of atonement. I was back in the States, decompressing from the very hatred that motivated men like Morgan, but the killing and the maiming were still going on. I felt suddenly very guilty that I was no longer with my platoon, but I was glad that I was no longer Morgan's platoon leader.

On Christmas Day my father-in-law drove Toddy up from Fort Belvoir to be with me for a few hours while her mother watched the baby. It was the first time she had been separated from our son, and she was apprehensive about missing several feedings. I was frustrated that Lewpy seemed to require so much of her time when I craved attention of my own, and Toddy was faced with the impossible task of nursing an infant and simultaneously stroking a sick husband when the two of us were several hundred miles apart. Colonel Todd dropped his daughter off in my room, wished me a merry Christmas, and made up a story about running errands so that Toddy and I would have some time together.

When we were alone, she told me about the fulfillment of being a new mother and the joy of watching our son begin to develop. I made no attempt to hide my jealousy of Lewpy, and as I switched the subject to the progress I was making, it must have been apparent to her that our newborn son and I both were trying to overcome helplessness. Despite our mutual frustration and the strangeness of our situation, the afternoon went fairly smoothly. By the time Colonel Todd returned several hours later, the awkward halts of our early conversation had disappeared, and we were interrupting each other and laughing as we had early in our courtship. I could not believe that the time had passed so quickly, and as Toddy kissed me good-bye, I whispered to her to be certain to bring some contraception when she returned for a longer visit on New Year's. She squeezed my arm and told me there was no way I would get her pregnant so quickly this time. As she left my sickbed on our first Christmas together as an old married couple, she looked astonishingly gorgeous, and I was buoyed by the prospects of the upcoming end-of-year celebration.

The week between Christmas and New Year's seemed interminable, and because so many of the staff and patients were on leave, the hospital was half empty. I worked hard at OT and PT, which I had almost to myself, and the skeleton crew that remained on duty through the holidays was able to give me extra attention. Commander Shaughnessey taught me an exercise to strengthen my atrophied gluteal muscles by pretending that a coin was positioned between the cheeks of my buttocks and then trying to squeeze it, and as I concentrated on the exercise, I imagined Toddy doing the same thing. Within seconds I was forced to roll to my side to relieve the pressure in an area I was not even exercising, and Shaughnessey wryly noted that I was definitely making progress.

In response to a wire service article that had been run nationwide earlier in the month, I got a lot of mail from strangers that Christmas. One elementary school teacher in the Midwest had her entire class send me drawings and notes they had prepared for me in class, and I was touched by their kindness. Someone also sent Lewpy a garish red velvet Santa suit, which cracked up the remaining patients and gave visitors a subject to focus on when first confronted with my appearance. Finally, there was a short note and a Christmas card from Lieutenant Zier, who I was delighted to hear had rejoined our old unit.

"Thought you would like to see what passes for poetry among Marines," he wrote. "I heard this from one of the troops and pass it on as a comment on the times."

> *Jingle bells, shotgun shells,*
> *VC in the grass,*
> *Merry Christmas, Uncle Charlie,*
> *Shoot you in the ass.*

I saved the letter and poem for his wife, Linde, who was working at the Vietnamese Embassy in Washington and who had become friends with Toddy after John and I had become close in Vietnam. The ward staff decorated my room that Christmas with cards from well-wishers and the drawings my adoptive class had sent. I also received a book inscribed anonymously: "To Lewis, with velvet love." Although we never learned the identity of the mysterious donor, Toddy questioned me for months about forgotten liaisons.

Our plan for New Year's was for the Todds, Toddy, and Lewpy to drive up from Fort Belvoir on New Year's Eve morning and check into a motel near the hospital. That way Toddy could spend the afternoon with me, go back to the motel to eat and to nurse the baby, and return to the hospital for the evening. When SOQ 12 learned what we were up to a couple of days before New Year's Eve, our simple little plan began to take on a life and complexity of its own. I gave my corpsmen fifty dollars for wines, including sherry, and by the beginning of the holiday, there was enough alcohol in my closet to intoxicate an army. I had instructed the corpsmen to buy only wines because I knew that in my debilitated condition I could not handle anything stronger, but I was surprised at the care they put into the assignment. There was a variety of good white and red wines, a nutty sherry to get us started in the afternoon, and a fine bold port to cap the evening. Although McMonagle was no longer assigned to me, I began to sense his fine hand in the selection of wines, and by New Year's Eve I realized that I was buying for more palates than just Toddy's and mine.

A decorating committee was also formed, and by the time the Todds arrived, the room had been festooned with streamers, balloons, party hats, and noisemakers. I thought that I detected a look of disapproval on Colonel Todd's face as he surveyed the decorations, but he made no comment and soon departed. Our little celebration was the nearest thing to a real party since before Vietnam, and Toddy wasted no time in joining in my mood. We toasted each other with the sherry, and after several glasses of early-afternoon tippling, she moved from the chair to my bed. The staff had been alerted that my door was to remain closed, and although Toddy was nervous about being interrupted, our need for each other gradually prevailed over her inhibitions. At first we touched each other tentatively, but when she sensed that I was not as fragile as I seemed and I realized that I could still perform, we forsook caution and made love with the eagerness of young lovers who had been apart for half a year.

Later in the afternoon, after we had opened the door, other patients and staff began dropping by, and the word quickly spread that there was a party on SOQ 12. Someone commandeered the ward's portable ice dispenser, and it was hidden in the closet with the booze supply and used to chill wine bottles. Toddy went back to the motel to have dinner and feed the baby, and when she returned, McMonagle had come over from his new assignment to sample his wine selection. After a few good-natured toasts from our visitors and some heavy-handed allusions to what was assumed to have happened behind our closed door, we got rid of our guests and picked up where we had left off. By the time midnight came, Toddy had me feeling like a man when there was little else I had been feeling manly about, and we reveled in our reacquired intimacy and my heightened image of myself.

My twin sister, Martha, and her fiancé, Mike, called at the stroke of twelve to wish us a happy New Year and tell us of their marriage plans, and I, flushed with wine and awe at my newly found stamina, embarrassed Toddy by bragging about the day's events. When we had finished our phone conversation, Toddy reminded me that a marine acquaintance of ours who had been wounded in Vietnam had managed to get his wife pregnant while he was immobilized in a full body cast. Her reproof had no effect on my soaring spirits, and when Colonel Todd returned for his daughter, I clapped him on the back and thanked him for giving me Toddy.

On New Year's morning, Toddy came to say good-bye and let me see our son before returning to Fort Belvoir with her parents. Lewpy did not look much different to me from the way he had when I first saw him, but Toddy proudly pointed out the signs of growth she considered especially significant. The Todds wanted to get started before the holiday traffic became heavy, so our visit was a brief one, and I, with a hangover from too much after-dinner port, did not try to alter their plans. I had reopened a bed sore on my spine during our lovemaking the previous day, and though it was a minor price to pay for my overenthusiasm, Toddy smiled sheepishly when I told her of the damage her eagerness had caused. As we parted, she told me that she was going to begin making arrangements to move up to Philadelphia, and I resolved to work harder at therapy so that I could hasten my change in status to outpatient. I knew that the hospital would become more bearable if I could spend my nights with my wife and baby, and as I saw them to the door, I felt blessed to have a family.

I worked hard at my rehabilitation and gradually began to get stronger. One day at PT, as I was straining against the exercise table in the push-up position, I surprised myself by pushing my entire body into the air, where I hung suspended for a second with only my hands touching the table. I collapsed onto the table almost immediately; but my nosedive was the result of lack of balance rather than lack of strength, and an excited Commander Shaughnessey hurried over to the table to congratulate me on having just completed my first real push-up. I was also getting to the point where I could hold my own against Shaughnessey in arm wrestling, and I almost drooled at the prospect of being able to slam her knuckles onto the tabletop where she had beaten me so many times. Later in that week, after a particularly exhausting workout, I daydreamed absentmindedly about moving into an apartment with my wife, while the blue-bathrobed pusher from patient escort wheeled me back to my room.

When we had gotten about halfway back to the ward, he suddenly exclaimed, "You don't remember me, do you, Lieutenant?" and I turned in my chair to look him in the face.

It was Higgins, the same marine who had stood up in the firefight in the Riviera the time we were mortared. He told me that he was being treated on the neuropsychiatric service for the head wound he had suffered, but our conversation was strained and surreal. I sensed that he blamed me in some way for his situation, and I was uncomfortable because he was now pushing me, whereas I had formerly had the upper hand in our dealings. When I called the neuropsychiatric service later in my stay to check on his progress, I was told that he had been medically boarded out of the service, and I never saw him again.

In the course of my hospitalization several other enlisted patients who had been in my company in Vietnam were admitted, including one who had been in my platoon, but none affected me as strongly as Higgins in our brief encounter. My discomfort may have been caused by the strange way he acted in not identifying himself when he first came for me or by my failure to recognize him, but I believe it was caused by our reversal of roles as much as by anything. That same reversal of roles carried over into every other aspect of my hospitalization and was at times maddening. In Vietnam I had had the power of a god, with lightning and thunder only as far away as the nearest artillery battery. My commands may have been questioned, but they were always followed; and although I came to despise the life-and-death decisions I was forced to make, I had learned to make them professionally and competently.

All that was taken from me at the moment I was wounded, and it was difficult to adjust to being totally powerless. Many times I struck out blindly and irrationally at the corpsmen and nurses who were trying to help me, and it only increased my frustration that in my weakened state I was unable to inflict any damage on them. I now had to ask for everything, and it was damnably difficult to maintain a self-image when I was still soiling my bed.

======= ☆ =======

Shortly after New Year's I also had the first of many identical dreams. In it I was back in Vietnam, and my platoon and I were preparing for a combat mission. As I gathered up my gear for the engagement, I could not find some of the equipment I needed: an ammunition clip, some socks, or a helmet. The particular lost item varied with the dream and was not nearly as important as the life-or-death situation we would be facing shortly, but frustration over its loss rather than apprehension of impending danger was the dominant emotion associated with the early part of the dream. The middle sequence was hazy, but as the dream ended, we had engaged a unit of enemy soldiers, and I had become separated from my men. The soldiers chased me through the surrounding area, and as they closed in on me, I awoke, covered with perspiration and certain that I had barely avoided that last look into my soul that surely will precede my death.

I have had the dream many times since it first roiled up from my subconscious in the winter of 1969, and each time it has been as terrifying as if I were experiencing it for the first time. I am able to see now that the dream is a reenactment and playing out of the events leading up to my wounding, but my understanding of the dream's origins does not ease the terror associated with it. In fact, it serves only to remind me anew that had I chosen to confront the enemy on that now-distant battlefield where I almost died, I would perhaps have come to know myself better or to have proved myself my father's son.

=== ☆ ===

For the first weeks of January I was afforded a measure of privacy that was rare for SOQ 12, since Paul Barents had been discharged and I had not yet been assigned a new roommate. As a consequence, Toddy and I could be alone in my room when she was able to come up from Fort Belvoir. Our time together was hurried because she made mostly day trips and had to get back in time to feed Lewpy, but if too brief, it was at least put to good use. It got to be a joke on the ward that the Pullers were again behind closed doors; but we really had no choice, and the furtive element of our lovemaking actually seemed to kindle our reborn passion.

One day Linde Zier took a day off from her job at the South Vietnamese Embassy and drove Toddy up for a visit. I liked her immediately and was delighted to see that she and Toddy had struck up such a good relationship. We all got a chuckle from John's Christmas poem, which I shared with the women, and when it came time for them to leave, Linde promised to get us a case of scotch through the embassy. The next time I saw her she delivered twelve imperial quarts of Johnnie Walker Black Label, and until early summer, when it ran out, I indulged myself with the expensive scotch.

=== ☆ ===

By mid-January I had gotten to the point at PT where I could do push-ups in sequences, and Shaughnessey continued to drive me with her usual refrain of "Balance and strength, Lieutenant, balance and strength." I also began to notice for the first time that there was an ebb and flow of patients both at PT and OT and on the wards. Many of the patients who were just getting back on their feet when I arrived two months earlier had been discharged or were preparing for physical evaluation boards prior to discharge, although there was no lack of newly wounded men to take their places.

From what I could see, it seemed that the average patient stayed in the hospital from four to six months, and I decided early on that I would be ready for discharge by the end of the summer. I knew that I had been wounded more severely than most of the people around me, and with typical youthful naiveté I decided that I could be patient and give Uncle Sam another eight months.

I was transferred in mid-January to the hand service, where I was placed in the care of a brilliant and profane young surgeon named Sandzen. After he had studied my hands for several minutes without comment at our first meeting in his clinic, he suddenly asked me if I liked women. I had been prepared to answer a series of questions on the degree of use of my hands, and caught off guard, I stammered something about liking them so well that I had married one.

"Good," he replied, "because I am going to restore your hands to the point that you can do everything with your wife that you could do before."

I knew exactly what he meant, but I did not know whether to rebuke him for being a dirty old man or hug him for addressing directly an unstated concern that was much on my mind. When, later in our conversation, he told me that the restoration of my hands would take a year to eighteen months and numerous operations, I was incredulous, but as I later thought about our meeting, his words seemed to make sense. I would be trying to learn to walk while having my hands repaired, and since I was going to have to get about on crutches if at all, each hand operation was going to cause several weeks or months of downtime from my effort to learn to walk.

I had hardly had time to absorb the news that my length of hospitalization was going to be more prolonged than I had thought when more bad news arrived. SOQ 12 had a new patient, a badly burned lieutenant who had crash-landed a helicopter with a defective tail rotor while he was in flight training in Pensacola, Florida. The chopper had burst into flames on impact, killing one of the crew members and leaving Lieutenant Jim Crotty with legs that resembled charred beef.

I got the word that he was to be my roommate about five minutes before he was wheeled into my room, delirious from pain and Dilaudid injections and reeking of infected dying flesh. I knew immediately how Paul Barents had felt the day I entered his life, and as I watched the nurses and corpsmen maneuver Jim's bed into the area that Paul had occupied, I also knew that I would never again be able to make love to my wife on SOQ 12.

If Jim had any idea of who I was or even that he had a roommate, he kept it a well-concealed secret for the first several days we lived together. For the most part I watched him sleep and take injections of Dilaudid, a painkiller several times as powerful as morphine. I didn't have a clue to what he would be like as a roommate when he was no longer consumed with pain, although I did know almost immediately that if he did not start smelling better, I was going to have to go back on morphine. A fan was installed on his side of the room that blew warm air over some sort of scented crystals to disguise the smell, but the only satisfactory way to deal with the problem was to leave the room.

Having learned my lesson in my own dealings with Paul, I did not attempt to force conversation with Jim, and for several days he seemed to communicate only by grunts, groans, and bowel sounds. As I watched him, I began to realize how pain forces a man to focus on himself, often to the exclusion of the things that he holds most dear, and I realized how difficult it had been for Toddy to go through the healing process with me.

On the fourth day of our new arrangement I received a visit from a saleswoman for Great Books, who came because McMonagle, as a joke, had filled out in my name and mailed in an ad for a free art reproduction. In order to receive my free painting, I had to listen to her sales pitch. When she arrived at our hospital room, Jim was flying high on Dilaudid. The poor woman was aghast at Jim's odor and my appearance, and since I had no intention of buying her product, I was not the least bit comforting as she began her spiel. To her credit, she managed to get through her delivery without faltering too badly, but when she concluded by saying that ownership of the Great Books was tantamount to four years at a first-rate college, Jim gave a loud Bronx cheer. I was as startled as the saleswoman since Jim had not even appeared to be listening, and when he next pulled himself to a sitting position and announced that I would be a fool to fall for such a pitch, the saleswoman began to pack her props. As she left our room, Jim and I dissolved in laughter. The ice had been broken, and from that day forward, Jim Crotty and I had no trouble communicating with each other. As it turned out, we both had been liberal arts majors at college, and we spent the rest of the morning doing a postmortem on the poor saleswoman's mispronunciations of her subject matter.

=== ☆ ===

Shortly after Jim became my roommate, Toddy managed to move to Philadelphia. She packed a suitcase and a portable crib into our VW and, with Lewpy in the backseat, drove to the Philadelphia Naval Base, where she was temporarily lodged in a one-bedroom attic flat. For ten days she slept on a lumpy bed, cooked on a hot plate, and tried to get by with a semifunctioning toilet. She made arrangements for Lewpy at the base nursery and visited me every chance she got, but the thought that sustained us both for that time was her move into an apartment two floors below that would make my coming home a reality.

When the day arrived, I had surprise visitors in the morning just as I was scheduled to begin subsisting out from the hospital. Jeff Steinhoff, the fraternity brother who had visited me earlier, came up from Washington with Dave Ware, another fraternity brother with whom I had also gone to high school. Jeff and Dave caught me just as we were leaving the hospital, and I was so anxious to make good my escape that we paused just long enough to instruct them to follow us in their car to our new apartment. As I got into our car, it occurred to me that I was breathing fresh air for the first time in three months. It was also the first time in more than six months that I had been in a car, and the initial experience of transferring from a wheelchair to a car required all my strength. Years later I learned from Jeff that Dave Ware, who had not seen me since before my wounding, had cried for most of the way to our apartment.

When we arrived, Jeff and Dave carried me up the steps in my wheelchair to our new digs on the second floor. They then moved the Spartan government furniture down from the attic, and after setting up the bed and depositing me, they arranged the other furnishings as Toddy directed. Someone broke out a six-pack of beer, and for the rest of the visit Dave and Jeff were so busy arranging furniture and admiring Lewpy that neither of them had time to become preoccupied with me. I was exhausted from so much activity, and after a decent interval they sensed my weariness and departed. I thought I noticed an unfamiliar tightness in Dave's smile as he bade us good-bye, but at the time I did not give it much thought. I came to know that look well as I reestablished contact with my old chums later, but for now I was touched to have seen an old friend with whom I had played high school football, ridden motorcycles, and chased girls.

After they had gone, Toddy sat on the bed beside me and cradled Lewpy in her arms. The three of us were finally alone, and as I reached for her hand, conversation seemed completely unnecessary. I did not know how I was going to get back down the steps on Monday morning for my first day on outpatient status at the hospital, but then again I didn't really care.

For the next six weeks we settled into a pattern that was as close to normal as we could manage. The Marine Corps had promised us the ground-floor apartment just below us when it became available the first of March, and in the meantime, the captain who had the other apartment on the second floor carried me down to our car in the mornings and back up at the end of my day at the hospital. Toddy did the driving back and forth to the hospital, and we quickly learned to synchronize our departures and arrivals so that we would be ready when Captain Dick Morey left for and returned from work. The commanding general of the base also gave us a phone number that we could use to summon help when we got stranded, and although the arrangement was not ideal, it was far better than being in the hospital. When I first got home, I was unable to sit on a commode alone, and Toddy had to assist me with my most basic functions. Degrading though it was, we developed an intimacy rare in a couple who had been together such a short time, and we learned together to diffuse our tensions with laughter rather than tears. For a while Toddy was wiping the rear ends of everyone in the apartment, and when I got to the point that I could go to the bathroom unattended, it was a close question as to who was more thankful.

At the hospital I kept my gear in Jim's room and used SOQ 12 as a base of operations for my clinic visits and therapies. I talked Dr. Sandzen into releasing me from occupational therapy since I was able to perform most of the tasks that were taught there, but I also doubled up on physical therapy and rapidly gained stamina. On the strength of Toddy's cooking and tender loving care I put on another fifteen pounds and got to the point where I could do fifty push-ups without stopping or becoming winded. After one weight-lifting session during which I had vastly exceeded my personal best, I even boasted to Commander Shaughnessey that I could probably bench-press her if she didn't start giving me a little more respect. She shook her head knowingly and told me that it was just about time to begin my prosthesis training.

"Balance and strength, Lieutenant, balance and strength," she said as she fired a rolled-up towel in my direction and, turning toward her logbook, scheduled me for my first visit to the limb and brace shop.

When I got back to Jim's room, I could hardly wait to tell him that I would have my legs before his lazy butt was out of bed, but he was in no shape to share my enthusiasm. He had almost lost his own legs to a persistent infection that had dogged him since the first day we met, and the constant debridement of his wounds and painstaking skin-grafting procedures had necessitated his remaining on narcotics for far too long. He was now being weaned from the Dilaudid, and his withdrawal symptoms were such that for several days I ventured into his room only long enough to assure myself that he was not dying.

One night in early February, as Toddy prepared Lewpy for bed and I scanned the newspaper for news of the war, our routine was interrupted by a hysterical phone call from Linde Zier. Toddy answered the phone, and after trying to calm Linde down for several minutes, she handed the receiver to me. John had been seriously wounded by a land mine, and Linde had just received word that he was going to be medevacked to the Philadelphia Naval Hospital. He was not critical, but he had lost one leg, was in danger of losing the other, and had multiple shrapnel wounds to his upper extremities.

I tried to reassure Linde as best I could, and I repeated Toddy's invitation to Linde to stay with us after John arrived. All I could think of when we finished our conversation was that it must have been a hell of a large land mine to bring John Zier down. He had almost completed his time in the bush when he was wounded, and I was reminded that the first month and the last month in the field were the most dangerous times for infantrymen. Linde did not know where he had been wounded or any of the details, but I would have bet money that when it happened, he had just crossed the big rice paddy into the Riviera.

In the week before John's arrival at the hospital, I was fitted for my artificial legs at the limb and brace shop, located in a cluttered building adjacent to physical therapy. It was connected to the hospital by a ramp so that patients could more easily wheel over from therapy for adjustments or modifications. The shop was largely staffed by amputees, some veterans and some not, who had gravitated into the business as a result of their own needs, and they were as salty and profane a bunch of South Philadelphia rowdies as could be imagined. They showed no pity for the patients, and most of them were not above accepting gratuities in exchange for quicker or more efficient service.

My case was assigned to Eddie, a double amputee with a huge

potbelly and a booming voice, and when he leaned over from his workbench to introduce himself, I sensed that he was a man devoid of subtlety. "We are all out of Caucasian legs, Lieutenant," he began, "but if you don't mind, we can fit you with some nice Negro ones." His belly shook with laughter as if he were telling his little joke for the first time instead of the hundredth or five hundredth.

Despite his crudeness, Eddie knew his job, and in the next two hours I got a pretty good assessment of his plan for me. He first casted my left stump with plaster of paris so that he would have a mold from which to fashion a socket for the upper part of the prosthesis. Since I had no right stump, the procedures for my right prosthesis were more complicated. They required that Eddie make a mold of my lower torso that extended halfway to my armpits. When it had almost hardened, he cut it down the middle with a cast saw and I wriggled free. Eddie explained to me that when the upper part of the right prosthesis was completed, it would resemble a rigid corset with a hinge on the bottom to which my artificial leg would be attached. I could not imagine being comfortable, much less walking, with such a device, but I had no choice except to trust Eddie. He concluded our appointment by telling me to return in ten days for my training legs, or "stubbies," as they were known in the trade. The legs would be only about two feet long and would have no knees, but they would be more stable without the knee joints, which could be added later when I became accustomed to them.

Also, instead of having standard feet, my stubbies would be equipped with rockers on the bottom so that if I started to fall over backward, I could more easily catch my balance. The entire apparatus was almost too bizarre to be real; but I had seen other patients practicing on stubbies at PT, and while they looked like hideously deformed midgets, they were at least walking. When I left the limb and brace shop, I was tired from the strain of being fitted and covered with bits of plaster, but I was in an upbeat mood.

=== ☆ ===

My sister Martha and Mike Downs were getting married that weekend at Quantico Marine Base, and Toddy and I were going down to stay with her parents at nearby Fort Belvoir. I had been begging the doctors for weeks to let me go on this first trip away from the hospital, and in a moment of weakness Dr. Sandzen had consented. Our trip meant that I would not see John Zier for several days after he arrived, but I did not think that he would begrudge my wanting to see Mike and Martha get married. Besides, if John was going to be anything like the way Jim and I had been when we first were rotated up to SOQ 12, he would still be adjusting to his loss and would want to lick his wounds in solitude.

It was obvious that our Volkswagen would not hold the three of us plus my wheelchair and Lewpy's infant seat and assorted baby gear. To solve our problem, Toddy's younger brother had driven down from Princeton and exchanged his Pontiac for our smaller car, an arrangement we continued until we could buy a larger car. I rested on the backseat with Lewpy for most of the trip down while Toddy drove, and I quickly discovered that with my legs gone, I could get quite comfortable stretched out on the backseat of a car. There was a rehearsal dinner Friday night at the base officers' club, but it was small and intimate and was not too taxing for either of us.

Since the wedding was military, all the groomsmen were marine officers, with tours in Vietnam under their belts. During the dinner one of the groomsmen, a major with a degree from Harvard, suggested to me that I consider a run for political office as part of my future plans. I tried to brush aside his conversation as idle cocktail talk; but he persisted, and as he described the perspective he thought I could bring to national office, I found myself both flattered and fascinated. Toddy said nothing, but I could see that she was listening intently while Major Caulfield speculated on a future political campaign. Later, as we were driving back to Fort Belvoir, she brought the conversation up again, and while I could not even fathom the idea of a career in politics, I could tell that our future was very much on Toddy's mind.

The wedding was at four on Saturday afternoon, and we arrived in plenty of time to get me seated with Toddy's parents in the base chapel just ahead of the crowd. Aside from Mike's immediate family from Massachusetts and his groomsmen, most of the guests were family friends from Virginia who had known Martha and me since we were children. Many of them still referred to us out of habit as "the twins," and most of them had not seen me since before I left for Vietnam. For that reason the Todds and I had decided to leave the chapel just prior to the conclusion of the service so that we would not get caught in a crush of well-wishers. There would be plenty of time to talk at the wedding reception at the officers' club, and I did not want to create a bottleneck or upstage the wedding party outside the chapel.

As the bridesmaids took their places, they all looked splendid with their blue-clad military escorts, and I wished for a moment that I were capable of escorting Toddy down the aisle on my arm. Martha appeared radiant on our father's arm, and his medal-bedecked chest put to shame the meager, by comparison, decorations of every other uniformed man in the chapel. At the entrance to the chapel he turned to his daughter and told her that if she did not feel like going through with the ceremony, he could easily have it converted into a cocktail party, and she squeezed his hand silently as tears of joy brimmed in his eyes. As a concession to our mother, the service was conducted jointly by an Episcopal minister and a priest, but there was never any doubt that whatever children resulted from their marriage would be raised in their father's Catholic Church. The issue was a sore point with our mother; but it was readily acceptable to Martha and our father, and when Mother realized that she had no say, she abandoned her protest.

When we got to the club, the receiving line was just beginning to form and the first guests were trickling in. I got caught at the entrance to the ballroom trading chitchat with some early arrivals, and by the time I was able to excuse myself, the room was half full. Suddenly I was surrounded by a sea of outstretched hands, and as I tried to work my way across the room, I felt completely alienated from the family friends I had known for most of my life, who were now crowding in on me. As I was about to explode, Bev Williams, one of Martha's old boyfriends and my best boyhood friend, saw the expression on my face and ran interference for me until I found a safe corner.

Shaken, I downed several quick drinks and mechanically returned the greetings of the guests who continued to press in. When we had stayed long enough not to appear rude, I had Bev take me up to one of the bedrooms reserved for the wedding party, where I rested until Toddy could join us. Even then several well-meaning family friends sought me out, but the exhaustion I used as an excuse not to see them was real and was understandable to most. As I continued to drink, the emotion I had felt downstairs eased, but I had learned that I was not prepared to deal with social situations so quickly on the heels of my war and hospital experiences.

Later that evening, long after Mike and Martha had left for their honeymoon and the wedding guests had returned home, Toddy and I and a few other stragglers went down to the officers' club bar for sandwiches and a few rounds of drinks before returning to Fort Belvoir. As we sat at our table nursing our drinks and discussing the wedding, several captains who had instructed me in Basic School stopped by our table to let me know that if there was anything I needed, not to hesitate to look them up. I tried to thank them for their concern without appearing ungrateful, but I could not get over how much younger they looked than they had in Basic, now that we had shared the same war experience.

Later in the evening a colleague from Basic School, one of those who had been kept stateside to be a witness in a trial, came over to fill me in on what other members of our class were doing. As we chatted, he told me almost as an aside and without any change of inflection in his voice that Terry Pensoneau had been killed just before Christmas and that Ken Shelleman had been killed at the beginning of February. The casual revelation of their deaths so numbed me that I was able only to repeat their names and nod my head in acknowledgment. I could not believe that Terry, the gentle schoolteacher who had lent me his Glenn Yarborough albums when I was courting Toddy, was dead, or that Kenny Shelleman, the free spirit whose antics with his red Lincoln Continental and Lancer's wine we had all cheered at Basic School, was also gone. I drank as much as I could in the next two hours and left Harry Lee Hall on the day of my twin sister's wedding with tears streaming down my cheeks, dead drunk, and much in need of spiritual repair.

=== ☆ ===

When we returned to Philadelphia, John Zier had been assigned a room on SOQ 12, and as I had thought, he was not in much of a mood for company. The first time I entered his room, Linde was at his side, and he appeared to have been crying. I stayed only long enough to tell him that I was glad he had made it back alive and to let him know that I was available when he wanted to talk; but he was embarrassed that I had caught him with his guard down, and he could only manage a weak smile in response. He had lost his left leg above the knee, and the right one had a large section of muscle missing from the calf area. In addition, he had a nasty gash where his left arm met his torso, which in a smaller man probably would have severed the arm.

Despite his wounds, he still looked like a mountain lying there in his hospital bed, and I felt certain that he would make as full a recovery as possible. Linde followed me out of the room, far more composed than when we had last talked on the phone. She told me that she was just grateful to have him back at all, but I knew that it must have been particularly difficult for her, considering the wonderful athlete that John had been.

=== ☆ ===

Later that week I went back to the limb and brace shop to get my stubbies. Eddie was busy at his worktable when I wheeled in, and he motioned to me to pull my chair up to the parallel bars in the center of the room while he brought my legs over. They looked more like tree limbs than legs; but Eddie was proud of his work, and I did not comment as he placed them between the bars in front of my chair. For the right side he had me remove my shorts and put on a body sock before wiggling into the plastic bubble that was the top part of the prosthesis. When I had gotten it around my waist, he helped me fasten it to my body by two leather belts attached to the bubble. I then pulled myself to an upright position between the bars, and as the hinge connecting the bubble to the lower part of the device locked into place, I found myself standing for the first time in five months. Eddie then wrapped my left stump with an Ace bandage, guided the stump into the socket of the left stubby, and pulled my stump down into the socket by pulling the elastic bandage off the stump and through a small hole at the bottom of the socket.

When he finished, I was standing wobbily between the parallel bars, leaning heavily on them for support and soaked with perspiration. I was only eighteen inches from the floor, although the distance seemed more like ten feet. For the rest of that session I did nothing more than balance on the stubbies and point out to Eddie pressure points that needed sanding for a better fit. Once or twice I experimented with letting go of the parallel bars on either side of me, but each time I did so, I almost toppled over and quickly had to grab the bars to restore my balance.

When I sat down for the first time with the stubbies still in place, I was exhausted, and Eddie could see that I had had enough for one day. The stubbies stuck straight out from the seat of my chair like miniature battering rams, and I found out later that I could use them very effectively as such in wheeling through swinging doors without slowing my speed.

When we were finished, I wore the stubbies back to Jim's room in order to get used to wearing them while seated in the chair. They added a good twenty pounds to my weight, and my arms were aching by the time I pulled into the room; but the look on Jim's face was worth the effort. He had finally kicked his narcotics dependency but said he felt he was still hallucinating when he watched me take off my stubbies and store them for the weekend in his closet. On Monday morning I was to begin the next phase of my rehabilitation at PT by going to a session called stump rounds. For now I was in an optimistic mood and anxious to get going, although I had not yet taken a single step with my new legs.

=== ☆ ===

Stump rounds were held at nine o'clock on Monday mornings at PT and were supposed to be mandatory for all patients undergoing prosthesis training. Most patients complied because they were anxious to complete their rehabilitation and get discharged, but there were always a rowdy few who for one reason or another were consistently absent without leave. Some got into trouble on weekends and could not make it back by Monday morning, and some took the attitude that the hospital and by extension the government could not hurt them any worse than they already had and that missing rounds was a way of thumbing one's nose at authority. "What are you going to do, send me to Vietnam?" was a frequent refrain heard from belligerent young men whose lives had been shattered. The doctors, therapists, and staff had no answer, and I began to take a perverse delight in seeing some well-educated young doctor tongue-tied by a semiliterate marine or sailor.

For my first attendance at stump rounds, I stopped by Jim's room just long enough to pick up my legs, which I carried down to the session balanced on my footrests and leaning against the seat of my wheelchair. I was a few minutes late arriving, as were a good many other patients, but the staff ignored our tardiness. There was a row of chairs alongside the parallel bars and they were occupied by a representative from the limb and brace shop, Commander Shaughnessey, and a doctor who seemed to be in charge.

The patients sat, stood, or leaned on crutches in a large semicircle at the opposite side of the bars, and as their names were called, they came forward and performed for the staff. The more surefooted among them, usually men who were missing only one leg or who were fairly far along in their rehabilitation, paced up and down outside the bars, while the staff suggested gait corrections or adjustments to their prostheses. The bilateral amputees and the more newly injured usually walked between the parallel bars and leaned heavily on them for support. Altogether there were about fifty patients, about half of them, like myself, in wheelchairs. As each patient was checked off the list, he either left the room or stayed to work on some aspect of his training, and the routine moved fairly rapidly.

It was the first time I had seen the in-training amputee population of the hospital assembled in one place, and as I waited for my name to be called and watched the men pop wheelies and ignore the staff, I was fascinated by the variety of injuries present. The most common disability was an above-the-knee or a below-the-knee amputation, but there were also multiple amputations involving upper and lower limbs. The prostheses used by the patients were in various stages of completion and ranged from stubbies similar to mine to completely well-formed, shiny pink or brown plastic limbs.

Several of the patients who were in wheelchairs had graffiti scrawled across the backs of their chairs, and I saw one that read "Another project sponsored by your federal tax dollar" and another that said, "The Marine Corps builds stumps." I was surprised that such comments would be tolerated in a military hospital, but no one seemed to give them as much as a second look, since they were considered a form of speech protected by the First Amendment to the Constitution.

When my name was called, I wheeled over to the parallel bars expecting that Commander Shaughnessey would help me put on my legs. Instead she conferred with the limb and brace shop representative, made some notes on her clipboard, and told me to return for some one-on-one therapy after rounds were completed. I was relieved not to have to try out the stubbies in front of everyone, but I also realized that Shaughnessey was about to begin cracking the whip.

After rounds, Shaughnessey came over to the exercise table where I was lifting weights and told me that my regimen was going to be twice as demanding now because in addition to weight lifting, I was going to learn how to walk. She motioned for me to follow her over to the parallel bars, and as Eddie had done earlier, she placed my stubbies between the bars where I could reach them. I managed to wiggle into the right prosthesis using the same technique as before, but when I waited for her to begin wrapping my left stump, she handed me the elastic bandage and told me that there was no point in her doing it for me.

After several attempts I managed to don the left stubby while balancing on the right one, and when I had finished, I leaned against the bars and caught my breath. Shaughnessey then demonstrated the proper gait for my situation, and I had to restrain myself from laughing as she thrust her pelvis forward to simulate what I would need to do in order to start my gait. When I tried it, the right stubby moved forward about four inches. As it came to rest, I advanced the left stubby by pushing forward with my left stump. I then moved my hands forward on the parallel bars and repeated the process; after an agonizing ten minutes I had worked my way the length of the bars. I was able to reverse my direction by moving my hands to the opposite bars they had been gripping and then lifting and rotating my body. After I had completed the turn, I retraced my steps and lowered myself wearily into my wheelchair.

Shaughnessey tossed me a towel for my dripping face and congratulated me on my first steps, but I knew that I had a long way to go. I had seen several bilateral above-the-knee amputees walking without crutches or canes shortly after they were fitted with stubbies, and their progress was inspiring. On the other hand, I had never seen anyone use my type and combination of prostheses with anything approaching a normal gait, and I could not imagine trying to walk without the help of the parallel bars. Real-world situations, I knew, did not have parallel bars, nor would they have firm, flat surfaces. Shaughnessey could read the self-doubt on my face, but rather than patronize me, she announced that she would have some crutches shortened for me after I had mastered the parallel bars.

As I headed back to my room, I was proud of myself for having taken my first steps and anxious to tell Toddy about the experience. I had no idea what was going to happen a month or two down the road, when knees would be added to my legs. As I wheeled along, a refrain from a popular song by the Rooftop Singers stuck in my mind, and I sang it several times while a couple of startled visitors stepped aside for me to pass by. "Ev'rybody's talkin' 'bout a new way o' walkin' . . . baby, let your hair hang down." It seemed appropriate, and I decided to adopt it as my theme song while I was learning to walk.

=== ☆ ===

In early March the first-floor apartment below us became available, and we moved downstairs. There were five or six steps leading up to the quarters, but the Marine Corps built a ramp for my wheelchair, which Toddy and I were able to negotiate without help from a third party. We were both greatly relieved to gain an added measure of independence, as was the poor marine captain who had dutifully carried me up and down several flights of steps for the previous six weeks. Toddy was happy to have a more or less permanent place to call home, and as she began fixing up the baby's room and decorating the rest of the apartment, we both felt some sanity returning to our lives.

The first time that my parents came to visit us after my move out of the hospital, we all were amazed to discover that by coincidence we were living in the same apartment that they had moved into thirty years earlier as newlyweds. At that time Marine Corps officer basic training was given in Philadelphia rather than Quantico, and my father, an instructor in the school, was beginning to build his reputation as a young man who was going places in the Marine Corps. My future was going to have to take a different direction, but that did not prevent us from enjoying my parents' sense of déjà vu when they found themselves back in the apartment where their marriage had started.

It was also particularly heartwarming to watch Father play with his grandson that weekend and to share his pleasure each time that the baby would reach out to grasp his extended finger. My father was in many ways a simple man with simple needs, but high on the list of his priorities was his often-stated wish to see the Puller name perpetuated. Young Lewis was the last of his bloodline, and Toddy and I were deeply moved to see this wonderful old man become a witness to his namesake's emerging sense of self.

=== ☆ ===

As the harshness of winter gave over to spring in the early months of 1969, the quality of life in our family became more endurable. I spent my days at the hospital undergoing therapy and came home every evening much like any other man working at a normal job. We socialized with the patients who were able to leave the hospital and with the other marine families in our apartment building, with the nearby officers' club a frequent meeting place and the principal watering hole for both groups. We rarely discussed the war or the divisiveness that it had engendered in the country, but as I read the papers and watched the evening news on television, I began to think that something was going terribly wrong.

For the previous four months I had been almost totally helpless, consumed with pain, my mind blurred by drugs. Now that my pain was manageable, I became less self-absorbed and began to focus on external realities, and I was discomforted by my perceptions. It seemed that the entire country was at odds over Vietnam, and as the debate raged, students demonstrated, and politicians railed, I became more and more confused. Had I not been wounded, I would still be putting my life on the line in defense of a foreign policy that many were now calling misguided or even immoral, and if they were correct, my sacrifice and the sacrifices of my fellow servicemen were worthless. It was small wonder, then, that as America's opinion of the war began to shift, those of us who had been shattered by an involvement more real than intellectual had difficulty giving voice to our feelings or otherwise participating in the dialogue.

A month after I began living out of the hospital, Jim Crotty got a new roommate, and the seemingly endless cycle of admissions and discharges of war casualties was repeated. When I first met Lieutenant (jg) Bob Kerrey, he had just been assigned the bed space I had formerly occupied, and the doctors were evaluating his injured right leg to determine the level at which it would be amputated. Bob, who had been a navy Seal team leader in Vietnam, was wounded by an enemy grenade in a firefight in which his team had destroyed a North Vietnamese Army squad. He had continued to lead his men for several hours despite his injuries, and the scuttlebutt in the hospital had it that he was about to be recommended for the Medal of Honor.

The morning I entered my old room and discovered Bob, he was listening to an Aretha Franklin tape played several decibels above what the ward rules allowed, and he was trying to take pictures of his mangled leg with an Instamatic camera. He seemed oblivious of pain, and after I introduced myself, he handed me the camera and asked me to snap a few pictures of his leg for the American Legion folks back in his home state of Nebraska. Jim and I exchanged glances, but neither of us could tell if Bob was delirious or just marching to the beat of a different drum. I took the pictures while Bob joined Aretha in singing "Respect," and I sensed immediately that life on SOQ 12 was about to undergo a rejuvenation.

Within days Bob was taken to the operating room, and when he returned, his leg had been removed at mid-calf. During the first few days after the amputation he fought taking the kind of pain shots for which Jim and I had begged, and his stoicism, though unnerving, was a source of amazement to all. Jim and I had learned how to dull the pain with narcotics, and though Bob's wounds were not as severe as mine or his pain as great as Jim's, we wanted to see him more comfortable and to have our view confirmed that morphine was indispensable to recovery. Instead Bob asked for a fungo bat with which to beat back the phantom pains in his missing limb, and Jim and I were left to conclude sheepishly that some people had higher tolerances to pain than others.

During the time that Bob Kerrey was recovering from his surgery, John Zier was also beginning to mend. For several weeks after he arrived on the ward, he had run a high fever that was finally diagnosed and treated as a rare malarial strain. At first the doctors had thought that the fever was an infection from his injuries, and by the time the mystery was solved John had taken on the coloring of the enemy soldiers he had been fighting for most of the previous year. We chided him about his resemblance to his North Vietnamese cousins, and his response was always to hurl articles from his nightstand and disclaim any kinship with "those yellow bastards."

After his malaria was brought under control and he became well enough to roll about SOQ 12 in his wheelchair, the kidding came to an abrupt halt. With his massive chest and arms, John looked like a gorilla on a tricycle, and while the initial reaction to meeting him in the hall was to burst into laughter, most of us were wise enough to save our mirth until we were safely out of sight. Linde Zier, in the meantime, was not able to get base housing, but she took an apartment just across the river in New Jersey, and she spent many nights with Toddy and me while she was getting settled in. We were never able to relieve completely the anguish she felt for John, but having people around with whom she could commiserate was healthy for all of us and disastrous to my scotch supply.

═══ ☆ ═══

In PT Shaughnessey continued to ride herd on me, and when I warned her that Zier and Kerrey would soon be reinforcing me, she shrugged her shoulders and worked me harder. For several weeks I practiced walking up and down between the parallel bars, raising and lowering myself from a seated position and trying to balance without holding on to the bars. I also tried to wear the prostheses for increasingly longer periods of time, but they were so heavy and cumbersome that it was always a relief to take them off. In many ways I had more freedom of movement without the legs than with them, and I often wondered if there was going to be any payoff to the rigors I was undergoing.

One day when I arrived at therapy, Shaughnessey was waiting with my new crutches. They were similar to standard under-armpit support crutches except that they had been designed for a four-and-a-half-foot-tall person. As we adjusted them to my exact height, she ignored my comments about donating the crutches to the circus after I got regular-length legs, but she stood close to me as I attempted to take my first steps outside the bars. I was amazed at how much more difficult it was to swing each leg forward without the support and stability of the parallel bars, and as with my initial venture between the bars, I managed only a very short walk my first day on crutches.

I was tired and sore by the time I had crossed the room and returned, and as I lowered myself into my wheelchair, I heard a familiar refrain from Commander Shaughnessey, "Balance and strength, Lieutenant, balance and strength." As usual, my first impulse was to reach out and strangle her, but my hands were so sore from gripping the crutches that I would never have been able to complete the crime.

After several days of walking with my new crutches, it became apparent that the injuries to my hands were going to interfere seriously with my walking. When I practiced between the bars, I was able to push against the rails without gripping, and I could also rest my hands each time I took a step forward by simply removing my hands from the rails and bringing them back down as my step was completed. With the crutches, it was necessary to maintain a grip on the handles at all times, and when I could no longer maintain the grip, I could no longer walk. Shaughnessey sensed that I was discouraged, but she did not want to modify the handles on my crutches until the surgery on my hands was completed. We explained the problem to Dr. Sandzen, who had been waiting for me to gain as much strength as possible before going to work on me, and by late April he scheduled me for the first of a half dozen operations on my hands.

Sandzen decided to start with the least complicated procedure and to work on only one hand at a time so that I would not be completely helpless. I checked back into SOQ 12 with considerable trepidation the day before the surgery was scheduled, although my fear of the surgeon's scalpel was eased by the knowledge that I would be an inpatient for only a few days. After my preoperative workup and a consultation with the anesthesiologist, Sandzen dropped by my room to discuss the operation and obtain my signature on the consent form.

Since there was so little remaining of my left hand, he did not anticipate an extended stay in the operating room. He explained that his purpose in operating was to restore as much function as possible to the hand and to give it a more cosmetic appearance. To that end he planned to remove as much scar tissue as possible, smooth and straighten the remaining bones in the hand, and bring the skin together so that there would be only one scar line. What remained of my forefinger was now S-shaped, and he explained to me that he would also strengthen the finger by inserting two steel pins, which could be removed when the hand had healed.

The surgery went smoothly, and when I was returned to SOQ 12, Toddy was waiting for me. For several days my hand throbbed as if it were on fire, but unlike Bob Kerrey, I demanded morphine every three or four hours as the previous injection wore off. Toddy told me that I raved deliriously about Vietnam and carried on animated conversations with my old platoon members; but I had done that after each of my earlier surgeries, and the ward staff had come to expect it. As the pain subsided, the morphine was replaced by Darvon, and when Sandzen realized that his surgery was going to have no untoward consequences, he allowed me to return home to bed rest.

Toddy took me home from the hospital armed with a supply of Darvon for pain and enough bandages to change my dressings until I returned to the hand clinic ten days later. I was instructed to keep the hand elevated, and we rigged a sling to the bedside lamp so that I would not lower my hand inadvertently while I slept. Once again I was rendered dependent on Toddy for most of my needs, but my bad humor notwithstanding, she repeatedly assured me that she would rather tend to me at home, where she could keep an eye on both me and the baby, than visit me in the hospital.

After I had begun to feel better and the swelling in my hand had partially subsided, she would place Lewpy on the bed beside me, and the three of us passed the time amusing each other and visiting with the other apartment dwellers who stopped in to chat. I was never able to overcome completely the dread that accompanied my loss of independence after each surgery; but Toddy realized that I was more comfortable calling on her for help than I was calling on strangers, and she made a special effort to bring me home as quickly as was safe after each of my reconstructions.

When I returned to the hand clinic to have the pins removed, I had expected that Sandzen would anesthetize me before beginning the procedure. Instead and to my horror, he took a pair of needle-nosed pliers from his medical kit, immobilized my hand between his own arm and side, and yanked the pins out as if he were withdrawing nails from a piece of wood. I was so surprised that I did not have time to protest, but there was no pain and only a few drops of blood oozing from the exit holes. As I studied my hand, he expressed his complete satisfaction with his handiwork, and when he began photographing the hand for his files, I had to admit that despite its strange resemblance to a lobster claw, it looked a good deal better than the misshapen appendage of three weeks earlier.

Dr. Sandzen decided to give me a month's rest before starting to work on my right hand, and I renewed my physical therapy a few days after he removed the pins. Shaughnessey realized that we were in a holding pattern with my more serious hand operation coming up, and we spent the month between operations doing maintenance work rather than try to make any real progress.

One weekend I decided that my stubbies needed something to make them more attractive, and I spent hours cutting paper roses and ivy leaves from several gardening magazines, which Toddy then laminated onto the legs. I reasoned that while the Marine Corps may not have promised me a rose garden, there was nothing to prevent me from enjoying flowers. When I showed up at stump rounds the following Monday, the doctors and staff decided to ignore the bouquets that adorned my stubbies, but the other patients cheered and whistled as I strutted my stuff. I never knew if the hospital authorities feared that I was making a political statement unbecoming an officer and a gentleman, but my wounded comrades, many of whom had had similar figures tattooed onto their bodies, loved it. It was always a mystery to me why the powers that be became upset when a patient returned from liberty with a new tattoo, while the horrible scars and mutilations incurred in battle went largely unquestioned.

===== ☆ =====

During the time that I was undergoing the restoration of my left hand, Bob Kerrey and John Zier had begun to enhance morale on SOQ 12. Kerrey, irrepressible to begin with, had a freer hand than most of the other patients because of his status as a war hero. When some of his antics began to outrage the staff, the rest of us urged him on. To monitor possible internal bleeding, he was on output/input status, which meant that all the fluids entering and exiting his body were checked. To counter what he considered a gross invasion of privacy, he stole a pair of forceps from the dressing cart, bought a bag of jelly beans, and began inserting different-colored beans into his bowel movements. The corpsman whose job it was to strain the fecal matter was incensed when he realized what Bob was up to, and he complained loudly that Lieutenant Kerrey was setting a poor example for the navy enlisted personnel for whom he should be a role model. When confronted by the head nurse, Bob threatened to encase his car keys in the offensive matter, and until the monitoring was halted, the ward made bets on what would pop up next in Bob Kerrey's stools.

Later in his stay he, Jim Crotty, and John Zier spent hours making airplane gliders that they then launched from their window on the twelfth floor into the parking lot below. At first the military police patrolling the lot returned the errant missiles on the incorrect assumption that they had fallen from the window. Eventually, however, when the trio began coating the wings of the wooden gliders with lighter fluid and lighting them prior to takeoff, they were threatened with courts-martial under the Uniform Code of Military Justice.

Many other patients behaved in similar fashion when they realized that their military service was over and that they were going to spend the rest of their lives crippled and set apart as a result of that service. Others like the lieutenant who had lost his legs and testicles became more militaristic rather than less so. In his case, that meant wearing his uniform around the hospital and parking his wheelchair next to the paymaster on payday to make certain that enlisted amputees did not receive their paychecks unless their hair was regulation length. I knew from the start that the Kerreys of this world had a far more healthy attitude than did the Goodmans, even if pain and suffering were the common denominators that motivated them both.

When Zier and Kerrey began attending physical therapy, Commander Shaughnessey did not know what to expect. Word of their exploits on SOQ 12 had spread throughout the hospital, and I had given Shaughnessey fair warning that they were coming. Both men, however, took their rehabilitation seriously and did not behave as outrageously as they did on the ward, where boredom often prompted excesses. Kerrey, who was missing just one leg below the knee, did not require extended therapy, and he made it clear from the beginning that he was only interested in getting the right prosthesis and then getting on with his life.

John Zier, on the other hand, was a problem. When he started his rehabilitation, his badly mangled right leg was in a cast that made it difficult for him to train with his left prosthesis. He was also so large that when he first began walking, several attendants paced nervously along with him, knowing full well that if he started to fall, it would require all their combined strength to right him. On the exercise table he was world class, and when he first started weight training, the rest of us stopped whatever we were doing and stared at him in awe. From the beginning he could lift more than any man who had ever undergone therapy with Shaughnessey, and he worked so diligently that by the end of his rehabilitation his upper body was a mass of bulging muscles. He was definitely Shaughnessey's star pupil, and although none of the rest of us had his musculature, John Zier motivated everyone to push himself harder.

One day the three of us returned to SOQ 12 from PT to discover that the ward had a new admission. Lieutenant Jackson Roark was a navy meteorologist who had been scheduled for admission to the psychiatric service for alcoholism. While waiting for his paperwork to clear, the navy had lodged him temporarily in the base bachelor officers' quarters, where his room was conveniently located just a stone's throw from one of the busiest bars on the base. Lieutenant Roark had promptly gone on a bender, attempted suicide by slashing his wrists, and then suffered massive brain damage when he passed out from loss of blood and fell against the sink in his room.

When Zier, Kerrey, and I first met him, he was confined to a wheelchair and unable to communicate except to utter a few words that related to his military occupational specialty. "Turbulence, turbulence" was all he could manage when he first saw John, and while Zier scratched his head and tried to come up with an appropriate rejoinder of his own, Kerrey and I burst into laughter. The fall that had cost Roark his speech also affected his ability to reason, and for the few weeks that he was a patient on SOQ 12, he often tried to propel his wheelchair by leaning forward and pushing against the small wheels on the front of the chair. While his method of propulsion was unique, he could negotiate only about ten feet an hour, and the staff never had to worry about his wandering off from the ward.

Roark's most remarkable feature, however, was his penis, which was of such prodigious size that Kerrey was given to remarking that if it were an inch longer it would be a foot rather than a penis. When a corpsman placed him on the commode, the organ hung into the water of the toilet bowl, and as word spread of its size, nurses from all over the hospital began showing up to observe this anatomical wonder. The accident or his alcoholism had also rendered him impotent, and although his instrument, even in its permanently flaccid state, resembled a battering ram, it would never again breach any strongholds. Roark, of course, was utterly unaware of his endowment or his inability to profit from it, but the irony of his situation was not lost on those of us who had seen patients whose penises had been blown off but who nevertheless still had a strongly felt need for sex.

＝＝ ☆ ＝＝

In early June, just before the reconstructive surgery on my right hand was to begin, Phil and Sally Leslie came up to Philadelphia to spend a night with us. Phil had recently completed his tour in Vietnam, and I was anxious to see him and to get word of the platoon. He had written me from Vietnam, and he had also sent me a First Marine Division sweatshirt and some other mementos while overseas; but because he had been hospitalized when I was wounded, he had not yet seen for himself the extent of my injuries. Toddy warned me that the weekend might be difficult for him, but I was so excited to be seeing my old platoon sergeant that I hardly gave her warning a second thought.

When they arrived, Phil was wearing a sport jacket and tie and carrying a bottle of Jack Daniel's, and I was so used to seeing him in dirty jungle utilities that I almost did not recognize him. He had gained fifteen or twenty pounds, and he had lost the gaunt, sunken-eyed appearance that had made him look so formidable when I had first met him. As he handed me the whiskey and we shook hands, he seemed stiff, and I knew that he was struggling to accept my condition. Toddy and Sally sensed it also, and they took up the momentary slack in the conversation with small talk about babies while Phil and I tried to get over our discomfort.

Our wives connected from the start; but Phil's and my relationship was now on a different footing, and neither of us had expected it to be so difficult. While the women busied themselves with dinner preparations and tending to Lewpy, Phil and I repaired to the den, where we could talk. We broke out the Jack Daniel's and were well on our way through our second drinks by the time Toddy and Sally joined us. Several times I had to remind Phil that it was no longer necessary to call me "sir" or "Lieutenant," and as the liquor began to loosen us up, we got to the first-name basis that had been impossible in Vietnam.

Phil told me how he had gotten the news of my wounding and how sick it had made him, and for several seconds I thought we both were going to cry. He seemed to harbor some guilt that my wounding had taken place because he was not at my side, and though I assured him that there was nothing he could have done to change what had happened, it was clear that he felt otherwise. As the evening wore on, I tried to show both Sally and Phil that Toddy and I were making the most of our situation and that I could see a productive life ahead for us. He gradually relaxed, and by the time we had finished dinner and gone back to the den for after-dinner drinks, I felt as if I were again talking to the man who had shared some of my most powerful and frightening experiences.

As we discussed our time together in Vietnam, Phil told me that Corporal Morgan, the young squad leader who had written me at

Christmas, had gone berserk and killed several Vietnamese women while patrolling in the Riviera. When Phil rotated out of country, Morgan was being charged with murder, and it was expected that he would do time in Portsmouth prison. I was not surprised by the news, and although I could not forgive the atrocities, I felt that I understood the feelings that had caused him to lose control.

Phil also told me that Captain Woods had been wounded and medevacked but that he would be able to remain in the corps after his recovery. I was distressed to hear of the skipper's wounding, but his injury completed the circle. Every officer I had known who had spent time in the Riviera had been wounded there, and I once again thanked the Lord my time in that God-forsaken wasteland was over.

When the Leslies left the next morning, we exchanged phone numbers and promised to stay in touch, but I felt that it would be some time before our paths would cross again. While in Vietnam I could not have asked for more in a platoon sergeant than I got from Phil Leslie, but now that we were home and he was still following the military calling while I was facing retirement, our previous relationship was irrevocably skewed. The reunion had been painful for both of us, and moved as I was that he had come to visit me, I was exhausted by the experience.

When I told Toddy after they had left that I could not get over how strange Phil had looked in a coat and tie, she shrugged and asked me if I could imagine how strange I must have appeared to him. The most painful part of the visit for me, however, was the need I felt to convince him that I was happy and doing well despite what had happened to my life. It was almost as if I also had to convince myself, and the effort exacted an emotional toll.

VI

★

IN EARLY JUNE I checked back into the hospital for the reconstruction of my right hand. There was not enough remaining of my thumb or little finger to be useful, so Dr. Sandzen had decided to remove the little finger and attach it to the thumb in an effort to give me additional length and more of a grip. He explained that the operation was not always successful, but he did not think that we had much to lose since the stub of my little finger was almost useless anyway in its abbreviated state.

After he had explained the risks to me and I had signed the consent form, he paused for a moment and then told me that he wanted to show me something that had nothing to do with my surgery but that might affect the future course of my hospitalization. He then handed me a letter from the navy surgeon general in Washington to his subordinate commands that stressed the need to retire as quickly as possible all active-duty Vietnam casualties who no longer met the physical or mental qualifications for retention. The letter went on to state that these injured servicemen could be better cared for by the Veterans Administration, but it seemed clear to me that the military departments, having no further use for men like me who had almost died in the service of our country, now wanted to get rid of us as quickly as possible.

Sandzen had an ulterior motive in showing me the letter: The kind of reconstructive surgery he was performing would be seriously curtailed by his having to turn cases like mine over to the VA. I was furious and told him that I would try to bring the letter to the attention of Marine Corps Headquarters if he would provide me with a copy. Intellectually I understood that the navy and Marine Corps had limited fiscal resources and that the care of wounded veterans was not a primary concern for either branch. On a more visceral level, I had just been confronted with stark evidence that I was merely refuse to be discarded, and I was uncomfortable with the growing feeling that I had been used by my country. I was also apprehensive, to say the least, about the possibility of being warehoused at age twenty-three in an antiquated VA hospital with a bunch of geriatric patients. As I left Sandzen's office, I was uneasy about the next day's surgery and my future plans.

The operation itself went quickly, as Sandzen expected. By now I had had surgery so many times that I was becoming a master at maximizing my comfort before going under the knife. To that end I always tried to get on the surgical schedule as early in the day as possible so that I would not have to fast for too long a time after the previous midnight. I also asked for a strong sleeping pill for the night before my operations, and I requested an injectible sedative an hour prior to being taken to the operating room. The surgeons tried to honor my first request, and the anesthesiologists, sensitive anyway to the concept of pain, were usually willing to provide the latter. For this particular operation Sandzen wanted to use local anesthesia, but after the anesthesiologist had tried unsuccessfully to block the nerves radiating from my right armpit down into the arm, I was finally given general anesthesia. When I awoke in the recovery room, I had the usual dry mouth and a headache, but they were minor inconveniences compared with the pain that began in my right hand and coursed upward through my arm. The hand throbbed as if it had been put through a meat grinder, and I made a conscious effort to appear alert enough that the anesthesiologist would begin my postoperative morphine.

When I was returned to SOQ 12, Toddy was waiting for me, but for the next several days I was only intermittently aware of her presence beside my bed. Sandzen stopped by to reemphasize his orders to the staff that it was crucial to keep my hand elevated above my head, and the hand was tied into a sling above my bed so that I could not release it. Everyone on the ward knew that the first couple of days would determine whether the transplanted digit would take, and the other patients stopped in frequently to see how I was doing and to make certain that my hand was still elevated. Again I rambled incoherently about my experiences in Vietnam, but for the most part I slept fitfully between pain shots.

On the afternoon of the second postoperative day, the thumb began to darken, and Sandzen's worried look and more frequent visits alerted Toddy that the operation was failing. By the end of the week my pain was manageable, and I had been switched off the morphine injections and on to Darvon capsules. The blood supply to the transplant site had also failed, and the by now necrotic digit had taken on the appearance of an overripe banana. A disappointed Sandzen finally accepted the failure of his surgery and had the staff release my hand from the sling. He apologized profusely to Toddy and me, wrote me a refillable prescription for Darvon capsules, and sent us home for several weeks of convalescent leave. He told us that he did not intend to remove the blackened thumb for at least a month, when the rest of my hand would be fully healed and I was stronger.

In the meantime, I had to contend with a useless reminder of the inexact science of medicine. Besides the operation's having been unsuccessful, the transplanted digit had been attached to my thumb in such a way that it lay across the palm of my hand. It was impossible for me to resume walking since I could not take any pressure on the hand, and as had happened so many times before, Toddy again had to assist me with many of the simplest tasks of daily living.

When I considered my physical condition in the early summer of 1969, there seemed to be little cause for celebration. The operations on my thumb had stymied my efforts to gain independence, and I would, in fact, have been better off without the last one. Zier, Crotty, and Kerrey, like me, all had arrived at the hospital flat on their backs and almost totally helpless, yet each was now walking. I understood that my wounds were more extensive than those of any other officer I had encountered on SOQ 12 and that I would never again be a whole man, but it was still demoralizing to see arrive on the ward men who were sicker than I yet who were recovering more quickly.

Kerrey had, in fact, already been discharged, and he was about to be awarded the Medal of Honor by President Nixon in a White House ceremony. Legitimate heroes from my generation's war were rare and often unrewarded, and it was good to see Bob get the recognition and the honor he deserved. I confessed to Toddy that I was a bit jealous of Bob's success, but at the same time I felt enormous pride that when he stood in the White House and received his medal, he would in a sense be representing all of us who had served honorably. Toddy's response to my admission was to suggest that we schedule a party for Bob at our apartment after his trip to Washington, and I quickly agreed.

The second week in July we went on vacation with Martha and her husband to his family home on Martha's Vineyard, in Massachusetts. Toddy had sensed that I was frustrated and depressed, and when Mike and Martha offered to include us in their vacation plans, she set about convincing me that it was a good idea. I had been lying about the apartment feeling useless and brooding about the war, and at Toddy's urging, I finally agreed to go.

Just a month earlier President Nixon had met with President Thieu of South Vietnam on Midway and announced that twenty-five thousand American troops were to be withdrawn from Vietnam. A few days later the first American servicemen were pulled out, and although the numbers were small, the effort was symbolic. I was pleased that some of our servicemen were coming home unscarred, but I was confused by the strategy and the rhetoric of the withdrawal. I knew that even with more than half a million men in Southeast Asia we were not winning the war, and it seemed implausible that we were going to improve our odds by scaling back the effort. There was also something patently disingenuous about the explanation that we had trained the South Vietnamese armed forces to the point where they could now defend themselves. I knew that a year earlier that had not been the case, and it seemed that the administration was preparing to cut its losses and was lying to the American people in the process.

Martha's Vineyard was the first vacation Toddy and I had taken since before I left for Vietnam, and it was also the first time we had left Lewpy. Toddy's parents watched him for the week we were gone, and I knew that he was in good hands; but Toddy had a mother's natural apprehension about abandoning her infant and called her parents almost every night while we were away. Michael's parents and his brothers and sister were wonderful hosts and did everything they could to make our visit pleasant, but I clearly had not adjusted to being without my legs. The amount of effort involved in sightseeing from a wheelchair was overwhelming, and I finally got to the point where I made excuses to sit in the car rather than go through the frustration of being helped up steps or curbs.

It also seemed to me that not a single tourist on Martha's Vineyard was aware of or affected by the Vietnam War. When the curious among them stared at me, I stared back so defiantly as to make all but the rudest gawkers avert their eyes. I could not, however, get used to young children tugging at their mothers' arms and yelling, "That man doesn't have any legs." It also seemed odd to me that although my brother-in-law and I were so recently back from Vietnam, no one in his family wanted to talk about it. We had delightful conversations with them and spent considerable time watching the Boston Red Sox on television and idling over huge family meals, but it seemed as if the topic of Vietnam was taboo. Michael had four brothers, none of whom served in Vietnam, and they may have been sensitive to the sacrifice demanded of him and the fact that they had never been called; but I thought that my presence was the main factor that inhibited discussion of the war. It was not the first time I had felt as if people chose their topics carefully when they were around me, and it certainly would not be the last.

By the end of the week Toddy and I were ready to return to Philadelphia despite the more than ample food, drink, and Yankee hospitality. Martha and Michael drove us to Boston to catch the plane home and insisted that along the way we see Plymouth Rock, as well as Harvard Square and Fenway Park. The vacation had been a good break from the regimen of the hospital, but we both were exhausted and anxious to see our son. When we got home, Toddy's mother proudly showed us how she had taught Lewpy to sit unassisted while we were away. His first tooth had also come in, and he was saying "Da-da, Da-da" to everyone in sight. I knew that his words did not refer to me alone, but I was still as proud as if he had recited the Gettysburg Address.

On Sunday night Michael and Martha, who were spending several more days on Martha's Vineyard, called to make certain that we had gotten home safely and to tell us how the island was reacting to the news that Senator Ted Kennedy had driven a car off a bridge on Chappaquiddick Island, resulting in the drowning of his passenger, Mary Jo Kopechne. I had already begun to sense that the wisdom and veracity of our politicians were open to question because of the way Vietnam was unraveling, and the news of Chappaquiddick fueled a disrespect that prior to the war would have been unthinkable for me.

On the day after our return from Cape Cod I had a consultation with Dr. Sandzen at the hospital. He seemed in no hurry to remove the transplanted digit from my right thumb, but by now it was oozing a brown liquid, had turned completely black, and smelled terrible. I was irritated that he had been so enthusiastic about doing the initial operation but now seemed reluctant to try to straighten out the mess that my right hand had become, and when I voiced my displeasure, he put me on the operating room schedule for the following week.

When I got home later that day, Toddy told me that her brother would be driving down from Princeton the next day to drop off our Volkswagen and reclaim his own car. We had ordered a new car through a dealership in nearby Wilmington, Delaware, earlier in the summer, and it was supposed to be ready by August 1, so the timing was perfect.

Rob arrived for dinner the next night, and in the course of the meal filled us in on antiwar campus unrest. I had been reading about draft card burners and takeovers of administration buildings for months, but when he told us that nobody seemed to get upset when American flags were burned and that students wore American flag patches on the rear ends of their blue jeans, I was appalled. Rob was a senior at Princeton, hardly a bastion of radicalism, and only two years younger than Toddy and I were, but his college experience seemed to be light-years away from ours. I suddenly felt very old and wondered what my attitude toward the war would have been if I had been only a few years younger and had not been raised in a military family.

After dinner we moved to the den to watch television and listen to Walter Cronkite, who, in addition to doing his regular stint as CBS's anchor, had become his network's spokesman for the space program. On July 20, 1969, *Apollo 11* had landed on the moon. On our black-and-white portable television, Toddy, Rob, and I were watching footage of Neil Armstrong walking on the surface of the moon and making his now-famous comment to the world, "That's one small step for a man, one giant leap for mankind."

We all had wondered what he would say to mark such a historic occasion, and though we knew that the words were carefully planned and rehearsed, they seemed appropriate, and we lifted our glasses in tribute to him. It seemed incredible to me that Armstrong could walk on the moon, but that I could not do the same on earth—such an ordinary task that most of humankind did without a second thought. I cheered as loudly as Toddy and her brother that hot July night in Philadelphia, but my hope was that the same technology that put the Apollo crew on the moon could someday restore my missing limbs.

=== ☆ ===

Dr. Sandzen's second and last surgery on my right hand was far less ambitious than his earlier effort and was also more successful. I was taken once again to the operating room, given general anesthesia, and the thumb was debrided of the rotting digit that I had lived with for most of the summer. A skin graft taken from a donor site on the inside of my upper arm was used to cover the bone that Sandzen had to shorten in order to close the remaining stump. I tolerated the procedure well and endured a normal postoperative course in which I was initially given morphine and gradually weaned to codeine and Darvon. When Sandzen was certain that the graft had taken, I was sent home for another month of convalescent leave, with instructions to return to the clinic for a follow-up consult before resuming physical therapy.

Sandzen was resigning his commission in order to parlay the skills he had perfected operating on the mangled hands of Vietnam veterans into a sizable fortune, but I had no complaint with the care he had given me. My left hand was in as good shape as was possible, considering how little of it was still there, and the operation on the right hand had been a long shot from the beginning. Additional operations would be necessary before I was finished, and when Sandzen bade me farewell, I wished him luck as a civilian and told him that I only wished he could do my remaining surgery. I also wished that my knowledge of an infantry platoon commander's duties were as marketable as Sandzen's knowledge of surgery, but I kept that thought to myself.

The car we had ordered now arrived, and we went to Wilmington to pick it up from the dealer, and to have lunch with relatives who had helped arrange the deal. Thomas Evans, my mother's cousin, and his wife, Hannah, had made numerous trips to see me and to bring me food in those dark early days of my hospitalization. As we lunched, I commented on how much more pleasant it was to see them in their home than in the sterile environment of the Philadelphia Naval Hospital, and Hannah, ever the gracious hostess, told me that she wanted to give me something to memorialize the occasion. She then took a pair of crystal wine decanters from the sideboard and handed them to Toddy. I was deeply moved that she thought enough of us to make a gift of family heirlooms, and Toddy, embarrassed by such generosity from people she barely knew, tried to refuse the gift until I nudged her under the table.

Before we left, Hannah told us that she had wanted to have us over earlier in the summer but that her dog had been run over and killed by a school bus, and she was just getting over the experience of losing her beloved pet. As we drove back to Philadelphia with Toddy at the wheel of our shiny new Buick, we discussed the wonderful support that Thomas and Hannah had given us and the obvious distress that Hannah felt for the loss of her dog. By now more than thirty-five thousand Americans had been killed in Vietnam, and I wondered if I was losing my humanity not to be able to summon any more compassion for the loss of Hannah's dog. It took me years to realize that Hannah's grief was skewed in favor of the dog because she had known and loved the animal well but had never met a single one of the thirty-five thousand dead American boys.

When we got back home, I was anxious to have hand controls installed in the car, but I had no idea where to purchase them. I decided to write the local newspaper's action line, and it not only found me a dealership that would install the controls but arranged for an American Legion post to foot the bill. After my inquiry to the paper and its answer to my problem had appeared in print, I took a lot of ribbing from most of the other patients about using my injury to manipulate the press, although Jim Crotty thought the idea was ingenious.

On the day that we had the controls installed, the officers of the legion post met me at the dealership and presented me with a check. Pictures were taken of various legion dignitaries shaking hands and posing with me, and I felt thoroughly self-conscious, but I did my best to maintain a smile through the picture taking. I had never felt comfortable with any of the traditional patriotic organizations, primarily because they seemed to view war without any of the self-doubt I now had. On those occasions when their members had come to the hospital and reminisced about the glory days of World War II, I had purposely avoided them. Now, however, I realized that nothing was ever free, and I tried to give them a grateful appearance as we posed for their newsletter.

That afternoon a marine captain who lived in our apartment building and I went out to a little-traveled part of the base, and I tried out my new controls. It was the first time I had driven a car in more than a year, and I was apprehensive about what it would be like to drive with my hands rather than with my feet. My fear proved to be groundless, and I found out within ten minutes that I could drive as well with the controls as I ever had before. I did tend to slide across the seat to the passenger side when I turned too sharply to the right; but a seat belt corrected that problem, and I spent the rest of the afternoon driving around the base with the enthusiasm of a boy who had just learned to ride a bicycle. The freedom and independence were so exhilarating that when I got back to our apartment, I felt like jumping up and down.

Toddy was as delighted as I since my newly regained skill meant that she no longer had to chauffeur me to the hospital. Also, we could now spell each other on weekend trips to Virginia. When I saw Toddy was getting tired on long trips, I had been keenly frustrated by not being able to help. That evening, as we put Lewpy to bed, she remarked that our son would be walking before Christmas and that both her men were becoming so mobile that she could hardly stand it. Lewpy had started to crawl, and as I watched him make his way about the apartment, I looked forward to the day when he would stand alone and take those first tentative steps toward his own independence.

=== ☆ ===

In August 1969, as the Philadelphia summer humidity reached its zenith and I was recuperating from my surgery, I began to look more closely at the Vietnam War and the leadership in Washington that had shaped its course and so profoundly altered my life. Before Vietnam I had been essentially apolitical, accepting without question the judgments of our elected politicians. Now I was not so sure of the infallibility of the democratic process, and the closer I looked, the more it seemed that something was terribly wrong. Intelligent young men and women from stable family backgrounds were demanding an end to our involvement in a war that many experts were now saying was misguided from the start, aspiring politicians were building their careers on anti-war platforms, and a beleaguered president and his administration seemed to be less than candid in their statements about the war.

On a more personal level, it seemed to me that the Vietnam veteran was being made the scapegoat for everything that had gone wrong with our foreign policy, and each time I read a story of another returning veteran being spit upon or being similarly ostracized by those same Americans he thought he had been serving, I recoiled in disgust. In early August I read in the newspaper that Colonel Robert B. Rheault, a former commander of Green Beret forces in Vietnam and a West Point graduate, and seven other soldiers in his command had been charged with premeditated murder in the shooting of a Vietnamese man. The details were murky, and there were charges and countercharges that the Vietnamese man had been a double agent; but the implication of the editorials that followed was that American servicemen in Vietnam were cutthroats and murderers and that such atrocities were common-place. I began to waver in the very patriotic tenets that my father had sought to instill. When on August 9 the news broke that Sharon Tate, Abigail Folger, and three others had been found brutally murdered in Beverly Hills, I prayed that the murderer not turn out to be a Vietnam veteran.

When Bob Kerrey went to the White House that summer to receive his Medal of Honor, it seemed to me that the press was far more interested in chronicling the dark side of the war than in giving credit to its few acknowledged heroes. I remembered Sergeant York and Audie Murphy from my childhood, and the contrast between their triumphant returns from the First and Second World Wars and that accorded Kerrey and others like him was a painful reminder of the low esteem in which Vietnam veterans were held.

Like Bob Kerrey, my father had gone to the White House to be honored, at that time by President Kennedy, but the climate of the country in the early and late sixties was altogether different. President Nixon seemed to be a hostage to his own foreign policy, and I found it pathetic that he found himself in the role of honoring Medal of Honor winners in little Rose Garden ceremonies, while simultaneously trying to extricate us from the war that a growing number of Americans were now saying was dishonorable.

Bob came up to Philadelphia after the ceremony, and Jim Crotty, Toddy, and I had a party in our apartment in his honor. We decorated the house in red, white, and blue, bought an extravagant array of food and drink, and invited over as many patients and former patients as we could squeeze into the apartment. Bob regaled us with White House anecdotes, including comments on President Nixon's bad breath and Secretary of Defense Melvin Laird's diminutive size, but I noticed that he did not allow his medal and its silk-lined box out of his sight for the entire night. The medal had elevated Kerrey from the ranks of ordinary mortals, and I remember thinking that it could eventually prove to be a heavy burden to carry through life. I also remember wishing that I had as meaningful a symbol of accomplishment for my service, but I was nevertheless happy for Bob and felt that he had the strength of character to handle his new status. Earlier in his hospital stay, before he had actually received any of his medals, he had made a trip back to Nebraska. He had worn his uniform because it got him a reduced air rate, and he had considered borrowing my ribbons to wear. At our party, as I thought about the incident in light of what Bob Kerrey had just experienced, I had to smile, but beneath the smile I realized that we both were searching for any evidence that might validate our war experience and the terrible beating we had taken.

The liquor flowed, and we celebrated until we could no longer raise our glasses. At one point Paul Barents, who with his wife had driven over from New Jersey, tried to demonstrate that even with wooden legs he could still get into the baseball on-deck stance. Much to Kathy's mortification, he wound up flat on his face, but we applauded his effort and helped him to an upright position. John Zier showed up in an Italian suit with a purple shirt and white tie, and when Jim Crotty asked if he had gotten the outfit from a fire sale for the Sons of Italy, he replied that we would have to ask his wife because she was the one with the good taste in the family and bought all his clothes.

Late in the evening, as I went into the kitchen for more ice, I happened on to a serious conversation between Bob Kerrey and one of our guests who was a career marine. Kerrey was making the point that the war protesters should be allowed to engage in peaceful nonviolent demonstrations and that if illegal or immoral policies were being carried out, he could understand the use of illegal means to protest them. By the time I intervened the marine lifer was apoplectic, and when I reminded him that Bob had just come from the White House, where President Nixon had draped a Medal of Honor around his neck, he mumbled something about the war tearing the country apart and stalked out for another drink. I do not know if Bob was simply baiting his companion of the moment, but I had never heard him make such a radical statement. His thoughts about the political process had obviously gone beyond mine.

The following week, after half a million young men and women had gathered at a farm in Bethel, New York, to listen to Joe Cocker and Joan Baez, smoke dope, and embrace the concepts of peace and free love, I ended my convalescent leave and resumed physical therapy at the hospital. While I envied the Woodstockers their freedom, I felt a generation removed from them, even though most were my age or only a few years younger.

═══ ☆ ═══

The first time I donned my stubbies after a layoff of several months, I discovered that I had outgrown the left stump socket and a new one had to be made. That involved several trips to the brace and limb shop for fittings and a week's delay, but I used the time to lift weights and try to get back into shape. Shaughnessey's plan was to have me spend only a couple of more weeks on the stubbies and then move me up to rough legs by the end of September. Her plan held up, and after I had walked for a couple of weeks with the new socket, I went back to the limb shop with an order for full-length legs.

There Eddie complained that working on my legs was getting to be a full-time job and that he was considering writing a letter to Ho Chi Minh to reprimand him for not having me killed while he had the chance. When I pointed out to him that the president of North Vietnam had died at the beginning of the month and that he was going to have to take that particular joke out of his repertoire, Eddie looked sheepish and muttered that if I had died at the beginning of the month, it would have saved him a lot of work.

On the last day of September my rough legs were completed, and I got a call from Eddie telling me to come over from PT for a test walk. He had used the same sockets that had been on my stubbies, so there was not much of a problem with the fitting, and I put the legs on without any trouble. I sat in my wheelchair between the parallel bars for a few moments to get the feel of the legs and to screw up my courage before trying to stand up. As I sat there admiring my new knees and looking at the shoes that I had given Eddie to get the correct foot size, he suggested that we get the show on the road, and I took a deep breath and pulled myself up by the bars to an upright position.

When I looked down at the floor, my shoes seemed a dizzying distance away, and when I looked forward, I was looking Eddie straight in the eye. It was the first time in almost a year that I had been on eye level with an upright male, and Eddie smiled knowingly as I relished the moment. I then realized that Eddie was only five feet eight inches and that I had been about six feet before being wounded, and my elation gave way to disappointment. Eddie had made me about four inches shorter than my normal height, and as I started to point out his mistake, he put his finger to his lips and told me that I could walk more easily with shorter legs. After a few minutes of heated debate, during which I told him that I did not want to be five feet eight inches, and I called him every name in the book, he finally threw up his hands and agreed to add several inches to my height if and when I ever learned to walk.

For the next twenty minutes I made my way up and down the bars, as I had when I first got my stubbies. The walking was much more difficult since I now had two knee joints to master, but I found that by using the same type of motion I had used with the stubbies, I could ambulate after a fashion. The trickiest part was making certain that the knee on one side was locked before I brought the opposite limb forward. After a few turns at the bars I began to develop a rhythm as Eddie watched for a few more minutes and then stopped me. He told me that the right leg needed to be shortened one inch, but when I protested that I was already too short, he placed a one-inch board under my left leg and had me walk a few feet. The difference was amazing, and I agreed that a modification was necessary, although I did not understand why Eddie could not lengthen the left leg rather than shorten the right one.

After I had finished walking, I could not figure out how to get from a standing position to a seated one in my wheelchair. Eddie had to teach me how to back up to the chair, buckle the knees, and lower myself by the handrails on the parallel bars into my seat. It was difficult to do, and I knew that it was going to be next to impossible without the bars, but that problem was for later in my rehabilitation. Eddie handed me a towel for the perspiration on my face and neck, and I took the legs off and left them with him for readjustment. He told me that they would be ready for me to pick up before stump rounds on Monday, and as I left, he reminded me to bring the detachable footrests to my chair when I returned. Otherwise I would not be able to wheel anywhere while wearing the legs, and Eddie told me that he did not want me stuck in his shop all morning. I gave Eddie the finger when I wheeled out the door.

The first Monday in October 1969 I began training in earnest with my new legs. At rounds Shaughnessey checked my gait to make certain that Eddie's adjustment had been accurate, and after I had walked up and down the length of the parallel bars a few times, she made a notation on her clipboard. She then gave Eddie's work her seal of approval and told me that although there was no hurry, I should consider buying some lightweight shoes with rubber soles before the legs were finished. For the next several weeks I went to morning and afternoon sessions of therapy, and I continued to lift weights and exercise when I was not walking between the parallel bars. I tried to wear the legs while sitting in my wheelchair between sessions, but they were uncomfortable and severely restricted my mobility. They also added thirty pounds to my weight and at the end of each day at the hospital, I needed no coaxing to store them in my locker until the next morning.

On weekends the physical therapy department was closed, so Toddy, Lewpy, and I were free to come and go as we pleased. Several times that fall and winter we made trips to Virginia since both sets of parents as well as both my sisters and their families were living there. On our first trip south in mid-October I drove, and Toddy tended to our son, who also enjoyed riding in the car but required a lot of attention. From the beginning of my driving I always felt less helpless and more like a man when I was at the wheel, and Toddy, sensing my need to be in control, was always willing to let me drive. We had planned to spend a quiet couple of days with her parents in Fort Belvoir, and we were also going to visit briefly with Martha and Michael.

Halfway there we stopped for lunch at a restaurant on the interstate. As Toddy was getting my wheelchair out of the trunk, I noticed that the parking lot was crowded with buses and vans but gave the matter only passing thought. Once inside, however, we quickly realized what was happening. The restaurant was packed with young men and women wearing blue jeans and army field jackets. Many of them wore red bandannas over shoulder-length hair, and peace signs were prominently displayed on all but a few. They were going to Washington to participate in the October 15 Moratorium that Sam Brown and other leading antiwar activists had called for in major cities throughout the United States. By the end of the demonstration 250,000 of them had marched on Washington alone, and lesser but significant numbers had gathered up and down the East Coast and westward as far as Detroit.

I had begun paying a lot of attention to the antiwar movement as it was reported in the print media and on television, but up until I entered that Hot Shoppes cafeteria on Interstate 95 that October afternoon in 1969, I had never come face-to-face with an organized group of people whose attitudes toward and perceptions of the Vietnam War were the opposite of mine. The moment was emotional, and I toyed with my food, half hoping that one of the protesters would do or say something to which I could respond. Instead I was ignored or perhaps consciously avoided.

The air seemed to me to hum with an electric anticipation of purpose, and as I watched the faces of these obviously intelligent young men and women, I wondered how our backgrounds could be so similar and our paths so different. I had thought that by going off to war, I was protecting their right to protest, and they now thought that by protesting my going, they were protecting any future warriors on both sides of the conflict. Between the two views there had to be a core of truth, but I was not capable of grasping it. Once we were back in the car and on the road again, Toddy was unusually quiet, but I knew that she was thinking about the incident. Lewpy babbled happily in the backseat as if the world were perfectly normal, and after a long while Toddy reached over and squeezed my arm.

I drank too much at the Todds' home that evening and banged my head while trying to climb up onto a toilet seat in a bathroom whose door was too narrow for my wheelchair. I fell, scaring Toddy's parents and embarrassing me, but they quickly forgot about it, and as first-time grandparents spent most of our stay doting on Lewpy. It seemed that everywhere we went outside our apartment or the hospital there were narrow doors or steps or curbs with which to contend, and it was enervating to be planning constantly for such previously unknown obstacles.

We slept on a fold-out sofa in the den that evening rather than in the upstairs guest bedroom, where we had spent our last agonizing night together before I went to Vietnam. Before going to sleep, I thought about the protesters we had encountered that afternoon, and I was curious about what sort of play their march on Washington would get in the media. As I compared myself with them, I knew that only a couple of years earlier I would not have had the political activism or the interest that seemed to drive them, but I also thought that they were naive and idealistic in their view of our enemies.

I had seen firsthand the calculated acts of cruelty and vengeance of which men at war were capable, and if nothing else, I knew that there were very few lofty ideals at the level of conflict I had experienced. It made me angry to see these college kids, with no frame of reference outside a classroom, second-guessing the decisions that had almost cost me my life, and it made me angrier still to think that they might be right. That night I again had the dream in which I was separated from my men and was pursued by a unit of enemy soldiers. This time, however, I was wearing my wooden legs, and I was running as fast and as effortlessly as if they were real legs.

We spent the next night with Martha and Michael, who were stationed at Quantico. When we arrived, Michael was out running an errand, and since their apartment was on the second floor, we were faced with a dilemma. I finally hopped out of my wheelchair and hoisted my body up the several flights of stairs, using a modified push-up motion. I was out of breath and the seat of my pants was dirty when we entered the apartment, but I was proud of myself for having bested the stairs. After Michael returned, I told him that his apartment steps were a warm-up for my upcoming climb of the Washington Monument, and we half-seriously discussed the idea until Toddy announced that she would leave me if I ever tried such an egotistical stunt.

Captain Clyde Woods was by now also stationed at Quantico, after having recovered from his wounding, and Michael had invited him over for a drink before dinner. He seemed stiff and ill at ease when he arrived, much as Phil Leslie had when he first saw me in Philadelphia, but my old skipper seemed to loosen up as we drank my brother-in-law's liquor and discussed our time together in Vietnam. When he realized that Martha was holding dinner for us, he apologized for having delayed us and declined Michael's offer to stay for supper. On the way out he paused at the door, hesitated, and then told me that I should be proud of the job I had done for him in Vietnam. He went on to say that he had had serious misgivings about having Chesty Puller's son in his outfit but that I was a credit to the corps and that I should call on him if there was ever anything he could do for me. We shook hands on the landing, and as I watched him walk down the steps, I wondered if he felt in any way responsible for what had happened to me. When I turned to reenter the apartment, Michael had discreetly gone into the kitchen to carve the roast beef.

Later that evening, after we had eaten and the dishes had been cleared and stacked, Michael and I went into the den for after-dinner drinks. Seeing Captain Woods had loosened my tongue about my war experiences, and I knew that I could talk to Michael because we both had led troops in combat, been wounded ourselves, and seen men die under the most hideous of circumstances. Michael had mounted my ribbons and given them to me while I was in intensive care, and in those bleak early days, when my life was hanging in the balance and my pain was all-encompassing, I often focused on the Silver Star ribbon on the bedstead beside me as if it could ease my suffering. I now told him what his kindness had meant to me and how the Vietnam experience had been so intense for me that I relived a part of it every day and did not think I would ever get over it.

After I had finished, he got up from his chair, went into his bedroom, and returned with a notebook in which he had written the names of all the men in his command who had become casualties at the battle for Hue. He explained to me that he had written the names down to be sure to remember them always. As he shared the notebook with me, I could see that he was telling me to give myself a little time. When the evening ended, he carried me down the steps I had climbed on my own earlier, and Toddy drove us back to her parents' home.

The newspaper reports after the October 15 Moratorium seemed to me to indicate a seismic shift of opinion. Theretofore antiwar protesters had been presented, by and large, as left-wing ideologues, Communist sympathizers, or student radicals. Now, however, the center seemed to have shifted, and I was discomfited to read that middle-class housewives and even some veterans had participated in the marches. Indeed, I had a cousin who had carried a candle in the White House vigil led by Coretta Scott King to protest the war and honor our war dead, and while I knew that his politics were decidedly more liberal than mine, I also knew that he had America's best interests at heart.

On a Monday night in early November President Nixon went on television to try to counter the growing force of the antiwar movement, and I listened carefully when he alluded to the silent majority of Americans who supported the administration's policies in the face of a shrill minority. I wanted to believe him, but his words seemed to have a hollow ring, and when it was reported after his speech that calls and telegrams to the White House had been overwhelmingly in his favor, I wondered if the support had been orchestrated. I felt increasingly alienated, and unable to side with either the American Legion types and hard hats on the right or the draft card burners on the left, I drew into myself and on too many occasions drank away my evenings.

At the hospital, where I had now been a patient for more than a year, there were changes in personnel that affected my recovery. Dr. Sandzen was replaced by a navy captain named Leo Willett, who, though lacking Sandzen's specific experience in hand reconstruction, was a fine orthopedic surgeon. He had a realistic, no-nonsense approach to his calling, and he quickly gained the respect of his patients by never promising more than he could deliver. At our first meeting he made it clear that I would get no special attention from him because I was my father's son. He then explained that he would, however, do everything in his power to assist in my rehabilitation because in his opinion the severity of my wounds entitled me to all that he could offer. I liked Dr. Willett from the start, and although we knocked heads a few times, I always knew where I stood with him.

Shaughnessey was also scheduled for reassignment, and one day, after she had put me through a particularly grueling workout, she informed me that she would be leaving sometime after the first of the year. Her announcement came as a real blow to me not only because I had learned so much from her but also because she was a person who cared deeply without ever pitying. Her method of operation had been the perfect tonic for me and I resolved to maximize my effort before her transfer came through. In response to her announced departure, I tried to bluster through a mock hurrah, but we had gotten too close to each other for the bravado to disguise my true feelings.

On November 10, 1969, just a week after President Nixon's "silent majority" speech, Toddy and I went to a ball at the officers' club to commemorate the 194th anniversary of the founding of the Marine Corps. Marine birthday balls are a cherished tradition of the corps and the main event on every base's social agenda for the entire year, and Toddy and I were looking forward to our first one together. The previous year I had been in intensive care and Toddy eight months pregnant; but this year neither of us was indisposed, and she looked dazzling in a white strapless gown. Our party consisted of several other couples who shared our apartment building, and the men, all marine captains, wore their dress blue uniforms.

When we arrived, the club was appropriately decorated with crimson and gold bunting, and the mood was festive. I had to be carried up the steps into the main ballroom in my wheelchair, but once we were situated at our table, it was not too difficult for me to get around. After a prime-rib dinner, during which carafes of white and red wine were freely passed from guest to guest, a retired marine general, the guest of honor, made a brief patriotic speech complete with allusions to bombs bursting in air and the rockets' red glare. He then cut the birthday cake, and as is customary at birthday balls, the first two pieces were given to the oldest and youngest marines present. After the ceremonies and throughout the rest of the night, there was a steady stream of well-wishers stopping by our table to chat, and many of the men danced with Toddy and brought us drinks from the bar. As had happened before, I was envious of the sea of uniformed men who could glide about the ballroom so effortlessly, but I was grateful that Toddy got a chance to dance.

As I sat on the sidelines and watched, however, I began to get the uneasy feeling that despite the pageantry and hoopla, what was taking place bore almost no resemblance to my own Marine Corps experience. Almost all the marine officers assigned to the Philadelphia Naval Base and its support activities were in supply and logistics, and as I scanned their medals, I was struck by the lack of combat decorations. Once again I was reminded that I had been taught, both as a boy and as a young officer at Basic School, that marine officers were combat platoon leaders first and that whatever else they did was incidental. I could see now that the lessons I had learned were only partly true, and I brooded over my perception.

It seemed to me that the traditions of sacrifice we had gathered to commemorate on this special date did not include most of the people in the ballroom, and until Toddy returned from her dance, I felt alienated and totally separate from the crowd. To make matters worse, young marines were still dying in Vietnam, and I suddenly felt guilty to be feasting on prime rib and drinking chilled wine while real marines were trying only to make it through another day in the arena I had just left this time a year earlier. Toddy did not notice my change in spirits when she came back to the table, but for the remainder of the evening and for some time afterward, I wondered how I was going to handle myself in civilian life if I could not even be comfortable with fellow marines.

At the hospital I threw myself into my rehabilitation in order to get the benefit of Commander Shaughnessey's experience before she left, but the effort was demanding and often unrewarding. When I first ventured out from between the parallel bars on my new full-length legs, I found that I was unable to take even one step without leaning heavily on my crutches, and my hands were in such poor shape that I could not hold on to them properly. We experimented with different types of crutches and different types of grips for my hands before settling on crutches that attached to my forearms and had molded plastic pockets into which I inserted my hands. Even customized, the crutches were cumbersome and unwieldy, and there were many times I would have quit in disgust had it not been for Shaughnessey's encouragement.

In mid-November there was another antiwar march on Washington, which the media described as being larger and more successful than the one a month earlier. The following day, November 16, it was reported that Lieutenant William Calley had been indicted by the Department of the Army for the massacre of South Vietnamese civilians at My Lai, and as the details of the atrocity began to unfold, I felt both sickened and tainted by the revelations. Americans from all walks of life now seemed to be saying that the war was immoral, and Calley, in addition to allowing innocent women and children to be slaughtered, had validated the stereotype of Vietnam veterans as bloodthirsty killers and misfits. I waited in vain for any report about American servicemen in Vietnam who had actively helped preserve the lives of civilians. Indeed, that was the major premise for our being there, but examples of the humanitarian concern I had witnessed were almost never to be read or seen.

As Christmas approached, I began to see that I was never going to attain a level of proficiency with my new legs that could even remotely be described as normal walking, and the realization was devastating. When I first started walking, I had been motivated by Paul's example, but as I worked with my prostheses, it became apparent that Paul's situation and mine were totally different. As severely disabled as he was, Paul still had two good stumps, and no amount of work on my part was going to compensate for my more severe disability. After I had gotten my new crutches, which I could handle more easily, I eventually reached the point where I could walk for fifty or sixty feet on the flat, smooth surface of the PT room, but any distance beyond that was outside my range. In addition, there were surfaces on which I could not walk at all, such as sand, gravel, and grass, and the slightest variation of slope in a terrain caused almost insurmountable difficulty.

When Shaughnessey realized that sixty feet was my limit, she stopped concentrating on distance and gait, and we worked on sitting, rising from a seated position, and climbing and descending curbs and stairs. I knew that I had to develop a technique for each of these functions or my ability to walk would be useless, and often Shaughnessey and I had to improvise and experiment together since she had never trained anyone with my combination of disabilities. To sit and rise, I found my wooden legs almost useless, and I had to learn to muscle my way into and out of chairs with my arms, using the back of the chair for leverage. I also found that I could use my arms to climb stairs as long as the steps had a handrail, but without that simple device all my effort was in vain.

One day Shaughnessey announced that it was time for me to learn to raise myself from a prone position, and before I could object, she and an assistant wheeled me over to an exercise mat and lowered me to its surface. She then placed my crutches beside me, pushed the wheelchair out of my reach, and moved off to the edge of the mat while I pondered my predicament. Since there were no supports for me to pull myself up by, I quickly realized that I was going to have to use the crutches to get back on my feet, but the practice was more difficult than the theory. For the next hour I tried to position a crutch perpendicular to the mat and walk my hands up its length, and each time I got to a semierect stance I toppled over. By the end of the session I was as wet as if I had just emerged from the shower and the muscles in my arms and upper torso were as taut as banjo strings.

"Balance and strength, Lieutenant, balance and strength," she repeated when she finally relented and helped me back into the chair, and had I not been so exhausted I would have struck a woman for the first time in my life.

Shaughnessey did not need to remind me that if I could not get back on to my feet after a fall, I was going to be as helpless as a turtle on its back, and for several weeks we practiced on the mat. Many times I got tantalizingly close to regaining my feet, and each time I did so I could tell by Shaughnessey's clenched fists that she was rooting for me. The end result was always the same, however, and as I was helped back into my chair for the umpteenth time, I wondered why I was putting myself through such humiliation.

At the same time that I was bemoaning my lack of progress and watching other patients effortlessly perform feats that for me would have been miraculous, Lewpy began to strut his stuff. For weeks he had been pulling himself to an upright position by whatever piece of furniture was handy and then bouncing up and down like a jack-in-the-box, while I looked on with a mixture of envy and pride. One day just before Christmas he absentmindedly let go of the coffee table in our living room and discovered that he was standing on his own. He then tottered toward the sofa only a few feet away and, still on his feet at the end of his journey, grinned broadly in my direction as I stared in amazement. My son had just taken his first steps, and as his mother and I hugged each other and clapped him on the back, I felt a surge of emotion with which only a small percentage of fathers could identify. To encourage him, Toddy then moved the coffee table several feet farther away from the sofa, picked Lewpy up, and stood him beside it, and we watched him retrace his path back to the sofa. Within days he was walking as if he had never gone through the intermediate process of crawling, and we took an entire roll of film of him in full stride to send to both sets of grandparents.

That Christmas we moved about like nomads, spending part of the holidays with Toddy's parents and part with my two sisters at their homes in northern Virginia. My parents were spending the holidays with my older sister, and she made Christmas dinner so that my mother and father could be with all their children on Christmas Day.

Before we drove down from Philadelphia, Toddy had packed my

legs in the trunk of the car together with our suitcases and Christmas gifts for our families. When she went to gas up for our trip, she also asked the service station attendant to check the spare tire. When he opened the trunk and saw two legs protruding from the Christmas boxes, he did a double take, turned white, and slammed it shut. At first perplexed, Toddy then made matters worse by trying to explain to him that the legs belonged to her husband. By then, however, the poor man had completely lost his composure. She told him to keep the change and made a hasty departure. The spare tire never did get checked; but we both got a good laugh, and Toddy shared the story at dinner for years thereafter.

After we had finished the traditional Christmas turkey, candied sweet potatoes, and plum pudding, I told my father that I wanted him to see me walk, and my brother-in-law helped Toddy bring my legs and crutches from the car. I made the rest of the family wait in an adjoining room while Toddy helped me on with my legs, and when I was ready and standing, she summoned my mother, father, and two sisters. For the next ten minutes I paraded up and down the length of the room while my father looked on and held Toddy's hand. After I had finished, he came over to my side and I put my arm around his shoulder for support, as Toddy took pictures of us standing side by side. Not a word had passed between us, but I could tell by the tenseness in his back muscles and the way that he set his jaw that he was moved. I knew and had known for some time that I would never be able to fill his shoes, but it was gratifying to be able to look him in the eye.

Later in the evening, as we ended the reunion and prepared to head back to Toddy's parents' house, my father took my wife aside and told her that he thought I was going to be all right. She knew that his cup was full from having seen the son and grandson who bore his name both walking on the same day, and on the way home she told me that we could not have given him any better Christmas presents. For my part, I felt that even if I never walked again, I had gotten sufficient payoff for the months of physical therapy that had led up to that one moment when my father and I stood together on Christmas Day of 1969.

By the early part of 1970 the Vietnam War, after years of steady escalation, was beginning to wind down. In December sixty thousand more troops had come home, and politicians and administration spokesmen continued to mouth hollow phrases about "Vietnamization" and the increasing ability of the Vietnamese armed forces to fight their own war. It seemed incredible to me that the American people would swallow such claptrap or that our leaders, both military and civilian, had become so jaded by the war that they were willing to go on record with their hypocrisy. I also came to feel that I had given myself to a cause that, in addition to having robbed me of my youth and left me crippled and deformed, allowed me no pride for having been a participant.

Everywhere I looked, it seemed that Vietnam veterans were being shunned and reviled, and again I could not reconcile my father's generation's triumphal return from World War II with my own experience. I understood that the protected element of society tended to want to avoid sharing the horrors suffered by its warriors, but society did not seem to understand that those of us who fought the war needed to talk through our feelings and to receive some form of validation for our sacrifices. When I finally came to understand that my contemporaries did not want to share the pivotal experience of my life, I learned to keep my silence. I also attempted to ease my own frustrations and insecurities about the future by turning more toward alcohol, and for a long while my overindulgence allowed me to postpone coming to grips with the war.

The decreasing number of American boys fighting in Vietnamese rice paddies and jungles was measurable on SOQ 12 in terms of empty beds. When I first got to the Philadelphia hospital in late 1968, wounded veterans were crammed into every nook and cranny. Now, in the first months of 1970, new arrivals were far less common, and they were no longer a logistical nightmare for the hospital.

Those of us who remained got the attention that a staff, heretofore taxed past its limits, now had the capacity to provide. I was grateful that the level of carnage was being reduced, but I was also painfully aware that the war was ending and that I had no place to go where I would fit in. I had gotten used to the hospital and to the camaraderie of wounded men who at least did not have to explain to each other the reasons for their hideous disfigurements. On the outside, I knew that my mere presence would provoke questions anywhere I went, and I was reluctant to venture into situations where revulsion or pity was going to be a commonplace reaction toward me.

In February Commander Shaughnessey showed up at PT one morning with a pink-cheeked lieutenant (jg) in tow. Lieutenant Bill Smithers was to be her replacement, and the two of them were to work together for a couple of weeks before she was reassigned. As she introduced him to the staff and patients who were just getting started on their morning routines, I could sense that he was going to have to work hard to earn any respect. No one wanted to see Shaughnessey leave, and because she was such a seasoned professional, Smithers's lack of experience was even more apparent. In addition, he was in the same age group as most of the veterans in rehabilitation, and none of us was in a mood to take orders from a green officer who had not paid his dues in Vietnam.

By the end of the week it was clear that Smithers was getting only perfunctory cooperation from his new charges, and Shaughnessey took me aside and told me that we were only going to be hurting ourselves by not giving him a chance. She also told me that I owed her for the months she had spent putting up with my bullshit and that she was now calling in her chips. I knew better than to provoke her Irish temper on a matter she considered important, and I also knew that she had me dead to rights on the IOU. The next time I lifted weights, I asked Smithers rather than Shaughnessey to give me a hand getting started on my workout, and when I caught Shaughnessey's eye after my routine, we exchanged winks. After my first overture other patients began responding more positively to Bill Smithers, and by the time Shaughnessey left it was clear that her rehab unit was going to continue to function.

On her last day Shaughnessey showed up for work in her uniform rather than in the blue smock I had been accustomed to, and she transparently busied herself with last-minute paperwork at her desk rather than with direct patient care. I left her alone while Smithers and I worked on getting me upright from a prone position on the exercise mat. I was no more successful under his tutelage than I had been with Shaughnessey, and after I had finished, I wheeled by her desk to get a towel. As I was drying off, she rose from her chair, took the towel from my hand, and mopped my face.

"I want you to know, Lieutenant," she said, "that even if you never make it out of a wheelchair, you have come farther than any of us expected, and you have given meaning to my work."

Embarrassed by her openness, I took the towel from her and told her that I never could have done any of it without her help. For an awkward moment we stared at each other, and I extended my hand to grasp her arm in the same gesture she had made to me the first time we met.

"Now get out of here, Lieutenant, before I start crying," she said in breaking off our farewell, and I headed for the door as she turned back to her paperwork.

I never saw Commander Shaughnessey again, but if ever there was a lady who was the personification of her pet expression, "Balance and strength, Lieutenant, balance and strength," she was Irish with green eyes and red hair, and she had just passed out of my life.

After Shaughnessey's departure I continued to work with Smithers on my walking, but I seemed to have reached a point of diminishing returns. I could not rise from a prone position, could not negotiate curbs or steps without a handrail or support, and I could walk only on fairly level, smooth surfaces. In addition, the prostheses became extremely uncomfortable after an hour or two and actually made me less mobile overall. I thought seriously about giving up on walking altogether, but each time I entertained the thought, I felt guilty because I knew that if I quit, I was consigning myself to life in a wheelchair.

Without Shaughnessey's dominating personality, the mood of PT changed. Because I was not pushed as hard, I did not work as hard. Many of the newer patients had injuries that were incurred stateside rather than in Vietnam, and I had trouble relating to them. The newer patients were also usually less severely injured since as a rule motorcycle accidents do not cause multiple amputations, and toward the end of my hospital stay I had a difficult time finding anyone with a disability that remotely resembled mine.

When Dr. Willett next conferred with me about the last series of operations on my right hand, he sensed my discomfort and, before turning to the surgery, asked me if he could speak frankly. At my nod he told me that he had been monitoring my progress since I had become his patient and that in his opinion I was never going to be able to walk well enough that my prostheses would become a practical means of locomotion. He then told me that the ultimate decision to stick with the wooden pins was, of course, mine, but that I should not harbor any guilt if I took the path that every similarly circumstanced amputee he had ever treated had taken.

When I protested that what he was really telling me was that all my work had been in vain and that it was unfair to have allowed me to nurture false expectations, he said that I was perhaps correct but that part of the healing process was self-awareness of one's own new limitations and that I had to reach that perspective on my own. Since Dr. Willett was only corroborating what I'd known but up until then had not admitted to myself about my walking, I did not really have my heart in rebuking him further, and I was almost relieved when he steered the conversation to my upcoming operation.

To begin his discussion, Willett drew a crude right hand on the chalkboard in his office and then erased half of the thumb to approximate my hand. He explained that since the effort to add length to the thumb had failed, he now proposed to increase the web space between the thumb and the remainder of the hand so that I would regain some of the grasping ability I had lost. In order to accomplish his objective, he would have to split the tissue between my thumb and forefinger in toward my palm, sew the exposed hand to the left side of my abdomen for a two-week period, and then use flesh from my torso to increase the web space. The operation was called a pedicle flap graft and would be followed up a month after the flap was detached by a much shorter and simpler operation to revise the graft. After Dr. Willett had finished his explanation of the procedure, he erased the chalkboard and, putting his hands in the pockets of his smock, asked me if I had any questions.

I was already familiar with the operation from earlier discussions with him, and I had seen similar procedures performed on other patients, so my questions were superficial. As with any operation, I knew that there were minuses to be weighed against gains, and I asked Willett about the downside.

"Apart from the possibility of an operative mishap or a postoperative complication, Lieutenant," he answered, "the principal drawbacks will be extensive scarring at the donor site on your left side and more tender flesh where the graft is applied to your hand. Also," he continued, "you will probably have to shave your hand every couple of days if the donor flesh is hirsute."

As he rose from his seat to see me to the door, I knew that I had my priorities wrong to be worried about shaving a section of skin on my hand when I had just been told that I was going to spend the rest of my life in a wheelchair.

The operation was scheduled for mid March. Toddy was particularly solicitous of my wishes, knowing that I was about to be bedbound in the hospital for two weeks with my hand sewn to my side. The prospect of impending helplessness was a condition with which I was all too familiar, but it was appalling nevertheless. I was still brooding over my conversation with Willett about walking, so I was doubly depressed and Toddy had her work cut out in trying to cheer me up. She reminded me of how far we had come in our recovery and of how short a period this hospitalization was, and on the weekend before I was admitted, she cooked several of my favorite dishes and bought a bottle of expensive scotch.

It was Lewpy, however, who provided the catalyst that lifted me from despair. He had been babbling for months, but after the novelty of hearing "Da-da, Da-da" had worn off, I had stopped paying serious attention to his endless but unrecognizable chatter. Then, on the last day home before I was to return to SOQ 12, Lewpy toddled into the den, where Toddy and I were watching television, and said the name of the little girl who lived in the apartment above ours. "Ristine, Ristine," he repeated as we completely forgot our television program and gave our son our total concentration. Although he had left off the *Ch* from the beginning of her name, there was no mistaking his meaning, and he beamed with satisfaction at his accomplishment. I could not have been prouder, and we quickly summoned the little girl's parents to show them how he had honored their daughter and at the same time demonstrated an unparalleled gift for oratory.

When I was returned to my hospital room after the operation and several hours in the recovery room, I had a splitting headache from the anesthesia and the inevitable cottony mouth. As usual, Toddy was waiting for me, but since my right hand felt as if it had been filleted, I was not much company. She stayed just long enough to be assured that the danger period was over, and after brushing my mouth and parched lips with a lemon-flavored swab, she went home to take care of Lewpy.

I accepted the first of a half dozen postoperative morphine injections from the ward nurse without hesitation as soon as Toddy had left, and I welcomed the bite of the needle, knowing full well that the next ten minutes of euphoria would be followed by blessed unconsciousness. After the first couple of days the pain subsided, and the painkiller was reduced accordingly. Dr. Willett decided to try me on a new drug in lieu of morphine, and although it eased the discomfort in my hand and side, it slurred my speech and distorted my sense of space and distance. Immediately after I took the analgesic, objects appeared elongated to me, and when I closed my eyes, my hand felt as if it were on the other side of the room instead of only a foot from the end of my nose.

The unpleasant side effects of the narcotic were also accompanied several times by a return of my dream about being chased by enemy soldiers, and the combination of the dream and the hallucinatory effect of the pain shots was truly terrifying. After I woke from the dream, my pajama top was always soaking wet, and the intensity of the dream was as profound as my relief that it was over. I finally complained to Dr. Willett, who switched me to sixty-five-milligram Darvon capsules during the day and a strong sedative at night to keep me from thrashing about and compromising the graft. The worst parts of the recovery, however, were the helplessness of having only one free hand to care for myself and the boredom that resulted from being so confined.

When I groused to Toddy about my situation, she cheerily reminded me that the appendage on the end of my left wrist did not really qualify as a hand but that in any event I had obviously forgotten how much worse off I had been during the early part of my hospitalization when neither hand was free. Her jogging of my memory was enough to silence me, but I continued to pout as I let her feed me the homemade dishes she brought in on a regular basis. My spirits always revived when at dinnertime each evening I heard the familiar sound of her footsteps on the tile outside my door. Toddy put up with my carping and did the things for me that I could not do for myself. She also on occasion brought in with her a small vial of bourbon so that she could have a cocktail while she was feeding me my dinner, and the nurses and corpsmen were more than willing to allow her a breach of the rules since they were spared having to deal with me.

═══ ☆ ═══

Midway through the ordeal of having my hand sewn to my side, I received an urgent and alarming phone call from my older sister. She had just gotten off the phone with our mother, who had called to report that our father had awakened that morning confused and disoriented. The family doctor had come immediately and made a preliminary diagnosis of a minor stroke or cerebral accident, but he had decided to leave Father at home for the present rather than send him to the Portsmouth Naval Hospital, where his medical records were maintained. He was having some trouble recalling or using certain words, a condition known as aphasia, but other than that, he was stable and displayed no physical signs of having had a stroke.

As we talked, Virginia told me that the doctor believed that the strange surroundings of the hospital would add to Father's confusion and that it was too early to tell how badly his ability to communicate had been affected. Virginia also said that Mother and she had discussed a similar but less serious incident a few months earlier, after which Father was unable to recall for a few hours that I had been wounded and was in the Philadelphia Naval Hospital. Virginia and I both were aware that a ghastly pattern might be developing, particularly since a stroke had forced our father's retirement fifteen years earlier in 1955, and there had been recurrences since then; but neither of us wanted to pursue the matter, and as we ended our conversation, she promised to keep us abreast of his condition after she got to Saluda.

When Virginia hung up, I could not get the phone back onto its cradle with my one free hand, and frustrated at my helplessness and the news about my father, I let the phone fall to the floor and sank back onto my pillow. At a time when my father was most in need of help, I was unable to do any more than lie on my back like a turtle and wallow in my own self-pity. I felt guilty and useless. As I thought about the bad news, it seemed ironic that my own son was gaining an ability to speak just as my father was losing his, and I wondered if they would ever converse together. After a few minutes a corpsman appeared in my doorway to scold me for keeping the line into the ward tied up, and I pointed to the receiver dangling on the floor and told him where he could stick it. He shrugged and put the phone back on its cradle; he had better sense than to engage me further.

Later in the afternoon, when Dr. Willett came by to check my graft, I was in a more civil mood and badly in need of someone to talk to about my father. Standing at the foot of my bed, Willett listened politely as I described my conversation with my sister and my father's past history of strokes. After I had finished, he volunteered to establish a line of communication with the doctors who would be treating my father at Portsmouth if and when it later became necessary to hospitalize him. He also told me that he had experienced a similar situation with a close family member, so that his perspective was more than that of a dispassionate doctor. He finished his commentary gently but firmly by telling me that my father would probably endure a number of these insults until he finally stroked out.

I had never heard the phrase *stroked out*, and as I began to grasp the significance of what Dr. Willett was saying and of what Virginia and I had refused to acknowledge in our earlier conversation, the term struck me as obscene. For a moment I wished that I had never initiated the conversation with Dr. Willett, and as I turned my head on my pillow away from him and toward the wall beside my bed, he sensed my discomfort.

"For what it's worth, Lieutenant Puller," he said, "your father might die this year or he might live another ten years without a recurrence. You should know, however, that from my reading of what you have told me, his prognosis is poor."

When I turned back to him, he placed his hand on my shoulder and looked me in the eye.

"You should also know," he said, "that your being at his bedside now is completely out of the question and would also serve very little purpose except to make you feel better."

After he had left my room, closing the door softly behind him and leaving me alone, I allowed myself the luxury of tears for the man who had tried to teach me that it was unmanly for grown men to cry in the presence of other grown men. It was Good Friday evening and I knew that two days hence, on Easter Sunday morning, whatever joyful noises were made unto the Lord would be made tentatively, if at all, in the Puller family.

=== ☆ ===

A week later I was taken back to the operating room and given general anesthesia while Dr. Willett detached the flap from my hand. When he looked in on me after I had recovered sufficiently to be taken back to SOQ 12, he told me that the graft had taken beautifully and that I could go home in a few days. My side and hand were killing me, and I was too groggy from postoperative morphine to share his enthusiasm; but I was so grateful to be able to move my arm freely that I returned his thumbs-up when he told me that the next operation would be the last of more than a dozen. Before I went home, Willett removed the dressings from the donor site on my left side and from my hand, and as I watched him work, I was appalled that he considered the operation a success.

My left side was a mass of scar tissue surrounding the wound where the hand had been attached, and although it had been scarred from previous grafting before he started, it now looked even worse. Toddy later reminded me that one more scar hardly made any difference and that at any rate my newly acquired sculpting looked terrific compared with the terrible mess that the booby trap had made of my right side. My hand, however, alarmed me the most, and after Willett had unwrapped it, I turned it from side to side and flexed my fingers to work out the stiffness. Between the thumb and forefinger was a ball of healthy-looking pink flesh that to me looked misshapen and terribly out of place. In addition to its being hideous, I could not see how the graft was going to make my hand more functional or how Willett could possibly be pleased with the outcome.

"In a month, Lieutenant," he said, without even noticing my uneasiness, "we will bring you back in, pare away the excess flesh from the graft, and you can then start thinking about what you are going to do with the rest of your life."

241

His comment to me, although probably made to get my mind off my hand, was a pertinent reminder that there was life after SOQ 12. Willett had repaired a lot of broken marines and sailors in his years as a surgeon, and it was encouraging to know that he expected us to do something productive with our lives after he had finished with us. I was not at all certain that the rest of society shared Willett's expectations, and I had heard horror stories from several veterans who had begun looking for jobs as they were making the transition out of the hospital.

Paul Barents, for example, a bright and personable college graduate, had been turned down for entry-level management positions with several major corporations before finally finding a job. He told me that when he first started looking, he was shocked at how suspiciously Vietnam veterans were regarded. He had expected to encounter an attitude of doubt on the part of potential employers about his ability to function effectively with wooden legs, but he was not ready to have to justify his role in Vietnam as well.

John Zier wanted to work for himself and thus avoided the Vietnam stigma in preemployment interviews. He had decided that the sheer force of his own will was going to make him a millionaire before he was thirty. He had begun practicing his salesmanship techniques on fellow patients, and with my hand sewn to my side, I was an ideal sitting duck for his spiel. Although I thought most of his schemes were outlandish, he was entertaining, and I envied him his confidence as he expounded on the wealth to be derived from various franchises, pyramid schemes, and other pie-in-the-sky investment opportunities.

Many of the patients found the idea of further schooling less depressing than job hunting, and I was among those who thought they could recapture some of the innocence they had lost in Vietnam by returning to the campuses of their college years. In addition, because I was totally disabled as a result of a service-connected injury, the government would pay for all my schooling. In the fall I had gone to the Veterans Administration regional office in Philadelphia and been counseled on the benefit options under a vocational rehabilitation program. When I discovered what was available, I had hurried home to share the news with Toddy, and we quickly made a decision to contact the College of William and Mary about the admissions process for law school. I had taken the law boards my senior year there; but I had not scored well enough to compensate for a mediocre academic record, and with the prospect of military service hanging over my head, I wondered why I had bothered to take the test at all.

Now, almost three years later, I was glad I had my test scores; the rest of the application process was mostly routine paperwork and hard lobbying by one man. Jim Kelly, an old family friend who was in charge of alumni affairs, promised to help with law school admission. Jim was a former marine who thought the world of my father. While I was in college, he had been a loyal supporter and confidant despite my failure to take school seriously. Now I was leaning on him again.

When Dr. Willett decided that I was in no danger of postoperative complications, he sent me home for a month of convalescent leave. I would have to return to the hospital for my final surgery, but that would take only a week. My right hand would appear much more normal and more functional after he had given it his finishing touch. With a month of leave to look forward to and the arrival of spring, I was in good spirits when I got home. My father had stabilized following his stroke, and I did not yet know how I was going to react to seeing him with his speech impaired; but Mother was holding up well, and my sisters reported that his aphasia was mild although very frustrating for everyone.

On my first visit home Jim Kelly called to say that I could officially consider myself a member of the law school class of '73. I was elated and at the same time humbled by the news because I realized that I would never have been given an opportunity to become a lawyer had I not been so badly wounded. I was grateful that some good might be forthcoming from my war experience. I was also immensely relieved just to have a place to go following my release from the hospital, and Jim's phone call provided a focus to our lives that I knew would ease the transition into the civilian community.

Toddy was as excited by our prospects as I was, and when I had finished my conversation with Jim, she could tell by my grin that I had been accepted. She gave me a congratulatory hug, and we immediately decided to call our parents to let them know of our improving fortune. When I got through to my mother in Saluda, she told me that she could not have been happier for me, especially since her own father had been a lawyer, and I could hear her explaining the news to my father before she gave him the receiver.

As I explained to him that our old marine friend Jim Kelly had gotten me into law school, I instinctively raised my voice several decibels to compensate for the deafness he had developed as he grew older. He seemed to understand me perfectly and murmured his approval each time I paused. When I had finished, he told me that he was proud of me and that he would get the details from my mother. It was the first time we had talked together since his latest stroke, and I ended the conversation by telling him that I was glad he sounded so well. I did not mention his illness, and when I got off the phone, I realized that he had struggled for and been unable to summon several words during our brief conversation. Toddy told me that I had spoken too loudly into the receiver, and I wondered if my father was having as much trouble dealing with my disability as I was with his.

Later that night several of the couples in our apartment building dropped by to welcome me home from the hospital, and we shared our news of law school with them and made them stay for drinks. I was on an emotional roller coaster with good news coming on the heels of news of my father's stroke. After our guests had gone, Toddy and I looked in on Lewpy and then sat up in bed and talked for a long time about where we were headed.

At the end of April 1970 I had the final reconstructive surgery on my right hand, and the operation, compared with the countless others I had endured, proved to be a snap. Dr. Willett had me in and out in a week, and although my hand was bandaged and elevated for several days after the operation, the inconvenience was more tolerable because I could now see an end to my ordeal.

My roommate for this last surgery was a former army warrant officer helicopter pilot who had returned to Vietnam to work for U.S. AID after he had gotten out of the service. Unlike most of us who had viewed our commitment to the war in terms of years or months, Ken had, in his words, "signed on for the duration." He had not suffered a scratch in several dangerous tours as a combat helicopter pilot, but as a civilian peacekeeper he had stepped on a booby trap and had his insides rearranged. When I first met him, he appeared to be able-bodied; but his bathrobe concealed a colostomy bag, and he was impotent. A piece of shrapnel that had entered his abdomen and exited near his spine was the cause of his misery, and while he was mending, he did not know if his condition was temporary or permanent.

Ken and I liked each other immediately. Because he was ambulatory and anxious for distraction, he was more than willing to help me with the little chores I could not handle by myself. In fact, he was so obliging and handled his own predicament so gracefully that it became easier to overlook both the clouds of smoke created by his ever-present black cigar and the sickeningly sweet smell from the mint pellets that he used to disguise the odor of his bag.

On the morning of my release from the hospital Dr. Willett came around to write my discharge orders and remove my dressings for the last time. He had cut away enough of the excess flesh from the pedicle flap that the web space no longer appeared bulbous, and I complimented him on his work as we examined my hand together. It would never be a thing of beauty; but it certainly looked better than it had a week earlier, and at least the operations were finally over. Willett felt obliged to tell me that there were a number of other procedures that could be undertaken to restore more function to my hand but that they would be time-consuming and he could not guarantee success. When he mentioned another year of being a patient on the hand service, I shook my head and waved him off. On Monday morning I would resume my prosthesis training at PT, and by the fall I intended to be a law student at William and Mary. Ken puffed on his cigar in the background as Willett and I concluded our conversation, and when Toddy arrived to pick me up, he carried my bag out to the car. I was not free of the hospital yet, but I had spent my last night as a patient on SOQ 12.

On the day that Dr. Willett performed my final surgery, April 30, 1970, President Nixon had made a televised speech to announce that United States and South Vietnamese forces had attacked Communist sanctuaries across the border from South Vietnam in Cambodia. His announcement caught the Congress and the country by surprise and aroused such enmity within the antiwar movement that within days college and university campuses were awash with organized protests. Militarily I thought that the attacks were justified if indeed the Cambodian sanctuaries were being used as launching sites for NVA incursions into South Vietnam, and I was amazed at the vehemence and extent of the protests.

I wanted the war to end, and I was fearful that Nixon's decision could expand and prolong our involvement; but I still had a small-unit leader's perspective. I knew that our troops along the border, if they could not come home, at least wanted to be able to respond to enemy attacks. What bothered me the most, however, was the shift in the mood of the country. Increasingly the war seemed to be regarded by more and more Americans as just not worth fighting, and if that were so, I had lost my legs and several good friends for nothing.

Four days later and a day prior to my release from Dr. Willett's care, the growing protest occasioned by the foray into Cambodia reached a startling climax. On May 4, 1970, national guardsmen activated to monitor antiwar protests at Kent State University in Ohio shot and killed four student demonstrators. It was not made clear why the guardsmen had responded to a student protest with such deadly force, but the graphic footage of the shootings aired on television screens across the country galvanized the protesters and shocked the conscience of America. I, too, was appalled by the senseless killing, but I could not understand why my countrymen seemed to react so much more heatedly to the four Kent State killings than to the killings of more than fifty thousand Americans in Vietnam.

As summer arrived in 1970, I began to distance myself from the hospital and look toward the future. I continued to go regularly to PT, but by now I had accepted the fact that barring some miracle of modern medicine, I was going to spend the rest of my life in a wheelchair. My performance was therefore perfunctory, and I attended sessions more for the exercise and to get away from our cramped apartment than to improve my walking skills.

Most of the old crowd except for Jim Crotty had moved on, and as an old man of almost twenty-five I had little in common with the newer and mostly noncombat patients. During the spring the PT facility had been moved into a new area of the hospital, and even though it was more spacious, it had more direct exposure to the sun and was not air-conditioned. As a result, there were days during the summer when the temperature inside exceeded ninety degrees, and Smithers threatened to cancel therapy rather than make newly injured patients exercise under such intolerable conditions. I was angry that virtually every doctor in the hospital had an air-conditioned office while the patients had to suffer through stifling heat, but I also knew that at least some of my testiness was based on my fear of leaving the hospital and my growing disillusionment with the Vietnam War.

On far too many evenings I fortified myself for the nightly news with an extra drink or two, and news of the war was always depressing. In June a marine private, Michael Schwarz, was convicted of murdering a dozen Vietnamese women and children, and again I felt that the media and much of the country viewed the heinousness of his crime as typical behavior of combat veterans. The administration and the Pentagon continued to stress their timetable for U.S. troop withdrawals, and more troops were coming home. At the same time the rhetoric surrounding their return seemed designed to placate voters and avoid the reality that we were both losing the war and condemning our South Vietnamese allies to unspeakable terror.

Indeed, while Private Schwarz was being tried for his crimes, Vietcong forces had murdered more than a hundred innocent civilians in a little village near Da Nang, the same area where I had fought, and I could see that this atrocity was but a precursor of carnage on an even more massive scale. I was getting to the point where I could barely stand to watch or read news of the war, but like a moth drawn to a deadly flame, I could not force myself to turn off the television, stop reading the paper, or put the war out of my mind.

Early in the summer we made a trip south to spend a night with my parents in Saluda and look for housing convenient to William and Mary. We managed to find a small rental home on a day trip to Williamsburg, and the owner agreed to hold it for us despite the uncertainty of my discharge date from the hospital. The overall trip, however, was difficult.

I had not seen my father since his stroke, and I was apprehensive; but my mother and my wife managed to keep the conversation going despite my awkwardness and my father's faulty speech. He seemed to understand most of what was said to him, and he tried to take part in conversations; but often Mother or one of us had to supply the word he was struggling to produce. He tired quickly and seemed to have the most trouble late in the afternoon and in the evenings. Our efforts at communication were so tense and exhausting that by the end of the weekend I was actually looking forward to getting away from the man I loved most in life. That, of course, made me feel acutely guilty. On the way back north on Sunday evening I was despondent and slept part of the way while Toddy drove and Lewpy babbled happily in the backseat. His vocabulary was progressing by leaps and bounds, and every day he surprised us with a new word or phrase. It continued to amaze me that what was now coming so easily for my son was all but impossible for my father.

By midsummer Smithers and I had reached an understanding that I had nothing further to gain from physical therapy. Eddie had completed work on my legs, and I had bought a suit, several pairs of slacks, and some shoes to accommodate my new size. Toddy sewed zippers into the pant legs so that I could pull them over the rigid feet of my prostheses, and we both got a laugh when we realized that I was now going to have to zip my pants up in three places before I would be presentable.

I gave Eddie a carton of cigarettes for the work he had done on my legs, but I balked when he overplayed his hand by asking me to write a character reference for his personnel file. I had heard too many stories about his moonlighting with government prosthetic supplies, and I was finally fed up with his constant hints that he worked faster when his patients showed their appreciation with small favors. The last time I left his shop, he was earnestly telling a wide-eyed Caucasian patient that he was all out of white legs, and I shook my head and wondered how he could still find that story amusing after so many repetitions. The hospital seemed smaller to me now and less overwhelming than it had when I was a new arrival. I knew that it was time to be moving on; but I was scared to go, and I cursed the war, my country, and the Marine Corps for making my journey so difficult.

When the Philadelphia Naval Hospital concluded there was little more it could do for me, a three-doctor panel led by Dr. Willett was convened to document my disabilities. The findings of the Physical Evaluation Board filled three typewritten pages; Willett told me he had never seen a more extensive narrative of combat-sustained injuries in one individual. Most patients hoped to be rated for as high a degree of disability as possible because their retired pay or disability compensation would be based on the Physical Evaluation Board's findings. In my case, the combination of injuries was enough to qualify me for total disability several times over, and there was never any question that the government was going to compensate me at the maximum rate.

I was, of course, found unfit for further military duty and ordered to the retired list effective on August 31, 1970. Toddy and I spent our last several days in Philadelphia saying good-bye to friends and acquaintances and preparing for the move. Most of the patients with whom we had experienced our most painful times were long since gone; so were most of the hospital personnel who had nursed me back to health, but I felt a need to visit the hospital one last time.

On the morning the movers came, I drove over to the hospital by myself to check out for good and take care of a few last-minute details. A marine staff sergeant in patient affairs made sure my paperwork was in order, issued me a retired officer identification card, and gave me my honorable discharge and a Marine Corps lapel pin. The pin was no larger than a dime, and I rubbed it between the stump of my right thumb and forefinger while the staff sergeant counseled me on career opportunities. He was efficient, emotionless, and deferential to my status as an officer, but I had to restrain myself from snickering when he suggested that I was now qualified to teach small-unit tactics in a military school.

Dr. Willett was in surgery, so I left a message with the secretary that I had been by to say good-bye. I then made a quick tour of the hospital, stopping briefly at PT, OT, and finally SOQ 12, where there was the usual midmorning huddle of corpsmen and nurses at the nurses' station. I was six weeks short of two years as a patient in these familiar environs. Looking at them for the last time, I realized that the certainty of my eventual release had helped me survive the ordeal. Without further fanfare I took the elevator down to ground level and wheeled out the swinging doors of the emergency room into the parking lot over which I had been carried in a stretcher a lifetime ago.

By the time I got home, the moving truck was loaded, and all that remained was to pack the car and turn the apartment key in to base housing. I got behind the wheel while Toddy strapped Lewpy into his seat and put my wheelchair into the remaining space in the trunk. Toddy said her good-byes to the neighborhood wives gathered in our driveway. Then, by noon, we were on our way. As we cleared the sentry box on the way out of the base, a young marine on duty saluted the officer's sticker on the bumper of my car, and I absentmindedly acknowledged him by touching my hand to my brow.

Within minutes we had passed the hospital and were headed south toward Virginia and home, and I watched the gray central spine of the hospital in my rearview mirror until it passed from sight. For a long time neither of us spoke. When I finally turned my head toward Toddy, she smiled and squeezed my arm just above the elbow. I was a civilian for the first time in our marriage, and she was two and one half months pregnant with our second child.

From the car radio a line from a song by Creedence Clearwater Revival interrupted my reverie, and I wondered if it augured well for our family: "Tryin' to find the sun, I went down Virginia seekin' shelter from the storm."

Part Two

★

VII

★

IN WILLIAMSBURG we settled into our rented bungalow on a treelined street adjacent to the William and Mary campus. I had been accepted into the law school class commencing in the fall; but once in Williamsburg, I quickly realized that I was not yet emotionally ready for the rigors of law school, and I arranged with the dean to begin taking classes in January 1971 rather than in September.

For the first several months I felt completely adrift and cut off from the support I had had while I was in the hospital. No one in the world outside the hospital had experienced the Vietnam War the way that I had. Alone and isolated, I began to bottle up my feelings rather than try to share them with others. I felt they could not possibly understand. On those few occasions when I stumbled into conversations about the war, my presence seemed to make others so ill at ease that more often than not the conversations abruptly halted or shifted to safer topics. I even helped change the subject, but I raged inside at the unfairness of my situation. Having fought a war that cost me so dearly while leaving virtually all my new acquaintances untouched, I was now told in countless subtle ways that I could not vent my grief and frustration by talking about the war because it made society uncomfortable.

To make matters worse, I discovered that my new environment made almost no concessions to the wheelchair. I was so hampered in my ability to navigate that I frequently chose to stay at home rather than venture out. My reclusiveness meant that there were fewer occasions to subject myself to the stares of curious onlookers, but it also made me a prisoner in my own home and increased my despondency. I remembered with despair my earlier student days when I trod barefoot on the hot bricks of campus walkways and the only checks on my freedom were self-imposed. Frequently I left the house alone in my car and drove aimlessly for hours throughout the countryside, and it was only when I started classes that my black moods improved. By then, however, I had begun to take solace increasingly in drink, and by the time second semester classes began, I had to curtail a daily routine of half a dozen drinks between the cocktail hour and bedtime.

At the Philadelphia Naval Hospital my therapists had told me about a hydraulic knee joint that made walking easier for some amputees. When I began to realize how inaccessible Williamsburg was and how troubling my appearance was to people who were not prepared for it, I decided to make one more effort with artificial limbs. My sister Virginia had told me in a moment of candor that caught me off guard that when I began law school, I should consider using artificial legs for their cosmetic effect whether I could walk or not. Her advice jolted me in a way that the stares of strangers never could. Her comment also made Toddy so angry that for several days she railed about certain people, who were not related to her side of the family, minding their own business. The nearest VA hospital that could accommodate my needs was in Richmond, and early in September I began traveling back and forth twice a week for fittings and more physical therapy.

I had never been inside a VA hospital before, and on my first visit I was shaken by the sight of so many men sitting around in wheelchairs doing absolutely nothing. There was a concourse in the hospital with a cafeteria, a recreation area, and banks of tables along each of its walls. At each table there were several wheelchairs containing men in hospital bathrobes or casual civilian attire, and they all seemed to be smoking cigarettes and passing the time of day by talking to each other and watching the traffic in the center of the concourse.

At the end of my first day, after the VA had arranged for a private contractor to make new limbs for me, many of the men I had observed earlier were still sitting in their places as if waiting patiently for the day to end. On the drive back to Williamsburg I vowed that I would never let myself be warehoused in such a fashion. Many of the men were older, and some were obviously in the hospital temporarily; but a fair number were my age or only a few years older, and I could not understand how their circumstances could have so depleted their motivation. In the military hospital I had just left, we all were trying to escape our confinement; but here things were completely reversed, and I wondered what these men could have experienced that would have caused such a change. I did not like the picture I had just seen of life at the end of the road, and when I got home, I needed no encouragement to break out the scotch bottle.

I drove to Richmond twice weekly until I started law school, but it was apparent to me the first day I got up on my new legs that hydraulic knees were not going to improve my walking. I had undertaken this last rehabilitation effort solely because I was so frustrated by my physical condition, and now I knew that when I called it quits this last time, I would never walk again.

In the five months that I took therapy at the VA hospital I met only one other amputee who had lost his legs in Vietnam, and there were days, as I watched the geriatric patients around me, when I felt as if the Vietnam War existed only in the dim recesses of my mind. It seemed remarkable to me that my country was so vast that it could simply swallow up the dead and maimed from my generation's war and continue to march as if nothing was amiss. Because I had not yet made any friends in law school and had no outlet for my frustrations, I was miserable to be with at home, and if nothing else, my trips to Richmond at least got me out of the house.

During our first several months in Williamsburg, we were invited to a few social functions, but my resentful mood was such that I concentrated on my drinking and made no attempt to sort out my feelings. At one poolside party I overheard a group of local businessmen discussing the lack of respect the younger generation had for its elders, as if the issue were of paramount concern. I felt I was never going to fit in anywhere for the rest of my life. On another occasion an old college acquaintance, who was now selling life insurance in Williamsburg, took me out for a few beers with two women we had known as undergraduates. After an hour of mindless chatter about the hard life of unmarried female graduate students, I knew that time and distance had so altered our perspectives that the joyful escapades of only a few years earlier were no longer common ground for conversation. After another hour and several more beers I made an excuse for leaving and went back to my pregnant wife and child, convinced that I was at least a generation older than the two young women who had once been my contemporaries.

═ ☆ ═

During the second week in October 1970, the same week in which I had been wounded two years earlier, my father suffered a massive stroke and was rushed to the Portsmouth Naval Hospital. My mother and Virginia took a room at a motel nearby and used it as a base while Father hovered unconscious and near death in the intensive care unit of the hospital. I drove to Portsmouth as soon as I got the news. As I wheeled my chair through the swinging metal doors into intensive care, I overheard two marine gunnery sergeants who had come to pay their respects, discussing my father's situation.

"It looks like the old man has bought the ranch this time," one of them said, and there were such painful looks on their otherwise stoic faces that I steeled myself for the worst.

My mother and sister were already at his bedside. Mother held a balled-up handkerchief in her right hand with which she periodically made absentminded swipes at her nose. Virginia seemed to be doing her best to keep Mother from collapsing.

My father lay bare-chested on his back in the middle of a sterile field of starched white sheets, and his hands were secured to the chrome rails of his bed by restraining straps. He was struggling hard against the straps, but his movements were convulsive, and he seemed unaware of his condition. He was hooked up to the usual assortment of tubes, with which I had some familiarity, and the respirator tube that was taped to his nose made an obscene rhythmic sucking noise that for a few moments was the only sound in the room. My first impulse was to pull the tube from his nose and untie his straps, but after I had regained my composure, I hugged my mother and sister. The three of us were then joined by a white-gowned doctor, who escorted us out of the room, where we could talk with less distraction.

The doctor told us that there was nothing to be gained by our presence and advised us to go back to the motel and get some rest. The next forty-eight hours would be crucial, he said, and he promised to phone us promptly if there were any dramatic changes to report. I despised his cool efficiency and lack of emotional involvement, but I knew he was right. Virginia and I went to work prying our mother loose from her husband's bedside.

For the next couple of days Virginia and I took turns making short trips to the hospital. At the end of the second day Father's eyes seemed to focus for an instant on my sister and gave us a glimmer of hope for his recovery. We did not know yet if he was going to live or how much quality his life would have if he did; but Mother prayed now only for his survival under any circumstances, and Virginia and I did not give voice to our other concerns.

The next morning I left them at the hospital and drove back to Williamsburg for a business appointment. During the night Father had made some negligible improvement, but beyond saying that he was probably going to survive, the doctors were unable to say to what extent he would recover. On the way home I played and replayed my first sight of him in intensive care. I did not know if it would be more merciful to let him go now than to see him robbed of all dignity by the inevitable future strokes about which Dr. Willett had warned me. I did know that I needed his help in coming to terms with my own experience, and I allowed myself the luxury of self-indulgent tears as I reflected that there was very little strength left in my father on which I could draw.

My father survived his October stroke, and as with the earlier ones, there was no damage to his brain other than a marked worsening of his aphasia and a new tendency toward outbursts of temper. He was in the hospital for several months, and when he finally came home, he required constant supervision, which took a heavy toll on Mother. At first we tried round-the-clock nursing shifts, but the logistical problems associated with getting skilled practitioners in remote Saluda proved to be a nightmare.

One night he became enraged at the officiousness of a male nurse and tried to throw the man out of his house, which he was still proud enough to regard as his exclusive domain. Despite his speech difficulties, he made it clear that he would tolerate strange females in his home but that he was not about to share his home with any other adult males. Finally Mother was able to find Mrs. Gillen, a good practical nurse with whom he got along well, and she fired the shift nurses.

I tried to visit as frequently as I could, but the effort required to commiserate with Father in his first months at home was exhausting, and after each trip to Saluda I felt depressed and guilty that I had left my mother with such an impossible situation. She devoted all her time to my father in his final months at home, often reading to him until late in the night, lighting and relighting his pipe, and trying desperately to understand his garbled words. The attention that she lavished on him was the most noble endeavor I had ever seen her undertake.

═══ ☆ ═══

On November 12, 1970, at Fort Benning, Georgia, the court-martial of Lieutenant William L. Calley, Jr., for the murder of civilians at My Lai began. The trial lasted for more than four months and was the focus of such intense media coverage that it became, in effect, a forum for debate over American involvement in Vietnam. Calley was portrayed by supporters of the war as a maverick acting alone and without orders, whose actions, brought on by the stress of prolonged combat and casualties in his own unit, were an aberration from the rules of engagement. The opposing viewpoint held that his actions, if not sanctioned by higher authority, were at least tolerated and were typical of the conduct of ground units in the war.

I was deeply offended by the notion that the hideous atrocities committed by Calley and his men were commonplace in Vietnam, an inevitable consequence of an ill-advised involvement in someone else's civil war. The men I had led in combat were, like any cross section of American youth, capable of good and evil, and I felt we all were, by implication, being branded as murderers and rapists. Throughout the proceedings the reportage seemed to me to accentuate the monstrous evil of a group of men gone amok without any effort to depict fairly the discipline and courage that existed along with the forces of darkness in most units.

Lieutenant Calley was ultimately found guilty of the premeditated murder of twenty-two civilians and sentenced to life imprisonment, but I felt his punishment could never right the evil he had done or the perceptions he had helped foster of America's soldiers and marines as bloodthirsty killers. At the end of the trial I wrote letters to several local newspapers protesting that it was unfair for the Calley case to have so influenced public opinion, but the grisly photographs of murdered civilians lying in a ditch at My Lai, which had been so prominently displayed in newspapers across the country, spoke far more eloquently than my feeble words.

=== ☆ ===

Starting law school distracted me from my preoccupation with the Vietnam War. Toddy was by then in the last trimester of her pregnancy and near her wits' end with young Lewis and me underfoot most of the time. Nevertheless, she had bought me a shiny new briefcase as a send-off for law school, and before my first days of classes we both were optimistic that our situation was about to improve. I had stored my artificial legs in the closet; but I at least knew that I had given walking my best effort, and I was now ready to focus my attention on other matters.

When I arrived at law school the first day with a briefcase full of law books wedged between my chin and the seat of my wheelchair, I was uneasy about being able even to get into the classrooms; but several students hoisted me up the front steps of the building, and after that I rarely had trouble finding someone to help me in and out. The first time I was called upon to brief a case, the professor, unaware that I was in a wheelchair, asked me to stand to recite. For a long moment the class became completely still, and I could feel the color rise in my cheeks while I struggled for a response. When I finally managed to reply that nothing would give me greater pleasure than to comply with his request but that I was in a wheelchair, he quickly apologized, and I briefed the case without further distraction. That one exchange seemed to break the tension for the rest of my classmates, and once I had addressed my disability directly, albeit not by choice, communication was less painful from then on.

Although I perhaps should have expected it, the most surprising common denominator among my fellow classmates was their lack of direct Vietnam involvement. A majority of them had no military service whatever, and those who had served were usually reservists, stateside, or held noncombatant assignments in Vietnam. Of the almost 150 students in my law class, only 2 or 3 had experienced the terror of war in a way with which I could relate, and they, like me, seemed unwilling to share the experience. On the other hand, many of those who were untouched by the war seemed to hold the strongest opinions about it and were the quickest to voice their views.

During my first semester in law school, as a group of us milled about waiting for a class to begin, I overheard one student, who had never served, comment that soldiers had it easy because they got free meals and shelter, got to see the world, and did very little work. Having just come from living with so many torn young men, who had never had it easy and never would, I was too dumbstruck to respond. I was even more enraged that the rest of the group allowed the remark to go unchallenged. When I got to my seat, I had to steady my hands before I could open my briefcase, and I wondered if just I or the rest of the world was out of sync.

I was also bothered, but to a lesser extent, by the grousing of the reservists who had joined up mostly so that they would not have to serve in Vietnam. It seemed incredible to me that at the height of the Vietnam War there was a military option available that assured its takers that they would never see the war. Then to have to listen to them complain about the inconvenience of weekend drills or the hair-length requirements of their particular service was galling at first, until I forced myself to remember that it is a serviceman's privilege to complain, no matter how incidental that service might be.

My strongest resentment was reserved for those who had no service at all. By 1971 the war was winding down, and there were a fair number of students who made the transition directly from undergraduate school to law school without having undergone any intervening displacement. Most of them were blissfully unaware of how fortunate they were, but I bore them none of the ill will that I held for my contemporaries who had manipulated the system to avoid military service. The most common dodge was a teaching deferment, and my class seemed to be loaded with former teachers who had decided after conveniently spending a few years in the classroom that they now wanted to be lawyers.

There were also students who had obtained medical deferments, some of which were legitimate and some of which were, if not fraudulent, at least questionable. One student, who in all other respects seemed to me like a decent young man, made no effort to hide the fact that he had force-fed himself a high-calorie diet in a successful effort to flunk the draft physical. I was delighted that he was finding it far more difficult to take off the seventy pounds he had gained than to put them on, but I was also amazed that none of our peers thought any the less of him for his course of action.

There was, in the academic environment in which I found myself in 1971, a prevailing attitude that American involvement in the Vietnam War was, if not downright immoral, certainly a mistake of epic proportions. From that premise flowed a corollary that any effort to avoid involvement in the war was justifiable or even laudable. As I came to believe in the spring of 1971 that this attitude was representative of the thinking of an increasing percentage of the American public, I also began to feel that my own sacrifice and that of all of us who had fought the war were meaningless. Unable then to discover any higher purpose for the wasted lives of the dozen men whom I counted as friends who had not come home, I began to despise the government and the Marine Corps, which had asked of many of us everything we had and given back almost nothing.

I felt used up and discarded, and as I tried to dispel with alcohol the magnitude of the obscene fraud of which I had been a willing victim, I was assailed by conflicting and unresolved emotions. On the one hand, I wished that all the unscathed young men from whom I was now hearing a different view of the war had been forced to endure the war experience firsthand. On the other, I wished that none had been called to serve and that the insanity still unraveling in Southeast Asia would simply stop. In an effort to break with the military traditions that had so defined much of my earlier thinking, I let my hair and sideburns grow to the length that was currently popular in the civilian community; I ordered wire-rimmed granny glasses to replace my horn-rimmed ones, and I wore the flowered shirts that Toddy brought home from the shopping trips on which she went to escape from me and my depression.

Midway through our first semester in law school I awoke one morning to find Toddy calmly packing an overnight bag. It was March 11, her father's birthday and also the day on which we were scheduled to settle on the traditional brick rambler in a Williamsburg suburb, which we had bought with a VA specially adapted housing grant. Toddy had been having labor pains for several hours when I woke up, and when she told me that it was time to go to the hospital, I needed no further prodding. I had missed my son's birth; but I was not going to be left out this time, and I got Toddy to the hospital as quickly as possible. She signed the settlement papers for the house closing while she was on the delivery table, and by noon we had both a healthy new baby girl and a new home.

We had not given my father the second grandson with the Puller name that he had hoped for earlier, but Toddy and I were delighted with Maggie, and my father communicated his approval as best he could when I called to give him the news. On the way home from the hospital later in the week, I drove, and we allowed Lewpy to sit between us and hold his little sister so that he would not feel left out. When we got home, Toddy placed Maggie on the sofa in the den and took a few minutes to survey the way in which I had had the movers position our furniture. While we were occupied in the living room, Lewpy, either out of curiosity or resentment, tried to stuff a fistful of Cheerios down his sister's throat. Toddy smoothed over the situation by taking both children to our bed, where Lewpy could see his sister being fed properly, and I for a change felt right with the world as I watched my family settle into our new surroundings.

Shortly after Maggie was born, we invited my parents for a day visit so that they could see our new house and their new grandchild. They arrived with Mrs. Gillen, my father's nurse, who had become my mother's alter ego and was a godsend in helping with Father, and the five of us sat in the living room, where we showed off Maggie. Father tired easily, and it was impossible to tell how much of the conversation he was taking in; but he beamed proudly when Toddy let him hold the baby. After we had visited and Maggie went down for her nap, Toddy took my mother shopping, and Mrs. Gillen and I tried to entertain Father.

He seemed agitated after we were left alone, and his faltering efforts to begin sentences made it obvious that something was bothering him. As usual, he had more difficulty finding nouns than verbs, but I gradually became aware that he was trying to discuss the war with me. When I realized how important the conversation seemed to him, I tried desperately to fill in the gaps in his phrases and to anticipate what his questions were, but the effort was heart-wrenching for both of us. He seemed to understand that the United States was not winning the war, a situation he found bewildering, and he wanted to know how I was handling our lack of any positive results. I tried to assure him that I was fine; but my words had a hollow ring even to me, and I realized that this dear sick old man knew the agony in my heart and what trouble I was having finding meaning in my experience.

By the time my mother and wife returned, we both were emotionally drained, and as I exchanged hugs with my father and then watched Mrs. Gillen help him down the front steps and into the car, I was relieved to see him go. It was the only conversation my father and I ever had about the war. As I look back on it, I find it excruciatingly sad that while my father was ready to talk about it, he was unable, and while I was able, I was unready.

=== ☆ ===

The third week in April of that year more than a thousand Vietnam veterans gathered in Washington to protest American involvement in the war. On Sunday, April 18, 1971, they began assembling in West Potomac Park, and their activities over the next five days, reported extensively on national and local television and in newspapers throughout the country, came to be known as Operation Dewey Canyon III after two similarly named earlier military operations in Vietnam. I was not a part of the antiwar movement and indeed thought that the motives of many of its leaders were self-serving and destructive to the country, but as the week wore on and I watched my former comrades give vent to their feelings and frustrations, I was almost persuaded to go to Washington and join them.

In the course of the week they conducted a ceremony for the war dead near the Tomb of the Unknowns in Arlington Cemetery, established a campsite on the Mall, demonstrated at the Pentagon and at the Supreme Court, and staged a candlelight march around the White House. Throughout the week they lobbied on Capitol Hill for an end to the war. One articulate young combat veteran named John Kerry delivered a moving address before a special session of the Senate Foreign Relations Committee that, for me, summed up the sense of betrayal and the disillusionment I felt toward the administration and the leadership that had directed the course of the war from the safety of its Washington power base.

On Friday, April 23, in a culmination of the events of the week, the protesting veterans were scheduled to march to the steps of the Capitol and discard their medals in a symbolic gesture of their feeling of having been discarded themselves by the nation. These were my brothers, not starry-eyed intellectuals or malcontents dedicated to the overthrow of our form of government, but soldiers and marines, many of whom had paid for their perspectives with shattered lives and shattered limbs. They were now saying that their sacrifices had been meaningless, that my sacrifice had been meaningless, and that the precious blood spilled by our dead and maimed fellow veterans had been meaningless. For years I had been hearing similar rhetoric from antiwar spokesmen whose ideology was foreign to me; but I was now hearing it from those young men whose kinship with me had been forged in the bloody crucible of Vietnam, and its impact, like a fog lifting from a shrouded landscape, stripped me of my remaining self-delusions.

On Thursday night, before the climactic last day's events in Washington, I took my medals from our bedroom closet and debated whether I should drive to Washington to throw them away. As I sat silently in the dimly lit closet feeling the weight of bronze and silver in my hand and studying the red, white, and blue stripes of my Silver Star and the majestic cameo of George Washington on my Purple Hearts, I knew that I could never part with them. They had cost me too dearly, and though I now saw clearly that the war in which they had been earned was a wasted cause, the medals still represented the dignity and the caliber of my service and of those with whom I had served. I could no more discard them than I could repudiate my country, my Marine Corps, or my fellow veterans. As I put them away, I was very sad and very tired but grateful nonetheless that my children were asleep in their beds in America rather than anywhere else in the world.

=== ☆ ===

One Saturday night later that spring I drove up to Saluda for a visit with my parents. It was a clear, balmy day that held the promise of a stretch of good weather, and I was feeling good about the way my law school classes were going and about the upcoming break after I had taken my first examinations. When I arrived, my father was in the bathroom shaving, and my mother helped me into the house before he knew I was there. As I wheeled down the hall toward their bedroom, my mother went ahead to tell Father that I was there, and I heard him excitedly call my name as he came out to meet me.

When I reached up to take his outstretched hand, his face suddenly contorted, and for a moment he stood motionless in front of me while his head jerked spasmodically. Mother realized immediately that he was having a stroke, and we managed to ease him into a chair; but all the animation had gone out of his face, and a thin line of spittle formed in the corner of his mouth and made its way down his chin. After several minutes the episode passed; but his head lay heavily against his shoulder as he sat slumped in the chair, and when we stood him up to move him into his bed, he urinated helplessly on the floor. After we got him into bed, he seemed to rest easily either because he had lost consciousness or because the warring forces in his head had completely exhausted him, and Mother called the family doctor while I stood watch.

By the time she returned, he was sleeping like a baby, and she held his hand and kept repeating that he would be better after he had gotten some rest. I wanted desperately to believe her; but I had now seen my father twice locked in the throes of a death grip within a period of six months, and I was unable to give her any comfort.

Father was next taken by ambulance to the Portsmouth Naval Hospital, and though he survived, this stroke stripped away the last vestiges of his dignity. When I saw him again several days later, he did not recognize me, was incontinent, and had become verbally abusive to most of the staff on the ward. As with the previous strokes, his physical impairment was not as great as was the change to his faculties; but he now took short, hesitant steps, and he was frail, sallow-looking, and oddly bent at the waist when he stood. When I entered his room and moved toward him to kiss his cheek, he became convinced that I was trying to run him down with my wheelchair, and he climbed onto his bed and curled up into a ball to shut me out. For an hour I tried to communicate with him, but when I left his room, it was obvious that my visit had been meaningless to him and that I would never hear him call my name again, as he had only moments before his last terrible stroke.

Mother continued to believe that his mind would return if she could only get him back into familiar surroundings, but his doctors were adamantly opposed to his going home. They eventually decided to let me have the final word on whether or not he should be transferred to a Veterans Administration nursing facility or return home. For a week I agonized all day and drank all night in an effort to choose the right course of action. I felt that by committing my father, I would be turning my back on the only man whose love for me had been boundless and unqualified, but in the end I realized that I had no real choice. Mother could not take care of him at home despite her protestations to the contrary, and I knew that he would want me to be strong enough to let him go. When I signed the paperwork to have him transferred to the Hampton, Virginia, VA hospital, I used my left hand to steady my right and keep it from shaking. My decision, though time has proved it wise, was among the hardest I have ever had to make.

The domiciliary unit where Father was housed at the Hampton VA hospital was only a fifty-five-minute drive from our home in Williamsburg, and I tried to visit him on a regular basis after we got him admitted. His situation was so depressing, and our ability to make any difference in the quality of his life was so circumscribed, that I went mostly out of a sense of duty and to ease the necessity of more frequent visits on Mother's part. Early in his stay he was warehoused in a remote adjunct of the hospital, where he spent most of his waking hours wandering aimlessly in a large dayroom with a few attendants and several dozen other patients who were in similar shape. The first time that I visited I was awed to see so many men in such close proximity to each other who were unable to communicate and were seemingly unaware of each other's presence. A retired judge sat near my father with a blank expression on his face, and one or the other of them would get up from his chair periodically and begin circling the room oblivious of any efforts by staff or visitors to hold their attention.

On each successive visit I concentrated on trying to find some glint of awareness in his eyes, some change in facial expression, or some familiar gesture that would indicate comprehension on his part, but there was never the remotest sign that he recognized me. In a way I was grateful that my father was unaware of his circumstances; but I still felt that we had unfinished business, and I knew that I was now going to have to define our relationship without any further input from him. After several more such visits I began to wish the end would come, and as his deterioration quickened through the spring and summer, it began to appear that my wish would soon be granted. Each time I left him I made a conscious effort to put the memory of what I had just witnessed out of my mind, but little reminders of his nearly helpless state kept ambushing my psyche and adding to my despondency.

$$=\!=\ \text{\textasteriskcentered}\ =\!=$$

At the end of the summer a local newspaper reporter requested an interview for a story on my view of the war in Vietnam. When he arrived, I was preoccupied with my father's impending death and with the contrast between the public support of the military in his time and mine. My father had returned triumphant to the accolades of a grateful nation, while my peers and I had been either scorned or ignored, and I now wondered how my country's perception of military obligation could have so changed. The reporter and I sat in our living room, where after some preliminary chitchat he produced a pad and pencil and began asking questions that he had prepared in advance. At first the questions were general and exploratory, and as he jotted down background information on my family and our adjustment after Vietnam, I talked freely and openly.

Toward the end of the interview, however, the conversation became focused on my feelings about having served in an unpopular war, and as I gave vent to my frustrations, there seemed to open within me an emotional floodgate that surprised us both. While I was talking, I knew that I would probably be misquoted or that my words would be taken out of context, but I had remained silent and introverted about how I felt for so long that I now spoke unguardedly and from the heart. I told the young man that if my son were older and about to be sent off to a combat unit in Vietnam, I would do everything in my power to keep him at home, and I rashly concluded by saying that knowing what I now knew, I myself would refuse to go if called again.

When the article appeared in the paper a day or two later, it was picked up by the wire services and run in papers across the country and even abroad. A typical headline reading GENERAL PULLER'S SON WOULD NOT GO was used as a background prop on the prime-time comedy show "Laugh-In" for several weeks, and in the space of a few days and on the basis of a forty-five-minute interview, the media had moved me across the political spectrum. Now I was cast as a wild-eyed radical, and I felt that my willingness only a few years earlier to sacrifice my life for my country and my hideous disfigurements were cheapened by the about-face ascribed to me.

In the wake of the article I received phone calls and hate mail from total strangers, who accused me of selling out my country and being disloyal to the Marine Corps, and I was angry and hurt by what I regarded as unfair criticism. Throughout it all Toddy tried to show me that the only perception that really mattered was the one that I had of myself, but it took me, fettered by resentment, years to see the wisdom of her counsel. After a few weeks I got over the stream of ill will to which I was subjected as a result of my comments. Unfortunately they also made me suspect in the eyes of many career marines and in so doing increased the disenchantment that I was feeling toward the organization to which I was so strongly bonded.

=== ☆ ===

By the time the fall session of law school began, my father's condition had worsened to the point that he could not walk, and he had to be shifted to the main part of the hospital. Because he could no longer communicate, it was impossible to gauge the frequency or duration of the small strokes, and Mother warned me before my first visit to his new quarters that I should be prepared for the worst. Nevertheless, his physical surroundings were much more airy and cheerful than in the dingy old domiciliary unit, and I had a false sense of optimism as I wheeled down the hallway to his room. When I arrived, he had been propped up in a chair, strapped in, and he was being fed what passed for lunch by a nurse's aide. He was clean, freshly shaved, and his hair had just been combed as if in preparation for my visit; but beyond that there was little resemblance to the man who had once been so widely regarded as a tower of strength. He had lost a lot of weight since my last visit several weeks earlier; he now wore a metal brace on his left arm, and he was blind. The only stimulus that he responded to was the feel of the feeding spoon against his lips, and I was struck by the similarity of the sucking motion he made toward its contents and the instinctive movement that my daughter had made toward her mother's nipple when she was nursing. After several minutes in his room I could stand it no longer, and I thanked the woman who was caring for him and went home to my wife and children.

=== ☆ ===

In September, as I was beginning my first semester of law school as a full-time student and getting acquainted with my classmates, the war in Vietnam continued to unravel. The troop withdrawals went on, and by Christmas fewer than 140,000 men remained of a 500,000-man force. Peace talks in Paris proceeded at a maddeningly slow pace with endless posturing by statesmen on both sides while American and Vietnamese boys continued to slaughter each other, and on September 23, 1971, Army Captain Ernest Medina, Lieutenant Calley's commanding officer in Vietnam, was acquitted of all charges of involvement in the My Lai massacre. I believed that his acquittal helped contain the guilt-by-association aspect of Calley's crime that besmirched all of us who had served honorably, but many in the country thought otherwise and chose to view the outcome as part of a continuing military cover-up.

══ ☆ ══

On the morning of October 11, 1971, three years to the day after I was wounded in Vietnam, I received a phone call from my mother saying that Father had developed pneumonia and had been transferred to the intensive care unit of the hospital. He was not responding to treatment, and the doctors expected the worst. I drove to the hospital as soon as I got off the phone, and my sisters and mother joined me later in the morning. When I first arrived, Father was prostrate in his ICU bed. Aside from difficulty breathing, he did not appear much worse than when I had last seen him. After we all had gathered, however, his breathing became more labored, and he was fitted with an oxygen mask.

His doctor took me aside and told me that he was dying but that it would probably be at least nightfall before the pneumonia had run its course. Mother was distraught and tried to hold herself together by talking nonstop about any topic that entered her mind as long as it did not relate to her husband. My sisters were far better able to console her than I, and at their urging I drove back to Williamsburg in the afternoon to shave and shower and have Toddy make arrangements for standby baby-sitting for Lewpy and Maggie. When I returned to the hospital in the late afternoon, Father's breathing was again becoming labored despite the oxygen mask, and my mother, sisters, and I sat in a small room together and waited as darkness began to fall. After what seemed an eternity, Father's doctor came in to say heroic measures were now pointless, and Mother, sensing the doctor's next request, told my sisters that she wanted to be taken home.

I sat in the hallway outside the ICU with the doctor while my mother and sisters went to my father's bedside to say their last good-byes. Their visit was brief, and when my mother emerged, balled-up handkerchief in hand, she was supported on either side by Martha and Virginia. Choking back tears, she came over to me, brushed my cheek with her lips, and, without saying a word, turned to leave the hospital. Father's doctor saw them to their car, and while he was gone, I sat smoking a cigarette and wondered how my mother was going to get by without her husband.

When the doctor returned, he asked me for permission to remove my father's oxygen mask, and I nodded my assent and continued to sit by myself in my wheelchair in the hall. My father was dying in the next room, and other than being glad that I was going to be alone with him when he passed away, I felt numb and emotionless. After a few more minutes the doctor came out of the unit and beckoned to me to go to my father's side. When I wheeled up to his bedside and locked the brakes on my chair, he looked frail and delicate in the dim light and deepening shadows around him, and holding his unresponsive hand, I saw that his reservoir of strength, once seemingly inexhaustible, was now almost used up.

At the other end of the room two nurses busied themselves with a logbook, and feeling that they had no business sharing this last moment of intimacy with us, I fought back an impulse to scream at them to get out of the room and leave us alone. Instead I reached up and pulled the curtain around my father's bed as far forward as I could reach. After several more minutes he struggled to take a few shallow breaths, his chest rattled through one last exhalation, and he was still. As I watched, a single tear formed in the corner of his right eye and trickled slowly down his cheek. Although I knew it was involuntary, I saw the tear as his parting gift to his only son, and I laid my head on my dead father's chest and wept for a lifetime of missed opportunities to get to know him more fully.

After I had regained my composure and witnessed his death certificate, I called Saluda to give my family the news and tell them to allow the funeral home to issue a press release. Mother wanted to know if there had been any recognition or if he had suffered at the end, and I tried to assure her that he had died peacefully in his sleep. I then called Toddy to tell her that I would be driving back to Williamsburg to pick her up for the trip to Saluda, and when she asked me how I was, I realized for the first time how relieved I was that it was over. On my way out to the car, one of the orderlies caught up with me in the parking lot to give me my father's slippers and the hideous brace he had unknowingly worn on his left arm for the last weeks of his life. I thanked him, put the slippers on the floor of the backseat, and dropped the brace into a trash bin before heading home.

On my way back up to Williamsburg on the interstate I went over the day and tried to analyze the relief I was feeling. I knew that part of it stemmed from the culmination of a long and protracted ordeal, but I also hoped that now that he was dead I could stop feeling as though I were living in his immense shadow. Already I missed my father terribly, but I missed the man who had nurtured me through my youth and early manhood, not the legend against whom I had measured myself for so long.

Father was buried in a simple military funeral in the graveyard adjacent to the church in which he had married my mother almost thirty-five years earlier and in which, from the time of his retirement from the Marine Corps until his illness, he had attended Sunday services regularly. For twenty-four hours prior to the funeral his body lay in state in the church chancel, a marine sentry in dress blues posted at either side of his flag-draped casket. Throughout the vigil a steady stream of admirers came from up and down the East Coast to pay homage.

I drove down to the church by myself near midnight on the eve of his funeral, purposely waiting until late in the evening so that I might avoid the condolences of other mourners and have some solitude before the actual interment. When I arrived, several groups of men and women were standing in the churchyard talking quietly with each other, and while I was getting my wheelchair out of the car, several people came out of the church and joined the late-night throng. Once inside, I was surprised to find as many people sitting or kneeling in the church's pews as were outside, and the minister who conducted the funeral service later told me that he had never seen such a large and diverse group of people come from such distances to pay their respects.

While in the church, I shook hands with a few of the local parishioners whom I had known from my boyhood an eternity ago, but for the most part the strangers among them gave me my distance. After I had prayed for the strength to make it through the funeral without falling apart, I wheeled to the foot of my father's bier and thanked the two marine corporals who stood at parade rest flanking his casket for volunteering as members of the honor guard. I knew that my father would have wanted their contribution to be acknowledged, and I felt his presence with me as I left the church and began to steel myself for the day ahead.

The funeral took place at noon on a crisp fall day whose chill was softened by a high overhead sun. I rode to our parking space in front of the church with my wife and mother in the lead car of a cortege that contained the rest of the family, and when we arrived, several camera crews from local television stations were positioned outside the brick wall around the church and its graveyard. The major networks had agreed to honor my request not to film the service; but the word had apparently not filtered down, and after we had gotten out of our car, I asked the funeral director to inform the camera crews that they were not to film inside the wall.

As we made our way toward the church, the overflow crowd, which had spilled out into the churchyard, parted to accommodate my wheelchair, and Michael helped me up the two steps into the church. As he did so, Martha spotted Jones, my father's driver from Korea, at the edge of the crowd, and she went over to ask him to join the family in the reserved pews near the front of the church. Every seat was taken. As I scanned the congregation, my eyes locked on those of a large red-faced man in an ill-fitting suit whom I had never seen before. Tears were streaming down his face, and realizing that I would never hold up through the service if I shared the emotions of the crowd, I fixed my gaze on the casket at the front of the church until we reached our seats.

With my mother seated on my left and Toddy on my right, I bowed my head for a moment's prayer before the service began and then risked another look around the church. Across the aisle there was seated a contingent of Marine Corps generals, three dozen strong, many of whom had come down from Washington on a specially arranged helicopter to honor one of their own. Most of them were contemporaries of my father, still ramrod straight in their retirement and now assembled to mark the end of an association that for some had spanned five wars and fifty years.

"I am the resurrection and the life, saith the Lord: he that believeth in me, though he were dead, yet shall he live: and whosoever liveth and believeth in me shall never die," began the minister.

For the next twenty minutes I shared a prayer book with my mother and took comfort from the familiar language of the Order for the Burial of the Dead. We sang the hymns my sisters and mother had selected, "A Mighty Fortress Is Our God," "O God, Our Help in Ages Past," and "The Son of God Goes Forth to War." During the singing of each hymn I admired the resonant baritone of my older sister's husband behind me and remembered how terrible yet energetic my father's singing voice had been.

At the conclusion of the indoor part of the service an honor guard of four marine sergeants from the Marine Corps Barracks at Eighth and I streets in Washington, D.C., bore my father's casket from the chancel, and as they passed our pew, my mother clutched my hand, and we followed the procession to the family burial plot adjacent to the church. Outside, the wind stirred the stately elms and oaks of the churchyard, and as we passed through a cordon of marines standing at attention with their white-gloved hands raised to the brims of their hats, I watched the brown and gold dying leaves of autumn skip merrily across the route to my father's grave.

After the family members were seated in the folding metal chairs parallel to the grave and the honor guard had placed the casket on the lowering device, the crowd from the church filed in around us, and the minister began again. "Man, that is born of a woman, hath but a short time to live, and is full of misery. He cometh up, and is cut down, like a flower; he fleeth as it were a shadow, and never continueth in one stay."

When the minister completed his devotions, a firing squad of marines positioned near the casket fired three volleys at five-second intervals, and I again took my mother's hand. Immediately a lone bugler raised his burnished instrument and transfixed the assemblage with "Taps," and I tried to ignore the ache in my throat by concentrating on my mother's viselike grip on my hand. After he had finished, the members of the honor guard positioned themselves at either end of the casket and, with deliberate precision, folded the flag into a tightly wrapped triangle. One of them then handed the flag to the commandant of the Marine Corps, General Leonard Chapman, who presented it to my mother, and the ceremony was completed.

The family stood around awkwardly for a few minutes acknowledging the condolences of friends and strangers, and we were then led toward our cars with my mother holding her husband's flag tightly against her chest.

As we neared our car, I spotted Phil Leslie, my platoon sergeant from Vietnam, who seemed to be trying to decide whether or not to approach our car. I wheeled over to him, thanked him for coming, and invited him over to the house to share in the family table. He demurred for a moment, explaining that he would be uncomfortable in the presence of so much brass, but he then took my hand and told me that he would always regret not having had the opportunity to meet my father and tell him what a good lad his son had been. I lingered for a moment as the by now familiar ache returned to my throat, thanked him again for his kindness, and wheeled back to Toddy and my mother for the ride back to Saluda.

While we were at the funeral, the ladies of the community had mobilized in true southern fashion to lay out a feast. From outside I could smell the home-baked bread and fried chicken. In the kitchen every available resting place seemed to be filled by platters of ham, bowls of salad, plates of deviled eggs, and at least a dozen pies and other assorted desserts. A large borrowed coffee urn perked ferociously from its unaccustomed spot atop the washing machine, and Mother tried in vain to direct the activities of the half dozen ladies who were carrying food to the dining table. We were quickly shooed into the back parlor, where for the next hour and a half I sat by Mother's side and received our guests.

Most of the marine generals who paused briefly to share some personal reminiscence about my father wore Navy Cross lapel pins on their suit coats, and several of them were Medal of Honor recipients; but none had come close to matching my father's combat record. In addition, they all were old and courtly, and I could not visualize any of them as ever having been anything like the young men who had fought with me in Vietnam. After they had paid their respects, most of the mourners then returned to the front part of the house, where they were given plates and told to partake of the dining table's bounty. General Chapman had his hands full trying to round up all the generals for the return trip to Washington, but by midafternoon they and most of the other guests had departed.

One of the last to leave was Sergeant Jones, who requested a minute alone with me before he left. I headed out onto the porch to get away from the remaining guests, and while I was pushing myself through the dining room, he excused himself briefly and went to his car. When he returned, he gave me the two-star flag and stanchion from the official car he had driven for my father. I knew how much the flag meant to Sergeant Jones, how much he and my father had been through together, and how very like a father and son their relationship had been. I tried not to take the flag; but Jones was adamant, and after he had left, I realized that in lieu of being able to speak for the last several moments we were together on the porch, we had communicated by nods and gestures.

When the family was finally alone together, my brothers-in-law and I wanted to open a bottle of bourbon, but my mother felt that drinking would sully the occasion and uncharacteristically refused to let any of us imbibe. I desperately wanted a drink; but I could see that my mother was reestablishing control after having had most of her decisions made by others for several days, and we honored her wishes. I was concerned that she was not going to be able to live alone after all these years, and it was a good sign to see her take a stand even if it meant that I would have to forgo a much-desired drink.

Before Toddy and I returned to Williamsburg, I drove down to the churchyard alone to visit my father's grave one last time. The grave site was ablaze with floral arrangements of every size, shape, and color, and its gaudy patchwork of vivid hues contrasted starkly with the dying leaves of the surrounding trees and brown autumn grass. I was at last alone with my father, my God, and my thoughts, but I was as yet unable to sort out the conflicting strands of a desolation that had been building within me since that last tear had run its course down my father's cheek. He was gone now, and I was grateful that Toddy had gotten to know him, however briefly, and to see the kindness in him before he died. I knew that my children would have their lives touched by the recognition that history had given him, and I wished that they, particularly my son, could carry some memory of him that was more than vicarious. I also wished that I had been more like him, and I wondered if I would always find myself inadequate when I compared myself with him. He had been a wonderful father, and I was fortunate to be his son; but it had not been easy living in his shadow. As darkness fell and I took leave of his grave, I wanted him back and I wanted him gone.

After we got back to Williamsburg that evening, I looked in on my sleeping children and then at last fixed a drink. For a long time after Toddy had gone to bed, I sat in the darkness of our family room, periodically going to the kitchen to replenish my glass, and waiting for the blessed numbness that would wash away the turmoil.

＝＝ ☆ ＝＝

Following my father's death and for years thereafter, I tried to put the Vietnam experience behind me and to disassociate myself from the military community. By concentrating on my studies, tending to the increased demands of a growing family, and maintaining an almost compulsive social agenda with my classmates, I was able to keep my disillusionment about the war from becoming a preoccupation. Nevertheless, my feelings about the war continued to smolder beneath the surface and sometimes vented themselves in self-destructive and occasionally surprising ways.

As 1972 began, President Nixon continued to withdraw troops from Vietnam while Le Duc Tho and Henry Kissinger exchanged peace proposals in Paris. At home the Democrats and Republicans began to gear up for their national conventions, and the Vietnam War was a principal topic of debate for presidential aspirants.

At the end of January, just as I was beginning examinations, John Zier died of cancer, after having been diagnosed only a short time earlier, and I was dumbstruck that he had gone so suddenly. Aside from having been such a physically strong man and having lived life so fully, John was the one officer I knew whose Vietnam service most closely resembled mine, and I had begun to think that since we had once survived death, it would not again become an issue until much later in our lives. In dying, he took a part of my experience to his grave, and I felt cheated and betrayed that the man could no longer bear testimony to our ordeal.

Several times while I was in law school, classmates approached me about running for student government positions. At first I considered their propositions a flattering but transparent gimmick to garner sympathy votes, but as the encouragement continued, I began to realize that my peers might be seeing something in me that I did not see in myself. Ultimately I decided not to become involved as a candidate, but for three years the would-be politicians in my law school sought my advice and support, and I accepted an appointed position on the Honor Council in my last year. It all served to whet my appetite for politics, and I began to consider the possibility that at some later date I might want to run for office. My thinking was based not so much on the premise that I had unique qualifications as on my growing awareness that the kind of leadership that got us embroiled in Vietnam and was keeping us there was not worthy of the esteem with which I had formerly viewed it.

One of my classmates was the son of Tiny Hutton, the administrative assistant to my congressman. Scott Hutton and I had become friends early in our first year of law school. Scott, in total contrast with my background, had grown up in a political family, and as our friendship grew, he shared his knowledge with me and enlisted my help in supporting his father's boss. Congressman Tom Downing was an old-line conservative southern Democrat who had parlayed a distinguished

World War II record into a political career that had extended over almost twenty years in the U.S. House of Representatives and made him virtually unbeatable. Although he had never sponsored any significant legislation, he had assured himself of reelection by providing capable, consistent service and looking out for the needs of his district, especially the Newport News Shipbuilding and Dry Dock Company, Virginia's largest employer. In my first semester of law school Congressman Downing saw to it that each member of the incoming class was given a free copy of the Federal Rules of Civil Procedure. Each book had a prominently displayed stamp that read "Compliments of Congressman Tom Downing," but even the politically jaded among us were grateful not to have to purchase the book.

Throughout the election of 1972 I followed the activities of the candidates and the evolving platforms of the parties with newfound attention. My background and my upbringing were solidly conservative and middle-class, but my war experience and events up to 1972 had surely altered my perspectives. Before the war it had never occurred to me to question the wisdom of our political and military leaders or the judgments of the leaders of corporate America.

Now, as I looked around and saw the brokers of policies that were causing the meaningless deaths of American and Vietnamese boys without any consequences to themselves, I became cynical and completely distrustful of the wisdom that I had heretofore taken on faith. When I began to see that my wartime comrades, most of whom were drawn from the lower rungs of society, had fought ostensibly to preserve institutions and ways of life from which they had no real expectations of benefiting, I questioned the democratic process and at the same time became more convinced that my allegiance lay with the Democratic party.

In early June 1972 I awoke one morning and read in the newspaper that Captain Fred Suttle, a highly decorated army combat veteran and a college fraternity brother, had been killed in Vietnam. I had lost touch with Fred years earlier, but as I read the account of his short life and death, I was filled with sadness and anger that another friend had sacrificed his life in vain. Because it came so late in the war, I was jolted by the news, and I wondered why Fred had decided to serve multiple tours of duty in Vietnam when it seemed to me that most of the rest of the country was past caring about his commitment.

Later that summer I got drunk at a cocktail party and embarrassed Toddy's parents and my mother by loudly announcing that I thought

President Nixon was up to his crotch, if not to his ears, in the shit from Watergate. I had already decided to support Senator George McGovern, but I was baffled that my family seemed more upset by my cocktail party accusations than by the carnage in Vietnam over which the president was presiding. I was never greatly enamored of Senator McGovern, but I was going to vote for him in November because I remembered Nixon's saying in 1968 that a president who could not end the war in Vietnam in four years did not deserve to be reelected.

That November I voted in my first presidential election and then spent the afternoon as a poll worker for Tom Downing. I knew very little about my congressman's stands on the issues, but I knew that he was a Democrat and that because of Vietnam I would always be voting for the party that I thought best represented the interests of the men with whom I had soldiered. After the polls closed, Toddy, Scott Hutton, his girlfriend, and I went to a victory party at the Downing for Congress headquarters and I was invited into the smoke-filled back room where Scott's father, Tiny, juggled half a dozen phones and tallied the returns from his precinct workers on a huge chalkboard.

From the moment I entered the room, I felt an electricity that charged my senses and held me spellbound. Tom Downing's reelection had never been in doubt, and there was none of the anticipatory excitement of a close race; but as the squares on Tiny's chalkboard began to fill up, I felt myself part of the process, and I saw for the first time how I might be able to influence the government that had so influenced me. Before Tom Downing went out into the glare of the lights and the whirl of the cameras to make his victory speech, I was already high from too many victory toasts, but the feeling of closeness to politics and power certainly added something new to the chemical mix already in my bloodstream. Tom Downing won his election in a landslide, but the next morning I realized that my political instincts might still need some honing when I read that George McGovern had managed to carry only Massachusetts and the District of Columbia.

To his credit, a newly reelected President Nixon was able to announce in late January 1973 that an agreement ending the Vietnam War had been reached in Paris, and on January 28 an official cease-fire ended the longest war in American history. Whether the agreement would bring the "peace with honor" that Nixon described was open to debate, but I was, of course, relieved that American boys would no longer be dying for a tragic involvement that was not of their making.

In February the first POWs, led by Navy Captain Jeremiah Denton, began coming home, and for the next seven weeks a jaded and cynical public had its pride in country rekindled by the sight of almost six hundred American servicemen and civilian POWs being reunited with their families and expressing their joy at finally coming home. I confess to being almost resentful that the POWs were recognized so positively for their sacrifices, given automobiles, appliances, and free sports tickets, and as I watched them being showered with confetti, I wondered what had happened to my parade. Whereas these men were now being treated by the media as conquering heroes, those same media for the previous five years had never passed up an opportunity to focus on atrocities of a few of my comrades-in-arms at the expense of those of us who served honorably. Even worse, society had treated us as dangerous malcontents after we returned, and no matter how many examples there were of former servicemen who were now contributing to society, we continued to be stereotyped as drug addicts and outlaws. Nevertheless, I held my tongue while the orgy of renewed patriotism was being played out, and at the end of March I hoped the focus would shift to less emotionally troublesome ground for me when our last twenty-five hundred combat troops were flown out of Vietnam and North Vietnam, agreed to release its remaining POWs.

Six weeks later, in May 1973, the Senate Watergate investigating committee began public hearings into the break-in and bugging of the Democratic National Headquarters in Washington, and a fickle public had something else to divert its attention, and I, a new focus for my frustrations and resentments.

By summer, during which the televised Watergate hearings held America in thrall, I worked as a summer intern in the general counsel's office of the Veterans Administration. I had decided over the course of my first two years in law school that I owed it to my fellow veterans to spend at least part of my career addressing veterans' concerns. Toddy and I found a town house on Capitol Hill that was available for a short-term lease, and in June we packed up the children and enough clothes and toys to get us through the summer and moved to Washington. My internship was the first office job that I had ever held, and the work was new and interesting, although I found it personally disheartening that the Veterans Administration seemed to have so few Vietnam veterans in its employ. As in law school, there was almost no one with whom I could share my war experience, and while my co-workers were hospitable, our recent backgrounds were worlds apart. It was also terribly difficult for Toddy, Maggie, and Lewis to live in a cramped town house with so little room for the children to play, and we quickly tired of living in a three-level house that was all but inaccessible for my wheelchair.

By the time I completed my internship in early August, revelations about Watergate had so depleted America's confidence in its president that his popularity was the lowest of any sitting president in twenty years. Every night the news seemed to lead in the direction of White House complicity in the burglary and its cover-up, and I, like many Americans, had my disillusionment over Vietnam augmented by signs of a "cancer on the presidency."

When we returned to Williamsburg, I realized that I was deeply depressed and that I had been dealing inadequately with my feelings and drinking far too heavily. Toddy and I talked it over, and when the fall term of my last year in law school began, I sought out Dr. Adams, an army psychiatrist at the hospital where Maggie had been born, and began weekly therapy sessions.

I remained his patient until the following spring and was at least able to try to work through my anger over Vietnam, an anger that he encouraged me to express but that the rest of society demanded I keep bottled up. When I first began seeing him, I was having trouble sleeping, my appetite had diminished to the point that most foods tasted and smelled the same, and I was beginning to feel as if I were an observer of, rather than a participant in, my own life.

As I described my symptoms to Dr. Adams, I recalled how as a teenager I had read in Irving Stone's *The Agony and the Ecstasy* about the custom in Michelangelo's day of amputating the lips of court jesters so that their faces were carved into permanent smiles. I was now expending so much energy keeping my emotions in check and protesting so vehemently to our friends and acquaintances how perfectly well adjusted I was despite the war and my physical condition that I had begun to feel like one of those unfortunate clowns. I was angry and bitter that my country had sent me off to be maimed for life in a senseless war and then failed to recognize my sacrifices, but I was angrier still that I was now reduced to pretending that nothing was wrong. It was one thing, I recognized, for my country to have forgotten who I was and what I had been through, but if I now allowed myself to forget, I would have lost my soul and with it whatever meaning my ordeal might have produced.

In the almost six months that I spent with Dr. Adams we were at least able to keep at bay the devils that tormented me. I came no closer to resolving my feelings about the war, my role in it, and the attitude of my country toward my commitment than I had been at the beginning of my therapy, but I did learn to try to open up with my feelings. I also learned that it is possible to reach contradictory conclusions in the heart and in the head, and that single lesson enabled me to remain functional through my last year of law school and to overcome my depression.

In October 1973 I began an intensive course of study to prepare for the Virginia bar examination, and for the rest of the fall and winter I was so busy cramming fine points of law into my head that I hardly had time to brood over my situation or the deplorable situation in Washington. Vice President Spiro T. Agnew was forced to resign from office for accepting bribes while governor of Maryland, and for the first time in our nation's history a new vice president assumed the second-highest office in government without having been elected. Just ten days later President Nixon ordered his attorney general, Elliot L. Richardson, to fire special Watergate prosecutor Archibald Cox in the infamous "Saturday Night Massacre." By Christmas a majority of Americans thought there was something deeply wrong with their country. The House Judiciary Committee was gearing up to determine whether the president of the United States should be impeached. I found it ironic that as I was studying to gain admission to the legal profession, many of its prominent members could not possibly be setting a worse example for the nation and for their potential brethren at the bar.

By late spring Toddy and I were feeling much more optimistic about our prospects than we had at any time since beginning law school. I had passed the Virginia bar exam, and the general counsel's office at the Veterans Administration where I had worked the previous summer had offered me a permanent position after graduation in June. With all American combat troops withdrawn from Vietnam, it was somewhat easier to avoid having to think about the war despite the fact that the carnage continued, and by the time Dr. Adams and I concluded that I was no longer in need of his services, I was looking toward my future as a young Washington lawyer.

=== ☆ ===

One Sunday afternoon in April, while Toddy and I were playing with the children, Tiny Hutton dropped by unexpectedly for a visit and asked if he could have a few minutes alone with me. After I had taken him into the living room, leaving a puzzled Toddy with

Lewis and Maggie, he took a seat on the sofa and in measured words started a conversation that caught me totally off guard.

"Tom Downing is going to retire someday," he said, "and when he decides to step down, I would like you to take his place as the next Democratic congressman from Virginia's First Congressional District."

Before I could protest or even open my mouth to reply, he launched into a long discourse on why he thought I would be electable. Most of the rest of the conversation was no more than a blur of words to me, but I was so stunned by his suggestion that I, a third-year law student still in his twenties, should entertain thoughts of a congressional race that I sat quietly and listened until he had finished.

"I know this comes as a shock to you," he concluded, "and there is no rush to start positioning yourself since Tom Downing will probably not retire for several more years, but take some time to talk it over with the people who are important to you, and I will stay in touch."

After he had left, I went to the refrigerator for a can of beer and, with my thoughts and emotions in turmoil, finished it off in half a dozen quick gulps. I then went to find Toddy, who had discreetly taken the children for a walk, and after I breathlessly told her the purpose of Tiny's visit, she shrugged as if he had stopped by to borrow a cup of sugar. When I remarked that she did not seem very excited by the news, she replied that I was a perfectly logical choice and that in any event, it didn't appear to her to require very much talent to be a congressman. She then gave me a more reassuring hug and told me that if running were something that I later believed I had to do, she would support me in every way possible.

For the remainder of my time in law school, I simply went through the motions of doing what was required to get through my final examinations. I had already passed the bar, and I had a job lined up for the start of my professional career; but for months I was preoccupied with the words of a savvy political professional who had seen in me possibilities about which I had only dared to dream.

=== ☆ ===

Within weeks of the time I started work as an attorney with the Veterans Administration, President Ford instituted a clemency program for Vietnam military deserters and civilian draft evaders. Sensing a need to "bind the nation's wounds and to heal the scars of divisiveness," he issued a proclamation and an executive order on September 16, 1974, that established a program of conditional clemency to be admin-

istered by a nine-member board headed by former Senator Charles E.
Goodell of New York. I realized when I first heard about the program
that it was going to be a significant but controversial undertaking, and I
wanted from the start to be a part of it.

At its inception the board was headquartered in the Old Executive
Office Building adjacent to the White House, and I was working just
across Lafayette Square in the Veterans Administration's central office.
It was an easy matter therefore for me to arrange an interview with the
general counsel of the board and to wheel across the park for a noon
meeting with him in early October 1974. I sensed that the board and
the president were going to be subjected to heavy criticism for establishing any sort of program. I also knew that because I was a wounded
and decorated veteran, I could lend some credibility to the board.
Lawrence M. Baskir, the general counsel, agreed, and the interview
turned out to be a mere formality to my being offered a position on the
staff.

When several days later the White House requested that I be detailed
to the Presidential Clemency Board from my position at the Veterans
Administration, the VA balked at letting me go. I thought for a while
that I was not going to be allowed to join the board; but Chairman
Goodell then made his request more emphatically, and by mid-October
I was ensconced in an office in the Old Executive Office Building and
taking an active role in the board's formative work. For the first several
months we decided very few cases, concentrating instead on the development of policies and procedures and laying the groundwork for the
hectic months ahead. By Christmas I had begun presenting cases to the
board, and I had gained enough of an overview to see the hugeness of
our task and to appreciate the divergent perspectives of the nine board
members.

They had been chosen as much for their prominence as for their
ability to evaluate cases. Their individual philosophies covered the
political spectrum. Father Theodore M. Hesburgh, president of Notre
Dame University, and Vernon E. Jordan, executive director of the
National Urban League, were widely regarded as the liberal board
members, and General Lewis W. Walt, former assistant commandant of
the Marine Corps, and Dr. Ralph Adams, president of Troy State
University in Alabama, were considered conservatives. The viewpoints
of the other members generally fell somewhere between, but it was not
uncommon to see board members struggling to divorce themselves
from their own perspectives and decide the cases impartially. I knew by

the time I had presented several cases that I wanted to be deciding cases rather than working them up for the board's evaluation, and by late winter I had begun to see a way toward my objective.

As word of the Clemency Board spread to the American public and to potential applicants, the board suddenly found itself flooded with applications. The controversy over the board's work created by a liberal element that thought we were offering too little and by a conservative element that took the opposite view, while discomfiting, was good for business because it increased our visibility among the potential beneficiaries we were trying to reach. We did our best to increase that visibility even further by taking our program to the people through radio interviews and television appearances by board members in major cities across the country. We also sent tapes to radio and television stations and mailed informational literature to organizations that we thought could reach potential participants. In January 1975 alone we received three thousand applications for clemency, and by mid-April 1975 the number had grown to about twenty thousand cases. What had begun as a trickle back in September, when the program was first announced, had become a torrent, and the staff had to be increased by a factor of ten and the board size doubled to handle the work load.

When I realized that the board was going to be doubled, I started my own campaign to have senior staff members lobby for a position for me. I was proud of the work that the board was doing, and with one or two exceptions, the members were dedicated, hardworking men and women who had the best interests of the country and the applicants at heart. On the other hand, there was not a single board member who had paid the price that I had or who was more entitled to have a say in the fate of the veterans we were judging, and I was not going to be denied a position on the board when it was expanded.

I asked for and got an interview with Chairman Goodell, and when I explained to him that I was prepared to resign my position on the staff rather than continue to work for new members who were less deserving and less competent than I, he puffed on his pipe and regarded me soberly for several seconds. He then grinned broadly, came out from behind the desk, and placed his hand on my shoulder and told me that he had already sent my name over to the White House with his unqualified endorsement. I suddenly felt very foolish that I had taken a stand when none was needed, but after I had thanked him and backed out of his office, my whoops of joy brought several curious office workers out into the cavernous halls of the solemn Old Executive Office Building to see who was making such a spectacle.

In late April 1975 the Ford administration selected the new members of the Presidential Clemency Board, and we were invited to the White House for an orientation session. The meeting was convened at noon in the Roosevelt Room on the second floor of the White House, and as I took my place, I felt humbled to be part of such an important endeavor but a little light-headed to be meeting in such a grand setting. Despite my good fortune and the surroundings, however, I also was saddened over the news coming out of South Vietnam.

In March the Communists had begun a major offensive in Vietnam's central highlands, and on March 11 the key city of Bau Me Thuot was captured. President Nguyen Van Thieu responded by ordering his army to abandon the northern two-thirds of South Vietnam, and as his troops retreated, the operation turned into a rout. By the end of March cities where American marines and soldiers had fought and died were toppling like dominoes, and Pleiku, Quang Tri, Hue, and Da Nang all were overtaken by the advancing North Vietnamese Army. In addition to our having to witness the personal tragedy of uprooted refugee families being deprived of their homes and possessions, it was now crystal clear to me that America's involvement in Vietnam and my own sacrifice had been for naught.

President Thieu resigned on April 21, and a week later the remaining Americans in Saigon, with the North Vietnamese Communists closing the loop around the capital, were evacuated by helicopter. On April 30 Saigon surrendered without a fight, and for the first time in three decades there was no fighting in Indochina. The American war effort had cost us in excess of $140 billion, had produced more than two hundred thousand American military casualties, including more than fifty thousand deaths, and it had created a grotesque scar on the American people that was as palpable and would be as long-lasting as the scars that I would carry to my grave. The cost to Vietnam was, of course, immeasurable, and although the Ford administration attempted to accommodate the Vietnamese refugees who poured out of their ravaged country in the six months following the end of the war, such measures could never atone for the consequences of our misadventure or set right a fifteen-year record of a tragic involvement that was as ineffective as it was ill conceived.

With the unraveling of the war in Vietnam as background for the Clemency Board's initial meeting in the White House, I was beginning to find it unconscionable that so many of the young men on whom we were going to be sitting in judgment should continue to be penalized for their actions. President Ford had established the clemency program with the best of motives and in the spirit of forgiveness, but it was unsettling to me that the individuals most directly affected by the war should now require forgiveness while the architects of the war bore no stigma at all.

Having been promoted from a staff position on the board, I was far more familiar with the profiles of our applicants than were most of the new board members, and I wondered how they would approach their task as our briefing began. Of our eighteen members, only four were Vietnam veterans, and when it came time for the new members to introduce themselves, it was difficult to get a reading on any of them. When it came my turn to speak, I dispensed with the biographical format most of my predecessors had used and simply said that my name was Lew Puller and that we all would know each other much better all too soon.

Over the course of the next five months I reviewed the case histories of more than five thousand military deserters and draft evaders. The program was structured so that staff attorneys prepared case summaries on the applicants, which then were furnished to the board members prior to our deliberations. We read the summaries ahead of time and then met in three-member panels to make case dispositions. If the panel recommendation was not unanimous, the dissenting member could refer the case to the full board, where it would be considered anew, but overall the panels were able to reach agreement most of the time. Usually the only issues to be decided were whether the applicant should be granted clemency and, if so, whether a period of alternative service should be required as a condition of receiving clemency. As a result of our deliberations we granted clemency in almost 95 percent of the cases we evaluated, and in those cases where we required a period of alternative service, the average length stipulated was a little less than six months. In exceptional cases we recommended that veterans' benefits be restored to some of our applicants, but those cases were extremely rare and usually involved individuals who had been decorated for heroism in Vietnam and then gotten into trouble after returning to the United States.

Once the board became fully operational with a staff of more than six hundred employees borrowed from other agencies, there was tremendous pressure on it to complete its work by September 15, 1975, the deadline imposed by President Ford. During the spring and summer months we made nearly fifteen thousand case recommendations, which meant that the individual panels were collectively processing almost a thousand cases per week at the peak of our productive phase. Because we worked at breakneck speed and because the board members had such divergent political views, tempers sometimes became frayed, and a few of our sessions were explosive.

After I had reviewed cases for several weeks, I began to realize that the majority of our military applicants were the by-products of both a terribly unfair conscription system and a tragic war that never should have been fought. Out of the general population of draft-age men during the Vietnam era, fewer than one in ten ever served in Vietnam, yet many of those same Americans whom chance and coincidence had conspired against to require the heaviest sacrifice were now doubly burdened by stigmatizing military records that would follow them for the remainder of their lives. Unlike the civilian applicants, who made up less than 15 percent of our eligibles, the average military case fitted a profile that was all too often heartbreaking. Generally, he was from a broken home, had not completed high school when he joined the service, and had personal and family problems that severely limited his ability to perform his military duties in a productive manner. There were, of course, gross examples of applicants, both military and civilian, whose behavior was manipulative, cowardly, and without any redeeming features, but by and large, the men on whom I sat in judgment were the unlucky detritus of a flawed system and in many cases were truly spoils of war.

I gradually came to the conclusion that it was better to err on the side of leniency than to take a hard line with most cases, and my attitude did not sit well with some of the less forgiving of our members. Among them was General Walt, who had served in the Second World War, Korea, and Vietnam and who had been a protégé of my father's for much of his distinguished career. General Walt had driven down to Saluda to comfort my family immediately after I was wounded, and his close relationship with my father made our differences of opinion on Clemency Board matters doubly painful for both of us. The first few times we were assigned to the same panel, we each made an effort to accommodate the other's views, but our differences were so profound that eventually the chairman made certain that we were kept apart when sessions were scheduled.

General Walt, like many of the board members, was hardest on the applicants from whom he expected the most, in his case marines, and the higher standard to which he held them drove me up the wall. In one case, at the end of a session on which we had gone head to head for several hours, he voted "No clemency" for a marine because the man had in his record a nonjudicial punishment for going to sleep at his duty post in a rear area of Vietnam. When I moved to have the case forwarded to the full board, he stormed out of the room, leaving a dozen startled lawyers waiting to present cases, and paused only long enough to let me know that with my liberal tendencies I was never going to make it very far in Washington, D.C. After that episode all pretense of civility between us was destroyed, although I took a callow satisfaction from then on at full board proceedings when my views prevailed over his. To this day I believe that General Walt was deeply hurt that he could not bring the son of his lifelong hero around to his own views, but I think he also understood and admired me for standing up for my own convictions.

Although we made most of our case dispositions on the basis of abstracts prepared by staff attorneys, applicants were afforded the opportunity to make personal appearances before the board, and in those rare cases when applicants chose to exercise that option, the sessions were always highly charged. In one particularly memorable case a conscientious objector who had fled to Canada during the war came back to appear in person, and sitting in the audience at the hearing were his mother, who had not seen him in several years, and another woman, whose son had been killed in Vietnam. After we had decided to grant the applicant clemency, the two mothers embraced, and as their tears intermingled, I was overcome with emotion that they could be so bonded by the common pains of their sons' divergent experiences.

Unfortunately such understanding was all too rare. In retrospect I am dubious that our effort went very far toward healing the scars of the Vietnam War. Although the staff and board members were for the most part conscientious, hardworking men and women who brought skill and focus to a difficult assignment, toward the end of my tenure I began to see that our work bore political ramifications that were given far more consideration than the welfare of our applicants. I continue to believe that the primary purpose of the president and his advisers in setting up the Clemency Board was to quiet some of the political controversy over the Vietnam War and that anything we might have done for our applicants was secondary. That realization, in the last weeks of my service, gave me an uneasy feeling again that I was being used and turned much of the pride I had taken in my work on the board to ashes.

In the weeks just prior to the disbanding of the Clemency Board, we were given some paybacks for our time and effort. The first was a river cruise and cocktail party aboard the presidential yacht, *Sequoia*. On a sultry afternoon in early August the board members and senior staff and their spouses gathered at the Washington Navy Yard, where we were welcomed on board by a crew of naval officers and enlisted men. For the next three hours we cruised up and down the Potomac River, pretending that we were important dignitaries and availing ourselves of the president's mess and well-stocked bar. While we cruised, four navy speedboats, two fore and two aft, kept curious river traffickers from approaching us, and by the time the party ended, I could see clearly, despite the Pouilly Fuissé and elegant finger food that I had consumed, that all was not sacrifice and hard labor at the upper echelons of government service.

A week later we journeyed to Camp David in the Catoctin Mountains to spend a working weekend putting the finishing touches on a report to the president. Again we were wined and dined, this time amid the majestic pines and gorgeous foliage of the Maryland mountaintop. We were housed two by two in rustic green clapboard cabins, but our working sessions and meals took place in the lodge, with high-vaulted ceilings and an unobstructed and breathtaking view of the mountains. For diversion there were skeet shooting, swimming, bowling, and horseback riding and at night first-run movies.

Amid such luxury it was tempting to take a charitable attitude toward the administration that hosted our weekend, and the report that emerged as a result of our labors on Sunday afternoon was considerably more sanitized than the working version that the staff had forwarded to us on Friday evening. Most of the board members present had been picked, among other factors, for their loyalty and allegiance to the Republican party, and as had been the case so many times in our deliberations of the last several months, party loyalty and a desire not to embarrass the administration were as strong a motivation as our search for an objective and truthful rendering of our experience.

One chapter that was highly critical of the inequities in the draft that had persisted for much of the Vietnam War was deleted in its entirety, and as we debated its removal, I was again seized by a strong feeling of being manipulated. Nevertheless, I could see some merit to the argument that it was not within our charter to pass judgment on the Selective Service System, and I acquiesced in the majority vote and continued to accept the bountiful food and drink of our hosts.

After we had completed our work on the Clemency Board and turned over to the Department of Justice the remaining cases on which we did not have enough information to proceed, the board members were invited to the White House Cabinet Room to be personally thanked by President Ford for the work we had done. Special parking was arranged for me near the White House, and as I entered the room, most of the members were already seated in the leather chairs around the polished antique conference table. Each chair at the table bore a brass plaque that identified the cabinet secretary for whom it was normally reserved, and as the board members waited nervously for the president to make his entrance, I parked my wheelchair next to the door at the head of the table and read as many of the plaques as were within my view. Five minutes later, when President Ford was announced, he strode through the door beside me, and startled by my appearance, he locked his eyes on my lap before they rose to meet my own curious stare. The moment was over in a split second, and he quickly regained his composure and went to his seat, where he gave us an impromptu talk on the fine work we had performed on his and the nation's behalf, but I found it amusing that the president of the United States had been more taken aback by me than I by him.

After his little speech he shook hands all around, and we then proceeded to the Rose Garden, where he made the same type of speech for the benefit of the press and the Clemency Board staff members who had been invited to the outside ceremony. Before he began, however, Chairman Goodell, without asking my permission, moved my wheelchair to the dais from which President Ford addressed the crowd, and although his intentions were probably honorable, I felt taken advantage of and not unlike a trophy placed on display for the press. I said nothing; but I was resentful that I was being used as a prop for a presidential photo session, and my resentment did not abate when we were politely but quickly hustled out of the Rose Garden by the Secret Service after the ceremony to make room for whatever delegation the president was going to address next.

Looking back, I think we may have done some good for the applicants whose cases we heard, but that good was insignificant when weighed against the irreparable harm caused by the four administrations that mired us in Vietnam and then refused to acknowledge any wrongdoing or culpability. To this day I think we, as board members, were in the business of determining the guilt of the wrong people, and it was for me as shattering an experience as the loss of my legs and a dozen good friends in Vietnam to discover face-to-face the arrogance and the blindness that so often passed for leadership during the Vietnam era.

VIII

★

WHEN THE CLEMENCY BOARD was disbanded in the summer of 1975, I returned to my old job at the Office of General Counsel of the Veterans Administration, but I was restless and out of tune with the bureaucratic regimen of mid-level government lawyers. At the Clemency Board I had been a player in an exciting venture, but after having been back at the VA for a few months, I began to feel like a pawn in a game over which I had no control. To make matters worse, many of the old-line veterans who had been working for the VA since coming out of the service at the end of World War II or the Korean War were suspicious of and hostile toward anyone who favored clemency for Vietnam deserters or draft evaders.

On a few occasions I allowed myself to be drawn into arguments with some of the more vocal critics of President Ford's program, but eventually I got to the point where I simply fixed my antagonists with a stare and reminded them that until they had experienced combat, they would do well to keep their mouths shut. My approach usually ended the arguments, but it did not win me many hearts and minds, and after having experienced several such confrontations, I knew for certain that I did not want to spend the rest of my life working for the Veterans Administration.

═ ☆ ═

Sometime after the first of the year Tom Downing, the congressman from Virginia's First Congressional District, unexpectedly announced that he would not be seeking reelection. I had been keeping an eye on Congressman Downing's seat since Tiny Hutton's surprise visit, but his announcement in early 1976 caught me, most of the political junkies around the state, and even Tiny Hutton himself totally unprepared.

I knew that if I quit my job and moved back to the district in response to Tom's announcement, I would be viewed as an upstart who had not paid his dues and that in all likelihood I would never be able to wrest the Democratic nomination from whomever the First District party regulars decided to put up. For several weeks I vacillated, talking late into the night with Toddy and making phone calls to people back home. Their advice was almost uniformly to sit out 1976, see how the race turned out, and, if I was still interested, move back to the district in anticipation of running in 1978. It was maddening to realize that I had no way to get into a race for an open seat and would have to wait two years to challenge an incumbent, but I finally saw the wisdom of the advice I was being offered.

As I had anticipated, the Democrats nominated a good old boy from one of the two most populous cities in the district who had been active in political and community affairs for many years. Bob Quinn was a decent and honorable gentleman; but he totally lacked the killer instinct, and he made the mistake of assuming that his nomination was tantamount to victory because the district had elected his predecessor, a Democrat, for nine consecutive terms. His opponent was an ambitious young commonwealth attorney from rural Essex County who would use every opportunity to parlay his first elected office into a seat in the House of Representatives. His quest for the Republican party nomination was not difficult because most political observers initially shared Bob Quinn's view that the Democrats would continue to hold the seat. Nevertheless, as the campaign developed, it quickly became apparent that Paul Trible, the fair-haired young prosecutor who had come out of nowhere, was going to be a force to be reckoned with by election day.

Tappahannock, Virginia, the seat of Essex County, was only thirty miles up the road from Saluda, yet I had never heard of Paul Trible when I was growing up. Curious about this brash young newcomer, who in the course of his campaign proudly proclaimed himself a son of Essex County, I watched him closely as he covered the seventeen counties and several cities in the district.

In the course of my research I soon discovered that he had not lived in my district until two years previously, when he had been appointed Essex County commonwealth attorney. Prior to that he had worked as an assistant district attorney in northern Virginia and in the Nixon administration on the Committee to Re-elect the President. I also discovered that Trible, who was one year younger than I, had obtained a medical deferment from his local draft board that insulated him from any of the fallout of the Vietnam War.

According to the accounts of his medical condition that I read in the newspapers, he had reported for his draft physical after receiving his notice from the Selective Service System, at which time it was discovered that he lacked full range of motion in one of his arms, a condition of which he had been unaware until the physical. After reading the account, I had no doubt that Paul Trible, who was now loudly proclaiming the necessity of a national defense second to none and a hard line toward communism, had engineered a questionable deferment to avoid the war that had killed a dozen of my friends. I despised him for having been spared the most catastrophic episode of our generation, and I vowed that if he were to be elected, I would oppose him in his bid for reelection.

In early August 1976, as my frustration at the VA increased along with my feelings of impotence over political developments in the Tidewater, I received a phone call from Jim Maye, the executive director of the Paralyzed Veterans of America. Jim had been a fellow Clemency Board member, and I had developed an enormous respect for his judgment and for the way he handled the devastating paralysis with which he had returned from Vietnam. We met for lunch the following day with several of his colleagues from PVA. After a round or two of drinks and some good-natured chitchat about our time together at the Clemency Board, the conversation took a more serious turn, and before I knew what was happening, Jim had offered me a job at almost twice what I was making as an attorney with the VA.

Jim wanted me to take over as national service director of PVA. When he explained to me that it was one of PVA's top two or three paid positions and that I would be reporting directly to him, the job began to sound more and more attractive. His only stipulation was that I agree to work for him at least one full year. I told him that I would need a few days to consider his offer. Jim knew that I was interested in running for Congress, and he had added the one-year requirement to protect his organization. Over the weekend I decided that I could do more for my fellow veterans as a critic of the Veterans Administration than as an entry-level attorney, and with Toddy's blessings I called Jim and told him that I would come work for him for one year. On Monday I gave my notice at the VA, and within two weeks I was immersing myself in the problems of a group of veterans whose injuries made the loss of my legs appear almost inconsequential.

In November Paul Trible defeated Bob Quinn by a razor-thin margin in a come-from-behind victory. He achieved his success by garnering most of the votes of his core Republican constituency and by building a coalition of urban black and rural white voters who usually voted Democratic. In winning his election, he was the only Republican congressional candidate in the South who was able to wrest a seat from the Democrats, and despite Jimmy Carter's successful presidential race, I felt as if a part of my heritage had been purloined. On the day after the election an ebullient Paul Trible, flush with victory, was at the main gate of the Newport News Shipbuilding and Dry Dock Company for the morning shift change, and in the months succeeding his oath taking, he took every possible step to solidify his hold on his seat.

By virtue of his association with the shipbuilding company, one of the nation's largest producers of military vessels, he was able to gain a seat on the prestigious House Armed Services Committee. It did not go unnoticed in the local press that his predecessor had been unable to achieve such an assignment during a nine-term career. Trible also wasted no time in extending the olive branch to most of the political brokers who had opposed his candidacy, often calling or writing them personally to solicit their support and asking them to serve on his finance committee. Finally, in the year following his successful bid, he spent virtually every free weekend in the district, holding a town meeting at a different location each Saturday morning and making certain that the media were supplied with press releases.

While Trible was busy with his new position, I smoldered on the sidelines at his success and threw myself into my work on behalf of the Paralyzed Veterans of America. It seemed incredible to me that a man who had avoided military service by virtue of what I considered a spurious medical condition could now occupy a seat on the committee that directed policy and conducted oversight for the military services. As I reflected on the irony of the situation, I was grateful for the distraction of my new job.

In the year and three months that I worked for PVA, I gained a new perspective on the enormous personal sacrifice that is demanded by war. Older and more mature than I had been in the hospital, I was able to step back and survey more critically the spoils of war in a dozen different spinal cord injury units in Veterans Administration hospitals across the United States. Like the victims of catastrophic injury anywhere, the patients I encountered handled their disabilities with a range of behavior varying from the pitiful and pitiable to the most dignified and courageous imaginable.

On one ward I encountered a young man who had been blinded and paralyzed from the neck down in Vietnam five years earlier. The enormity of his injuries had so defeated him that for years he had lain in his bed and lashed out bitterly at anyone who attempted to draw him out. His only solace appeared to be the pint bottles of bourbon with which his fellow patients kept him supplied. When I had left his bedside after attempting futilely to make contact, I felt anew and uncomfortably the old bitterness toward the architects of our Vietnam policy that until then I thought I was successfully keeping at bay. On the other hand, I also met patients who were pursuing careers, raising families, and attending school without any apparent concessions to their disabilities, and I tried to concentrate on the successes and downplay the failures as, in the course of my employment, I visited and revisited the wake of destruction left by the Vietnam War.

After a while I began to feel more strongly than ever that individuals who shared my experiences and perspectives were needed in Washington, and on more than one occasion when I saw Paul Trible wave the flag and call for increased defense spending, I wondered where the boy wonder had developed his perspectives. If he indeed had the remotest idea of the dangerous potential of drumbeating and Red-baiting I was not able to ascertain it, although it was clear to me that he fully appreciated the vote-getting potential of a patriotic speech. Shortly after he was elected, he donned a fighter pilot's suit and helmet and went for a test ride in an air force fighter jet at the invitation of the commanding general at Langley Air Force Base in nearby Hampton, Virginia. The next day his picture appeared in all the local papers with an article attesting to his patriotic achievements. As I studied the photograph of a smiling young congressman sitting at the controls of a jet and giving the thumbs-up sign, I wondered how many readers had noticed in the accompanying article that he did not know his own boot size when he was being outfitted for the flight.

In Virginia there is an election every year, the state and local elections coming in the odd years and the national elections taking place in the even years. After I had been at PVA for a year, I realized that if ever I was going to become more than a bystander in my political dreams, I was going to need an entry into First District politics. Charles S. Robb, son-in-law of President Lyndon Johnson and himself an aspiring politician, provided the opening I needed.

Chuck had decided to begin his political career by running for lieutenant governor of Virginia in 1977, and the Democrats had obligingly nominated him. By the late summer he had opened an office in almost every district in the state, and although most were staffed by part-time volunteers, he needed more help. Because he had been an officer in the Marine Corps and had served a tour in Vietnam, there was already a bond between us, and when I called him to ask if he would like my help in his campaign, he invited me out to his home in McLean, Virginia, the following Sunday to discuss my offer.

He and Lynda were holding a fund-raising party, and it was not until the end of the evening that we could repair to his study. After I explained to him that I wanted to test the political waters for the run against Paul Trible—about which he already knew—and that I thought by helping him I could help myself, he nodded his consent. He agreed to give me office space and to cover my expenses if I would move into the district for the six weeks prior to the election. I would be working without pay, but I knew that in representing Chuck Robb, I would gain some valuable speaking experience and I would get to know who the political operatives were in the district where I intended to stake out my own claim.

Back at PVA, Jim Maye was less than exuberant about giving me a six-week leave of absence, but I had kept my end of the bargain, having given him a year of honest work. I had also trained a deputy who could fill in for me, and in September I gave my colleagues at PVA a phone number where I could be reached on a daily basis, bade farewell to my wife and children, and headed to the Tidewater and an exciting new venture about which I knew almost nothing.

For the six weeks that I worked on the Robb campaign, I lived with Toddy's parents in Williamsburg and commuted daily to a makeshift campaign headquarters in nearby Newport News. The headquarters was shared by volunteers for several local candidates as well as the statewide office seekers, and I was given a desk, a telephone, and a free hand to conduct my affairs as I saw fit. For the first couple of weeks I tried to visit as many local politicians and community leaders as I could, to introduce myself and get a feel for the lay of the land, and to assess Robb's popularity. If by chance the conversation shifted over to

Trible and the job he was doing, I also had a place to file that information, but for the most part I tried to present myself as a Chuck Robb true believer and nothing more. As I became more familiar with my candidate and his platform, I also began standing in for him at high school assemblies and civic group meetings when he was unable to be present.

After speaking for Robb a few times, I began to realize that the campaign stump had a powerful attraction for me, and by the end of the campaign I often wished that I could speak for myself rather than as a surrogate. Midway through the campaign I also did a newspaper interview that gave the impression that in addition to assisting Robb, I was conducting a dry run for a future unspecified candidacy of my own. After the article appeared, my access to the local politicians improved, and I could sense that I was being judged for myself as well as for what I was doing for the Robb campaign.

On election day in November Chuck Robb handily carried Virginia's First Congressional District as well as most of the state, and I no longer had an excuse to gad about the district on his behalf. I had all but made up my mind that I was going to try to challenge Paul Trible in just a year. Although I returned to PVA for the remainder of the year, my heart and mind were really elsewhere, and over Thanksgiving and Christmas I spent most of my time preparing myself for the ordeal ahead. I had returned home with a yellow pad full of names and phone numbers of prominent men and women I had been unable to reach while I campaigned for Robb, and when I was not huddling with friends and acquaintances whose judgment I respected, I was frequently making phone calls back to the district to introduce myself and solicit support for my candidacy.

Many of the people with whom I conversed were unequivocal in their belief that Paul Trible was making all the right political moves and, as an incumbent, would be difficult to beat. Nevertheless, I was undaunted in my enthusiasm to take him on, and like many political novices, I paid more attention to the encouraging words I heard than to the discouraging ones. I knew in my heart that I could not get an accurate reading of my own chances until I entered the race, and in the meantime, I was tantalized by the thin margin that had carried Trible into office.

Following President Carter's inauguration, I decided that if ever I was going to make my move, this was the time, and I gave Jim Maye notice of my intention to leave PVA. The office had a little going-away party for me, and at the conclusion of the festivities the hat was passed and eighty dollars was collected for my campaign. The Puller for Congress Committee, which technically was not yet in existence, had its first donation, and I no longer had a job.

In January 1978 Virginia's First Congressional District consisted of seventeen more or less rural counties extending from just below Fredericksburg south to the border of Norfolk. The district also included two counties on the Eastern Shore and, back on the mainland, the cities of Hampton, Newport News, and Williamsburg. With two-thirds of the voting population concentrated in the Hampton–Newport News area, I knew that campaigning in the rural counties was not going to be the best use of my time and energy, but as an underdog I could not afford to write off any area of the district. Trible had established a domicile in Newport News when he ran the first time, and I now decided to make my residence in Hampton.

While I was looking for a place to move my family and making my first forays onto Trible's turf, Toddy stayed in Alexandria to let Maggie and Lewpy finish their first semester of first and third grades. In February a law school buddy, Ed Hubbard, found us a furnished beach cottage in Hampton overlooking the Chesapeake Bay that a client of his let us have gratis until summer. Toddy did her best to make the cottage look homey, to help Lewpy and Maggie with their adjustment to a new school, and to try to accommodate the insane conditions under which we were laboring. Despite her efforts, the early months of 1978 were an ordeal for all of us, and had I not been so single-minded in my pursuit of the political brass ring, I would have realized more fully what an enormous sacrifice I was asking of my family.

═══ ☆ ═══

I now picked up where I had left off with the Robb campaign. In February and March I kept up a ceaseless round of appointments, meeting with civic, religious, and political leaders and trying to lay the groundwork for a campaign. There was one other local politician who was interested in the nomination, and because he was an established local Democrat, I was frustrated in my efforts to get commitments from party regulars until early April, when he dropped out. More disturbing, however, than the delay his vacillation had caused was the number of supposedly loyal Democrats who had pledged their support to Paul Trible. Time and time again I set up an appointment with an influential businessman or civic leader only to be told that Congressman Trible had already visited and a commitment had been made.

One of the first visits that I made was to the owner of the *Daily Press*, the only daily morning newspaper in the district. Mrs. Bottom was an elderly widow who had run her domain for years without fear of competition. Unfortunately for me, she had a niece who had gone to school with Trible's wife, Rosemary, and Trible had skillfully used that connection to gain and then solidify the paper's support. When I met with Mrs. Bottom, she offered me sherry and macadamia nuts, and when we chatted in her spacious office on the second floor of the *Daily Press* building, she was effusive in her praise of Paul Trible and his family. Sensing that I was not going to be able to obtain her support under any conditions, I tried to steer her toward a neutral stance at least until the closing stages of the campaign. When our meeting was concluded, she rose from the couch and saw me to the elevator.

As I prepared to leave, she took me by the arm, and in what I am sure she meant to be encouragement, said, "You are a nice young man, Mr. Puller, and there will be time for you later."

I thanked her for the macadamia nuts and sherry and left her building shocked, in my naiveté, by what I had just heard but sadly wiser about small-town journalism.

With my Democratic opposition out of the way and an unimpeded route to the nomination in sight, Toddy and I began to assemble a staff, to formulate a campaign plan, and to begin raising seed money. I hired a campaign manager who, though active in Democratic politics and possessed of an impressive résumé, proved to be an unmitigated disaster. He was incapable of offending anyone and consequently could never make a decision, which in the pressure cooker atmosphere of a campaign could not have been a worse shortcoming. Fortunately the rest of the staff was all top rate and after a fashion capable of covering for Gary's inadequacy.

Dennis Lieberson, a senior at nearby William and Mary, had planned to run the campaign of my Democratic rival, and when that possibility evaporated, he came over to work part-time for me. He was as arrogant as Gary was conciliatory, but he was also remarkably self-possessed for a college student. Toddy recognized his value immediately, and by the time of his graduation she had talked me into firing Gary and giving Dennis the top job. His acceptance of the position meant that he had to postpone graduate school for a year, a considerable personal sacrifice on his part, but for the campaign it meant that we had an exceptional leader who could not be intimidated. Despite an occasionally abrasive manner, Dennis was fiercely loyal and never failed to do what he thought was best for me and for the campaign.

By then we had also hired a fund-raiser, a researcher, a driver, and an office manager–secretary, Margaret Thompson. She had impressed me when I was working for Chuck Robb, and she proved to be the hardest worker and least complaining person on board despite the fact that her job was one of the most difficult and least glamorous of positions. Tom Rastetter, my driver, was another William and Mary senior, but unlike Dennis and Margaret, he had no intention of burning himself out over my candidacy. He was, however, a handsome young man with an excellent sense of humor, and in the last months of the campaign I spent far more time with him than I did with Toddy. In fact, we even got to the point where we used a specialized vocabulary complete with inside jokes and arcane references that was gibberish to outsiders but easily understandable to the two of us.

In addition to the paid staff, the treasurer of the city of Newport News agreed to be my treasurer, and a law professor from William and Mary, Dick Williamson, filed our Federal Election Commission reports and helped out with legal questions involving finances. Another law professor and fellow Vietnam veteran, Tim Sullivan, served as an adviser to the campaign and was invaluable in helping me write speeches and articulate issues.

As is the case with most high-intensity ventures, the political campaign in its early stages had its share of ups and downs. Virginia's First District, with its naval and military installations, is highly dependent on defense spending. I had decided to accentuate my military background and commitment in an effort to demonstrate that I could continue to serve my country as a civilian as I had while in uniform. I also thought that the contrast between Paul Trible's background and my own would speak for itself in terms of our respective sacrifices.

He, however, proved far more adept than I at wrapping himself in the American flag, and the local media never once in the course of the campaign made any reference to the circumstances surrounding his draft deferment. In addition, in the spring and summer of 1978 the country was still too close to the war itself for much appreciation of its returning veterans.

If anything, my service was viewed with hostility in many quarters. It was also apparent to me that many young businessmen who were spared my war experience felt guilty about it. Early in the campaign I visited an old family friend who had been commonwealth attorney in Gloucester County and whose views as a patriot and as a conservative were well known.

"Don't try to run on your war record, Lewis," Catesby Jones had advised me, "because it will probably wind up hurting you more than helping you."

I was astounded when I first heard his words, and I fingered the mint in my julep cup and gazed out at the riverfront view from our vantage point on his front lawn. I said nothing then in response to his advice, but my mind was churning with the thought that if I could not run on my war record, my service had been in vain. On the up side, however, my first mail solicitation, a patriotic appeal to fifteen hundred political donors from around the country that stressed my military background, quickly pulled in over twelve thousand dollars. Even if the donors were outside the district, I knew that I had a significant source of funds for my campaign.

=== ☆ ===

I came face-to-face with Paul Trible for the first time in the early spring of 1978, before I had been selected to be the party's candidate. In honor of the founding of Yorktown, Virginia, there was a series of events culminating in a luncheon for several hundred dignitaries at Nick's Seafood Pavilion in Yorktown. The owner of the restaurant, Nick Matthews, was a Greek immigrant who had made a fortune in his restaurant by serving only fresh seafood and by being willing to work eighty-hour weeks. He had never forgotten what the land of opportunity had made possible for him, and now in his seventies, he was a generous backer of patriotic and philanthropic causes. He was also a great admirer of my father, and for years my family had limited its visits to Nick's Seafood Pavilion to one or two trips a year because it was embarrassing always to have Nick refuse to accept payment for our meal.

On this occasion he was picking up the tab for the entire party, and the governor of Virginia, the French ambassador, and virtually every local politician had gathered to feast on seafood shishkebobs and Greek wine. Congressman Trible was seated at the head table, and although he did not speak along with the governor and the ambassador I watched him far more closely than I watched either of them.

In his early thirties, with blond hair, a light complexion, and almost delicate features, Trible appeared even younger, although he and his wife worked the tables around them like seasoned professionals. I could see no evidence of any disability in either of his arms, and from the way he was shaking the hands and slapping the backs of the diners around him, he had apparently rehabilitated himself quite well. When the meal was over, the Tribles made a beeline to the restaurant's main door, where almost on cue a member of his staff suddenly materialized from a side door with their infant child. I watched in amazement as Paul Trible accepted the child from her caretaker, placed her against his shoulder, and continued shaking hands until the room had almost emptied. I wondered for a moment if I could use my own children in such a fashion and if, indeed, I was up to playing the political game the way I had just seen my opponent play it.

On a hot and humid Saturday morning in May, the delegates to the First District convention assembled at Gloucester High School to place my name in nomination as their congressional candidate. Since there were no other candidates, the outcome was foreordained, but we had nevertheless tried to orchestrate the agenda as carefully as possible to set the proper tone for our kickoff. Gloucester had been picked as the convention site because it was the geographic center of the district with easy access to Hampton, Williamsburg, and Newport News as well as the more remote rural counties.

Bob Quinn, the Hampton attorney defeated earlier by Trible, had agreed to nominate me, and Jessie Rattley, the vice-mayor of Newport News, and Tayloe Murphy, a member of the General Assembly from Westmoreland County, were going to second the nomination. Rattley was an imposing black woman who controlled much of the black vote in the east end of Newport News, but she had acquired that control by making a career of taking on the white establishment that ran the other end of town. Murphy, on the other hand, was a Virginia blueblood and the scion of a wealthy family that had owned a vast homestead since before the Revolutionary War. In an earlier era his family probably would have owned the family of Jessie Rattley, and as I watched them sitting side by side in the auditorium of Gloucester High School, I had to smile.

The convention was an hour late getting started, and Dennis spent his time placating disgruntled delegates who could not understand why some of their colleagues were late arriving. He also busied himself with the last-minute details of setting up the dais and positioning the camera crews. I used the time to rehearse my speech. I had worked hard on my acceptance speech because I wanted people to understand what motivated me to run.

Vietnam and its personal costs had not only bred skepticism but also taught me that even the most revered of leaders is human, and with that simple revelation came a growing awareness that young men like me, who had so scrupulously followed the mandate of older politicians, could seek to provide that mandate. My decision to run was but a logical extension of those premises, and now at the moment of my acceptance I burned with a passion to lead not where I had been led but toward some safer haven. When the seconding speeches were concluded, there was perfunctory applause, and Dennis gave me a good-luck pat on the back and a push toward the dais that he had purposely lowered to accommodate my wheelchair.

As I took the stand and the microphone, an unnatural calmness replaced the butterflies I had been feeling all morning, and I knew instinctively that the speech was going to go well. Looking out at my audience, I asked my mother, Toddy, and her parents to rise briefly, and I acknowledged the contributions they had made to my life and the influence they had exerted in bringing me to this point. I then thanked the people on the dais, began an explanation of how the troubled era of Vietnam had modified my strongly held conservative views, and concluded by reaffirming my faith in a country that, despite Vietnam and the troubles of our recent past, still held the promise of a blessed future.

When I finished, I realized for the first time that my arms were extended above my head, and I brought them back to my sides in some confusion. For five seconds my audience sat in stony silence while I wondered what had gone wrong, and then the crowd in the auditorium at Gloucester High School erupted with shouting, whistles, and applause as the delegates rose to their feet in unison. I did not know what the rewards of political service might be in the future, but as I allowed myself to bask for a moment in the crowd's adulation, I doubted if it could get much better than this. When I brought myself back to reality, Toddy was suddenly beside me, squeezing my hand, and on the periphery of the crowd I could see my mother dabbing at her face with a crumpled piece of tissue. Even Dennis had an animated look on his face that I had never seen before, and I grinned and wondered where all this might lead.

The next day the *Daily Press*, in a short statement with no pictures, reported that a strangely subdued crowd had nominated me to oppose Paul Trible. At the same time there was a laudatory description, complete with picture, of my opponent's convention, and Dennis and I fumed at the unfairness of the coverage. When Dennis called the paper to complain, he was told that Trible got the coverage because he was the congressman and I was just the challenger. The explanation did nothing to assuage our irritation, but at least we knew from the start how the game was going to be played.

══ ☆ ══

Following our respective nominations, interest in the race began to build, although Trible and I both knew that the pace would not really quicken until after Labor Day. In the meantime, it was necessary to raise funds to be able to finance a media campaign in the fall, and in June I was spending at least half of each day trying to buttonhole big givers, courting labor unions and political action committees, and attending small fund-raisers. As soon as I had the nomination in hand, we also commissioned a poll that not surprisingly showed that my name recognition was only modest and, more ominously, that Trible's support was greater and more solid.

After this poll Dennis and I hired a media consultant from Boston, who flew down for a week and designed a ten-page insert about me to be circulated with the district's newspapers. The brochure contained at least a dozen pictures of me, my family, and local supporters, and in large bold print tried to develop the theme that I had served my country on the battlefield and was now trying to continue that service in peacetime. It also contained laudatory quotations from Lyndon Johnson and Gerald Ford about my service and concluded by pointing out that these customary opponents agreed on me. The piece cost twenty thousand dollars, but it made hardly a dent in the results of a poll we ran afterward. It did prove useful in our fund-raising efforts and gave an early indication that we were dead serious about winning our race.

Though in the course of the summer's effort I occasionally became frustrated and despondent from encountering so many Trible supporters, there were moments of pure exhilaration. At an NAACP banquet at the venerable old Chamberlain Hotel in Hampton one night, a black minister of high local reputation got up to say a few extemporaneous words. I had visited with him earlier in his church office, as I had with most of the black church leaders in Hampton and Newport News, but he had remained noncommittal about my candidacy. Now I suddenly perked up when I heard the Reverend W. W. Brown say that despite the fact that the NAACP was supposed to be nonpartisan, he wanted to go on record personally as supporting the "young man in the wheelchair at the back of the room" in the upcoming election and that he would

304

appreciate it if I would share some of the thoughts with tonight's guests that I had shared earlier with him.

I had not prepared a speech, and my ears were burning from the unexpected support; but when I was handed a microphone, I again felt the calmness that conviction brings. I began by alluding to the strongly conservative heritage with which I had been nurtured and then spoke briefly of my baptism by fire in Vietnam and how the war and its aftermath had so irrevocably altered the underpinnings of my political philosophy. When I began to speak of the young men, both black and white but all poor and uneducated, who made up the bulk of the infantry and who took a disproportionately high percentage of casualties, the room became silent and the atmosphere heavy with expectation.

"Those same young men," I said, "who were called upon to sacrifice so much in the name of freedom then returned home to be locked out of the institutions and citadels of privilege that they had ostensibly been fighting to preserve. I vow here tonight that if elected, I will devote my career and my energies to opening those doors of opportunity, to making certain that if, God forbid, another war takes place, its burdens will be shared equally and that once in the corridors of power, I shall never forget my brothers-in-arms, who, though many died doing so, taught me the meaning of social responsibility and commitment without expectation of personal reward."

I concluded by stating that though I did not have the perspective of growing up black, I knew what it meant to be a member of a minority and to be judged on the basis of personal appearance rather than intrinsic worth.

"It has been a hard lesson," I finished, "but it has made me a more compassionate and more caring person, and because of that, I am now better able to serve you."

When I finished and handed back the microphone, Reverend Brown led the applause, which began at the head table and, picking up steam, rippled backward throughout the room, accompanied by shouts of "Amen, amen." Rough and callused hands reached out for mine later when, after the benediction, the crowd began to disperse.

"You hit a home run tonight," said one of the other black ministers as he shook my hand before departing.

I acknowledged his compliment, and while I did not disagree, I also knew that my speech would not play so well with the white establishment that was going to decide this election. It hurt me to realize that I now had more in common in some ways with people I had never really known than with people of whom I had heretofore always been a part. Paul Trible had sent his wife as a surrogate to this banquet, and I hoped that my reception at least caused him some consternation when she described it to him later.

══ ☆ ══

My wheelchair proved to be a huge drawback to my candidacy, as I knew it would be. In the protected environment of the hospital, law school, and my earlier jobs, people dealt with me on a more or less regular basis, and I had a chance to teach them to look past my chair and torso and to judge me on my own merits. But in the rush of a campaign, where so many judgments are formed on first impressions, I remained subject to the prejudices and misconceptions that many people have about the disabled.

Time after time, as I prepared to leave an appointment, the person with whom I was meeting would ask who had brought me to the meeting. A look of incredulity invariably followed my explanation that I had driven myself, and I realized quickly that the chasm separating me from the able-bodied was often unbridgeable. In addition, because I could not walk or perform some functions normally taken for granted, many were convinced I was unqualified to hold high public office. Finally, there were some people who, because of my disability, considered me inferior, and I could sense that they found it exceedingly galling that I would presume to present myself as a person who could lead them. Dennis realized the extent of the problem also, and he was as frustrated as I because having gotten to know me, he felt that though there were traits that might prevent me from being a good congressman, the loss of my legs was not one of them.

We devised some unusual stratagems to counter the wall of prejudice that we faced almost every day, and though they were often ingenious in concept, they had little overall effect on public perception. Every candidate for office needs a driver so that his time between campaign stops is free for studying issues or for resting, and Tom Rastetter did a capable job of chauffeuring me around the district. When people saw the two of us emerge from my jeep, however, they often decided that Tom was my attendant and that without him I could not get around. To put a stop to that foolishness, early in the campaign Tom and I started exchanging places in the front seat just before arriving at a campaign stop. In that way I was always at the wheel when we were first noticed.

306

One day Dennis decided that I should campaign door to door with a camera crew in an accessible neighborhood to demonstrate my mobility. After much searching he finally found a subdivision of houses built on slabs that I could negotiate. At the appointed hour a camera crew from one of the local television stations met us, and as the cameras began to roll, I opened the front gate of an appropriate house and rolled toward the front door. Before I had gotten ten feet, the door burst open, and a little old lady emerged and ran toward me with her hands outstretched, motioning me to go back.

When we met in the middle of her walkway, she cocked her head, looked straight into the camera, and as if on cue said, "He's in a fucking wheelchair, he's in a fucking wheelchair."

She then turned and ran back toward her house as if my condition were contagious, and as Dennis, the camera crew, and I dissolved into laughter, she slammed the door and drew her blinds. We never got a clip that was used on television, but for weeks I was referred to as the man in the fucking wheelchair.

=== ☆ ===

In the lull before the storm that preceded Labor Day, we tried to make an appearance at any occasion that generated a decent crowd. I pressed the flesh at assorted bull roasts, fish fries, shad plankings, barbecues, and other outdoor gatherings. Tom and I tried to arrive just as the chow lines were forming so that I could pick a vantage point and shake as many hands as possible while he passed out campaign literature and bumper stickers. Our standard operating procedure was to get in and out as quickly as possible so that we could get on to the next event and also so that we appeared to have momentum.

In the less populated counties it was difficult to cover more than two or three events in a day, but in urban areas we could usually take in half a dozen or more gatherings. If there was a radio station nearby we also tried for interviews, and if the event proved to be a total bust, we could usually salvage some of our effort by shaking hands in neighboring supermarkets, plants, or office buildings. I accepted all invitations to speak, and by the end of the summer I had honed my skills in enough chambers of commerce, Kiwanis clubs, veterans' organizations, and philanthropic groups that I was comfortable on the stump no matter what the makeup of the audience.

At an early press conference I issued the usual challenge to my opponent to come forth and debate me on the issues, and none of us was surprised when Trible countered with a press release indicating that his duties in Washington precluded acceptance of my offer. At that point he was so far ahead in the polls that it would have been foolish to give me an opening, but I wondered about the transparency of his excuse. For the previous two years he had spent almost every Saturday campaigning in the district, but now with an opponent for the first time and an election only three or four months away, he was too busy in Washington to accept my challenge.

As the campaign developed, a confrontation arose in the Newport News Shipbuilding and Dry Dock Company that, in the light of my newfound populism, pointed up a major difference between me and my opponent. For years there had been unrest in the yard over wages and fringe benefits. In the summer of 1978 a bitter battle was in progress between the Peninsula Shipbuilder's Association and the United Steelworkers. The PSA, which billed itself as the South's largest independent union, was in effect a management pawn. For as long as I could remember it had done nothing for its members, and in response the Steelworkers sought to take over representation. By early summer they had won an election, and as I began my campaign, they were waiting for certification from Washington as the official union of the shipyard. Trible had the support of the shipyard management and the PSA, and I had the Steelworkers' endorsement. However, it appeared that their support was not going to be of much value if they could not get certified before the November election.

As the economy of the shipyard went, so went the economy of most of the businesses in the community, and in the summer of 1978 business was almost at a standstill. Faced with a lack of work, the shipyard had been laying off its employees in increments of several thousand, and while morale was understandably low among the remaining workers, business and community leaders were scrambling to try to attract new shipyard business.

Trible had been touting his membership on the House Armed Services Committee as a position from which he could help channel defense contracts into the yard. It naturally followed that to deliver on his promises, he should be returned to office. I, on the other hand, in my standard stump speech was trying to hammer home the point that Paul Trible, as a freshman Republican congressman in a Democratic administration, was a political lightweight who could not possibly bring work into the yard. I, on the other hand, had paid my dues to the military, and when decisions that affected my constituents were made, mine was a voice that would be listened to by the brass in Washington.

One morning just before Labor Day I arrived at the office to find Dennis jumping up and down and pounding a folded copy of the local newspaper on his desktop. He was smiling from ear to ear, and as he handed me the paper and I saw the headlines, I realized that we had the makings of a real bread-and-butter campaign issue. In its commitment to a strong navy, the administration had developed a program called the Service Life Extension Program (SLEP), under which four ships were going to be overhauled at a cost of five hundred million dollars each. Each ship would provide enough work to keep our shipyard running for many months, and Newport News was the prime candidate for the job. In addition, the yard that received the contract for the first job would probably get all four of them. The morning paper's lead story and Dennis's reason for exultation was a report that Vice President Mondale had just announced that the first ship, the USS *Saratoga*, was going to be refurbished in Philadelphia. The story went on to report that he had announced it as a payback for the closing of the Frankford Arsenal, and Congressman Trible was already screaming political payoff and demanding an investigation.

For once I was in agreement with my opponent regarding the political aspect of the situation; but that was the point I had been trying to make for months, and Dennis and I quickly scheduled a press conference to condemn Congressman Trible's lack of clout and to bemoan the loss of the *Saratoga*. I began the press conference by stating that it was a black Monday for Virginia's First Congressional District when enough work to keep five hundred people employed for two years slipped through our hands with the loss of the *Saratoga* contract. I went on to demonstrate how a congressman who could work with rather than against the Carter administration would be in a better position to steer the remaining three contracts back to our shipyard, and I concluded by saying that "Remember the *Saratoga*" had unnecessarily become a slogan that would haunt those who had the best interests of the First District at heart. For all our effort we got one paragraph on a back page of the *Daily Press*, while Trible got a front-page story stating that he had made a personal trip to the White House to protest the *Saratoga* situation.

When we called the White House to verify his story, we were told that he had made a courtesy visit to the White House with several dozen congressmen on a completely unrelated matter and that the *Saratoga* had not even been discussed, but the paper that had printed his version of the story refused to do a follow-up when we brought the misstatement to its attention. Finally, because I had described the date of the

Saratoga's loss as a "black Monday," a letter appearing in the paper implied that I was a racist for using the word *black* in a pejorative way.

Dennis was furious that the other side could get away with such distortions of the truth, but he admired the way Trible played hardball. He immediately began a letter-writing campaign of his own, and we bombarded the *Daily Press* with so many letters written by our staff but signed by volunteers that three weeks before the election the paper took the unprecedented step of announcing that it would print no more letters to the editor of a political nature until after election day.

Because commerce in the shipyard had such a visible and vital effect on the local economy, we tried to keep the *Saratoga* issue in the forefront as long as possible, but without coverage from the *Daily Press* we were fighting a losing battle from the start. The shipyard itself remained an area of concern, however, for Democrats and Republicans alike, and by the time Labor Day arrived, I had worked shift changes at all of the yard's entrances and exits countless times. Even in a wheelchair, I had, by my third or fourth shift change, learned how to shake as many hands as possible in the frenetic fifteen or twenty minutes when the workers entered and left the yard, and I also got my political patter down so that I could handle friendly, hostile, or indifferent employees with equal alacrity. As expected, the yard bosses and management types greeted me much more coolly than the rank and file, but I even took a perverse pleasure in forcing the obvious Trible supporters to acknowledge my presence. So important was the yard that Trible had tried to put a district congressional office inside the plant itself, but even the yard's management viewed this as a political ploy too blatant to be allowed.

For our first televised political advertisement and my first effort at acting on camera, we decided to do a spot on the banks of the James River with the shipyard's main dry dock as a backdrop and the welfare of the yard's employees as our theme. Our media firm in Boston had written the spot that I was supposed to have rehearsed and memorized, and on the day of its filming Dennis and I and a film crew from nearby Norfolk assembled at the river to make the commercial. My spiel, consisting of only three sentences that had to be delivered in twenty-five to twenty-seven seconds, ended, "Who speaks for the pipe fitter and the welder and the other little men who get the job done? I'm Lew Puller, and in Congress I will speak for them."

It was designed mainly to let the voters get familiar with me, but it also gave the bland and nonthreatening message that I intended to represent all my constituency. I had thought that the making of the commercial would be a snap, but when the director cued me to look into the camera and begin my delivery, my lines headed for the hinterlands, while I sat looking helplessly into a rolling camera.

After half a dozen takes that showed only marginal improvement, the director wrote out my message on a piece of poster board and held it directly above the camera. We then spent another twenty minutes trying to get the rhythm down, and by the time we had an acceptable piece, my shirt was soaking wet and I felt as if I had just completed a day of hard labor. Dennis rolled his eyes and mumbled something on the way back to the office about my not being any Robert Redford. I was flabbergasted that something I had thought would be so simple had proved to be so difficult, and from that day forward I had a new appreciation for actors and actresses who made their living doing commercials.

When summer ended and the pace of the campaign accelerated, Toddy and I and the children took an apartment in town. We enrolled Lewis and Maggie in the Hampton public schools and found a sitter for after school, but both Toddy and I felt guilty that for the first time our children were being neglected. I tried to justify it by reasoning that the campaign would be over in a couple of months and that in the meantime they seemed to be adjusting well, but my rationalizations had a hollow ring. For days at a time I saw my children only after they had gone to sleep at night, and when I realized that I was finding out about milestones in their lives, if at all, only after they had passed, I told myself that I was going to do a reassessment when I had time. For the last three months of my campaign our family had only two or three dinners alone together, and although Toddy never complained, I could sense that the family disruptions bore heavily on her.

If I had misgivings about the way my political pursuit was affecting my family, I developed even more serious doubts about where I was headed as the daylight hours shortened and election day approached. Virginia's First District, with its dependency on government spending and its military heritage, was a bastion of conservatism. Paul Trible had learned how to wave the flag and embrace that heritage with a fervor that left his audiences clamoring for more, but I, despite my military background, was uncomfortable appealing to jingoism. Ironically, I, who had been raised in the Marine Corps and had fought a war and seen firsthand the death and destruction that cheap rhetoric can engender, was made to appear less patriotic than my opponent, who could fire up the most zealous flag-wavers, without ever having worn a uniform or heard a shot fired in anger.

One night Tom and I traveled to the Eastern Shore to address an American Legion post, people who should have been a natural part of my constituency, and I decided to give them what they wanted to hear. I began by recalling Nikita Khrushchev's banging his shoe on the table at the United Nations and later saying, "We will bury you," and I went on to outline our need for a defense second to none and a blue-water navy to support our forces anywhere in the world.

It was an impassioned but simplistic performance that had the post membership stamping its feet, and even Tom wondered aloud after it was over where my uncharacteristic zeal had come from. The roar of the crowd had felt good and energized me while I was speaking, but driving back to Hampton, I realized that I only halfheartedly believed what I was saying and that a generation of young Americans lay dead partly because for far too long politicians had been free to mouth patriotic platitudes without any regard for the consequences of their words. Early in the campaign a Trible supporter had told me that after one of his jingoistic speeches he had asked Trible if he really believed everything he'd said. The congressman's alleged response was that it did not really matter, in light of the speech's effect on his audience. After Vietnam I grew to feel that politics was too important for grandstanding, and it made me very uncomfortable to see how close I was getting to courting votes by slanting my opinions.

— ☆ —

At one end of the city of Hampton is Fort Monroe, which has been pumping money into the local community since before the Civil War. As I began my campaign, rumors had circulated that the administration had Fort Monroe on a short list for the chop. As far as I could see, the base had some historical significance as the site where Jefferson Davis was imprisoned after the Civil War, but other than provide graveyard tours for army officers about to retire, it contributed very little. It was indeed an obvious selection for termination, but for the fact that any politician who endorsed that view in the Hampton area would also be selected for termination.

I tried to finesse the situation by remaining silent, but Trible released a statement saying that the fort was vital to the defense of the Chesapeake Bay and that as a member of the House Armed Services Committee, he intended to see that it was maintained. I did not know that the Chesapeake Bay was so severely threatened by the Red Menace that some overweight army colonels at the end of their careers were needed to buttress its defense. When I made my observations known to Dennis, he reminded me that I did not have Congressman Trible's perspective as a member of the House Armed Services Committee. In any case, Fort Monroe was my introduction to pork-barrel politics, and I was beginning to see that if I had to make a career out of defending the indefensible, I was going to lose a part of myself.

=== ☆ ===

In September I had my first face-to-face encounter with my opponent on the campaign trail. A debate had been scheduled at one of the local high schools in Newport News, and I was to participate along with the two candidates for the United States Senate, John Warner and Andrew Miller. Both Miller and Warner sent surrogates, and our campaign had been informed that a stand-in would be representing Congressman Trible. A few seconds before the debate began, with the rest of us seated on the stage of the school auditorium, Trible appeared at the back of the room and began making his way through the students who were still milling in the aisles.

I was already apprehensive about my first debate, and my unease was increased by the unexpected appearance of my opponent. I tried to appear nonchalant as he passed me to take his seat. The format was standard, with a moderator asking each candidate a question, to which his opponent could then respond. The order of questioning was then rearranged so that the initial answerer could respond last, and finally there were a few questions from the audience. Trible began each answer with the preface "When this issue was addressed in the House of Representatives," and ten minutes into the debate it had become obvious that he was contrasting his legislative experience with my inexperience. In addition, I flubbed a couple of early answers on the Alaska pipeline and the future of the snail darter, although I finished more strongly.

After it was over, Dennis was livid because he felt that we had been set up, and he set about devising a strategy where we could return the favor. We both knew that from that day forward Trible would diffuse the issue of not being willing to debate me by pointing out that he had already done so, and as the challenger I needed to make a strong showing each time we appeared together. I had failed to do so in our first debate, and I resolved never again to be caught unprepared. I also learned as our first debate wore on that in rough-and-tumble political debating, where the rules are not rigidly applied, you can avoid answering a question that is not to your liking by simply rephrasing it or using it as a springboard to put your opponent back on the defensive.

In the weeks ahead I rarely saw Congressman Trible, although I learned a great deal about him and his campaign style. He seemed to run on the premise that his constituency was solid and that there was more to be gained by trying to make inroads into my natural constituency than by stroking his own supporters. To that end, he courted heavily the black voters who had provided the winning margin in his first race but whose legislative goals he had never advanced once elected.

Naturally he also tried to stress his agenda for a strong national defense and his role as a member of the House Armed Services Committee in an effort to win over the veteran community that should have been solidly behind me. In so doing, he obtained endorsements from several local veterans' organizations, and he used them to make it appear that their parent organizations on the national level supported him. On one occasion a local Veterans of Foreign Wars post gave him its man-of-the-year award, and I was invited to the banquet where he was to be honored. I accepted on the condition that I would be recognized and allowed to speak, but after I arrived, it was obvious that there had been a misunderstanding.

Trible, who was seated at the head table, was the center of attention throughout the evening while I was seated at a back table. After the meal was concluded, he gave his standard speech on national defense and then had his picture taken for the newspapers as he accepted a plaque from the post commander. My recognition consisted of having my name read from an alphabetical listing of the invited guests in the room, and I was not permitted to do anything more than raise my hand when named. After it was over, I forced myself to wheel over and congratulate the congressman on a fine speech, but what I really wanted to do was strangle him, the post leadership, and Dennis for putting me in such a humiliating position.

In a roomful of summer soldiers and sunshine patriots, I was probably the only man who had ever experienced combat or shed blood for his country, and they gave their highest award to a boy who did not even meet their own lax requirements for membership. Once again the facile politician had stolen the limelight while I was forced to sit and watch, and the next morning's newspapers would feature a beaming Paul Trible accepting the bounty of a grateful community of veterans.

After Trible and I had completed our first joint appearance, the pace of the campaign quickened. I addressed at least a dozen high school assemblies, and at each of them I began my presentation by describing how the Vietnam War had shaped my political views and kindled my desire to seek public office. After describing the affinity that the war had given me for the workingman's point of view and the tragic result of accepting unquestioningly the mandate of our leadership in Washington, I described how I had come to the realization that I was as qualified to lead as, if not more so than, those in whom I had so naively placed my trust.

The high school students whom I addressed, without any trace of the mixed feelings of guilt of the Rotarians, Lions, and Kiwanians to whom I also spoke, made wonderful audiences. At the same time it sometimes seemed to me that their lack of knowledge of events taking place less than ten years earlier made them dangerously susceptible to what I had experienced. After some of the assemblies there were mock elections, and it was gratifying to beat my opponent, even in a straw vote by students not old enough to vote. I realized, of course, that Trible was also winning mock elections at high schools I was not able to cover, but there was a thrill in trying to shape young minds.

I had three more joint appearances with Paul Trible before the election, and the first of these fulfilled Dennis's ambition to ambush the opposition. In the early fall we got a call at our campaign headquarters advising us that on the following Sunday afternoon Congressman Trible would be addressing an NAACP meeting in Williamsburg and that if we cared to participate, we would be given equal time to speak.

Our research into Trible's voting record for his first term in office had revealed that of twenty-odd legislative initiatives that the Congressional Black Caucus had picked as being of primary importance to them, Trible had not voted favorably on one. Despite that record, he had the audacity to campaign in black churches and before black audiences as a friend. Dennis and I were almost drooling at the thought of confronting Trible with the results of our research before a black audience.

When we arrived for the meeting, it was obvious from his look that Trible had not been advised of our invitation, and when he saw me, he asked lamely if the format was going to be changed to a debate. His apprehension was allayed only mildly when he was told that he would be given the promised opportunity to speak, but that out of courtesy I would then be allowed to speak. After he had given a recitation of the programs in Washington that he had supported that were favorable to blacks and that he intended to continue to support despite the political fallout, I was given my chance.

"My name is Lew Puller," I said softly, "and I have come here today to set the record straight with regard to my opponent's stands on issues of importance to blacks."

There were scattered nods of agreement and mumbles of "Amen" as I listed Trible's no votes on which I would have voted yes, but when I finished, the principal reaction was lukewarm applause. The crowd was confused and skeptical about the information I had just given it, and in light of Trible's high visibility and favorable impression in the black community during the previous two years, it was not inclined to take my words as gospel.

Trible left the meeting as quickly as possible, taking the microphone briefly on his way out to say that future debates would clarify the distortions I had made in his record, but that for now his duties in Washington required his return. I knew that we had wounded him, if only by planting a seed of doubt with a group of voters I had learned to value highly, and Dennis was elated that Trible was visibly upset when he left the confrontation. Politics could be gratifying, I thought, but I, too, was angry that my opponent was going to continue to garner black support that I thought was totally undeserved.

Before our next meeting, we began a flurry of activity that included speaking engagements and appearances of a diversity I would not have thought possible three months earlier. In just a matter of weeks I spoke to senior citizens' groups, philanthropic organizations of every sort, church groups, unions, veterans' organizations, and fraternal orders. I spoke in church and parish halls, from the steps and greens of county courthouses, in high school auditoriums, and at outdoor rallies, fish fries, barbecues, and picnics, and on one occasion from the back of a flatbed truck in a newly mowed hayfield. I shook hands at plant gates during shift changes, at high school football games and bingo games, and at grand openings of newly established businesses. In the mornings there were breakfasts to attend, followed by coffees, luncheons, teas, and dinners, and whenever there were lapses in the schedule, Dennis had me shaking hands at grocery stores or going from desk to desk in corporate buildings and industrial parks.

Toddy and the children rode with me in parades, and we passed out literature and bumper stickers to anyone who would accept our offerings. I appeared on television talk shows during interviews and panel discussions until the entire array of activity began to blur together like the scenery from a train. After being bombarded for so long with such intense stimuli, I began to block out all but the most unusual experiences, moving through them rather than lingering on any one event.

An episode that caught me totally off guard and moved me almost to tears took place in a warehouse in Newport News. The building had been converted into a tailoring establishment, and I had been told only that I was going to spend a few minutes shaking hands with the women who were doing piecework for an independent contractor. When I entered the building, I saw row after row of sewing machines, each of which appeared to be operated by a Vietnamese woman. When they saw me, all work suddenly stopped, and the familiar high-pitched cadence of Vietnamese women, excited by the interruption of their schedule, replaced the sound of the sewing machines and carried me back to my time in Southeast Asia.

The women had been told that I was coming, and as I wheeled down the rows between them, I was greeted by outstretched hands and smiling and sometimes weeping faces. A spokesperson for the group, the only one who appeared to be able to communicate in English, told me that they all were refugees who had come to Newport News from a relocation camp. They wanted me to know how much my sacrifice meant to them and how it would always be remembered. As I took her hand to acknowledge her words, I had trouble speaking, and I finally gave up and just nodded my head. For once I felt uplifted rather than degraded by the reactions of strangers to my service in Vietnam, and I spent the next half hour trying to shake the hand of every woman in the shop. Later I realized that none of them could vote, but the experience, far more enriching than a mere campaign event, helped me focus on why I was trying to become a congressman and kept my spirits buoyed for days.

⸻ ☆ ⸻

Sometime during the final weeks of the campaign a gradual sense of calm began to replace the apprehension I had felt early in the effort. Although I was dog tired most of the time and frustrated by the demands of conflicting constituencies, I began to sense that I was in command and that I could operate effectively no matter what the occasion. The feeling was not unlike the confidence I had gained in Vietnam after I had gotten used to my platoon.

I also saw that I really wanted to be a congressman, to go to Washington and try to make a difference, and not just to serve so that I could call myself a congressman. In the beginning I had been motivated by a strong desire to unseat my opponent, who I did not feel was worthy of his position; but that motivation had waned, and I came to see that I desperately wanted to fulfill my potential and give meaning to my being spared on the battlefield in Vietnam. Ironically, as I became comfortable with my status as an aspiring politician and as my thirst for office increased, I also began to realize that the odds were prohibitive.

The next audience Trible and I faced together was solidly in his camp. Sponsored by the Chamber of Commerce, the debate took place at a Newport News hotel. The conference room was so crowded with white middle-class businessmen and their carefully coiffed wives that Dennis had to run interference in order to let me wheel to the front of the room. As planned for the first debate, the two candidates for the United States Senate, Paul Trible and I, and several candidates for local office were featured, eight of us in all. We were seated at a long table to the right of the moderator on a dais. Since the debate was to last only an hour, no one was going to dominate the scene if we all got equal billing.

John Warner, the Republican candidate for the Senate and husband of Elizabeth Taylor, set the tone for the evening when he, as the first candidate questioned, addressed an issue that had not been asked by the moderator. After that it became a free-for-all, with each of us using our allotted time to try to draw a reaction from the crowd. After Trible and I had each answered several questions, it became clear that neither of us was going to be able to lay a glove on the other, and I decided to ignore him and engage Warner in a good-natured discussion of the relative attractiveness of our respective wives. Just before the debate ended, Dennis passed me a note that read, "You're doing great, but straighten your tie," and I acknowledged his encouragement with a nod before making my closing remarks.

When the final speeches were over, Dennis drove me home, and as usual he critiqued my performance. By way of encouragement he told me that he thought I had grown to the point where I could more than hold my own against Paul Trible. That, however, we both knew was not going to be enough to turn the election, especially since we had only one more joint appearance scheduled. What was truly alarming about the evening, we both realized, was the size of the crowd that had showed up to support its fair-haired congressman. The people had come to see him, not me, there was little I could do to change their minds, and they all would be voting come election day.

Because we had succeeded in selling our candidacy to the Democratic Congressional Campaign Committee, Virginia's First Congressional District race was targeted as a possible upset. That meant that we got some extra union money, but more important, it meant that we got cooperation from Washington. Dennis had commissioned a beautifully done prospectus that laid out our campaign strategy and convinced a lot of people that we were professionals who had a real chance of winning. He also developed contacts in the White House and on Capitol Hill, and in early October we scheduled a two-day trip to Washington to reap the fruits of his effort and to try to get some much-needed publicity.

On the morning of the first day we journeyed to the White House, where I was to meet with President Carter and Vice President Mondale. The White House staff had told our campaign that we would be permitted to bring one news reporter with us to chronicle the meetings, but when we extended the offer to the *Daily Press*, it declined, saying that the meetings were not newsworthy. I was incredulous, and while Dennis did the second best thing by finding a reporter from the Richmond paper who would accompany us, I cursed the Newport News paper and swore that if elected, I would someday get even.

When we arrived at the White House, there were four or five other invited congressional candidates, and we all were ushered into a conference room, welcomed to the White House, and given a briefing by a team of young staffers. After an hour of being taught how best to take advantage of the Carter connection and how to handle difficult questions that might surface while campaigning, we were moved to an anteroom adjacent to the Oval Office and given the order in which we would go in to meet individually with the president.

When my turn came, I wheeled nervously through the heavy door onto the plush carpeting, and a smiling President Carter came across the room to greet me. As we shook hands and he directed me to a sitting area, he told me that he had heard good things about what I was doing for the state of Virginia from Lieutenant Governor Chuck Robb and how much he enjoyed getting to meet me. I had prepared absolutely nothing to say in response to his introduction. While I wanted to discuss the USS *Saratoga* decision, I knew that that topic was not appropriate for the occasion. Instead I grinned like an idiot and mumbled something inane about what an honor it was to meet him. As we sat side by side in the Oval Office and posed for a photograph, I felt as stiff and unnatural as I had ever felt in my life. The president, with his legs crossed confidently in the chair next to me, was obviously much better at this than I was, and for some odd reason I could not stop staring at the thick rubber sole of one of his shoes, which seemed oddly out of place with his expensively tailored suit. Five minutes later the meeting ended and the president showed me to the door and told me that he hoped he would have the opportunity to work with me in the next Congress.

Outside, there was a twenty-minute wait while the president met with the rest of the candidates, and we were then led down a hall to the vice president's office. Instead of meeting with him individually, as we had with President Carter, we were taken into Vice President Mondale's office as a group and given seats in front of his desk. He made a brief welcoming speech in which he offered to provide whatever assistance he could to our campaigns, and then he asked us to introduce ourselves and come forward to his desk for a photo opportunity.

I had resolved, after having squandered my opportunity for meaningful dialogue with President Carter, to say something of substance to Vice President Mondale. Again I wanted to bring up the matter of the USS *Saratoga*. When my turn to speak came, I wheeled forward to his desk, told him that I was Lew Puller and that I was trying to become the congressman from the district that should have been awarded the *Saratoga* contract. Vice President Mondale had earlier made the announcement that the *Saratoga* was to go to Philadelphia rather than to Newport News, and when he heard my words, he good-naturedly offered to get under his desk while the picture was being taken. Again the meeting was adjourned before there was any opportunity for meaningful discussion; but I felt much better that I had at least mentioned the incident, and our reporter from the Richmond paper had witnessed the exchange and was taking notes as furiously as if the fate of the free world were under discussion.

Before we left the White House, Dennis called the *Daily Press* to let it know that the Democratic candidate for the First District had just met with the president and vice president of the United States and that it should seriously consider doing a story about the visit. The response was that the paper had no reason to believe we were even calling from the White House, and it dismissed Dennis and his offer of corroboration. The next day a picture of me shaking hands with Vice President Mondale appeared on the front page of the Richmond paper, but there was never any coverage whatsoever from the newspapers in my own congressional district. Dennis suggested that if I wanted free press at home, I was probably going to have to murder someone.

During the remainder of our trip to Washington we also met with Speaker Tip O'Neill and House Majority Leader Jim Wright. Having learned my lesson at the White House, I let each of them know that if elected, I expected and deserved a seat on the House Armed Services Committee. That night we capped our stay in Washington by holding a fund-raising reception at a downtown hotel, and Congressman Wright attended and gave Dennis a sizable check for my campaign. He also indicated that he did not foresee any problem with my getting the committee assignments that I wanted, and he offered to work vigorously on my behalf.

After the reception I was dead tired from such a momentous day, and as I reviewed our schedule, it was obvious that Dennis had performed splendidly in orchestrating the events. It was also clear that if elected, I was going to get the kind of assistance that is not generally available to a freshman congressman. I had paid my dues in blood, and after all these years it was gratifying to know that there could be some payback for my sacrifice. It was also obvious that we were still a long shot, but to contemplate defeat after having worked so hard required an acceptance of reality that would have stopped my campaign in its tracks.

=== ☆ ===

Our third and last joint appearance took place at York High School a couple of weeks before the election. This time Trible and I were the only debaters, and the give-and-take was sharp. The audience consisted of government students at the high school as well as members of the senior class, and my staff had been tipped off that Trible had agreed to the debate only because the head of the government department at the school was a Trible supporter. Supposedly she was going to see to it that we were asked some questions that were to Trible's liking, and when Dennis heard the rumor of another potential ambush, he started working. By pure coincidence, one of our best campaign volunteers had children who were friends of some of the York High School seniors, and by the time of the debate we had several students sitting in the audience armed with questions that my campaign manager had written.

The debate began innocuously enough: the congressman and I were introduced, shook hands, and then took our positions at the front of the auditorium while the rules of the debate were explained and several cameramen from local television stations positioned their equipment. After a few preliminary questions, during which neither of us was able to gain an edge, a young man with glasses, a slender build, and an otherwise unremarkable appearance rose from his seat in the audience and addressed a question to Paul Trible.

"Mr. Trible," he began in a quiet and almost monotonous voice, "we have been told that during the Watergate scandal you worked as a lawyer to keep President Nixon from going to jail. Would you care to defend your actions during that time?"

Within seconds the crowd, which until then had been only halfheartedly following the proceedings, became hushed, and in anticipation of Trible's response, many of the students leaned forward in their seats. Caught off guard by the question, Trible fumbled badly, and his explanation that in a democracy every man is entitled to legal representation and that he was proud of his service to the president elicited more boos and snickers than applause. When I was given the opportunity for rebuttal, I decided to attack by appearing to defend my opponent since he was already on the ropes.

"I remember Watergate," I said. "It and Vietnam were the main reasons I decided to enter politics, but I can assure you that Paul Trible had no impact on either. He experienced the war from the sidelines, and as an inexperienced attorney only two years out of law school during Watergate, his role in Nixon's defense was negligible."

If Trible's response to the question had cost him his audience, mine had made him look like a liar. Undone by Dennis's strategy, my opponent spent the rest of the debate in a futile attempt at damage control. When I made my closing statement, I emphasized to the York students that my opponent favored a minimum wage differential that would mean that in his mind their work was worth less than that of older workers. I also pointed out that although he had been spared military service, he now favored a universal draft for all the young men in the audience.

The debate ended with a crowd of students gathered around my wheelchair, Dennis and Tom clapping each other on the back as if we had just won the election, and Paul Trible making a quick getaway. I had finally drawn blood, and even if no one else ever heard about our skirmish at York High School, I at least had a sense of vindication.

=== ☆ ===

One night during the last week of the campaign I stopped by our headquarters to pick up some literature on my way home and found Dennis working late at his desk. When I wheeled into the office, he looked up from the figures he was examining and beckoned me over. I knew that he had been doing an end-of-campaign poll, and from the worried look on his face, I knew the results were not good.

"Trible's ahead with solid support in every area of the district," he said, pointing helplessly at the tangle of papers on his desk. "I'm going to run a negative ad attacking him for taking so much political action committee money, but at this point it looks pretty hopeless."

I nodded my understanding, and for an awkward moment neither of us said a word. Finally I put my hand on his arm and told him that it was important that we ride out the remainder of the campaign with the dignity that we had aimed for so far. As I prepared to leave, he handed me a letter from a contributor and told me that he had been saving it for an appropriate occasion. Instinctively I glanced first at the upper corner of the envelope and noted that the figure $100 had been penciled into the corner by Margaret to keep track of the amount of the enclosed contribution.

The letter, which had been mailed in Florida, was from a doctor who had treated me when I was brought in from the battlefield in Vietnam. He had by chance received one of my campaign solicitation letters, and he wrote to tell me that for a year he had treated battlefield casualties in Vietnam.

"Never," he wrote, "had I seen more severe traumatic injuries in a patient who had lived, and I wondered at the time if I was doing the right thing by allowing you to live." Continuing, he wrote, "Your survival had seemed to me a miracle of dubious value which severely tested the moral imperative of my Hippocratic oath." He concluded, "Your running for the House of Representatives ten years after our meeting in Vietnam reaffirmed the worth of my service there and is a source of great personal satisfaction to me."

When I finished the letter, I returned it to Dennis, who rose from his chair and told me that it should be some consolation that there were thousands more like the good doctor who had been inspired by my campaign. As I drove back to Toddy and my sleeping children, I was buoyed by the realization that the doctor had had his Vietnam service validated by my current effort, and I wished that the same held true for me. I was saddened, however, that I could do no more to justify the faith of the majority of my supporters, including Dennis, who of late seemed to be much more human.

=== ☆ ===

Election day was a clear, unusually warm November Tuesday, a good sign because traditionally Democrats are viewed as being more inclined than Republicans to stay at home when the weather is bad. Dennis had laid out for me an ambitious campaign schedule that basically involved shaking hands with voters at two dozen polling places throughout Hampton and Newport News.

I voted for myself and the Democratic slate at six in the morning, when the polls opened, and then with Tom began crisscrossing Hampton and Newport News in a frenzied effort to greet as many voters as possible. At each stop I first thanked those who were busy trying to make last-minute converts for me outside the polling places and then positioned my wheelchair so that I would have the best access to incoming voters. As Tom handed out sample ballots, I tried to concentrate on the voters who appeared undecided and to thank those who indicated that I had their support, and by noon my right hand had begun to ache from pumping so many outstretched hands.

In virtually all the black precincts in Newport News and Hampton, there were black women wearing straw boaters with Trible bumper stickers wrapped around them, who were being paid to campaign for the congressman. Throughout the day at least a dozen of these women apologized to me for what they were doing but told me that their families needed the money they were being paid. In fact, it became so commonplace to hear them greet voters with the expression "Ignore my hat and vote your conscience" that I wondered if this was standard parlance in the district at election time.

By the time the polls closed at seven o'clock I was so wound up from the day's pace that though physically exhausted, I was not certain I would ever sleep again. At the last polling place we visited in Hampton, I reached out mechanically to shake hands with a voter and then realized that he was an old law school classmate who had volunteered to work the polls on my behalf. I also realized that my right hand had begun to bleed from overuse, and for a moment I could not decide whether I was glad the handshaking was over or I wanted time suspended so that I could go on greeting voters into infinity.

By my nose count, the vast majority of voters I had encountered in the previous thirteen hours had favored my opponent, but there had been exchanges with some of my supporters that were achingly poignant. In addition to the law school classmate I had just encountered, there were friends along the circuit who had remained loyal despite the overwhelming odds against me. Paul Barents, my old roommate from the hospital, had driven down from Pennsylvania to pass out literature for me, and several other Vietnam veteran friends, seemingly undaunted by the sting of our defeat in Vietnam, had now taken on another losing effort for a comrade. Strangers also provided much-needed encouragement on the last day of my foray into politics. I will always remember one particular incident.

While I was soliciting votes that afternoon outside an elementary school in Newport News, a cab pulled up to the curb and the driver assisted an elderly, well-dressed lady out of the backseat. Leaning heavily on a walker, she gave me a peremptory smile and then began making her way toward the voting booths inside the school. While she was voting, the cabby told me that he often helped her on those rare occasions when she ventured outside her apartment and that for weeks she had been talking about going out on election day to vote for Lew Puller. When she returned, I wheeled over to shake her hand and to thank her for supporting me. As our eyes locked, she drew herself up grandly and admonished me to get back to my campaigning rather than waste so much time on a foolish old lady. I never got her name, but I will be moved by her for the rest of my life.

══ ☆ ══

When the polls closed, Tom and I packed our remaining literature into the jeep and headed for the Best Western motel in Newport News, where we were to meet Toddy, the children, and the rest of the staff. The motel owner had contributed a private room for my family and a party room for my supporters, and I had planned to spend some time alone with Toddy, Lewis, and Maggie before venturing out to make my statement. When I arrived, Toddy, who had been on her own campaign schedule all day, was waiting in the room with the children. For a few moments we exchanged small talk about the way the day had progressed, but as always we avoided any discussion of impending defeat. We both were exhausted, and beneath my wife's cheerful exterior I could sense that she was just as relieved as I that the madness of the last year was drawing to a close. Lewis and Maggie, with barely eighteen years of life between them, seemed to sense that the occasion was important, and they tried to appear nonchalant under bewildering circumstances.

After a few more minutes the phone began ringing, and a steady stream of visiting well-wishers, staff, and media types started to appear at the door. For once I was pleased that the commotion made intimacy impossible, and while Dennis did his best to fend off the onslaught at the door, someone turned the television on to catch the first returns. With one precinct reporting, I was in the lead, and for an instant a flicker of hope stirred inside me. Trible quickly took the lead as other precincts began reporting, and I watched in fascination as my slim lead became a rout. After another twenty minutes Dennis put his arm around my shoulder and awoke me from my reverie with a gentle reminder that I needed to thank my supporters and concede defeat.

With Toddy at my side and the children in tow, we made an agonizing trip from our room to the meeting room at the other side of the motel to face a subdued and somber crowd.

"By now," I said, "you know that our reach for the brass ring has fallen short. I want to thank all of you for your dedicated support in the face of almost insurmountable odds and to let you know that I will always cherish and remember you. Even in defeat I am proud of what we have accomplished together. I do not know if I will seek political office again, but I do know that if I had this race to run again, I would not do very many things differently. I am leaving you now," I concluded, "to drive over and congratulate the Trible campaign on its victory, but I want you to remember that while Pullers have been beaten, we have never been bowed, and I am going to hold my head high when I concede defeat."

When I had finished, the crowd applauded, and a dozen well-wishers gathered at the front of the room to offer condolences and encouragement. I shook as many hands as were within my reach while Tom pushed my wheelchair toward the exit and Dennis ran interference for the rest of us.

When we were seated in the car on our way to the Trible victory celebration, Dennis insisted that I limit my remarks to congratulating the Trible campaign and not say anything that could be taken as complimentary toward the congressman personally. I was in no mood to quibble over a choice of words that, however carefully chosen, were going to stick in my throat, so I nodded my assent. The rest of the car was silent for the fifteen-minute drive, although I noticed at one point that Maggie had her face buried in her mother's side and was crying quietly.

At the Holiday Inn, where the Trible party was being held, so many cars were packed into the parking lot that the overflow extended up and down the street for half a mile to accommodate the crowd. Dennis parked illegally, and we fought our way through the lobby and into the room where Trible was scheduled to make his victory speech. So many people were milling about that it took us ten minutes to get to the platform at the front of the room on which he and his wife were accepting congratulations. When they spotted us, they beckoned to us to join them on the stage, and I shook hands with each of them and resisted the urge to punch my adversary in the mouth when he kissed my wife on the cheek. I made a brief statement along the lines Dennis had suggested, and as quickly as we could, we left the stage and the laurels to the man who had bested us.

Unlike our entrance, the crowd now parted to allow our departure, and as we reached the blessedly cool air of the parking lot, I could tell by the roar of the people inside that their candidate had begun his speech and was giving them what they wanted. Toddy pressed my hand to her side and managed one of the tight little smiles that hid more than it revealed and had for years endeared her to me. We were going home, and Paul Trible would have the luxury of working the morning shift change at the Newport News shipyard without having to look over his shoulder to see if I was gaining on him.

IX

★

THE MORNING AFTER election night I awoke with a hangover, having stayed up half the night drowning my sorrows. We had invited a few key supporters over; but the gathering had been awkward, and I had been in no frame of mind to be a good host. When the party broke up, Toddy went to bed, leaving me alone with my misery and my scotch bottle. Because I was badly out of shape for drinking, the overindulgence cost me dearly, and now, even after the luxury of six hours of uninterrupted sleep, my temples throbbed. I knew that it would take a week or two to close down the campaign, but once that task was over, I had no job, no prospects, and an as yet undetermined campaign debt.

For the first time in months I was thinking past election day; but the process was frightening, and I welcomed the distractions of the telephone, which began ringing in late morning and by the end of the day seemed to have taken on a life of its own. Most of the callers, including Lieutenant Governor Robb, offered their condolences and a few words of encouragement and then sought a polite way to end the conversation. A few, however, wanted to know what was next on my agenda, and I could sense that my lack of focus was disturbing to supporters who had admired me for decisiveness. Unhappily I did not have a clue to what was next, other than to lick my wounds for a while and get reacquainted with my family.

On the second or third day of my moping around the apartment, Toddy decided that she had to get me moving again, and we went grocery shopping together. Because I had programmed myself to look for voters with whom to shake hands whenever I entered a crowded building, it was a strange sensation to be looking only for food in a supermarket, and I had to force myself to concentrate on the items on Toddy's list. At each of our stops I could tell that strangers around me were pointing me out and talking about me, and while the attention had not bothered me as a candidate during my campaign, it irritated me now that I had lost my race. On our way back to the apartment we talked about our situation and decided that it would be best for us and for the children to return as quickly as possible to our home in northern Virginia, where I could begin job hunting and we could try to restore some stability to our lives.

X

OVER THE NEXT FEW DAYS we closed down the campaign office, returned all the rented and loaned office equipment and furnishings, and laid off most of the paid staff. Margaret agreed to stay on at a nominal salary to handle unfinished business, and we retained our post office mailing address so that creditors could contact us and supporters could send checks to help retire our debt. Toddy also made arrangements to cancel the lease on our apartment and have our belongings moved back to Alexandria.

Although I drafted a letter to our supporters during this time asking that they help us with the twenty-five-thousand-dollar campaign debt, Toddy and Margaret took care of most of the other loose ends. I was still stunned at having been beaten by better than two to one, and hurt and disillusioned, I was able to do very little to come to terms with a disaster that I felt was largely of my own making. Toddy recognized that I was going through a grieving process in many ways similar to that which we experienced when I returned from Vietnam, and while remaining available, she wisely gave me a wide berth. Until the movers came, I slept late each morning, often drank my lunch with friends for whom I finally had some time, and ended my days by brooding alone in the darkness of our living room with a half-empty scotch bottle.

Our return to our old home just before Thanksgiving after an absence of almost a year provided each of us a new set of tasks and should have been especially beneficial for me because the move took me out of the arena of my political humiliation. While Toddy worked to undo the mess a couple of bachelor friends had made of the house and to reestablish contacts in the community, I concentrated on retiring my campaign debt, and I began making plans to start a job search after the first of the year. Lewis and Maggie were delighted to be back in their own home and with friends with whom they had grown up, but my readjustment was less successful.

I was able to pay off all the creditors and to reduce the debt by fifteen thousand dollars, but because I had not worked in well over a year, had maintained two homes for much of that time, and had incurred a personal loss of ten thousand dollars, Toddy and I were financially strapped for the first time in our marriage. When I began looking for a job, the process was laborious, and with no concrete prospects in sight, my depression over the campaign was compounded.

I felt worthless because I was not working, and with time on my hands, I brooded over the meaning of my political defeat and drank heavily most nights. As I looked back at my run for Congress, it seemed to me that my reward for having served was that I was forced to challenge an incumbent who, because he had been spared military service, was able to enter the political arena well ahead of me and to stack the deck against any political success on my part. In my depressed state I began to despise Paul Trible and his victory with an intensity I had never felt toward any other man, and my contempt for him expanded to encompass most of the young men of my generation who had found ways to avoid the war experience.

To make matters worse, Toddy came home from running errands one day shortly after our return and breathlessly announced that the Tribles had bought a house just around the corner from us. At first I thought she was making a joke, but when I realized she was serious, my incredulity gave way to indignation. It was bad enough, I thought, that I had been beaten by a draft dodger, but now he was going to rub my nose in my defeat. In all the vastness of northern Virginia's many suburbs, Paul Trible had chosen a home whose backyard was just a stone's throw from my own, and the cruel irony of having to watch him drive around the neighborhood with his congressional license plates was almost more than I could bear. On one occasion my wife even found his car parked in the handicapped parking section that I used at the local Safeway, and while I did not find it surprising that he would use a restricted parking space, I devoutly wished that I could make his use of the space legitimate.

═══ ✶ ═══

I now began to isolate myself from meaningful contact with all but my immediate family. I avoided social occasions and seized on any pretext to maintain my self-imposed exile. I also became *more* obsessed with the Vietnam War, and I dwelt endlessly on the unfair treatment and lack of respect that my fellow veterans and I received from the media, from society, and from our government.

By late winter it was not an uncommon experience for me to open a new bottle of scotch every other day, and while my drinking did nothing to improve my melancholy, I continued to search for the blessed oblivion I seemed to be able to find only at the bottom of a bottle. I could see that the pace of my drinking was accelerating, and on numerous occasions I told myself that I was going to have to give up my crutch before my children realized that their father was becoming a lush, but I always found some excuse to continue drinking. In the spring, still jobless, I contracted hepatitis and pneumonia, and for six weeks I could not have worked even if I had been employed. The doctor who treated me ordered me to admit myself to the hospital; but I knew that once admitted, I would be deprived of my favorite medication, and I unwisely stayed at home while my illness ran its course.

Warmer weather brought recovery, and finally, much to Toddy's relief, I began looking for a job in earnest. One day on Capitol Hill I ran into Pete McCloskey, a former marine and old family friend, who was a Republican congressman from San Francisco. Pete had been awarded a Navy Cross while serving under my father in Korea, but I most admired him for the way he had challenged President Nixon on the Vietnam War years earlier, a stand that left him a pariah in his own party but a hero to many others. When he heard that I was looking for a job, he told me that he had a slot for an attorney on the House Merchant Marine and Fisheries Committee and he would like to see me take it. He went on to explain that since Paul Trible was a member of the committee, his blessings for my appointment would have to be obtained, but Pete saw no particular problem with such a formality.

After our conversation I rushed home to tell Toddy the good news, and excited about something for the first time in months, I babbled on about how perfect the job would be for me. For starters, the job would give me Capitol Hill experience, and in addition, it would be highly marketable if I should decide to parlay the expertise I gained into a private-sector job. More important, it would allow me to remain in Washington yet keep my hand in business affairs in my old district, a perfect situation if I should decide to position myself for another political race.

Three days later Pete called with the news that Trible had vetoed the appointment and that out of professional courtesy there was no more he could do to help me secure the job. Pete refrained from expressing any judgments about Trible's decision in the matter, but after I thanked him for his help and hung up the phone, I began to wonder if I was going to be saddled with Trible's vindictiveness for the rest of my life.

═══ ☆ ═══

At the end of the summer of 1979 I was offered, with some help from the White House, a position as an attorney in the Office of the General Counsel at the Department of Defense, and at the beginning of October I took the offer and once more became a Washington bureaucrat. It had been almost two years since I had held a paying job, and while Toddy was relieved to have me out from under and earning a living, I had mixed feelings about the new job. On the one hand, I was dealing with challenging legal issues on a regular basis, but on the other, I had few illusions about changing the world as a faceless lawyer in the Pentagon. I was also drinking heavily almost every night, and my dependence on alcohol had become so fixed that my primary goal on rising in the morning was to make it home in the evening so that I could begin anesthetizing myself. For important meetings or projects that required a clear head, I was able, through force of will, to refrain from drinking altogether for up to a few days at a time, but when I drank, I always drank to excess. After six months on the job I could tell that I was becoming powerless over my ability to control my drinking, and though terrified by my situation in a way I had not felt since Vietnam, I dared not reveal my dark secret to anyone.

For years I had used alcohol to numb the pain of my Vietnam experience and the loss of my legs, and now in what I regarded as a cruel irony, alcohol was failing to bring the relief of oblivion. Angered by the realization that my old companion was turning against me, I drank more heavily and became even more depressed and withdrawn. Toddy sensed that something was severely wrong, but since she did not realize the extent of my dependence on alcohol, she attributed my darkening moods to depression and waited for me to pull myself out of it.

═══ ☆ ═══

Within six months of beginning the new job, I had reached such a state of despair that an especially difficult work assignment precipitated a crisis. Unable to complete the task on my own and too isolated to ask for help, I decided that I was a failure as a lawyer, a husband, and a father, and I began contemplating suicide. One morning, when Toddy was away from the house for several hours with the children, I began drinking straight shots of vodka to get the courage to take my own life.

After half a dozen shots I wrote Toddy a brief note telling her that I loved her and the children and that what I was about to do was not her fault. I then drank another half dozen shots and called a prominent Vietnam veteran in New York whom I barely knew to tell him what a rotten deal we veterans had gotten from our country. After the phone call I had one more drink, went out to my car, and tightly closed the garage and kitchen doors. I put the key in the ignition. For what seemed like an eternity I sat behind the wheel with my hand on the ignition key and tears streaming down my face and thought about never seeing my family again. Unable to turn the key and suddenly feeling the effects of so much vodka, I decided to put my head down on the seat for a few minutes before getting on with my plan. When I came to several hours later, Toddy was standing over me, screaming and slapping my face, and all I could think was that my suicide gesture, like my life, had been a failure.

After being sedated in the psychiatric ward of the nearest hospital, I was paired with a one-legged roommate named Jimmy Carter and poured into bed. When I awakened sometime late the next afternoon, I had missed most of a day and Carter was gone. A staff doctor interviewed me and told me that the next day I was being transferred to the psychiatric unit of Bethesda Naval Hospital for a period of rest and recuperation.

At Bethesda I was stabilized, diagnosed as clinically depressed, and introduced to a regimen of individual and group psychotherapy for the next week while strangers plotted the course of my future. Initially I felt humiliated and shamed to have so lost control of my life that professional help was needed to piece me back together; but as the week wore on, my flagging spirits revived, and I became more hopeful. With the alcohol out of my system, I was less depressed, and I even came to enjoy the give-and-take of therapy. Most of the other patients were young enlisted men and women, and without much education or life experience, they were easy to manipulate in group therapy. Unfortunately the verbal jousting in which we engaged was so facile that I gained no real understanding of my own problem.

For six months after my hospitalization, as a therapy outpatient, I saw Dr. Walter Kearney for one hour each Thursday evening for individual psychotherapy. At the end of my workday I drove directly to his office, where after an initial exchange of pleasantries, he sat quietly and I vented whatever was on my mind. I took our sessions seriously because I knew that suicidal depression was a serious matter, and I felt that I had been spared. However, since my gesture and subsequent hospitalization had resulted in so few adverse consequences, the two events did not convince me that any radical alterations in my life-style were necessary, and I thought I was doing enough by spending one hour a week with a psychiatrist.

After I had told him all I thought he needed to know about my childhood, parentage, and deepest inner secrets, I began to tire of our sessions and grew increasingly frustrated because I could never draw him into conversation. I began to feel better after a few months, but psychotherapy was hard work when half the team was putting out all the effort and I wanted my doctor to tell me that I was healing. On a few occasions I brought up the Vietnam War; but that topic, too, did not provoke any response from Dr. Kearney, and I decided that there was no point in pursuing it with him since he, like most young men, had never served and had no reference point for my feelings.

In the months just prior to my hospitalization, I had begun to hear about a veteran named Jan Scruggs, who had been wounded while serving as an army corporal in Vietnam. Scruggs had been to see the Vietnam movie *The Deer Hunter* in the spring of 1979, and the film had rekindled dormant feelings for those of his fellows who had died in Vietnam. He now wanted to build a monument to honor their memory, and while his ambitious project moved me, I had become too cynical to think it had any possibility of success. Nevertheless, I stored his name in the recesses of my mind, and in subsequent months, as I heard more about him and his mission, I began to hope that his effort would prove my judgment wrong. Dr. Kearney, I felt, could never share my growing excitement over the prospect of a monument in our nation's capital listing the names of every man and woman who had died in Vietnam, but I knew that there were millions like me who had been changed by the war and were desperately in need of some affirmation of our sacrifices and those of our lost brothers and sisters.

On Memorial Day 1980 there was the usual ceremony at the Tomb of the Unknowns at Arlington National Cemetery. I had attended the event on occasion in the past, but I had always returned home discomfited by the seeming emphasis on the two world wars and Korea and by the lack of participation by Vietnam veterans. This year I missed the observance, but on the evening news I was surprised to see that a group of Vietnam veterans had held their own memorial service across the Potomac River on the Constitution Gardens site where Scruggs and the Vietnam Veterans Memorial Fund wanted to build their memorial. The event was subdued and had none of the pageantry or cast of national figures as was gathered at the Tomb of the Unknowns, but it was a beginning. The next morning I eagerly read the news reports of Jan Scruggs and the cathartic quest he had begun, if too late, at least in pursuit of a worthy objective.

A short time later, on May 30, Toddy and I were invited to the White House by President Carter for a ceremony in honor of the first Vietnam Veterans Week. Several hundred Vietnam veterans, among them Jan Scruggs, were in attendance, and the president made a little speech acknowledging the nation's debt to us. He then unveiled a blowup of a stamp that the Postal Service was about to issue in honor of Vietnam veterans, and I began to wonder why and if, after all the years of neglect and outright hostility, my country was finally reaching out to acknowledge the Vietnam experience.

═══ ☆ ═══

A month later Jim Crotty, my old roommate from the Philadelphia Naval Hospital, got married in Philadelphia, and Toddy and I decided to drive up for the ceremony. It was to be a reunion of sorts since Bob Kerrey would also be there, and the following day we were going to drive over and spend a night with Paul and Kathy Barents, who lived a short distance west of the city. I had, in an unusual experiment for me, not had a drink for several weeks prior to the wedding weekend, and when I mentioned the upcoming events to my psychiatrist, we discussed whether I should break my abstinence. He shocked me by saying that I had been working hard in therapy and deserved the reward of being able to drink at the wedding.

As soon as we arrived at the Crotty home, I fixed myself a double scotch, and since I had my doctor's approval for a weekend of indulgence, I had finished off several more drinks by the time of the reception and dinner at a posh suburban country club. My dinner partner was a young woman who made no effort to hide her revulsion at either my physical appearance or my drunken state, I could not tell which, and I increased her disgust by getting even drunker as the night wore on. I remember bits and pieces of the early part of the evening, but after Jim and his bride had the first after-dinner dance, I blacked out for the rest of the evening.

When I awoke the next morning, I was back at the Crotty house with no idea how I had gotten there, an indignant wife, and a pounding hangover. Toddy told me that after dinner I had stationed myself by the coat closet near the entrance to the club and profanely reviled the departing guests until she and Bob Kerrey managed to dump me into the car and carry me away. I was chagrined that I had behaved so badly and alarmed to have no recall of the event, but not so alarmed that I refrained from sitting up half the next night drinking a bottle of expensive liquor with Paul Barents.

When we returned from Philadelphia, I decided that six months of therapy with Dr. Kearney was more than enough, and I broke off our relationship. I felt that he had been of some value in helping me overcome my depression, but I also thought that I had reached a point where our time together was yielding fewer returns.

Over the Fourth of July holiday Toddy and I were invited to the White House for a reception and an evening of patriotic music and fireworks, and I again drank to excess and behaved badly. Fortunately Toddy saw the warning signs as I began to lose control, and after I had engaged the secretary of defense and Kirk Douglas in inappropriate conversation, she took me home early and put me to bed. My drinking seemed to be reaching a point where I would sporadically become unpredictable and then black out. I would then resolve to moderate my consumption, and after going a few weeks without a repeat incident, I would feel I had overcome the problem. Inevitably, however, I always returned to the point of excess.

Over the course of the next fall and winter I drank myself into near oblivion almost every night, and while there were no obvious signs of my dark secret at work, I was becoming moody and withdrawn. I would awaken in the morning, shaky from overindulgence and badly in need of a drink. Once again my main goal on rising was to make it to the end of the day so that I could resume drinking. Ashamed of myself, I walled out my friends and family, and alone and isolated, I became increasingly bitter at the injustice I thought life had dealt me.

At a law school cocktail party in Williamsburg in November, I again lost control, and when Toddy brought me a plate of food to try to sober me up, I threw it across the room and created a scene. Again, I had no recollection of the event until my mortified wife described it to me the next day. Toddy did her best to maintain appearances and keep the family and our relationship going, but I was far too self-absorbed to grasp the heroism involved in her effort. When lovemaking became an impossibility during the nighttime, she accommodated me by accepting my advances after I had awakened in the morning, but there was no joy and no tenderness in my desperate attempts to prove myself still functional. On those rare occasions when my head was clear enough for self-reflection, my conscience reminded me that Lewis and Maggie were getting old enough to realize what was wrong with their father, but while I did not want them to remember me as a hopeless drunk, I was powerless to alter my self-destructive course.

═══ ☆ ═══

In January 1981 Ronald Reagan was inaugurated as president, and the American hostages who had been captured in the American Embassy in Teheran more than a year earlier were released. Tired of seeing our fellow Americans degraded at the hands of fundamentalist fanatics, the country embarked on an orgy of rejoicing and patriotic fervor. The attention, which lasted for months, was remarkable for its intensity. In short order the hostages were accorded heroic status and showered with free airline passes, admission tickets to athletic events, and gifts from corporate donors. A grateful nation held testimonial dinners and ticker-tape parades, there were invitations to the White House, and special legislation was introduced in the Congress to try to compensate the hostages for their ordeal. Suddenly thrust into the limelight, some of them embarked on speaking tours and considered running for political office.

Throughout it all I held my emotions in check and tried to appear approving of the catharsis that was being played out. Inside, however, I was beset by guilt over my inability to view the hostages as truly heroic and by my anger at the painful contrast between their confetti-strewn homecoming and the starkness of my own return. Confused and out of touch with the mainstream of America, I took my usual course of action by remaining silent, stifling my rage, and going to the bottle.

═══ ☆ ═══

Later in the winter I awoke one morning at two, having passed out in my bed earlier in the evening. Sitting bolt upright, I felt as if I were going to come apart at the seams if I didn't have a drink, and I quietly transferred into my wheelchair so as not to awaken Toddy and went out to the kitchen. I then filled a highball glass three-quarters to the top from the jug of wine I kept in the refrigerator and finished it off in three or four frantic gulps. As I waited for the wine to take effect, I thought how insane my behavior was and how I was going to have to work harder to discipline myself. Several nights later I repeated the pattern, and within six or eight weeks I was fixing myself a large glass of wine in the middle of the night almost every night.

By spring I was fast on my way toward needing alcohol in my system at all times just to feel normal, and I frequently had to resort to the wine bottle an hour or so before I shaved each morning in order to steady my hands. Once at work, I tried to do all my paperwork and take care of everything that needed my signature in the mornings before the tremors returned. I then spent the rest of the day fixated on the thought of that first drink after I got home in the evening and in terror that I was going to be found out.

=== ☆ ===

In May the design competition for the Vietnam Veterans Memorial was completed, and a panel of jurors selected what became a controversial submission from among the almost fifteen hundred entries. As I read about the winning entry, designed by a woman undergraduate at Yale named Maya Lin, I pictured the two black walls containing the names of all those killed in Vietnam. The walls were going to form a V shape and be built into a hillside on the Mall with one arm pointing toward the Lincoln Memorial and the other toward the Washington Monument. It seemed like a perfectly appropriate, albeit unconventional, design to me, although I would have preferred that it had been submitted by a Vietnam veteran. Little did I realize that a major battle would take place before the memorial became a reality, or that while the controversy raged, I would be engaged in a life-or-death struggle with some demons of my own.

I briefly considered calling the Vietnam Veterans Memorial Fund to offer my help several times that spring and summer and, in fact, was often chided by Toddy to do so, but I was too incapacitated to offer anything more than token support from the sidelines. Nevertheless, in moments of lucidity I realized that something important was taking place for all of us who had served, and as if it were a lifeline thrown a drowning man, I was buoyed by the effort that others were making on my behalf.

=== ☆ ===

By summer I had exhausted my defenses against the encroachments of alcohol. I knew that I was in serious trouble and that despite my best efforts, I could not stop drinking on my own. I had tried switching brands, drinking only beer or wine, drinking only after a certain time of day or no later than a certain time of day, or not drinking at all. No matter what new and feeble approach I seized on, I always seemed to wind up drunk and out of control, and my self-esteem plunged to such depths that I no longer considered myself fit company for friends or family. Toddy knew that I drank too much; but she had no idea of the extent of my drinking, and she tried to hold on to the illusion that my problem was a depression out of which I would eventually emerge.

One day during the summer we drove Maggie to a weeklong camp in the western part of Virginia. On the Saturday morning that we left I was so drunk that I slept in the backseat for the five-hour trip, and when we got back home, I was so ashamed that I decided not to drink until Maggie's camp was completed. For the first three nights I lay awake on the sofa all night, my clothes soaked in perspiration and my nervous system screaming for a drink. By the end of the week I had detoxified myself, and I proudly made a point of driving the entire trip when we set out to retrieve our daughter. On the night that we got home I decided to reward myself with two glasses of wine, and I again drank myself into oblivion and undid all of the sacrifice of the previous week.

A few weeks later I was asked to do a Vietnam veterans' segment to be used on the "Tomorrow" show, and I knew that in order to perform well, I would have to do the taping without alcohol in my system. I again detoxified myself, and again I spent several nights tossing and turning on the den sofa. The television piece went very well, and I resumed drinking as soon as it was completed; but I could now see that alcohol had such a grip on me that it was causing more pain than pleasure. I was drinking at a maintenance pace in order to keep an acceptable blood alcohol level in my system, and that meant that there were many times when I had to drink even though I did not want to.

For some reason, at about the time that I thought alcohol had betrayed me, I became even more obsessed with the Vietnam War. Perhaps I was using it as an excuse to justify my drinking, but in my blackest moods I always turned to the war. I felt that if I could only find some meaning in it or some positive consequences of my involvement, I could put my life back on course and get my drinking under control. When not a shred of solace resulted from my obsession, I became even more bitter and withdrawn. There were times when I felt as if I had fought the war all by myself, that no one could understand my pain, and that I was going to spend the remainder of my life, like the tragic Texas boy in the bubble, in near-total isolation.

In the mornings, as I wheeled to work along the corridors of the Pentagon, with my last drink only an hour or two behind me, I scanned the ribbons of the uniformed officers and enlisted men I passed. I was looking for evidence of the shared experience of combat in Vietnam, as if finding it in others would reaffirm what I had endured and would give meaning to my experience. When, as was usually the case, I failed to see a single chest that bore a combat decoration or a Purple Heart, I began to despise the rear-echelon soldiers I was encountering. What right had any of them, I thought, to draw pay or wear the uniform when they had been spared the hardship of real soldiering?

Unable to find what I was searching for among the military members with whom I shared office space, I often spent my lunch hour alone in the stacks of the Pentagon library. There, among the dusty monographs and military treatises on operations and campaigns in Vietnam that had once seemed of paramount importance, I relived in words and pictures experiences that for most Americans were, if not downright alien, now only dimly remembered. Yet despite the single-mindedness of my forays into the recent past of Vietnam, I was unable to form any judgments or reach any conclusions that eased the anguish I was carrying.

One Sunday night after a weekend of almost continuous drinking, I was sitting alone in the den watching television and dreading the thought of five consecutive days of work. Toddy and the children had read my black mood and wisely chosen to take refuge downstairs. As I absentmindedly switched the channels on the television set, I happened upon a documentary about Vietnam veterans, and I settled back, beer in hand, to see if the reporting was in accord with my experience. Ever sensitive to the distorted image that I believed most newscasters had given Vietnam veterans, I needed only a few minutes to become enraged at the narrator of this documentary.

Before I fully comprehended the consequences of my actions, I had picked up a poker from the fireplace and thrust it through the television screen. When Toddy and the children came running upstairs to see what the commotion was all about, I brandished the fireplace tool and, in an unnaturally calm voice that belied my emotional state, explained that the television had made me angry. The children burst into tears immediately, and as Toddy took them back to their bedrooms to comfort them, it dawned on me that I had just destroyed a four-hundred-dollar television set and I could not even remember the offensive words that had set me off. Later in the evening, when Toddy had gotten Lewis and Maggie to sleep, she joined me in the den and thankfully did not press me for an explanation. She did tell me, however, that my little rampage was the first honest emotion she had seen coming from me in months.

In the middle of August we traveled to Europe for a ten-day vacation with my twin sister and her family, who were on an overseas tour of duty in the Netherlands. Toddy had decided that a vacation might be just the right tonic for my melancholy state, and since we had a standing invitation to visit Mike and Martha, the opportunity seemed too good to pass up. I dried out for several days prior to our departure because I feared that I would not have sufficient access to alcohol to maintain my usual blood alcohol level while we were away from home.

Mike met us at the airport in Frankfurt, and while driving us to meet Martha and the rest of the family, where they lived in Holland, he explained that we would use their home as a base of operations for the next week and take day trips to Belgium, France, and Germany. When we got to their home, I was relieved to find that the refrigerator was stocked with enough beer and wine to hold me comfortably. I started drinking immediately and over the course of the next week had drunk enough of the native wines and beers of each of the countries we visited to qualify as an expert.

At the end of the week we parted company with Mike and Martha and, with our children in tow, boarded a plane for London and the last three days of our vacation. Because I had increased my intake of alcohol during the previous week I now needed alcohol more frequently to be comfortable. Unfortunately it was less available in our London hotel than it had been in Mike and Martha's kitchen. Hard liquor also cost twice as much in London as it did in the United States, and British law forbade our taking the children into pubs. Beaten at every turn, I was therefore miserable for most of our time in London. Toddy did her best to ignore me, but despite her best efforts to maintain a cheerful appearance in front of Lewis and Maggie, the vacation was quickly turning sour.

On the day before we were to return home, we stopped at a department store to buy a bottle of bourbon. Toddy went inside with Lewis to make the purchase, leaving Maggie and me on the street corner outside, and before she had been gone five minutes, a woman walked up to me and handed me money. Several times in the previous three days I had rejected similar offers, but this time I decided to play along. I unfolded the paper note the woman gave me and dropped it in my lap so that passersby could see it. Within minutes several more women handed me money, and by the time Toddy returned fifteen or twenty minutes later, I had gathered enough currency to cover the cost of the bourbon. Maggie was dumbfounded by the experience, the likes of which had never happened at home, but I took a perverse satisfaction from knowing that if alcohol made my life much worse, I could always move to London and eke out an existence as a street person.

As soon as we returned home and I resumed work, I started drinking more heavily than before. Within a short time I was getting out of bed at least twice a night to go to the refrigerator for wine, and the only relief from the pain I was feeling came from the bottle that was causing the pain. Often I just sat quietly in my wheelchair in the living room after I had refueled and waited for the blessed numbness of alcohol to spread throughout my body. At four o'clock in the morning, with the house silent and almost totally dark, I was now in a world of my own, and I wondered if I would ever rejoin the world of the living. I was now drinking to eliminate all feeling rather than drinking to feel good, as I had for so many years, and I knew that I lacked the energy to continue the charade for much longer.

On the Monday before Labor Day of 1981 I stopped off at a liquor store on my way to work and bought a pint of vodka. I had never before drunk at work during the day, but I had now gotten to the point that I seriously questioned whether I could last eight hours without a drink. On Monday and Tuesday I took small drinks from my pint throughout the day, and no one at work seemed any the wiser. On Wednesday at lunchtime I went back to the same liquor store and purchased another pint, and by Friday evening, when I got ready to go home, all but a couple of ounces were gone. By now I was leaving for work drunk every morning, staying drunk all day, and returning to my family drunk. I dreaded the weekend. I did not know which way to turn, but I knew I needed help badly. Somehow I managed to make it through Friday evening without giving myself away, and on Saturday morning Toddy had a political meeting that kept her away from the house for most of the morning. While she was gone, I drank the better part of a half gallon of wine, and when she returned home, she found me incoherent and back in bed. My drunken state was no longer a secret, and she immediately called the psychiatric unit at Bethesda Naval Hospital, where I had been a patient almost two years earlier.

══ ☆ ══

On the way to the hospital Toddy, steering the car with one hand and wiping away tears with the other, asked me over and over why I was drunk and out of control on a Saturday morning. It was a fair question for which I had no answer, and when we got to the emergency room, the admitting doctor very wisely chose to separate us as soon as possible. Toddy was told that there was nothing more she could do to help, and she was sent home to await a prognosis on the miserable wretch she had married. I was given a preliminary interview, about which I remember almost nothing, and a blood alcohol test that measured more than twice the legal limit for intoxication in Virginia. I was then escorted back to the same ward where I had previously been a patient and unceremoniously poured into bed in a private cubicle at the end of the ward. Sometime later that afternoon I was awakened by a navy corpsman for more questions, after which I slept until the next morning.

I remained in isolation for another two days and went through the by now familiar shakes and cold sweats associated with withdrawal, and I was then assigned a bed in the main part of the unit. With the alcohol out of my system I actually began to feel pretty good physically except that for the first two weeks of being alcohol-free I was able to sleep for no more than an hour or two a night. Mentally, however, I was a complete wreck and was convinced I would never again be able to hold my head up. I also knew that I would never be able to drink again. That realization, signifying the end of a relationship that had sustained me for twenty years, triggered in me a sense of loss that I was not at all certain I could handle. I was truly terrified at the prospect of living the rest of my life without alcohol, and I mourned its loss with a grief as palpable as any I could have mustered had a loved one been taken from me.

On my first day out of detox a doctor stopped by to give me his diagnosis of my condition. He was accompanied by an army colonel whose ribbon-bedecked chest bore testimony to heavy combat in Vietnam but whose role in my recovery was beyond my understanding. As my eyes darted back and forth from the doctor to the colonel, the doctor informed me that his review of my record indicated that I was a mid- to late-stage alcoholic. No one had ever called me an alcoholic before, and I was appalled to be hearing that at age thirty-six I had already advanced to the latter stages. He then told me that I was to be transferred to a twenty-eight-day civilian alcohol rehabilitation program downtown and that I had best take it seriously if I expected to survive to age forty. Before I could protest or ask any questions, he told me that he thought I might benefit from what a recovering alcoholic who was dealing successfully with his illness had to say, and he introduced the colonel.

For the next twenty minutes I listened to a tale of degradation and violence-filled anecdotes the likes of which I had seen only in the movies. The colonel described blackouts that lasted for days at a time, shoot-outs with policemen, and automobile wrecks that left the highways strewn with human carnage. When he had taken himself to the very depths of despair, he then described a conversion that had freed him from alcohol and a rebuilding of his life. He concluded by telling me that he had not had a drink in more than three years, and he gave me a book with a blue jacket and told me to read the first seventy pages.

After the doctor and the colonel had left, I put the book on my nightstand and tried to analyze what had just taken place. Other than the fact that the colonel was a decorated Vietnam veteran, I felt that we had very little in common, and I could certainly not see myself doing any of the things that he had done in the late stages of his alcoholism. By the time my tray arrived for dinner I was still smarting from having been called a mid- to late-stage alcoholic, but while I might quibble over what stage I was in, there was no doubt in my mind that I was an alcoholic.

What really stood out from the visit I had just been paid, however, and what I could not get out of my mind were the doctor's description of alcoholism as an illness and the colonel's not having had a drink for more than three years. If what I had was an illness that could be controlled by abstinence from alcohol, perhaps it was possible that I could someday resume a normal life. Certainly, I thought, the colonel was living proof that it could be done.

If my hopes for the future had been rekindled by my visitors that afternoon, they received a setback after dinner when I picked up the book I had been given and read the assigned pages. The beginning of the book made the point that any attempt to recover from alcoholism had to start with an admission by the alcoholic that he was, in fact, an alcoholic.

"So far, so good," I thought, but as I read on, the next stage in the recovery process seemed to be predicated on a belief in a higher power that could restore the shambles I had made of my life. Although I finished reading the seventy pages suggested by the colonel, what there was of my spiritual stock had been so depleted over the last couple of years that I was not certain the concept of a higher power had much bearing on my situation. I still believed in God, but I had not prayed since Vietnam and my hospitalization, and if this higher power concept required adherence to any formal religion, it was not for me.

Putting the book back on the nightstand, I lay against the pillow on my bed and considered my situation. I had just been detoxed for the third or fourth time of the summer, and every time I resumed drinking I drank myself into oblivion. Things had gotten so out of hand that I was now a virtual prisoner in a psychiatric ward, and the next step was four weeks in a rehab unit. I knew that my life was at a crossroads and that I badly needed directions or alcohol was going to take everything from me. Already my self-respect was gone, and it was a miracle that I still had a job and the love of a wonderful woman and two fine children.

"God help me," I thought, and as tears began to roll down my cheeks, I said the words aloud for the first time in years in a desperate plea for help.

At the end of the week arrangements were completed for my transfer to the Psychiatric Institute of Washington, and Toddy picked me up for the trip across town. She had been advised to take me directly to the facility without any stops where I might be tempted to drink, and I did not argue the point. During the ride our efforts at conversation were hesitant and strained, almost, it seemed to me, as if we had been apart for years and were just getting reacquainted. I asked about the children, who Toddy assured me were getting along fine, and she made small talk about what other items I would need other than those that she had packed for me. When we got to PI, she stayed just long enough to see that I was checked in, kissed me lightly on the lips, and prepared to leave. At the door on the way out she turned and waved good-bye, and although her familiar tight-lipped smile was firmly in place, I now knew it masked many months of pain and disappointment.

After I had filled out the admissions forms and been given a physical, I was taken to the elevator and delivered to the staff of the alcoholism unit on the second floor. A counselor met me as I exited the elevator, introduced herself, and showed me to a room containing two single beds separated by a desk and two dressers. As I unpacked, I could see ten or fifteen people sitting in a circle of chairs in a dayroom across the hall from my room. The group was about equally divided between men and women and appeared to range in age from mid-twenties to late sixties. The counselor explained to me that the patients across the hall were having a discussion session as part of their therapy and that I would be joining them the next morning.

During the remainder of the afternoon I was interviewed by a staff psychiatrist, who jotted down notes while I gave her a history of my life, and by the head of the unit, himself a recovering alcoholic, who explained what was expected of me and what I could expect from my stay at PI. Basically the program seemed pretty simple and not unlike what I had encountered at Bethesda. Each week the schedule would be posted on the bulletin board in the hall, and I, like everyone else, was to show up on time for activities, and refrain from drinking or using drugs. By the time I got back to my room the meeting in the dayroom had broken up, and the other patients were back in their rooms or milling about in the hall, waiting to be summoned for dinner in the cafeteria downstairs.

As I entered my room, Bob, my roommate, got up off the far bed and came over to shake hands. He told me that he, too, was a Vietnam veteran and that he had two more weeks of rehab remaining of his twenty-eight days. He also told me that all the other patients had been informed that a double amputee in a wheelchair would be joining their group today. I understood that someone had probably paired us because we both were Vietnam veterans; but I took an immediate dislike to Bob for the familiarity he assumed with me, and I was glad he would be gone in two weeks.

Before I had a chance to revise my first impression, half a dozen other patients stopped by to welcome me to the group, and when the signal was given for dinner, we all went down together. During dinner I was surprised at how openly my newfound companions talked about their alcoholism as well as how full of hope they seemed for the future. They were only a week to a month ahead of me in their sobriety, yet it seemed to me that they were aeons ahead on the route to recovery. I decided that the prudent course was to say as little as possible and keep my ears open, and no one seemed to take my silence for unfriendliness.

After dinner I was told that we would be allowed half an hour of free time, divided into two groups, and then driven by buses to evening meetings of recovering alcoholics somewhere in the Washington area. When I pressed for more details, I was told that there were eight hundred such meetings a week in the metropolitan area and that evening meetings generally started at eight-thirty and lasted for one hour. There were discussion meetings, at which some topic relevant to alcohol was the subject; speaker meetings, where two recovering alcoholics would each take half an hour to tell their stories; and step meetings, at which one of the twelve steps to recovery would be the subject. I had no idea what the twelve steps were, but since my group was going to a speaker meeting that evening, I decided to save further questions for later. There was an embarrassing moment before we boarded the bus for the meeting at a church in downtown Washington until I showed two of the stronger-looking young men in our group how to assist me with the wheelchair. After that, locomotion was never a problem, as volunteers scrambled to help me whenever I got on or off the bus or needed help with steps at meetings.

When we entered the church for my first meeting, our little group of eight or nine patients was quickly absorbed by a crowd of at least a hundred well-dressed men and women. Self-conscious at first, I quickly realized that my presence had little, if any, effect on the congregation, and I found an inconspicuous spot at the back of the room and studied the revelry taking place about me. Everywhere I looked people seemed to be hugging each other, laughing, and conversing as if in celebration of some special occasion. I had expected a group of joyless unshaven old men in gray raincoats, and I was astounded to find a fairly typical cross section of men and women, each one an alcoholic, who seemed to be not only getting by but thriving without alcohol. Before I could reconcile my astonishment, a young woman stepped up to the podium at the front of the room and rapped her knuckles against its wooden top.

The crowd immediately fell silent, and she began the meeting by saying, "Hi, I'm Jill, and I'm an alcoholic."

"Hi, Jill," the crowd roared back, and I was struck by the collective enthusiasm of the response.

She then read from a palm-size card a brief passage about sharing experience, strength, and hope and helping others recover from alcoholism. As she read, she appeared absolutely radiant and completely at peace with the world, and I knew that I wanted what she and the others in this hallowed place had found. After she had finished, she announced that she was celebrating one year without a drink, and the assemblage again burst into tumultuous applause. When it had quieted, she introduced a speaker who told a story in the same vein as the one I had heard from the army colonel, and he was then followed by a second speaker.

So absorbed was I with the strange phenomenon I was witnessing and the profound effect it had on me that I paid very little attention to the actual content of the two speeches. When it was over, the crowd rose from their chairs, and the strangers on either side of me extended their hands to grasp mine. Within seconds a human chain had formed involving every person in the room, and the young woman leading the meeting began reciting the Lord's Prayer, in which everyone joined.

When it was over, my hands were squeezed by the strangers beside me, and the crowd shouted in unison, "Keep coming back. It works." I thought: "Indeed, it does work," and I desperately hoped I had found safe passage from my wayward course.

Later that night, as I lay wide-awake in my bed at the Psychiatric Institute while Bob snored across the room, I could hardly wait for dawn and the start of a new day. I felt suffused with energy and alive in a way that I had not felt in years. I also knew I was being given a third chance at life, and though apprehensive that I would not avail myself of it, I longed to succeed. It had been just a few hours short of one week since my last drink, and I suddenly realized that the compulsion to drink, which for years had occupied most of my waking hours, had miraculously been lifted from me. Now if I could just get some sleep, I thought, I would truly be a new man.

The next several days kept me occupied learning the routines of life in an alcohol rehabilitation unit, but while I was intellectually curious about the process, I resented the limitations on my freedom. Essentially a loner, I did not adapt easily to the emphasis on group activity, and I despised several of the staff members who seemed to revel in the authority given them. Nevertheless, I was aware that the present constraints on my liberty would be short-lived, and in any event, they paled by comparison with the slavelike existence to which my dependence on alcohol had reduced me. Each evening we were taken to a meeting in a different part of town, and my anticipation of those nightly trips helped sustain me during the day.

At the first discussion meeting I attended, a group leader began by reading the same paragraph I had heard at my first meeting. He then gave a brief description of his alcoholism, introduced a topic, and called for volunteers to speak. As the volunteers were called upon, they prefaced their remarks by saying their first names, followed by the phrase "and I'm an alcoholic" or "I am powerless over alcohol" or something similar. After the leader had run out of volunteers, he began picking people at random, and ten minutes before the meeting ended, he called on me.

Self-conscious at being singled out, I could feel the color rising in my cheeks, but before I knew what I was doing, I had blurted out, "Hi, I'm Lew, and I'm an alcoholic." For years I had known that I was, but until that moment I had never acknowledged my alcoholism to another person, much less a group of strangers. Despite the awkwardness of the moment, I was overcome by such a feeling of relief following my initial admission that I spoke easily for the next couple of minutes about some topic related to alcoholism for which I was hopelessly unprepared. When the meeting ended with the customary hand holding and recitation of the Lord's Prayer, there was no doubt in my mind that I was in the right place.

Late in my first week a new patient arrived, and she was a painful reminder of how I had been two weeks earlier. Lucille came in kicking and screaming, and like me, she had to endure two days in the relative isolation of detox before she was anything approaching fit company. Sometime during her second day another patient, who had almost completed rehabilitation, came back from an afternoon pass with a single flower, and she had the flower placed in a Dixie cup at Lucille's bedside. It was a simple act, one alcoholic reaching out to share with another, and despite the fact that they did not know each other, I felt as if they had been friends all their lives. I do not know to this day if the placing of that flower on Lucille's nightstand had any effect on her, and I have long since forgotten the name and face of Lucille's benefactor, but her gesture of kindness is with me forever.

As I emerged from the alcoholic fog of years, my physical and mental state began to improve. On the physical side the tremors, which of late had so frequently sent me to the bottle well before breakfast time, abated almost immediately after I arrived at PI. I took so much satisfaction in being rid of the shakes that for several weeks during and after my rehabilitation, I would practice writing my signature over and over on a blank piece of paper and marvel at its legibility. I also stopped throwing up after meals and quickly came to see that while I had been blaming my queasy stomach on the ulcer surgery I received after being wounded, I was really practicing a form of denial of my alcoholism. My senses also seemed to sharpen as I put more distance between myself and my last drink, and there were times when my restored sensitivity to colors, shapes, textures, sounds, and tastes was so joyously exquisite as to be almost uncomfortable. Several of the patients had radios, and I found new pleasure in old songs that for ages had meant no more to me than background noise. Similarly, the simple act of biting into an ordinary hamburger became for me a celebratory act.

Mentally the first and most noticeable improvements were the restoration of my memory and a renewed ability to grasp detail. After a couple of weeks of working with the group and going to meetings every night, I realized that I could recall not only the names of everyone who had spoken but entire sequences of conversations. As I improved and became more sure of myself, I also began to open myself to further stimulation, and I could almost feel the wall I had carefully constructed toward the end of my drinking to keep outsiders at bay begin to crumble. As it collapsed, I began to look outward rather than inward, and my isolation gave way to an intense curiosity about the other patients with whom I was forced to mingle and to a growing admiration for the strangers I saw each night.

During my twenty-eight days in rehabilitation, proximity and the common bond of alcoholism drew many patients together into a tight-knit group, and in reaching out and trying to share their perspectives, I gained new insights into the nature of alcoholism and the alcoholic. Most of us were in treatment because we had reached rock bottom and, in the parlance of alcoholics, because we were sick and tired of being sick and tired. Some came voluntarily, some were committed, and a few, it seemed to me, had become patients not because of problems with alcohol but because of problems with life. An alarming, though small, number of the patients were among us because of relapse, and toward the end of my stay a middle-aged woman arrived who had been through ten twenty-eight-day programs.

My roommate, Bob, I discovered early, was a repeater who had checked himself in after drinking one beer at the end of a year's sobriety. When he narrated the circumstances surrounding his second admission, I was incredulous that he had taken such a drastic measure over something so seemingly trivial. My impression was soon confirmed that he was one of those whose problems with life had driven them to a safe but temporary haven.

Two days before Bob was supposed to be released and after a week of being alternately subdued or disagreeable, he raised his hand during a men-only group discussion meeting and began talking about his child-hood. As the story unfolded, he revealed that he and an older sister were frequently abused sexually at the same time by the single father who raised them. He then described how his own resulting sexual dysfunction had led him into having intercourse with farm animals, brutalizing his wife on their honeymoon, and most recently being seriously tempted to abuse their young daughter.

When Bob finished his confession, I glanced around the room to see if the other patients were as horrified as I. Most of the other men appeared impassive, and after a few moments another speaker shifted the conversation onto safer grounds. None of us ever mentioned the matter in my remaining days at PI, but over the years I have often wondered if I did the wrong thing by restraining my impulse to run screaming from the room. Bob was crying out for help, if not for himself, at least for his daughter, and we were unable or unwilling to provide it. Two days later he was gone, and I saw clearly that even three hundred dollars a day in a rehab program were not going to be enough to keep all our personal demons at bay.

Although during the first half of my rehabilitation I was apprehen-sive about the adjustments I was forced to make inside, I worried during the last two weeks about going back out into the world. I wondered how I was going to face life without the crutch of alcohol, and I wondered how I would deal with temptation when alcohol was again readily available. Fortunately all the other patients had the same concerns, and we spent hour after hour in discussion groups address-ing our fears. Our rehabilitation was geared toward returning us to an alcohol-free productive life, and in gaining an insight into my own alcoholism and the devastation wrought by my addiction, I was learn-ing valuable coping skills. Most of the counselors were themselves recovering alcoholics, and they tried to impart to us the lessons they had learned to ease our minds and help us prepare to leave.

From the start of my rehabilitation I was eager to learn all I could about alcoholism and the recovery process, but by my last few days as a patient I had been bombarded with so much information that I was having trouble keeping it all in perspective. We were lectured by medi-cal specialists and alcoholics, shown slides and educational movies, given endless books and pamphlets, drawn out in group therapy and discussion groups, and taken to every possible kind of evening meeting of alcoholics. The pithy phrase as a memory device seemed to be the common denominator of much of my education on alcoholism, and in my twenty-eight days I heard many of them over and over:

352

"One day at a time."

"Easy does it."

"Keep the plug in the jug."

"Don't drink and go to meetings."

"It works if you work it."

"Walk the walk instead of talking the talk."

"Turn it over."

"First things first."

"Live and let live."

Also, "Avoid getting hungry, angry, lonely, and tired (HALT)," and on and on until I felt I was being programmed.

Midway through my last week at PI I experienced the final and most dreaded ordeal that each patient had to endure before being released. A sort of trial by fire, it was called the hot seat and involved sitting in the middle of a circle surrounded by the group and a few key staff members. Each member of the group was free to criticize the person in the hot seat, to ask personal questions relating to recovery, or, in some cases, to offer encouragement. I had seen this process get nasty on a couple of occasions and knew just how unpleasant it could be if the subject deserved it and the inquisitors were skilled.

Not wishing to be given a difficult time, I had tried not to arouse any animosity preceding my turn, but I was still apprehensive. After I had moved to the center of the room and locked the brakes of my wheelchair, I made a point of trying to acknowledge as many of my comrades as I could by either gesture or eye contact before the start. One of the counselors led off by asking me if I thought I was ready for the outside, and when I responded that I was not certain but I hoped so, she nodded approvingly. The opening exchange helped set a favorable tone because each succeeding question or comment was either neutral or complimentary, and within five minutes it was over.

As I sat congratulating myself and wondering why I had spent days fretting over such an absurdly simple exercise, a small voice inside my head reminded me that on this occasion, like many others, my physical condition had probably blunted any potential slings and arrows. For more than ten years that same condition had discouraged friends and family from criticizing my drinking, I realized, and ultimately they had done me no favors by holding their tongues.

When Toddy picked me up on Friday afternoon, I was eager to put my time in rehabilitation behind me but mindful that I needed to keep using the tools I had been given. I was also worried that everyone I knew would be talking about me behind my back, but the counselor who had helped me through my hot seat told me that I was far less important than I thought and that most of my acquaintances would probably not even have missed me. She then told me, as I had been told countless times in the last four weeks, to try to go to ninety meetings in ninety days after I got home. I had been given a directory of times and places of meetings in the northern Virginia area, a phone contact in the Pentagon, and a prescription for Antabuse, a pill that, taken daily, would make me ill if I tried to mix it with alcohol. Finally I had a small book on living sober tucked away in my overnight bag.

"Read it for inspiration," the woman had said in presenting it to me at my meeting the night before. I had seen her on several occasions at meetings in the previous month, but I knew nothing about her except that she was a recovering alcoholic. Inside on the flyleaf she had penned a note of hope: "You are about to enter a new and wonderful life."

With only a portion of the weekend remaining, I tried to reintegrate myself with Toddy and the children before resuming work on Monday. I had talked to Toddy by telephone several times a week throughout my absence, and on one Sunday afternoon near the end of treatment she had brought the children out for a picnic at a grassy area near PI. At that time Lewpy had volunteered the opinion that he and Maggie did not think my drinking had been so bad, and I knew then that my children were trying hard to put the best twist on the discovery of their father's alcoholism.

I had been taught in treatment not to rush the topic of alcoholism with my family, and I knew that I could make better amends to them by remaining sober than by explaining my situation. Yet in those first weeks at home with all the newfound energy of a man freed of a terrible debilitating illness, it was difficult not to force my enthusiasm on the rest of my family. In addition, I had to remember that for the last month I had been living in an environment that encouraged frank and open discussion of alcoholism, while my family inhabited a world where the subject was still taboo. Nevertheless, by Sunday night I thought that we all were getting along reasonably well, and I knew Toddy could see that sober, I was going to be a better person to live with despite some adjustments each of us would have to make.

At work on Monday my boss and I had a frank discussion about the things I would be doing to maintain my sobriety, and the rest of the office did not seem to know or care that I had been gone for five weeks.

I had gotten a similar reaction from our next-door neighbors when we arrived home on Friday, and at least in these instances I was relieved to conclude that as my counselor had suggested, I was not as important as I thought. No one seemed to have missed me, and I was just as glad.

When I dialed the number I had been told to call for a contact within the Pentagon, a woman with a pleasant voice answered and identified herself as being part of a civilian counseling group. After I explained my situation, she told me that there were noon meetings on Tuesdays and Thursdays in the Pentagon. She then gave me a room number where the meetings took place, told me that her name was Karen, and said she hoped to see me the next day.

Several times over the course of the next few hours I opened my bottom desk drawer and looked at the vodka bottle I had not been able to finish before my last drunk at work. I thought it odd that the same bottle I would have moved mountains for only weeks earlier had now lost its allure. On the way home from work that evening I carried my bottle into the men's room and wheeled into the nearest stall. After a few moments' reflection, I backed out of the stall, deposited my cargo in the trash container, and with my errand completed headed out of the building toward my car. I had no desire to drink, but I was still too sick to pour perfectly good vodka down the toilet.

While a patient in treatment, I had been warned that many alcoholics, after breaking their addiction, experience a period of exhilaration commonly referred to as a pink cloud. I realized toward the end of my stay that I was experiencing the phenomenon. I also knew that it would probably not last long and that it could dissipate quite easily as a consequence of any sort of emotional upheaval. Oddly, even in the midst of my euphoria I began to turn again to my Vietnam experience and to the unresolved issues concerning it that my drinking had kept in abeyance. With a clear head for the first time in years, I felt robust and alive but also painfully compelled to come to terms with my past. I rejoiced in my sobriety, but I knew that I must use it wisely if I was ever going to achieve the serenity I had witnessed in other recovering alcoholics.

During my first week back at work I opened the newspaper one morning to discover that a troublesome controversy had surfaced over the design of the Vietnam Memorial. A disgruntled combat veteran had testified in a public forum that he viewed the memorial as a black gash of shame, which, instead of honoring those who had died in Vietnam, called their sacrifice into question. Although I did not know the speaker, I knew that with two Purple Hearts, he had paid the dues to express his beliefs. When I put the article down, I was confused and upset because until now I had viewed the memorial with hope as a symbol that would pull the country together and offer some reconciliation of the conflicting emotions about the war that haunted me. In the ensuing weeks and months I was relieved to find that the negativism about the memorial expressed in the news account was not shared by the majority of Vietnam veterans who expressed their views.

As my recovery progressed, I focused my attention more sharply on events leading to the construction of the memorial, and in a sense I came to believe that its progress and my own progress were twin facets of a divine plan and not mere circumstance. The healing process that was at work within me, I felt, also inhabited the granite and concrete that were going to take form in the memorial, and I was immensely hopeful about what was taking place.

Throughout that fall and winter my recovery, like the anticipated construction of the memorial, seemed to proceed by fits and starts. On my second day back at work I attended the noon meeting of alcoholics in the Pentagon to which Karen had invited me. The meeting was small, consisting of about eight or ten men and women, several of whom were in uniform, and I was ill at ease as a newcomer in a strange group. Karen came over as soon as I arrived and introduced herself. She was attractive with long brown ringlets and a ready smile, and although she was younger than I by half a dozen years, her bearing suggested an older woman. She, too, was an alcoholic and, as I was to learn, given to calling a spade a spade in language that would shame a combat marine when she sensed dishonesty. After the meeting she suggested that I spend several sessions with her as a follow-up to my time in treatment, and I accepted her offer readily. I had already decided not to participate in aftercare at PI, and time with Karen would be a convenient substitute since I would not need to leave the Pentagon.

Over the next months I ran myself ragged trying to keep up with my job and complete ninety meetings in ninety days. Fortunately I was able to locate half a dozen meetings within a two-mile radius of home, and with the two noon meetings a week at the Pentagon I was spared having to go out on Tuesday and Thursday evenings. Nevertheless, I was exhausted from putting so much effort into my recovery, and I breathed more easily when I had met my quota by January. After that I gradually settled into a routine of two to three meetings a week, and with the less hectic schedule I was able to achieve a satisfactory comfort level.

It is said of recovering alcoholics that their progress is noticed first by those with whom they come in contact rather than by themselves, and to an extent the observation held true in my case. Early in my recovery I was so grateful to have my evenings back that I would continue conversations with Toddy long past the time when we both should have been sleeping. Because our communication had been so poor while I was drinking, she humored me until I became less compulsive in my talking, but I knew that she was pleased to have me cheerful instead of brooding for a change.

One Saturday in January we went out to run an errand, and in the car we made small talk and joked with each other. It was an ordinary moment by most standards, a husband and wife exchanging pleasantries on a winter day, but my wife saw the occasion as being in such stark contrast with earlier trips we had made that she reached over and squeezed my hand.

"It is so good to have you back," she said, and I was warmed by her words and by the return to intimacy between us.

The children, too, saw the change, and though Lewpy was initially reticent about discussing my alcoholism, he became more vocal as I improved. Maggie asked almost immediately why I had stopped taking naps on the sofa after dinner, and Toddy and I exchanged smiles over our daughter's charitable use of the word *nap*.

While my sharing with other alcoholics in and out of meetings was crucial to the early stages of my recovery, it was by no means a panacea for the egotistical thinking and rationalization my abuse of alcohol had helped me sustain. I was sick, physically, mentally, and spiritually when I hit bottom and was finally made to confront my alcoholism. As I began mending, most of the other recovering alcoholics who reached out to me, like most people I encountered while a practicing alcoholic, tended to withhold the criticism I needed to get better. I knew that my physical condition led well-meaning people to be lenient in dealing with me, and just because I had stopped drinking did not mean that I had, all at once, become willing to forgo the manipulation of sympathy to obtain my ends. Karen was the exception. As a professional counselor, a recovering alcoholic, and a damned tough woman to boot she recognized self-serving behavior, no matter how well disguised, and she refused to tolerate it.

At our first counseling session together she told me that like me, she liked most recovering alcoholics but that my charm and articulation could less euphemistically be labeled bullshit. I tried to dodge her criticism by saying that I was glad we had gotten to be such friends so quickly, but she refused to be sidetracked.

"Lewis," she continued, "it has been my experience that you must change yourself to escape drinking again. You have got to learn to get outside yourself, or all the work you have done will be for naught."

At that moment and for some time afterward, I wanted to best Karen in the competition I thought she had begun, but I gradually came to see both the wisdom of her words and the fact that she did not regard me as an opponent.

═══ ☆ ═══

In the closing months of 1981 and the early part of the new year, I followed with keen interest the vicissitudes of the Vietnam Veterans Memorial. On the positive side, funding for the memorial topped eight million dollars, the majority of which came in individual contributions of ten dollars or less. It appeared to me that the wherewithal was in place to build the memorial, and I was most proud that the government that had shattered the lives of so many of us had not been called upon to contribute one red cent. We had gone to war to do our country's bidding, to offer up our lives and limbs without thought of personal reward. But we had come home to indifference and rejection on the part of the government that demanded of us so much, and I thought it particularly fitting that it now be excluded from taking any credit for such a powerful symbol of the healing process. I was also pleased to learn that in conjunction with the expected completion date of the memorial, November 1982, a national salute to Vietnam veterans would be held. Even if such an event was coming ten or fifteen years too late, it would at least help validate the service we had given.

On the negative side, a few art critics, writers, and prominent Vietnam veterans, including some for whom I had profound admiration, continued to voice criticism of the memorial's design. There was even an organized, though short-lived, movement within Congress to have the Reagan administration block its construction. A construction permit was needed from James Watt, the secretary of the interior, before the project could move forward, and he withheld his approval until mid-March after a series of gut-wrenching compromises were made. I was angry that so many professional critics, politicians, and government officials, most of whom had not been even remotely touched by the Vietnam War, now felt compelled to dictate the conditions under which the memorial should be built. Nevertheless, I had no real argument with the final decision to add an appropriately placed flag and statue. Against the political infighting and empire building that appeared to be taking place in Washington, however, the country seemed almost solidly behind the concept of a memorial and its basic design.

When the building permit was issued, Jan Scruggs, John Wheeler, Bob Doubek, and the dozens of others who had worked so tirelessly for the memorial knew for the first time that their dream was only months away from becoming a reality. The healing process that I and the country so badly needed would continue, and my sense of excitement and anticipation was becoming visceral in a way that would not have been possible had I still been drinking.

═══ ☆ ═══

In January, some four months after I had taken my last drink, I was asked to lead the Tuesday noon meeting at the Pentagon. I had never led one before, and I was apprehensive about sharing what I had learned with alcoholics who were light-years ahead of me in recovery, but Karen assured me that it was a sign of my progress that I had been asked to lead. Over the weekend before the meeting I picked and rejected half a dozen topics for discussion before deciding on the subject of serenity, how to find it and how to keep it.

At the appointed hour I wheeled to the head of the table from which the leader usually spoke, introduced myself as a recovering alcoholic, and began by reading the now-familiar preamble that starts most meetings. I then spent ten minutes describing to the group the journey that had brought me there, and I asked for further directions on the path to serenity. Several in the group suggested that serenity was most readily attainable by praying and by working through the prescribed twelve steps, and when the next speaker mentioned focusing on others rather than oneself, Karen nodded her head approvingly at the back of the room. When Karen's turn to comment came, she told me that the recovering alcoholic gets well first physically, then mentally, and finally spiritually. She went on to say that the spiritual aspect of recovery is the most difficult but also the most precious and that without a spiritual component, at least for her, serenity would be impossible.

Later that evening, before going to sleep, I thought about how the meeting had turned out, and I tried to sort through the advice I had been given. Several members of the group had complimented me on leading a good meeting after it was over; but that was fairly common, and I knew that they were trying to put me at ease. Karen's words, however, continued to echo in my mind as I thought about the three aspects of recovery she had cited. I knew that I was improving physically. After all, I no longer shook or threw up in the toilet, and I had even begun working out and lifting weights. Mentally I was alert and able to concentrate once more, although that was sometimes a mixed blessing since Vietnam was of late so much in my thoughts.

I was stumped, however, by the idea of spiritual recovery. It then occurred to me that perhaps the path to it began, as Karen had suggested, in getting outside myself. And if I could do that, I suddenly realized, my preoccupation with Vietnam might diminish and allow me some peace of mind. My radio operator had told me to pray years earlier when he had seen how badly I was wounded, and now years later, when I was wounded in spirit, I was getting the same advice.

"God, grant me the serenity to accept the things I cannot change, the courage to change the things I can, and the wisdom to know the difference," I said, repeating the words of the serenity prayer that is frequently recited in meetings.

Someone else at a meeting had told me that if I could not pray, I could at least act as if I were praying and that eventually I would find myself actually praying.

After four or five sessions with Karen we came to an understanding that I had stabilized to the point that I no longer needed to see her professionally. I knew it was a healthy development to be able to let her go, but she had been such a help to me in sharing her wisdom that a part of me wanted to continue the relationship. Initially I had viewed my time with Karen as a contest of wills, but she had declined to accept the challenge. In so doing, she had shown me that serenity for recovering alcoholics required an acceptance of one's powerlessness over people, places, and things in much the same way that it required an acceptance of powerlessness over alcohol.

"Victory is only possible through surrender," she had told me.

When I first heard her words, I was incredulous. I had been raised never to back away from a fight, to view surrender as the ultimate dishonor, and the Marine Corps had reinforced those childhood lessons. When I protested, she pointed out that I was not able to begin recovering from alcoholism until I recognized that alcohol had beaten me.

"Taking it a step further," she had continued, "you will come to believe that a higher power is at work in your life and that it is her will rather than yours that must be done if you are to remain sober and find serenity."

It did not bother me that Karen had attributed the feminine gender to my God, but I feared the path she was showing me was one I might be incapable of following. It was, however, a message of hope, and I knew that if it could help me in recovering, it could also help me with life and with the ghosts of my Vietnam experience.

═══ ☆ ═══

On March 26, 1982, three weeks after I had celebrated six months without a drink at my Pentagon meeting, ground was broken for the Vietnam Veterans Memorial. I drove over to the Mall from my job at the Pentagon and joined the crowd that had gathered just as the ceremony was getting under way. As I worked my way to the front of the assemblage, spectators moved aside to allow me access and an uninterrupted view of the proceedings. On the proposed site a five-hundred-foot-long red ribbon had been aligned along the V-shaped path of the monument with one end pointing toward the Washington Monument and the other toward the Lincoln Memorial. Along the length of ribbon 120 shovels had been evenly spaced, and beside each shovel a veteran stood waiting to participate in the historic groundbreaking. The day was sunny but cold and windy, and I sat shivering from the cold and from anticipation until a veteran standing near me noticed my discomfort and handed me his overcoat.

The ceremony itself was brief. Chuck Hagel, the deputy administrator of the Veterans Administration and a twice-wounded Vietnam veteran himself, spoke extemporaneously but movingly about a patrol he had participated in during which several members had been killed and how they would now be remembered. His comments were followed by a benediction, the singing of "God Bless America" by the crowd, and finally the actual groundbreaking. As the shovels completed their symbolic work, I returned the borrowed overcoat and headed back to the Pentagon.

It seemed altogether fitting to me that the principal remarks had been delivered by a Vietnam veteran who had shed blood in my war and that in speaking, he had stressed the suffering rather than the glory of war. The shovels had, that day, begun a tangible effort of binding the nation's wounds, and we all were to be enriched by what was coming. Later I learned that Robert Nimmo, the VA administrator, was playing golf on a Washington golf course while the groundbreaking was taking place; but he was not one of us, and I would not allow one insensitive act to dampen my enthusiasm.

═══ ☆ ═══

Over the next several months I came down from the pink cloud that had eased my transition into sobriety. The descent was gradual, however, and even while it was occurring, I realized that I was becoming more comfortable as a recovering alcoholic, growing as a person, and learning to deal with my long-unresolved feelings about Vietnam. At one meeting a speaker commented that when recovering alcoholics are troubled by a situation, the source of the trouble is usually internal rather than external.

Applying his comment to my Vietnam experience, I realized the Vietnam War had been over for ten years. If I were going to come to grips with it, I would have to change because events happening a decade earlier could not change. When I looked at it in that way, it became easier for me to accept the fact that I had lived while so many of my comrades had died and even eventually to take pride rather than feel guilty about having survived. I also came to see that while the Vietnam War was a tragic mistake and never should have been fought, my role in it had been as honorable as circumstances would permit. I had not performed perhaps as well as my father might have; but I had done the best I could, and it was time to move on to new challenges.

At another meeting the topic was "geographic cures," the relocation that practicing alcoholics often undertake as a futile solution to problems caused by their alcoholism. As the meeting progressed, several speakers mentioned the denial and dishonesty that they had practiced as a way to rationalize their drinking. Finally, one speaker described how like a nomad he had moved from place to place as his drinking progressed and how sad and foolish it had been to think he could outrun a problem that was part of him. As he talked, I was reminded of our move ten years earlier from Philadelphia to Williamsburg, and the words of Creedence Clearwater Revival replayed themselves in my head as they had back then: "I went down Virginia seekin' shelter from the storm."

Like alcoholics who tried geographic cures, I had been unable to find shelter from my strong feelings about Vietnam. I carried them with me all the time, I could not hide from them, and I could accommodate them now only by dealing with them honestly and forthrightly. I had finally discovered that a war that had ended for most Americans ten years earlier could continue to be waged in my head only as long as I would allow it. My meetings were giving me the tools to declare a truce, and I was optimistic that someday soon they would serve me well.

The next time I saw Karen at a meeting I told her that I was thinking about writing an autobiography in which I would surrender the Vietnam War. She looked quizzical, and I did not pursue the conversation; but I saw myself like some of the Japanese soldiers who remained in hiding on deserted islands for years after World War II had ended. If I could now summon the courage to forgive my government, to forgive those whose views and actions concerning the war differed from mine, and to forgive myself, I could perhaps move into the present, attain a degree of serenity, and find the reason for which I had been spared, first in Vietnam and then a second time, from an alcoholic death.

=== ☆ ===

Over the last half of 1982 work progressed on the memorial and on the planning for the National Salute to Veterans that was to accompany its dedication. During this period I was strictly an observer, but as I picked up information through newspapers, magazines, and television, my excitement grew. One day in early summer Toddy and I drove across the Memorial Bridge on our way into Washington to run an errand. As we passed the Lincoln Memorial, our view of the Vietnam Veterans Memorial site was cut off by a construction fence that had not been there the last time we traveled into town.

I realized there was a lot going on there, as with me, that was not discernible to the naked eye. In midsummer the first panel containing the names of veterans arrived in Washington, and by September a memorial, which I could only picture in my mind, was in place but for some finishing touches. All that remained was a ceremony to honor the fifty-eight thousand Americans who had died in Vietnam and further bind the nation's wounds.

=== ☆ ===

On the first Tuesday in September I led a meeting at the Pentagon to celebrate my having been sober for one year. But for the fact that we were celebrating a remarkable event, my having gone 365 days without having taken a drink, the meeting was very much like any other. A dozen or so recovering alcoholics sat around a table and shared their experience, strength, and hope with each other that they might solve their common problem and help others to recover from alcoholism. For my topic I asked the other participants to comment on where they were in their recovery. The responses varied from the fearfulness of the newcomer to the serenity of the old-timer, but the common denominator seemed to be that all were better off as recovering rather than practicing alcoholics.

The one-year celebration is a landmark in the recovery process, and I had been looking forward to this meeting for weeks. As it was ending, I told the group that I was not yet willing to introduce myself at meetings as a grateful recovering alcoholic, but I certainly understood the meaning of gratitude. It was hard for me to believe that a year earlier I had sat in a church at my first meeting, watched a young woman receive a chip for having completed a year of sobriety, and wondered if I could ever duplicate her journey.

Now, a year later, I not only had abstained from alcohol but had discovered a new and wonderful life outside myself. With the help of my higher power I was growing in new directions, and as I continued to progress, the painful thoughts and feelings about my Vietnam experience were becoming less intrusive. That night at dinner I told Toddy and the children about my anniversary celebration earlier in the day, and although they offered me their congratulations, I could tell that they attached no particular significance to it. It was better, I realized, that they viewed my abstinence as ordinary than that they saw it as miraculous, just as they and I had learned to make no particular concessions for the loss of my legs.

=== ☆ ===

While the work that I put into my recovery was paying handsome dividends in my first year of sobriety, work on the memorial and the Salute to National Veterans was once again beset by controversy in the months preceding the dedication. In early October "60 Minutes" aired a segment on the memorial that played up the differences of opinion over its design while suggesting that opposition was prompted by opposition to its designer, Maya Lin, who was Asian-American and a woman. While the suggestion of racism and sexism was, in my mind, unwarranted, it did have a grain of truth, as there were many veterans, including me, who would have preferred the memorial to have been designed by a Vietnam veteran.

Three days after the "60 Minutes" segment, the *Washington Post* ran a piece by Tom Wolfe that called the memorial a "tribute to Jane Fonda" and suggested that its design had no relationship to the casualties of the war it was supposed to honor. Against this background, the Fine Arts Commission, which had veto power over proposed Washington monuments, met to decide if the statue agreed upon as an addition to the memorial was acceptable. When the commissioners found it unanimously so, Secretary of the Interior Watt gave permission to dedicate the memorial, and the Vietnam Veterans Memorial Foundation had but three weeks remaining to see that the memorial was prepared properly for dedication and to finish organizing the national salute.

On the Wednesday, Thursday, and Friday before the dedication, there was to be a Candlelight Vigil of Names at the National Cathedral. During the vigil, as part of the dedication, volunteers working in shifts were to take turns reading in alphabetical order the names that would be memorialized in granite on Saturday as part of the dedication. I had not made plans to participate in many of the weekend activities, but when I learned of the vigil, I asked for and was sent a roster of names to read on Thursday afternoon.

Realizing that the vigil was the only time that the names would be read collectively and aloud and that a schedule had been publicized, I tried to go over the list to practice pronunciations for the names allotted to me. The task proved difficult, but it gave me a sense of the cultural diversity that made up our heritage and once again brought home how tragically the melting pot of America had become a caldron of fire in Vietnam.

On Thursday afternoon I drove over to the National Cathedral and with roster in hand was directed to a small chapel off the main part of the cathedral where the names were being read. Like the war that had been fought apart from the mainstream of America, the setting seemed appropriate, but I was not prepared for the sacred nature of my task as I paused at the back of the chapel and observed the setting. A dozen rows of seats, most of them unoccupied, separated me from the reader, whose intonations of the names, though made softly, were magnified by the stone walls and high ceiling of the chapel as they reached my ears. Candles and red roses added to the reverential aura, and for several minutes I sat transfixed and listened to the names.

"Are you Lew Puller?" a woman beside me asked, and when I nodded, she indicated that I was the next reader.

As I wheeled to the front of the chapel, a portly black woman with graying hair seated in the front row caught my eye, and I knew from that moment's contact that I would be reading the name of her flesh and blood. As I began reading from my list, an unexpected calmness settled over me, and I was able to complete my reading without breaking down. When I finished, I looked up and spied one of the regular attendees at my Pentagon noon meeting, but the woman in the front pew was gone. I had gotten outside myself in reading the names, I realized, but I now prayed devoutly that I had not mispronounced the name of that unknown woman's loved one.

Before I relinquished my space to the next reader, I called out in one final act of requiem the names of all the men I had personally known who had died in Vietnam: Lee Tilson Clarke, Michael Robert Barton, Ronald Walsh McLean, Michael Maurice O'Connor, Terry Pensoneau, Kenneth Hyde Shelleman, Byron Morrow Speer, Frederick N. Suttle, Jr., Cornelius Herbert Ram.

By Friday evening Washington had become a staging area for Vietnam veterans from all walks of life and all parts of America who had come together to honor their dead, validate their own service, and help the rest of the country atone for nearly two decades of neglect. They came singly, in pairs, and in groups, alone and with families, on foot, by motorcycle, car, truck, and bus. Some wore the uniforms they had worn in Vietnam or stateside, some Vietnam memorabilia they had purchased more recently, and some three-piece suits to demonstrate the successes they had made of their lives despite the odds against them.

The majority of them had been in their late teens and early twenties when they were called upon to give service in Vietnam, healthy young men with smooth faces and full, though closely cropped, heads of hair. In their thirties and forties now, they were again gathering to give service, but many of their healthy young bodies had been disfigured by war or were showing the effects of approaching middle age, and the once-smooth faces in many cases now sported beards or mustaches to compensate for the encroachments of baldness. They were older and wiser than they had been when they were called to serve, and the hard lessons of war and years of public disavowal may have dulled their expectations; but in most cases their love of country was stronger than ever.

Finally, on Saturday morning, after a night of hard-drinking camaraderie during which they held sway in most of the watering spots and hotels in Washington, the veterans held a parade for themselves. Fifteen thousand strong, they marched, wheeled, crutched, and hobbled their way down Constitution Avenue, reveling in the applause of the spectators and augmenting their ranks along the route yet achingly aware of the hallowed destination for which they were bound.

I had watched most of the morning's activities on television and by noon was badgering Toddy to get ready so that we would be on time for the two o'clock commencement of the dedication ceremonies. The day was cold and windy, just as it had been eight months earlier for the groundbreaking; but it was now also cloudy, and the November chill cut through my suit and overcoat. We had arranged to meet Linde Zier across from the Lincoln Memorial, and while she and Toddy caught up on each other's activities, I turned toward a crowd of 150,000. Back to back in reverential awe, they stood forming a huge half circle, facing the memorial and pressed against the temporary fences separating them from the rostrum and the monument. I had never been part of a crowd so large and yet so orderly, and as I made my way to an area reserved for wheelchairs, hands reached out over and over to touch my arms and shoulders, and the refrain "Welcome home, brother" echoed and reechoed.

Moved by the reaction I had gotten, it took me a few moments to gather myself after I reached my vantage point flanking the memorial and facing the crowd. My view of the memorial was unobstructed, but I was seated too far away to make out any of the names cut into its black panels, and for the next hour I felt myself being drawn into its center. I wanted to kneel at its apex, caress the names I had read during the candlelight vigil, and, like a mute given speech for the first time, run back and forth from one end to the other, screaming out the names for all the world to hear. Instead I sat silently in my wheelchair, shaking from the cold and my own ragged emotions until I felt Toddy's presence beside me and her calming hand on my shoulder. Like the service at the groundbreaking, this one was Spartan and brief, almost as if we could go only so far with our collective grief and ultimately had to make our peace individually, alone, or at best with the help of our own personal gods. When it was over, after the invocation, speeches, and the singing of "God Bless America," Jan Scruggs pronounced the memorial dedicated, and the crowd came to life, roaring its approval and surging toward the black granite panels.

I knew that given the crush of the crowd and the memorial's inaccessibility to wheelchairs, I would not that day get close enough to feel its healing power. I also knew that I now had the serenity to accept the things I could not change and that after a wait of almost fifteen years, a few more weeks or months would be tolerable. For the next hour I mingled on the outskirts of the crowd, exchanging handshakes, hugs, and greetings with my brothers and their families, and sharing the exquisite anguish we all felt on this blessed occasion. Just before we left, an intoxicated but well-meaning veteran staggered up and offered me a drink from a paper bag. Tears were streaming down his face, and though I rejected the drink, I drew him to my chest.

"But for the grace of God, there go I," I thought, repeating in my mind the words I had heard at countless meetings over the last fourteen months.

Not too long before I would have handled the situation exactly as he did, and tomorrow I would have had nothing to show for my effort. To feel the joy, I realized, one must remain open to the pain.

When Toddy and I got home, I was tired and, though exhilarated by the afternoon's activities, a little upset that the president and most of his administration had not seen fit to attend the dedication. The cold weather, the exertion required to negotiate the crowd, and the emotional toll had combined to wear me out, and I decided to take a nap. When I awoke, several hours had passed, and I was refreshed. On the spur of the moment I decided to drive back downtown to see if I could recapture some of the emotion I had gotten from my earlier contact with other veterans.

When I told Toddy of my plans, she said that she was going with me, and an hour later in darkness we found a parking place on the street in front of the Hotel Washington and headed inside. The hotel had been a weekend hangout for young officers when I had attended Basic School in the late sixties, although I had never been there. My first thought on wheeling into the lobby was that I had made a mistake in bringing Toddy. Raucous music blared from some distant jukebox, and half a dozen veterans lay sprawled on the floor, drinking beer, sleeping, or in various states of relaxation.

There seemed to be no one in charge, and when I finally found the manager to ask where the Marine Corps reunion was taking place, he shrugged his shoulders and pointed to a side room that seemed more ominous than the room we now occupied. When we entered, the location of the jukebox was immediately apparent. It was also apparent that we were interrupting a party that had been in progress for several hours. The room was so crowded with former marines, most of whom were wearing uniforms, that my first reaction was to turn around and go home. Then suddenly a pathway opened in the sea of bodies to allow me access, and again, as in the afternoon, hands reached out to touch my arms and shoulders. Although the words "Welcome home, brother" were repeated as Toddy and I made our way to a sitting area near the bar, no response seemed required of me. I was at last back among the men who had fought with me and protected me in the now-distant rice paddies and jungles of Vietnam, and I felt safe and at ease in their company.

For the next two hours we sat and received the attention and love of men who, though strangers, shared a kinship with me that surpassed time and place. Forged as it was in the bloody crucible of Vietnam, it was unnecessary for me to give my name or to offer justification for my physical condition. This blessed band of brothers and I had shared the worst and the best that life had to offer, and in our reaffirming our connectedness, words were, for the moment, superfluous.

Toward the end of the evening, when the crowd had begun to thin and the jukebox fell silent, one of the remaining marines began to play an ancient upright piano adjacent to the bar. Before the rest of us recognized his skill or thought to make requests, he had begun to play "God Bless America," and every man in the room picked up the words until we sang as one. He then played "The Marine's Hymn," again joined by his newfound chorus, and as the evening drew to a close, I wondered how, after a lifetime of contact with the Marine Corps, I could love and despise it with such equal ardor.

As we were leaving, Toddy, who was by now feeling comfortable with the group, turned to one of the marines and told him that I was Chesty Puller's son.

"Yes, ma'am," he replied without batting an eye, "and I'm John Wayne."

When we got back to the car, I took the wheel, and Toddy nestled down next to me, both of us tired but attuned to each other after a long but wonderful day. Heading south on Fifteenth Street, we crossed Constitution Avenue, where earlier in the day fifteen thousand of my brothers had affirmed their pride in service, and we then passed the Washington Monument, heading south toward home, Virginia, and shelter from the storm. Far off to our right the illuminated columns at the top of the Lincoln Memorial shone brightly in the darkness. Between these two landmarks now stood a third, the Vietnam Veterans Memorial, and though I could not see it, I knew it stood as a witness to history and a permanent part of the landscape of the Mall.

Later, in what became an often-repeated rite of homage, I returned to the memorial with a single red rose and, seeing my reflection in its polished stone, came to understand how inextricably linked the memorial and I were by the bloodshed of my brothers—I, an insignificant

369

speck on the continuum of history; the memorial, panoramic in its sweep, eternal, dark, silent, embracing all who would pause before its outstretched arms, in the end, comforting, spiritual, rooted in the present, but, like me, looking both backward in sorrow and anger and forward in hope and exultation.

Epilogue

★

ON WEDNESDAY MORNING, May 24, 1989, a dozen Soviet veterans of the war in Afghanistan gathered at the Vietnam Veterans Memorial to pay their respects to our war dead. Their visit to Washington was sponsored by the Vietnam Veterans of America, and I had been asked to meet them at the memorial for this stop on their agenda. I arrived early, driving over from the Pentagon, just across the Potomac River, where for the last ten years I had practiced as an attorney/adviser to the office of the secretary of defense. As I took one of the handicapped parking spaces adjacent to the Lincoln Memorial and wheeled over to the statue of the three soldiers facing the memorial, I felt apprehensive, yet excited at the prospect of meeting Soviet soldiers for the first time and on such hallowed ground.

Over the years I had fallen into a pattern of visiting the memorial at least twice a year, the first time on Memorial Day and again six months later on Veterans Day. On each occasion, despite some good-natured kidding from Toddy and our children, I would don my dusty bush hat with its fading ribbons and Marine Corps emblem, square my shoulders, and go off with a red rose to place at the apex of the memorial. Later, toward the end of my ritual, I would spend a few moments in remembrance of the dead whom I had known. Then, turning my back to those forever youthful ghosts memorialized in stone, I would go in search of the living among the holiday crowds with whom I might share some connection to the past.

Now, as I contemplated the arrival of the Soviet veterans in a different context, I wondered how I would react to them. All of my life I had regarded Soviets as my enemies, and I was pleased when their incursion into Afghanistan began to sour. Because of the many similarities between the Afghanistan War and the Vietnam War, however, I had for some time wanted to meet a Soviet veteran of Afghanistan. Consequently, I now felt a certain guarded empathy for the men I was about to meet. When they arrived, late and looking very much like everyday Washington tourists with open sport shirts and cameras, my first reaction was surprise that they did not fit my stereotype of Soviets. Most of them appeared to be in their mid to late twenties and several carried flowers, obviously brought along to perform the same type of ritual I had carried out for the last half dozen years. As I sat quietly and watched, they were ushered to a nearby grassy knoll that was inaccessible to me and given a short lecture on the background and meaning of the memorial.

They then proceeded down a path to the memorial, where they split up into twos and threes, placed their flowers at the base of the monument, and like many American visitors, seemed to become transfixed by its sanctity. When the first group of men completed its obeisance and approached me sitting near the statue, one young man asked a companion to ascertain if I were a Vietnam veteran who had been wounded in the war. Sasha, who himself had been horribly burned on his face and hands in combat in Afghanistan, spoke excellent English. When I answered affirmatively, he introduced Nicolai, and both men embraced me. Nicolai then took a Soviet medal from his pocket and, after asking permission, pinned it on my lapel. I do not know what I had expected on meeting Soviet soldiers for the first time, but it certainly did not include embraces and the gift of a treasured medal.

The three of us then began a conversation that gained intensity as it progressed, and by the time it was over, it had attracted a television crew, several reporters, and a crowd of fifty or sixty bystanders. As Nicolai and Sasha spilled out their feelings about their war experience, I became aware of how similar to me they really were. They wanted to build a memorial in the Soviet Union to their fallen comrades, whose sacrifice they regarded as having been for nothing. They felt alienated from their own countrymen, and they did not understand why the poorest and the least educated in their country had been called to fight

372

a war for which they were given no credit. Further along in the healing process than they, I tried to tell them that time and a homecoming more often rude than not had disabused me of the chauvinism with which I marched to war. I also told them that time would be their ally, and that I was able to find serenity only when I became capable of making a separate peace. My words were probably lost on Nicolai Knerick and Sasha Karpenko, two former soldiers fighting the battle for reconciliation that, partly because of them, I now see to be universal with men who have been to war.

Later that evening I attended a reception for the Soviet soldiers on Capitol Hill, to which I wore the medal I had been given earlier in the day. As I entered the room, a young Soviet officer whom I had not met at the Memorial hurried over to introduce himself. In near perfect English he explained that he had studied General Puller in military school and he considered it an honor to shake the hand of the son of one of America's great military leaders. Accustomed to receiving compliments about my father, I was nevertheless amazed to learn that he was admired in the Soviet Union. As I accepted the young man's praise, I realized with a mixture of pride and resignation that my father's shadow was longer even than I had thought.

When I saw Nicolai and Sasha, I gave them each miniature copies of two of the medals I had been awarded during the Vietnam War. As I proffered my Silver Star and Purple Heart to my newfound friends, a lesson I had learned in my fellowship meetings came to mind: "Often the only way to keep that which we hold most dear is to give it away."

Index

★

Adams, Dr. Ralph, 279, 280, 282
Afghanistan, Soviet veterans of, 371–73
Agnew, Spiro, 280
Agony and the Ecstasy, The (Stone), 279
Alaska pipeline, 313
America. *See* United States
American Legion, 203, 219, 228, 312
American Revolution, 29
Americans
  black-market products of, 106
  hostages, 338
  killed in Vietnam, 42, 46, 219, 246, 339, 363, 365, 366
  military records of, 286
  and presidency, 279
  and Vietnam, 64, 220–21, 230–31, 233–34, 258, 260, 262–63, 268
  and Watergate, 279, 280
  See also United States
Andrews Air Force Base (Maryland), 161

Antiwar movement, 30–31, 225–26, 228, 245, 246
Apollo 11, 217
Arlington National Cemetery, 263, 336
Armed Services Committee (House of Representatives), 294, 308, 312–13, 314, 321
Armstrong, Neil, 217
Army, Department of the, 230
Army–Navy game, 175
ARVN (Army of the Republic of Vietnam), 46, 116, 127, 128, 129, 131, 132, 134
  assignments with, 137–41, 145–46
Asia. *See* Southeast Asia

Baez, Joan, 222
Banana Wars, 19
Barents, Kathy, 169, 170, 173, 178, 222, 336
Barents, Lieutenant Paul, 174, 175, 188, 190, 222

Barents, Lieutenant Paul (*cont'd*)
   example of, 231
   friendship of, 177–78, 336, 337
   job hunting of, 242
   loyalty of, 324
   recovery of, 168–70
   surgery on, 171–73
Barton, Lance Corporal George, 101,
   102, 103, 116, 149
   death of, 150–51, 152–53, 156
Basic School (Marine Corps), 42–49,
   51–52, 54–55, 64, 68, 80, 88,
   110, 154, 160, 196, 197, 202, 230,
   368
Baskir, Lawrence M., 282
Bau Me Thuot (Vietnam), 284
Beatles, 89
Beatty, Warren, 38
Belgium, 342
Beltzer, Lieutenant Joe, 171
Bethesda Naval Hospital (Maryland),
   14, 15, 344
Bob (recovering alcoholic), 347, 349,
   351–52
Boston Red Sox, 216
Bottom, Mrs. (newspaper owner), 299
British, 29, 342
Brown, Sam, 225
Brown, Staff Sergeant, 34, 36, 39, 40,
   41, 42
Brown, Rev. W. W., 304–5

Cabot, Dr. Nicholas, 171–72, 176,
   177, 178, 182
Calley, Lieutenant William L., 230,
   257–58, 268
Cambodia, 245
Camp David (Maryland), 288
Camp 413 (Vietnam), 94, 97–99, 104,
   105, 108–12, 115, 116, 121, 125,
   129, 131, 133, 145, 150, 152
Camp Hanson (Okinawa), 63, 64

Camp Lejeune (North Carolina), 10,
   15, 16
Camp Pendleton (California), 1, 5, 22
Canada, 31, 287
Candlelight Vigil of Names, 365
Carter, Jimmy (roommate), 334
Carter, Jimmy (President), 294, 297,
   319–20, 336
Carter administration, 309
Caulfield, Major, 195
"CBS Evening News," 159
Chamber of Commerce (Newport
   News), 318
Chapman, General Leonard, 272, 273
Chappaquiddick Island incident, 216
Chesapeake Bay, 312–13
China Beach (resortlike military area),
   137–38, 139, 141
Chinese hand grenades, 89
Chosin Reservoir (Korea), 4, 5, 69
Christchurch School for Boys, 25–26
Civil War, 4, 9, 312
Clarke, Lee Tilson, 366
Clemency Board. *See* Presidential
   Clemency Board
Coast Guard, 56
Cocker, Joe, 222
College of William and Mary, 30, 32,
   33, 50, 242, 243, 258, 298
Committee to Re-elect the President,
   293
Communists, 21, 31, 99, 284
Congress, 245, 286, 293, 310, 320,
   331, 338, 358
   See also House of Representatives;
   Senate
Congressional Black Caucus, 315
Constitution, First Amendment to,
   200
Coswell (corpsman), 117
Cox, Archibald, 280
Cowboy (squad leader), 81–82, 116,
   141–42, 144

Creedence Clearwater Revival, 249, 362
Cronkite, Walter, 159, 217
Crotty, Lieutenant Jim, 192, 193, 195, 198, 199, 203, 207, 214, 219, 221, 222, 246, 336, 337
as roommate in hospital, 189–91
Crumpton (butler), 13
Cua Viet River (Vietnam), 68, 70, 82, 93, 94

Dabney, Captain William, 31–32, 69–70
Dabney, Virginia Puller (sister), 5, 9, 10, 16, 17, 28, 31, 41, 58, 165, 232, 233, 243, 254, 268
and father's confusion, 239–40
and father's death, 268–69
and father's stroke, 256–57
Daily Press, 299, 303, 309–10, 319, 320
Da Nang (Vietnam), 64, 66, 87, 95–96, 110, 126, 158, 160, 247, 284
TAOR (tactical area of responsibility), 94, 97–99, 149
Davis, Jefferson, 312
Deer Hunter, The (film), 335
Demilitarized zone. See DMZ
Democratic Congressional Campaign Committee, 318–19
Democratic National Headquarters, 278
Democratic party, in U.S., 275–76, 277, 281, 292, 294, 296, 298, 299, 308, 310, 320, 323, 324
Denton, Captain Jeremiah, 277–78
Department of the Army, 230
Department of Defense, Office of the General Counsel at, 333
Department of Justice, 289
Detroit Tigers, 163

DMZ (demilitarized zone) (Vietnam), 87, 91, 92, 93, 94, 114
Doan, Lieutenant, 135–36, 139, 140, 141, 142, 143–44, 145
Dong Ha (Vietnam), 70, 79, 87, 88, 92, 94, 97, 98
Doubek, Bob, 359
Douglas, Kirk, 337
Downing, Tom, 275–76, 277, 281, 292
Downs, Martha Puller (twin sister), 28, 41, 42, 45, 46, 49, 53, 57, 58, 185, 215, 216, 225, 226, 227, 232, 233, 243, 268, 342
athletic ability of, 8, 22
childhood of, 5–13, 16, 17
and father's death, 268–69
at father's funeral, 271
height of, 25–26
meets twin after wounding, 163
roommate of, 33
wedding of, 194–96
Downs, Michael P., 160, 163, 185, 215, 216, 225, 226, 227, 233, 271, 342
awarded Silver Star, 46
marriage of, 194–96
Draft dodgers, 31, 260
Dunaway, Faye, 38
Dunkel, Michael Robert, 366

Eddie (limb and brace technician), 193–94, 198, 200, 223, 224, 247, 248
Ellis, Doc (corpsman), 74, 85, 89, 91, 99, 103, 109–10, 114, 117, 123, 126, 134, 146, 148, 149, 150, 152, 157
Ernie (corpsman), 165
Esquire magazine, 18
Essex County (Virginia), 292, 293
Europe, 342

Evans, Hannah, 218–19
Evans, Thomas, 218, 219

Federal Election Commission, 300
Federal Rules of Civil Procedure, 276
Fine Arts Commission, 365
First Amendment to the Constitution, 200
First Marine Division, 63, 69, 210
  First Marine Regiment of, 4
  Second Battalion of First Marine Regiment of, 66, 70
Fleet Marine Force, 7
Folger, Abigail, 221
Fonda, Jane, 364
Ford, Gerald, 281–82, 285, 286, 289, 291, 304
Ford administration, 284
Foreign Relations Committee (Senate), 263
Fort Belvoir (Virginia), 52, 59, 159, 225
Fort Benning (Georgia), 257
Fort Monroe (Virginia), 312–13
France, 342
Frankford Arsenal, 309
Franklin, Aretha, 203

G Company. *See* Golf Company
Geneva conventions for conduct of war, 67
Germany, 342
Gillen, Mrs. (nurse), 257, 261, 262
Golf Company, 70, 71, 72, 98, 99, 131, 158
Goodell, Charles E., 282, 283, 289
Goodman, Lieutenant Cal, 171, 208
Green Beret forces, 220
Gretter, Captain, 34, 36, 37, 38, 39, 41, 42, 44, 45

Hagel, Chuck, 361
Haight-Ashbury section, of San Francisco, 62
Haiti, 19, 107
Hanoi (Vietnam), 51, 93, 94
Harris, Richard, 57
Hawaii, 137
Hemingway, Ernest, 32, 64
Hesburgh, Father Theodore M., 282
Higgins (marine), 114, 186–87
Hitch, Corporal, 82, 86, 89
Ho Chi Minh, 223
Hoffman, Dustin, 49
Holland, 342
Hollywood war wound, 64
House of Representatives, 276, 292, 313, 323
  Armed Services Committee, 294, 308, 312–13, 314, 321
  Judiciary Committee, 280
  Merchant Marine and Fisheries Committee, 332
  See also Congress
Hubbard, Ed, 298
Hue (Vietnam), 46, 95, 133, 227, 284
Hungarian Revolution, 21–22
Hutton, Scott, 275, 277
Hutton, Tiny, 275, 277, 280–81, 292

I Corps, 79
Indians, 10–11
Indochina, 284
  See also Vietnam
Iranian hostage crisis, 338

Jack (corpsman), 165
Jackson, Stonewall, 4
James, Dr. and Mrs., 17
Japan. *See* Yokosuka
Japanese soldiers, 363
Jill (recovering alcoholic), 348–49

Johnson, Lyndon, 296, 304
Jones, Catesby, 301
Jones, James, 64
Jones, Sergeant Orville, 5, 6, 7, 10, 15, 271, 273
Jordan, Vernon E., 282
Judiciary Committee (House of Representatives), 280
Justice, Department of, 289

Karen (recovering alcoholic/ counselor), 355, 356, 357–58, 359–61, 363
Karpenko, Sasha, 372–73
Kearney, Dr. Walter, 335, 336, 337
Kelly, Jim, 243
Ken (hospital roommate), 244, 245
Kennedy, John F., 15, 221
Kennedy, Ted, 216
Kent State University killings, 245–46
Kerrey, Lieutenant (jg) Bob, 203, 204, 205, 207, 208, 209, 336, 337
awarded Medal of Honor, 214–15, 221, 222
Kerry, John, 263
Kesey, Ken, 136
Khe Sanh (Vietnam), 70
Khrushchev, Nikita, 312
King, Coretta Scott, 228
Kissinger, Henry, 275
Kiwanis, 307, 315
Knerick, Nicolai, 372–73
Kopechne, Mary Jo, 216
Koreans, in Vietnam, 106, 154
Korean War, 3, 4, 5, 10, 16, 19, 32, 57, 96, 286, 291, 332, 336
ending of, 9
Koto-ri (Korea), 4

Lafferty, Mr., 23
Laird, Melvin, 221

Langley Air Force Base (Virginia), 295
"Laugh-In" (TV show), 266
Lee, Robert E., 4, 57
Lennon, John, 89
Leroy, Captain, 45
Leslie, Staff Sergeant Phil, 73–74, 75–76, 77, 86–87, 92, 94, 96, 97, 98, 100, 101, 103, 104, 105, 107, 108, 110, 112, 113, 115, 116, 117–18, 121, 122, 125, 126, 127, 133, 134, 136, 138, 141–42, 144, 145, 146, 182, 227
and ARVNs, 132
at Chesty Puller's funeral, 272–73
disciplining by, 93, 124, 128–29, 143
goodwill mission of, 83–85
guidance of, 81
helpfulness of, 79
professionalism of, 72, 78
seasoning of, 80, 111, 123, 140
storytelling of, 139
on Vietcong captive, 120
on Vietnamese, 106
Vietnam tour completed, 209–11
wounded in Vietnam, 147–48
Leslie, Sally, 209, 210, 211
Lieberson, Dennis, 300, 306, 313, 314
letter-writing campaign of, 310
and NAACP, 315, 316
personality of, 299
as political campaign chief, 299, 302–4, 307, 309–11, 315, 316, 318–21, 322–23, 325–27
after Trible victory, 326–27
and White House meeting, 319, 320
Life magazine, 22
Lin, Maya, 339, 364
Lincoln Memorial (Washington, D.C.), 363
Lions, 315
Lolich, Mickey, 155
London (England), 342, 343
Lucille (alcoholic), 350

McClary, Lieutenant Clebe, 171
McCloskey, Pete, 332, 333
McGovern, George, 277
McKenney, Colonel Tom, 159–60
McKenzie, Scott, 62
McKeon, Staff Sergeant Matthew C., 19–20
McLain, Denny, 155
McLean, Ronald Walsh, 41, 42, 366
McMonagle (corpsman), 168, 172
  dedication of, 166, 174
  departure of, 177
  personality of, 165, 167, 175, 176, 185
  as prankster, 190
Mai Xa Thi (Vietnam), 93, 94
Marble Mountain area (Vietnam), 116, 129, 131, 133
Marine: The Life of Lewis B. "Chesty" Puller, 55
Marine Corps
  anniversary of founding of, 229
  Basic School, 42–49, 51–52, 54–55, 64, 68, 80, 88, 110, 154, 160, 196, 197, 202, 230, 368
  birthday ball, 229–30
  emblem of, 3
  enlisted men in, 15
  fiscal resources of, 213
  generals, 271
  and Hue, 46
  influence of, 360
  lapel pin, 248
  and legend of Chesty Puller, 15–16, 19, 27, 28, 69, 74, 138
  mandatory briefings of, 64
  Officer Candidate School (OCS), 31, 32, 33–42, 43–44, 46, 54, 76
  Puller's ambivalent feelings toward, 137, 153, 166, 260, 369
  Puller's enlistment with, 30–31, 33
  retirement policy of, 18
  reunions, 8, 368
  training methods of, 19–21
  See also First Marine Division; I Corps; Second Marine Division; Third Marine Brigade; Twenty-seventh Marines
Marine Corps Barracks, 272
Marine Corps Headquarters, 15, 31, 213
Marine Corps Recruit Depot, 6, 7
Martha's Vineyard (Massachusetts), 215–16
Mary Washington College, 33
Matthews, Nick, 301
Maye, Jim, 293–94, 296, 297
Medal of Honor, 214–15, 221, 222
Medina, Captain Ernest, 268
Merchant Marine and Fisheries Committee (House of Representatives), 332
Michelangelo, 279
Midway, 215
Miller, Andrew, 313
Mondale, Walter, 309, 319, 320
Monroe, Fort, 312–13
Morey, Captain Dick, 192
Morgan, Corporal, 182–83, 210–11
Murphy, Audie, 221
Murphy, Tayloe, 302
My Lai massacre (Vietnam), 230, 257–58, 268

NAACP, 304, 315–16
National Cathedral (Washington, D.C.), 365
National Salute to Veterans, 363, 364
Navy Cross, 5, 35
Netherlands, 342
Newport News Shipbuilding and Dry Dock Company, 276, 294, 308
New York Times, 20, 41
Nicaragua, 19, 107
Nimmo, Robert, 361–62

Nixon, Richard, 214, 215, 221, 222, 228, 229, 245, 275, 277, 280, 322, 332
Nixon administration, 293
North Vietnamese, 32, 35, 64, 90, 115, 130, 131, 144, 156, 204, 223
    antiaircraft emplacements, 88
    vs. ARVNs, 141
    offensive, 45–46
    and POWs, 278
    See also NVA
Nui Kim Son (Vietnam), 131, 133, 145
NVA (North Vietnamese Army), 76, 80, 83, 88, 90, 92, 98, 140, 156, 203, 245, 284

O'Connor, Michael Maurice, 366
OCS. See Officer Candidate School
October 15 Moratorium, 225, 228
Office of the General Counsel, Department of Defense, 333
Officer Candidate School (OCS) (Marine Corps), 31, 32, 33–42, 43–44, 46, 54, 76
Okinawa, 63, 64
O'Neill, Thomas (Tip), 320
Operation Dewey Canyon III, 262
Order for the Burial of the Dead, 271

Pappy (Marine), 77, 82
Paralyzed Veterans of America. See PVA
Paris peace talks, 268, 275, 277
Parris Island (South Carolina), 7, 20, 21
Peninsula Shipbuilder's Association. See PSA
Pensoneau, Terry, 197, 366
Pentagon, 246, 263, 333, 341, 354, 355, 356, 359, 361, 363, 366, 371

Philadelphia Naval Hospital, 164ff
Phu Bai (Vietnam), 67, 68
Physical Evaluation Board, 248
PI. See Psychiatric Institute
Pleiku (Vietnam), 284
Popular Forces, 82
Portsmouth Naval Hospital, 28, 264
Postal Service, 336
Potok, Chaim, 136
POWs, from Vietnam, 277–78
Presidential Clemency Board, 281–90, 291, 293
Project 100,000, 77
PSA (Peninsula Shipbuilder's Association), 308
Psychiatric Institute (PI) (Washington, D.C.), 346–54, 356
Puller, General Lewis B. (Chesty) (father), 32, 33, 41, 42, 43, 47, 55, 57, 127, 128, 196, 232, 233, 301, 332, 362
    as commander of Second Marine Division, 10–12
    committed to VA hospital, 265–66
    communication with son, 29
    criticisms of military by, 8, 10, 14–15, 18
    death of, 268–69
    family background of, 3–4
    fragility in old age, 58–59
    funeral for, 270–73
    general officer status of, 6–7
    gentleness of, 26–27
    as grandfather, 175, 202, 233, 261–62
    grave of, 274
    health of, 11, 12
    heroism of, 4, 5, 19, 35, 69, 273
    honored at White House, 221
    hospitalization of, 28, 265–66, 267
    letters from son to, 94, 107, 136–37
    as Marine Corps legend, 15–16, 19, 27, 28, 29, 69, 74, 138, 373

Puller, General Lewis B. (*cont'd*)
  meets son after wounding, 162, 163
  as newlywed, 201–2
  promoted to major general, 9–10
  prostate operation on, 28
  relationship with son, 1–2, 17–18,
    22–23, 29
  retirement of, 14–15, 16–19,
    27–28
  son of, 31, 34, 36, 40, 67, 68, 69, 74,
    96, 138, 158, 172, 227, 228, 266,
    287, 369
  suffers strokes, 12–13, 14, 17, 239–
    41, 256–57, 264–65
  testimony at McKeon trial, 19–21
  and Toddy, 50–51, 53
  toughness of, 24–25
  tributes to, 138–39
  weakened condition before death,
    267
  weakened by strokes, 243, 244, 247
  after wounding of son, 161, 164
Puller, Lewis B., Jr.
  adolescence of, 23–29
  alcoholism of, 226, 255, 274, 276–
    77, 279–80, 328, 330–33, 337–
    44, 345–58, 359–61, 362–64
  arrival in Vietnam, 66–70
  article on, 266–67
  artificial legs of, 194, 198–201,
    204–5, 222–24, 230–31, 236,
    247, 254–55, 258
  bonding with father, 1–2, 17–18,
    22–23
  as Chesty Puller's son, 29, 31, 34,
    36, 40, 67, 68, 69, 74, 96, 138,
    158, 172, 227, 228, 266, 287, 369
  childhood accident, 13–14
  combat in Vietnam, 88–92, 101–4,
    109–10, 112–16, 123–26, 129–
    31, 142–44, 151–52, 155–57
  commits father to VA hospital, 265
  communication with father, 29

  courtship of Toddy, 38, 39, 41, 42,
    43, 45, 48–49, 50, 51, 52, 197
  near death after wounding, 158
  defeated for political office, 325–
    27
  before departure for Vietnam, 55–
    61
  depression of, 166, 169, 170, 179,
    213, 247, 254, 255, 279, 329,
    331–32, 334–35, 337, 341
  dreams of after wounding, 187–88,
    238
  early memories of, 3–12
  enlists in Marine Corps, 30–31, 33
  and father's death, 268–69
  and father's funeral, 270–73
  first combat in Vietnam, 88–92
  first command in Vietnam, 70–88
  flights to Vietnam, 61–65
  guilt over death of Barton, 150–51
  hate mail received by, 267
  hospitalization of after serious
    wounds, 162–201
  joins Marine Corps, 30–31, 33
  journey home from Vietnam, 161
  at law school, 242, 243, 255, 258–
    59, 270, 275
  letters to father, 94, 107, 136–37
  letters to Toddy, 78, 94, 107, 116,
    136, 153, 160
  and Marine Corps, ambivalent
    feelings toward, 137, 153, 166,
    260, 369
  at Marine Corps Basic School, 42–
    49, 51–52, 54–55, 64, 68, 80, 88,
    110, 154, 160, 196, 197, 202, 230,
    368
  at Marine Corps Officer Candidate
    School (OCS), 31, 32, 33–42, 43–
    44, 46, 54, 76
  marries Toddy, 53
  media coverage of, 266–67
  meets Toddy, 33

Puller, Lewis B., Jr. (*cont'd*)
morphine used by, 162, 163, 165,
166, 172, 205–6, 213, 239, 241
moves out of hospital, 201
as new father, 174–76, 183, 261
at Office of General Counsel of VA,
278, 280, 281, 282, 291, 293–94
operations on hands, 205–6, 212–
14, 218, 236–37, 238–39, 241,
244, 245
operation on ulcer, 161
in OT (occupational therapy), 178,
180–82, 183, 189
passes Virginia bar exam, 280
in politics, 281, 296–327
on Presidential Clemency Board,
282–90, 291, 293
at Psychiatric Institute, 346–54,
356
in PT (physical therapy), 178–80,
181–83, 186, 188, 189, 192–94,
198–201, 204–9, 222–25, 230,
231–32, 234–36, 245, 246
public reaction to disability of, 216
Purple Hearts awarded to, 126, 159,
160, 263, 373
at PVA, 293–97
recovery from alcoholism, 345–58,
359–61, 362–64
religious beliefs and practices of,
23–24, 360–61
reliving Vietnam, 206, 214, 227,
255, 330, 332, 334, 340–41, 355,
360, 364
and Robb campaign, 296–97, 298
self-image, difficulty of maintaining
after wounding, 166, 187
seriously wounded in Vietnam,
156–59
Silver Star awarded to, 159–60, 227,
263, 373
and Soviet veterans of Afghanistan,
371–73

speeches of, 303, 305
suicide attempt of, 334
surgery on stump of, 171–73, 176–
77
survival after hospitalization, 162,
164–66
therapy for, 279–80, 334–35
and Vietnam, coming to grips with,
362–64
and Vietnam, doubts about, 220–
21, 233–34, 246, 274–75, 279
and Vietnam Veterans Memorial,
339, 358–59, 361, 363, 367, 369
and walking, attempts at, 198–99,
200–201, 204, 223–24, 230–32,
236, 258
and wheelchair, limitations of, 253–
54, 259, 306–7
wounded in Vietnam, 125–26, 156–
59
Puller, Lewis B. III (Lewpy) (son), 175,
184, 185, 188, 191, 192, 193, 195,
202, 206, 210, 215, 225, 226, 244,
249, 258, 261, 278, 281, 325, 331,
343
baby-sitting for, 268
babytalk of, 216, 238, 247
birth of, 174
in crawling stage, 220
and father's alcoholism, 338, 342,
354, 357
growth of, 186
helplessness after birth, 176, 183
in school, 298, 311
at walking stage, 232
Puller, Maggie (daughter), 262, 268,
278, 281, 325, 326, 331, 340, 343
birth of, 261, 279
and father's alcoholism, 338, 342,
354, 357
in school, 298, 311
Puller, Martha. *See* Downs, Martha
Puller

Puller, Toddy (wife), 47, 54, 56, 62, 70, 128, 135, 217, 227, 228, 232–33, 247, 248, 249, 254, 262, 267, 274, 278, 280, 294, 298, 331, 332, 336, 339, 353, 354, 364, 371
  and Chesty's death, 268–69
  at Chesty's funeral, 271, 273
  courtship of, 38, 39, 41, 42, 43, 45, 48–49, 50, 51, 52, 197
  gives birth to Lewpy, 174
  gives birth to Maggie, 261
  and husband's alcoholism, 333, 337, 338, 340, 341, 342–43, 344, 346, 357
  before husband's departure for Vietnam, 59–61
  and husband's law school, 242, 243, 279
  and husband's suicide attempt, 334
  letters from husband to, 78, 94, 107, 116, 136, 153, 160
  at Marine Corps birthday ball, 229–30
  marriage of, 53
  meets husband after wounding, 162–63
  meets husband, 33
  after move out of hospital, 201, 202, 204, 207, 210, 211, 219–21
  and politics, 277, 281, 292, 299, 300, 303, 311, 316, 323, 325–27, 328, 330
  pregnancy of, 52, 55, 57, 58, 258
  supportiveness during husband's hospitalization and surgery, 164–67, 175–76, 178, 183–86, 188, 190–96, 205–6, 213–14, 218, 237–39, 241, 244, 245
  and Vietnam antiwar movement, 225–26
  and Vietnam Veterans Memorial, 363, 367, 369
  after wounding of husband, 157, 159, 160, 161, 162–63, 170

Puller, Virginia. *See* Dabney, Virginia Puller
Puller, Virginia Evans (mother), 16–17, 18, 19, 21, 25, 28, 32, 38, 41, 55, 196, 232, 233, 239, 261–62, 267, 270, 274, 276, 303
  and husband's death, 268–69
  at husband's funeral, 271–72, 273
  and husband's strokes, 256–57, 264–65
  after husband's stroke, 243, 244, 247
  meets son after wounding, 163
  as newlywed, 201–2
  singing voice of, 23–24
  and son's accident, 13–14
  before son's departure for Vietnam, 57–58, 59
  son's recollections of, 3, 5, 8, 10, 11, 12, 13–14
  and Toddy, 50–51, 53
Puller for Congress Committee, 298
Purple Heart, 126, 159, 160, 263, 373
PVA (Paralyzed Veterans of America), 293–97

Quang Tri (Vietnam), 284
Quantico (Virginia), 31, 33, 226
Quinn, Bob, 292, 294, 302

Ram, Cornelius Herbert, 366
Ranger School, 54
Rastetter, Tom, 300, 306, 307, 312, 322, 324, 325, 326
Rattley, Jessie, 302
Reagan, Ronald, 338
Reagan administration, 358
Red Chinese, 4
Red Cross, 160
Republican party, in U.S., 275, 288, 292, 294, 308, 310, 318, 323

Rheault, Colonel Robert B., 220
Ribbon Creek (Korea), 20
Richardson, Elliot L., 280
Riviera (Vietnam), 99, 102–5, 108,
    111, 113, 116, 117, 140, 145–47,
    149, 153, 182, 186, 193, 211
Roark, Lieutenant Jackson, 209
Robb, Charles S., 296–97, 298, 300,
    319, 328
Robb, Lynda, 296
ROKs, in Vietnam, 154
Rooftop Singers, 201
Rotarians, 315
Russia. *See* Soviet Union

Saigon (Vietnam), 284
Saluda (Virginia), 16–19, 22, 23, 25,
    26, 31, 57–58, 159, 175, 269, 273
San Diego (California), 10, 11
Sandzen, Dr., 189, 192, 194, 205, 206,
    212–14, 216–17, 218, 228
San Francisco, Haight-Ashbury section
    of, 62
Saratoga (USS), 309–10, 319, 320
"Saturday Night Massacre," 280
Schwarz, Michael, 246, 247
Scruggs, Jan, 335, 336, 359, 367
Seabees, 133, 134–35, 138, 139, 146,
    158
Seattle, 63
Second Marine Division, 10, 15
Secret Service, 289
Selective Service System, 31, 289, 293
Senate, 313, 318
    Foreign Relations Committee, 263
    Watergate investigating committee,
    278
    See also Congress
Sequoia, 288
Service Life Extension Program. *See*
    SLEP
Shakespeare, William, 60

Shaughnessey, Commander, 181, 182,
    183–84, 186, 188, 192, 199, 208,
    223, 224, 230
    and crutches, 204–5
    departure of, 234–36
    introduction to, 180
    reassignment of, 228–29
    supportiveness of, 231–32
    techniques of, 200–201, 206–7
Shelleman, Kenneth Hyde, 52, 69, 70,
    71, 197, 366
Shepherd, General Lemuel C., 15–16
Silver Star, 46, 159–60, 227, 263, 373
"60 Minutes" (TV show), 364
Ski (walking point in Vietnam), 82,
    119, 120, 121
SLEP (Service Life Extension
    Program), 309
Smithers, Lieutenant Bill, 234–35,
    236, 246, 247
Sorg, Sergeant, 34, 35, 36, 39, 40, 41,
    42
South China Sea, 64, 99, 100, 112,
    137, 139, 155
Southeast Asia, 30, 32, 44, 46, 55, 61,
    215, 261, 317
    See also Vietnam
South Korean allies, 153
South Vietnam, 64, 86, 215, 246, 284
    border of, 245
    civilians in, 121, 230
    escalation in, 45–46
    military units from, 129, 141
    See also ARVN; Vietnam
Soviet Union, 372, 373
    and Hungarian Revolution, 21–22
Soviet veterans, in Washington, D.C.,
    371–73
Speer, Byron Morrow, 33, 366
Stalin, Joseph, 21
"Stars and Stripes Forever," 161
Steinhoff, Jeff, 174, 191
Stewart, Jimmy, 41, 43

Stone, Irving, 279
Sullivan, Tim, 300
Supreme Court, 263
Suttle, Captain Frederick N., Jr., 276, 366

TAOR (tactical area of responsibility), 94, 97–99, 149
Tate, Sharon, 221
Taylor, Elizabeth, 318
Teheran hostage crisis, 338
Ten Commandments, 24
Tet offensive (Vietnam), 45–47, 51, 95
Thanh, Captain, 132–33, 134, 135, 136
Thieu, Nguyen Van, 215, 284
Third Battalion, Twenty-seventh Marine Regiment, 97
Third Marine Brigade, 5
Tho, Le Duc, 275
Thompson, Margaret, 300, 323, 330
Todd, Colonel Robert G. (Toddy's father), 53–54, 55, 59, 174, 183, 185, 186, 194, 261
Todd, Margaret (Toddy's mother), 53, 54, 55, 183, 194, 216
Todd, Rob, 217
Todds, the, 59, 60, 61, 159, 176, 184, 185, 186, 195, 215, 226, 232, 233, 276, 296, 303
Tomb of the Unknowns, 263, 336
"Tomorrow" (TV show), 340
Tompkins, Tommy, 159
Trible, Paul, 294, 296, 302, 306, 308
    background of, 292–93
    and blacks, 315–16, 324
    flag waving of, 295, 300, 311
    on House Armed Services Committee, 312–13, 314
    and House Merchant Marine and Fisheries Committee job, 332–33

    at NAACP meeting, 315–16
    and parking space incident, 331–32
    political ability of, 297, 301–2, 310
    press coverage of, 303–4, 309
    reelected, 325–27
    support for, 298, 299, 318, 322–23
    and Watergate, 321–22
Trible, Rosemary, 299, 301, 302, 306
Tu Cau bridge (Vietnam), 104, 105–8, 116, 127, 128, 131, 136, 145
Tu Cau River (Vietnam), 98
Turner, Corporal, 85, 116, 121, 127, 134, 136, 138, 139, 150, 152, 154, 155, 157
    as acting platoon sergeant, 148–49
    in combat, 124
    joking of, 123, 137
    leadership ability of, 74, 129
    patrol led by, 119–21
    strategy of, 122
    theorizing of, 141
Twenty-seventh Marines, 97, 98, 100

Uniform Code of Military Justice, 208
United Nations, 312
United States, 139, 285, 295, 342
    antiwar movement in, 225–26, 228, 245, 246
    and Cambodia, 245
    mailings to, 106
    mainstream of, 338
    medical supplies from, 92
    vs. Soviet Union, 21
    and Tet offensive, 46
    troop withdrawals from Vietnam, 215, 233, 246, 278, 280
    and Vietnam, 202–3, 215, 262, 276, 277, 284
    wounded from Vietnam to, 64
    See also Americans
United Steelworkers, 308

U.S. AID, 244
USO, 134
U.S. Congress. *See* Congress
USS *Saratoga*, 309–10, 319, 320

VA (Veterans Administration), 281,
    282, 293–94, 361
  hospitals, 212–13, 254, 255, 265, 295
  housing grants, 261
  Office of General Counsel of, 278,
    280, 291
  vocational rehabilitation program,
    242
VC. *See* Vietcong
Veterans, and Presidential Clemency
    Board, 285, 286–87
Veterans Administration. *See* VA
Veterans of Foreign Wars, 314
Victor Charles. *See* Vietcong
Viem Dong (Vietnam), 104, 111, 112,
    149–50, 153–57
Vietcong (VC), 32, 45, 76, 108, 110,
    115, 117, 119, 120, 121, 151, 182,
    184
  and booby traps, 112, 113, 145
  murder of civilians by, 247
  in Riviera, 98–99, 102–4, 145, 153
  snipers, 73, 145, 147
  and villages, 83–85, 150
Vietnam, 52, 54, 135, 140, 161, 170,
    184, 185, 187, 195, 199, 214, 226,
    235, 236, 244, 266, 272, 273, 302,
    305, 312, 318, 322, 333, 346, 373
  and Afghanistan, 372
  agreement ending war, 277
  Americans and, 64, 220–21, 230–31,
    233–34, 258, 260, 262–63, 268
  Americans killed in, 42, 46, 219,
    246, 339, 363, 365, 366
  Americans out of, 278, 280
  and antiwar movement, 225–26,
    228, 245, 246

  atrocities in, 211, 230, 257–58, 268
  attrition rate in, 44
  bloody crucible of, 369
  campus unrest over, 30–31
  casualties in, 40, 53, 167, 168, 178,
    212, 218, 293, 323
  children in, 84, 95, 101
  Communists in, 99, 284
  cordon and search operation in,
    153–54
  debate over, 202–3
  defeat in, 324
  destructiveness of war, 295
  frustrations of war, 51
  heroism and death in, 32–35
  leadership and, 275, 290
  malingering in, 146
  maneuvering around, 92–95, 97,
    105, 111
  money in, 64
  news of, 209–10
  night patrols in, 97–98, 133, 141–
    44, 149–50
  platoon sergeants in, 148–49
  and Presidential Clemency Board,
    281–90, 291
  Puller's arrival in, 66–70
  Puller before departure for, 55–61
  Puller's combat in, 88–92, 101–4,
    109–10, 112–16, 123–26, 129–
    31, 142–44, 151–52, 155–57
  Puller coming to grips with, 362–64
  Puller's doubts about, 220–21, 233–
    34, 246, 274–75, 279
  Puller's first combat in, 88–92
  Puller's first command in, 70–88
  Puller's flights to, 61–65
  Puller reliving, 206, 214, 227, 255,
    330, 332, 334, 340–41, 355, 360,
    364
  Puller wounded in, 125–26, 156–59
  Purple Hearts in, 128
  refugees from, 284, 317

Vietnam (*cont'd*)
and reservists, 259
service in, 286, 296
shaping power of war, 315
spare time in, 95–96, 107, 136–37
as stigma, 242
suffering in, 175
as taboo topic, 216, 253, 335
and Tet offensive, 45–47, 51, 95
troop withdrawals from, 215, 233,
246, 278, 280
trophies from, 144–45
troubled era of, 303
unraveling of war, 233, 267–68, 284
and U.S., 202–3, 215, 262, 276, 277,
284
vendors in, 106
veterans of, 234, 262, 263, 336,
344–45, 347, 361, 366, 369
veterans' protest in Washington,
D.C., 262, 263
villages in, 83–85, 100–102, 117–
19, 120–23
wounded from, to U.S., 64
See also ARVN; Indochina; North
Vietnamese; Southeast Asia;
South Vietnam; Tet offensive;
Vietcong; *specific towns*
"Vietnamization," 233
Vietnam Veterans of America, 371
Vietnam Veterans Memorial, 339,
355, 356, 358–59, 361, 363, 367,
369
Soviet veterans at, 371–72
Vietnam Veterans Memorial
Foundation, 365
Vietnam Veterans Memorial Fund,
336, 339
Vietnam Veterans Week, 336
Virginia, 295–96, 344
First Congressional District, 297,
298, 300, 302, 309, 311, 319
Virginia Military Institute, 22, 33

Walt, General Lewis W., 159, 282,
286–87
Ware, Dave, 191–92
Warner, John, 313, 318
Washington, D.C.
dedication ceremonies in, 367
march on, 225, 226, 230
Soviet veterans in, 371–73
Vietnam veterans' parade in, 366,
369
Vietnam veterans' protest in, 262,
263
Washington Post, 364–65
"Waste of an Old War Horse" (*Esquire*
magazine), 18
Watergate investigating committee
(Senate), 278
Watergate scandal, 277, 279, 280,
322
hearings on, 278
Watson, Corporal, 77, 81, 85, 88,
89, 119, 122, 126, 131, 132,
136, 141, 142, 143, 151, 152,
156
after Puller wounding, 157
Purple Heart request of, 123
as radioman, 74
Watt, James, 358, 365
Wayne, John, 32, 63, 114, 151,
369
Wheeler, John, 359
White House
and Medal of Honor winners, 214–
15, 221
and Presidential Clemency Board,
282, 283, 284, 289
and USS *Saratoga*, 319, 320
and Watergate scandal, 279
Willett, Dr. Leo, 228, 236–37, 238,
240–42, 243, 244, 245, 248, 249,
257
William and Mary. *See* College of
William and Mary

Williams, Bev, 196
Williamson, Dick, 300
Wolfe, Tom, 364–65
Woods, Captain Clyde, 76, 78, 80,
    81, 82, 86, 87, 92, 94, 95, 103,
    110, 111, 127, 143, 145, 150, 151,
    152
  and cordon and search operation,
    153–54
  introduction to, 72–73, 74–75
  leadership of, 89–91, 100, 116, 146,
    147, 155
  recovered from wounds, 227
  wounded in Vietnam, 211
Woodstock, 222
World War I, 19, 221
World War II, 19, 31, 32, 63, 159,
    219, 221, 234, 286, 291, 363
Wright, Jim, 320, 321
Wright, Major, 70, 71

Yarborough, Glenn, 52, 197
Yokosuka (Japan), 159, 160, 161
York, Sergeant, 221

Zatzerine, Commander, 167, 168
Zier, Lieutenant John, 94, 148, 194–
    95, 209, 214, 222
  Christmas card from, 184, 188
  confidence of, 242
  death of, 275
  hospitalized, 197
  hugeness and agility of, 87, 90, 96,
    208
  malaria strikes down, 203–4
  playfulness of, 207–8
  recovery after wounding, 146–47
  wounded in Vietnam, 115–16, 193
Zier, Linde, 184, 188, 193, 197, 204,
    367